BIRDS & BLOOMS'
Ultimate
Gardening Guide

BIRDS & BLOOMS
Ultimate
Gardening Guide

By Melinda Myers

MELINDA MYERS is a contributing editor to *Birds & Blooms* magazine. She has spent her career helping backyard green thumbs have more success and fun through gardening.

Melinda is a horticulture instructor at Milwaukee Area Technical College, hosts the "Plant Doctor" call-in radio program and the "Great Lakes Gardener" television series on PBS. She's also a garden columnist for the *Milwaukee Journal Sentinel* and a member of the Garden Writers Association of America.

In 1998, the American Nursery and Landscape Association named her Garden Communicator of the Year.

Editor: Jeff Nowak
Art Director: Bonnie Ziolecki
Associate Editors: Deb Mulvey, Susan Uphill, Mike Beno
Associate Artists: Jim Sibilski, Sandy Ploy, Lori Arndt
Graphic Art Associates: Ellen Lloyd, Catherine Fletcher
Photo Coordinator: Trudi Bellin
Assistant Photo Coordinator: Mary Ann Koebernik

Chairman and Founder: Roy Reiman
President: Tom Curl

©2002 Reiman Media Group, Inc.
5400 S. 60th St. Greendale WI 53129
International Standard Book Number: 0-89821-355-X
Library of Congress Catalog Card Number: 2002094601
Printed in U.S.A.

BIRDS & BLOOMS *BOOKS*

Cover photo: Dan Roberts; back cover photo: Faith Bemiss

Karen Bussolini

Foreword

WHEN MY FRIENDS at *Birds & Blooms* approached me about writing a book for our subscribers, I was thrilled. I love sharing what I've learned from experience, mistakes, other gardeners and professionals.

But when I heard the title, *Birds & Blooms Ultimate Gardening Guide*, the pressure was on. Who was *I* to write the definitive book on gardening?

Luckily, I had help from so many of you. When we asked *Birds & Blooms* readers to send us ideas and topics to be covered in this comprehensive guide, you didn't let us down. The ideas poured into our office. After combing through each letter, we shaped this book to address your needs.

The hard part was trying to organize all this information into one comprehensive gardening guide. After all, I have a library full of books on each of the topics you asked me to cover…somehow I needed to come up with a way to do it all in one volume.

Rather than get crazy about it, I took a deep breath and began thinking about what the *Ultimate Gardening Guide* really means to me.

It's All About Fun

The answer was simpler than I thought. Gardening should be fun, not a chore. As we sweat and toil, we should keep a smile in our hearts. If it's not there, we're doing something wrong.

So, read this book and try some of the new techniques you'll learn. They should help make gardening fun and the real "work" easier.

I myself am a low-input gardener (no, that doesn't mean lazy). I love being in my garden, but never have enough time in the day or season to accomplish everything. So I look for simple ways to do each task with fewer sore muscles—an underlying theme in this book.

I also tried to weave in a little of the sci-

ence behind growing a beautiful and productive landscape without making it intimidating.

When composting became the rage in the mid-1980s, many people were expounding on the science of compost. The intentions were good, but at the same time, it scared many gardeners from trying it in their own yard.

As you'll see, my approach is simpler—toss it in a heap and let it break down. For those who want quicker results, I've included several methods to speed things up without backbreaking labor.

When it comes to plants, I've found out writing a book is much like my garden—there's never enough space to include everything I'd like.

So, instead I'm presenting a palette of plants that would serve most readers, regardless of where they live. My selections have a wide range of heat and cold hardiness. And, since fun and success are the goal, I searched for reliable plants that put on a beautiful show with minimal attention.

Sharing What I've Learned

Throughout the years, I've learned gardening isn't as much about plants as it is people. I've learned lots from others who love to work in the soil—from professionals to neighborhood green thumbs.

Many have shared their successes, challenges, secrets and innovations that have helped me become a better gardener and horticulturist. And I've had a chance to pass on their knowledge and experiences through this book.

So, is this the *only* book you'll ever need to garden? Probably not. But it should be a great start or valuable addition to your garden library. In true *Birds & Blooms* style, it's a mix of research, experience and other gardeners' ideas for making backyard landscaping and gardening fun and successful—just as it should be.

So dig in—to both this book and your garden—and start creating your own beautiful backyard just for the fun of it. And before I forget…thanks for helping me write it!

Melinda

Melinda Myers

Table of Contents

Building Great Soil

Chapter 1

The Foundation of Your Garden *10*

Here's the dirt on beautiful gardens…you'll need to start with a soil test first. This extra step on the front end will pay off with brilliant blooming gardens for years to come.

Chapter 2

Laying the Groundwork *20*

Find out all you need to know about creating new gardens, working the soil and selecting the right supplements to make your garden the most productive in the neighborhood.

Chapter 3

Get Rich with Compost *36*

There's a reason gardeners call compost "black gold". It's one of the most valuable natural resources you can add to your garden. Here's how you can produce this rich additive. Here's how…

Basic Gardening Techniques

Chapter 4

Perfect Planting *50*

Now the real fun begins—planting. Find out how to have success with growing seeds, flower bulbs, bedding and container plants. We'll even help with the big stuff—trees and shrubs.

Chapter 5

Maintaining Paradise *70*

While nature takes care of itself, gardeners lend a helping hand. Providing the right amount of water, using the proper pruning and training techniques and knowing where and when to move your plants is all part of successful gardening.

Building Great Soil

- *Chapter 1*
The Foundation Of Your Garden

- *Chapter 2*
Laying the Groundwork

- *Chapter 3*
Get Rich With Compost

Chapter 1
The Foundation Of Your Garden

"What lovely soil. How long have you been growing it?"

This isn't typical garden talk. We all love to show our friends the latest additions to our gardens—the unusual annual, the tree with the spectacular fruit display—but few of us drag guests to the backyard to see our soil. And yet, while it might not have the same visual appeal as a flower, good soil is the foundation for all healthy gardens.

That's why building a beautiful garden requires working from the ground up. And believe me, it's work that always pays off. A friend of mine was able to raise five crops of lettuce every year in his Wisconsin garden, partly due to his season-extending techniques, but mostly because of the rich, fertile soil he'd worked so hard to build.

How Your Soil "Grows"

SOIL IS a combination of water, air and solid materials. The bedrock, or parent material, lies inches or feet below your garden. Over the years, temperature, moisture and plants break apart and wear down the rock to create the basis of the soil. The bedrock contributes minerals that influence the soil's fertility, structure and texture.

Bedrock breaks apart as plants find cracks and crevices in the stone and begin to grow. When the plants shed leaves and die, microorganisms, insects and earthworms move in, speeding up decomposition and creating organic matter.

As these living creatures work, they create a glue-like substance that helps the organic matter clump together. These clumps help the soil hold moisture, supply small amounts of nutrients and improve drainage.

The small spaces or pores created by the clumping process provide channels for two things every plant needs—air and water. Oxygen allows roots to absorb water and nutrients. Water, of course, is needed for plant growth and development.

When the pores fill with a mixture of water and oxygen, plants are able to take up water. If soils are flooded, air is crowded out of the pores. This prevents the plants from taking up water until the excess has drained and air returns to these small spaces. At the other extreme, plants growing in excessively dry soils have plenty of oxygen, but no water.

Soil Types and Textures

As the bedrock beneath your garden weathered and broke down, it left behind particles of various sizes. To better understand what type of soil is in your garden, and how you can improve it, you first need to know about the types of soils these particles create.

Clay soil, composed of the finest particles, feels smooth when dry and sticky when wet. Wet clay holds its shape when molded, much like modeling clay. I was working on a new garden once with some of my horticulture students and found them making sculptures out of the soil. No doubt about it—that stuff was clay!

Medium-sized particles, known as silt, feel smooth and floury when dry, but not sticky when wet. The largest particles are sand, which are visible with the naked eye and are rough to the touch.

The proportion of these particles determines the soil's texture. Fine-textured soils have a higher proportion of clay particles. They tend to hold moisture, warm up slowly in the spring and are easily compacted.

Medium-textured soils have more equal proportions of each particle size. Since they have a mix of large and small pore spaces, which allows for drainage and water retention, these soils usually provide good growing conditions.

Coarse-textured soils have a larger percentage of sand particles and feel gritty. They are often too well-drained to hold water well, so plants must be watered more often.

What's in My Dirt?

There are a couple of ways to find out what texture your soil has. The easiest way is to moisten a small soil sample with a bit of water, then rub it between your thumb and forefinger.

Coarse-textured soils will feel rough and gritty and will barely stay together because of the high sand content. Medium-textured soils will be less gritty and hold together well. Fine-textured soils, with their higher clay content, will be smooth and sticky.

To actually see all the different particles that make up your soil, try the particle-settling test. This is a fun

family project, especially if you have budding gardeners or scientists in your household. All you'll need is garden soil, a straight-sided 1-quart jar with a lid (pictured below left), water and some non-foaming detergent like Dash (or a similar product).

Gather 1 to 2 cups of soil and let it dry. Remove sticks, stones or other large debris from the sample and crush any large soil clumps. Fill one-fourth of the jar with soil. Add enough water so the jar is three-fourths full. Add a tablespoon of the non-foaming detergent, which will help separate the particles. Cover the jar with the lid and shake for about 3 minutes. (This is a great way to help young gardeners expend some extra energy.) Keep shaking until the soil particles have separated and the water appears cloudy.

Place the jar on a table where it can remain for several days. The heaviest particles, the sand, will settle within the first few minutes. The silt will come next. After several days, the water will clear as the fine, lightweight clay particles settle. Measure the portions of sand, silt and clay to estimate the percentage of each.

Now look at the soil texture triangle below and try

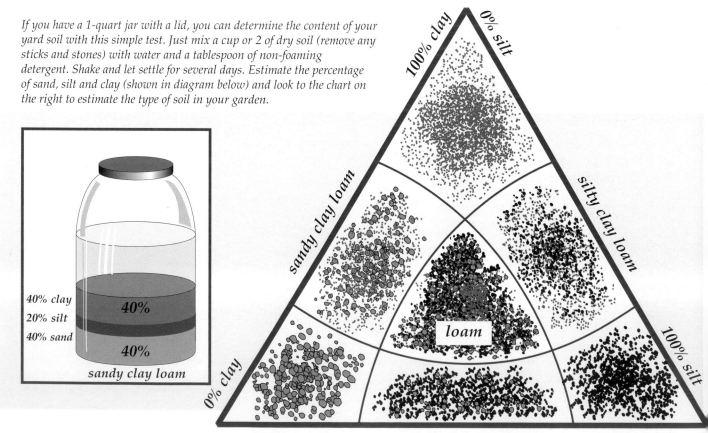

If you have a 1-quart jar with a lid, you can determine the content of your yard soil with this simple test. Just mix a cup or 2 of dry soil (remove any sticks and stones) with water and a tablespoon of non-foaming detergent. Shake and let settle for several days. Estimate the percentage of sand, silt and clay (shown in diagram below) and look to the chart on the right to estimate the type of soil in your garden.

40% clay
20% silt
40% sand

40%

40%

sandy clay loam

100% clay — 0% silt

sandy clay loam

silty clay loam

loam

0% clay — 100% silt

100% sand — **sandy loam or silt loam** — **0% sand**

to pinpoint the percentage of sand, silt and clay in your sample with those on the triangle. Loam with equal parts of sand, silt and clay is one of the best type of gardening soil.

Improving the Mix

Most of us start with less than ideal soil. The good news is, whatever your soil's texture, you can improve it by adding organic matter. Peat moss, aged manure or compost (see Chapter 3) can help boost water-holding capacity in sandy soils and increase drainage in clay soils.

Many homeowners have soil that has been disturbed by erosion and urbanization. When a new home is built, the precious topsoil that took centuries to form gets scraped away. During excavation, lesser-quality subsoil is dug up, and that's what gets placed around your finished house. This is covered with an inch or 2 of topsoil, some sod and maybe a few trees. Not surprisingly, this thin foundation of soil is not substantial enough for raising a healthy garden.

Many gardeners with soil like this just give up and buy topsoil to create a better growing environment. You can rebuild your soil, but you'll need to invest quite a bit of time, organic matter and sweat. See Chapter 2 for more information.

Soil Structure

Fighting clods? You need to improve your soil structure. Is the garden filled with very small, gritty particles that won't hold water? You need to improve your soil structure.

Soil structure is determined by the way its sand, silt and clay particles hold together. If your soil forms clumps that crumble, it has good structure. If it forms clods that hold together when the soil is wet, dry or cultivated, or is so gritty it reminds you of your last trip to the beach, you need to do some work.

Here's another way to check the soil structure. Dig a hole about a foot deep. Are there lots of small clumps about half an inch in diameter? Do the larger clumps break apart easily when tamped? If so, your soil has good structure.

Now pour water over the soil you removed. If this flattens out the clumps or creates puddles, you'll need to add organic matter and use organic mulches

Great garden soil doesn't just happen. It usually takes lots of work. You can improve your soil by adding lots of organic matter such as peat moss, aged manure or compost.

to help nature's cultivators build your soil.

Sand, silt and clay particles bind together with the help of soil organisms like earthworms, insects and fungi. Whenever organic matter is added to the soil, these creatures break it down into usable nutrients. In the process, they create a sticky substance that helps hold the soil particles into larger clusters or aggregates. As plant roots and fungi grow, they move the particles throughout the soil and create their own sticky substances, forming even more aggregates.

That's why you improve soil structure the same way you improve its texture—by adding organic matter. With mulches, compost and other organic matter to chew on, these organisms can get busy creating the glue-like substances that form aggregates...and improve the condition of your soil in the process.

When to Work the Soil

Soil structure is always changing. You can ruin it with improper or poorly timed cultivation. Never work soil that's either very wet or very dry. Wait until the soil is moist before breaking out the tiller or shovel.

In severely dry ground, cultivating breaks the pieces apart, creating a powdery soil that erodes easily and won't retain moisture. Tilling very wet soils creates clods and crusts that inhibit water penetration, drainage and plant growth.

How can you be sure your soil is ready to work? Take a handful of soil and gently squeeze. Now open your hand and see what you have.

If you're left with a clump of soil, tap it gently. Moist soil will break into smaller pieces and is ready to work.

Wet soil will stay in a mud ball (as seen in the photo below). In that case, go back inside, look at your garden catalogs and wait for the soil to dry.

If you end up with a handful of loose powder, the soil is too dry. Moisten the top few inches of soil and wait until the next day to cultivate.

Of course, waiting is easier said than done. We all have busy schedules, and it's often difficult to

find time to prepare the garden just when the soil is at the right moisture level.

When I worked as an Extension horticulturist, helping folks plant community gardens, it always seemed to rain for a week straight just before it was time to prepare the gardens for planting. The gardeners became impatient, and so did I. But anyone who has fought clods or cracked soil can appreciate the benefits of waiting.

Once you've worked the soil, you can maintain good structure all season long by mulching with shredded leaves, bark, pine needles or other organic material. Mulch protects the soil from pounding rain, which can ruin its structure. And the organic materials help build up soil structure by fueling the microorganisms that constantly improve it.

Soil Drainage

You might not have given much thought about the soil drainage in your garden. But understanding it helps you manage it and grow healthy and productive plants.

Drainage depends partly on the soil's texture and structure. Soils with a high clay content tend to hold water and drain slowly. This results in poor root growth, rot and, ultimately, an unhealthy, unattractive garden.

Sandy soils have the opposite problem—too much drainage. These soils don't hold on to moisture and require frequent watering.

Good soil structure creates channels for water to pass. The sticky "soil glue" that holds the particles

together also keeps some water in the soil for plants to use. Improving and preserving soil structure will help improve drainage. Once again, organic matter is the solution.

The slope of your yard also influences how water moves over and through your soil. Gardens planted on hills or raised areas generally have excellent drainage. Those growing on a slope are subject to runoff. Gardens in low spots serve as a collection point for water and often become waterlogged.

For the quickest, most manageable solution, take your cue from nature. Create raised beds or berms, mounding the soil several inches to several feet high. (For very large berms and higher raised beds, you'll need to bring in good-quality topsoil.) The deeper soil in raised beds drains more quickly. Since the beds are surrounded by air, they dry out faster, too.

That's exactly what the city of Milwaukee and other municipalities do. I worked on the staff that managed many of Milwaukee's small flower gardens located on grassy strips in the middle of city streets, surrounded by pollution, salt and cars. Talk

Good drainage is vital for healthy plants. The lush garden above undoubtedly has excellent soil that drains well.

about tough growing conditions! The soil also contained a lot of clay and was usually compacted.

To increase the visual impact and improve drainage, we created raised beds. As a result, we were able to prepare the soil and plant flowers sooner than other green thumbs in the surrounding neighborhoods.

Before you order that truckload of soil, though, check your soil's drainage. Dig a hole about 1 foot in diameter and 1 foot deep. Fill it with water (right), measure the depth of the water and record the time. Check and record the progress every hour. Well-drained soils will lose about an inch of water per hour. Those that drain more slowly need some work.

Check several areas in your yard or in each garden area. The soil texture, structure and drainage varies greatly within my own small city lot, and I'm sure in your yard, too. I have some loamy soil that drains well, but other sections have a high percent of clay and need lots of organic matter and careful watering.

Sweet and Sour

You may have heard farmers or seasoned gardeners talk about soils being "sweet" or "sour". They're referring to the soil's pH level—a measure of the soil's reaction with chemicals in the soil. The soil's pH influences which nutrients are available for plant absorption and growth.

Soil pH is measured on a scale of 0 to 14, with a pH of 7 considered neutral. Soils with a pH below 7 are acid, or "sour", and those with a pH above 7 are alkaline, or "sweet". Most plants prefer soil pH between 6 and 7.

To check how well your soil drains, dig a hole and fill with water. Well-drained soils will lose an inch of water per hour.

It's very difficult to change your soil's pH. You see, soil pH is measured on a logarithmic scale. That means a soil with a pH of 4.5 is *10 times* more acidic than one with a pH of 5.5. So raising or lowering your soil's pH is really a greater task than it might appear.

Since adjusting pH is a difficult task, your best bet may be to simply grow plants suited to the soil you have and avoid plants that aren't. For instance, gardeners with alkaline soils should stay away from blueberries, white oak, red maples, rhododendrons and other acid-loving plants. (For more details on adjusting pH and choosing the right plants for your soil, see Chapter 2.)

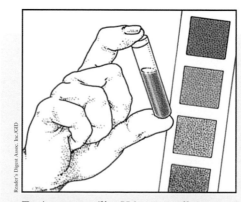

Testing your soil's pH is easy—all you really need is litmus paper, distilled water and a small soil sample. Dip the litmus paper and match it to a pH chart.

Testing Your Soil's pH

TO TEST your soil's pH, all you need is a soil sample, distilled water, litmus paper from a hobby shop or science supply store and the pH chart that's packaged with the litmus paper.

Mix a small bit of soil with the distilled water. Touch the litmus paper to the soil-water solution. Now match the color of the litmus paper to the pH chart. This will give you a fairly accurate reading, within half a unit. If you have your soil tested by a lab, compare the results to see how close you came.

Putting Your Soil to the Test

AS YOU have dug, planted and cultivated your gardens and landscape, you've probably discovered a variety of soil types. As I pointed out earlier, in my little city lot, I have some areas of clay, some of loam, others that are gritty and well-drained. There are even a few spots I suspect were used to dispose of ashes, bottles and other debris. All this variability requires different soil preparation in each area of my garden—and probably in yours—to get things in shape for a successful growing season.

To know exactly what your soil requires, you first need to know what's already in it. A soil test conducted by a state-certified laboratory will tell you what nutrients your soil contains and what you need to add for the plants you're growing. If you follow the lab's recommendations, you'll save time and money by adding only the nutrients your plants need, which will improve your garden's health and beauty.

Following these recommendations also minimizes the risk of over-fertilizing, which can give you huge green plants but no flowers or fruit. In extreme cases, too much fertilizer can damage your plants or even kill them.

Proper fertilization is better for the environment, too. Excess fertilizer leaches through or runs off the soil and ends up in our groundwater, lakes and streams. This decreases water quality and increases harmful weed growth in our waterways.

When Should Soil Be Tested?

Soil tests can be taken any time, as long as the ground is not frozen. The only time you shouldn't take a test is right after fertilizing the lawn or garden. That can give you false results.

I like testing the soil in fall. The labs are usually less busy then, and you'll get the results in plenty of time to improve the soil before the next growing season.

Test the soil whenever you're planning a new garden or landscape. The test will tell you what your soil contains

and what you need to add to provide the proper amount of nutrients to establish your plants. Retest the soil every 3 to 5 years so you can adjust your fertilizer regimen to best fit your plants' needs.

Consider a soil test whenever your garden's health and appearance start to decline. I use soil tests as a tool for diagnosing sick plants. The tests can expose nutrient deficiencies or rule them out. Either way, I obtain valuable information for improving the health of the garden.

Collecting the Samples

Your first task is finding a lab that's state certified. These labs' chemicals and equipment are evaluated regularly to ensure that they're properly calibrated—an essential step for accurate results. To find a lab near you, check the yellow pages or contact your local Extension service, listed in the County Government section of your phone book. The cost will vary depending on the lab and location, but it's generally around $10.

Before you collect your samples, check with the lab for any specific directions or recommendations. Remember, your test results are only as good as the sample the lab receives.

Soil test results are based on the plants you are growing, so you'll need separate tests for each plant-

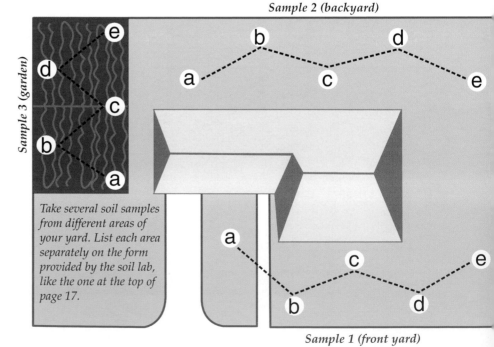

Sample 2 (backyard)

Sample 3 (garden)

Take several soil samples from different areas of your yard. List each area separately on the form provided by the soil lab, like the one at the top of page 17.

Sample 1 (front yard)

LAWN & GARDEN SOIL INFORMATION SHEET
(See back for instructions)

LAB USE ONLY	NAME AND ADDRESS	METHOD OF PAYMENT
	County from which sample was taken:	Amount paid: _____ or Acct. ID:
Date Rec'd_____	Name:	Cash ☐ or Check No. _____ PO#
County Code_____	Address:	Credit Card VISA ☐ MC ☐
	City _____ State: ___ Zip Code:	Credit Card No: ____-____-____-____ Exp: ___/___

If you would like to view your report(s) on-line please provide your E-mail address: _____

Choose *one* letter and number combination *per sample* from the Landscape Categories below:

L LAWN
1. Established
2. New from seed
3. New from sod

TOPSOIL
See back of sheet
for topsoil instructions.

G GARDEN
1. Vegetable
2. Asparagus

FG FLOWER GARDEN
1. Annual
2. Perennial
3. Prairie

T TREE
1. Hardwood shade
2. Hardwood flowering
3. Evergreen

S SHRUB
1. Bush fruit
   (viburnum, juneberry)
2. Rose
3. Azalea, rhododendron
4. Evergreen
5. Deciduous

M MIXED BED
1. Annual flowers &
   perennial flowers
2. Annual flowers & roses
3. Perennial flowers & shrubs
4. Annual flowers, perennial
   flowers & shrubs

F FRUIT
1. Strawberry
2. Blueberry
3. Grape
4. Raspberry (red, black, purple)
5. Bush fruit (currant, gooseberry, elderberry)
6. Apple
7. Pear
8. Cherry
9. Peach, apricot, plum

PC PERMANENT COVER CROP
1. Prairie
2. Native/Bluegrass
3. Vetch
4. Trefoil

AC ANNUAL COVER (Green manure)
1. Buckwheat, oat, wheat, rye, barley
2. Alfalfa
3. Clover

Lab Use Only	Sample No.	Your Identification of Area	Landscape Category
Example	1	Front	L1
	1		
	2		
	3		
	4		
	5		

All samples are analyzed for PH, organic matter, available phosphorus and available potassium.

Special Tests (additional fees):

Lead	Particle size (% sand, silt, clay)	Soluble salts	Other tests:

ing area. Have one test done for the lawn, one for the vegetable garden and so on. Consider separate tests for problem areas or those with drastically different growing conditions. This may mean separate tests for the front and back lawn, wet areas or the flower beds on the east versus the south side of the house.

To collect the sample, brush away any mulch or debris. Use a trowel to take a slice of soil from the surface to a depth of 4 to 6 inches. You'll need several samples from each area. I like to take one from each corner and several from the middle.

Mix all samples from the same test area in a clean bucket and allow the soil to dry for several days. This reduces mailing costs and the time needed to process your test. Measure and mail one cup of the soil to the testing lab. (The lab or Extension office usually provides the mailers.)

Now relax and enjoy the break before your work begins. The lab will process your sample and return a detailed report in about 2 weeks. The test will tell you what your soil contains and what you need to do to create a healthy environment for your plants.

Reading the Report

When your test results arrive, they'll tell you everything you need to know about your soil, from its texture and pH level to the nutrients it contains. The results also will recom-

University of Wisconsin
Madison - Extension
SOIL SAMPLE BAG

Name _____
Field _____
Sample No. _____

†Fill to this line with soil†

• Soil Fertility Testing—
  Farm, Lawn, Garden,
  Tree Plantation,
  Greenhouse
• Plant Nutrient Analysis
• Feed & Forage Quality
  Analysis
• Environmental Testing

Deliver to:
UW Soil & Plant Analysis Laboratory
5711 Mineral Point Road
Madison, Wisconsin 53705
(608) 262-4364
OR
UW Soil & Forage Analysis Laboratory
8396 Yellowstone Drive
Marshfield, Wisconsin 54449
(715) 387-2523

mend the type and amount of fertilizer to add for the plants you're growing. Here are some of the factors your soil test may measure:

• **Organic matter.** Most soil tests check the amount of organic matter, which influences water retention, provides some nutrients and feeds worms, insects and microorganisms that help improve the soil structure. Ideal soils contain about 5% organic matter.

Changing the level of organic matter in your soil is difficult. If you add 100 pounds to the soil, that breaks down to 10 pounds the following year, and 1 pound the year after that. This makes it a constant job just to maintain the level of organic matter in your soil, let alone increase it. Yearly applications of compost, peat moss or manure, use of organic mulches and minimal tillage can eventually lead to a slight increase.

• **Soil pH.** This tells you if your soil is acid, neutral or alkaline. This, too, is difficult to change. Though the difference in numbers may be small, it takes huge amounts of energy and materials to change them. Lime is used to raise pH in acid soils, and sulfur is often used to lower pH in alkaline soils. Always test the soil before trying to alter its pH and follow the lab's recommendations. The damage caused by improper application of lime or sulfur can take years to repair.

Jerry Howard/Positive Images

• **Nitrogen.** Plants use this nutrient for growth in relatively large amounts, and it leaches from the soil quickly. That's why nitrogen fertilizers are added on a regular basis. Since plant-available nitrogen does not stay in the soil, it's difficult to get an accurate reading in a soil test, so these recommendations are based on the needs of the specific plants you're trying to grow. The labs rely on years of plant and fertilization data to make these recommendations.

• **Phosphorous and potassium.** Plants use both these nutrients in smaller amounts. Since both move slowly through the soil, the lab checks the soil's level of plant-available phosphorous and potassium. The test results will tell you how much to add, if any.

• **Soluble salts**. This measurement reflects the amount of soluble chemicals, such as sodium, in the soil. A high level indicates over-fertilization, exposure to deicing salts or soils that are naturally rich in these chemicals.

Proper fertilization and drainage will help prevent salt buildup. Minimizing the use of deicing salts and rinsing these materials through the soil with a thorough watering each spring will reduce their presence, too.

Naturally salty soils require more extensive work, however. The soil test will recommend gypsum, other additives or changes in management practices to counteract the problem.

• **Calcium, magnesium and sulfur.** These nutrients may or may not be included in a standard soil test. Many soils have adequate levels of all three, and some labs will test for them only if a deficiency is suspected. In those cases, the results will recommend what you need to add.

Special Tests

In some circumstances, you may want to ask the lab about conducting special tests. Certain very specific tests may involve an extra fee. The directions you receive from the lab should provide guidance.

Trace nutrients like boron, zinc, iron, manganese, copper and molybdenum are not part of the standard soil test. Plants use these nutrients in such small amounts that they are generally not deficient.

Regular additions of compost or other organic matter usually provide the needed amounts of these nutrients. Adding more of the specific nutrients, even in small amounts, can be toxic to your plants.

Urban vegetable gardeners may want to request a special test for heavy metals like lead and cadmium, both of which can cause health problems. Fortunately, heavy soils with a high clay content and soils with a high pH tend to bind these metals so they're not absorbed by the plants we eat. To be on the safe side, always wash fruits and vegetables before eating them, and never allow children to put soil into their mouths.

The *Plant Doctor* is in

Q: *My lawn is lumpy from all the earthworm activity. How can I eliminate the earthworms and regain my smooth, level yard?*

A: A lumpy lawn is a sign of healthy soil. The earthworms are helping to aerate the soil, move organic matter to the plant roots and keep your lawn lush and healthy. Let the earthworms do their job. You can lightly roll the lawn if the lumps are too bothersome. Use an empty roller on moist soil to flatten the lumps without damaging the soil structure.

Q: *I heard lime will help improve the drainage in my clay soils. How much should I add?*

A: Lime can improve soil drainage, but it also raises the soil pH, which can cause other problems by limiting the nutrients available to your plants. Lime should be used only on acid soils, never on alkaline ones. Before applying lime, have your soil tested by a state-certified lab and follow its recommendations (then see Chapter 2).

Another option is to add organic matter to the soil before planting. Then mulch with shredded leaves, pine needles, wood chips or other organic matter to improve soil structure and drainage.

Q: *I would like to test my own soil. Are the home test kits as accurate as tests done by soil-testing labs? I'd like to save some money and speed up the results by doing the tests myself.*

A: When you have your soil tested by a state-certified lab, you know the results are accurate—and that makes it worth the time and money. The labs' equipment and chemicals are checked for accuracy on a regular basis. Home test kits, on the other hand, may

sit on a shelf for a long time or travel through various temperature extremes and get shuffled in the process. Combine this with your limited soil-testing experience, and your results can be off by small or large amounts.

Try some of the simple tests for pH and soil texture discussed in this chapter, but consider investing in a soil test, too. The results will include precise instructions for fertilizing your garden—advice that will recoup the time and money spent on the test.

Q: *My soil test says I have excessive levels of phosphorous and potassium. Will this hurt my plants? How can I lower the amount of phosphorous in the soil?*

A: High levels of phosphorous (P) and potassium (K) are common in urban and highly cultivated soils. Labs across the country are finding that years of adding 10-10-10 or other complete fertilizers to our landscapes has resulted in excess levels of P and K, which can interfere with plants' uptake of other nutrients.

You can't remove P and K from the soil, but you can avoid adding to the problem. Use ammonium sulfate, urea and other nitrogen fertilizers that do not contain phosphorous and potassium. Or select other synthetic or organic fertilizers that have little or no amounts of these nutrients. Your soil test should tell you how much or what type of fertilizer to use. Follow these recommendations for best results.

Q: *A gardening neighbor said the hardpan layer of soil in my garden is causing poor plant growth. What is hardpan and how can I fix it?*

A: Hardpan is a hardened layer of soil that occurs several inches below the surface, impeding root growth and the flow of water. I often find this layer in gardens that are frequently tilled. The tiller blades run through the soil at the same depth each season, turning the top 4 to 6 inches of soil, but compacting the earth beneath. After several years, this causes a hard layer to form.

Get out the shovel or pickax and start breaking up the hardpan. Keep adding organic matter to the soil to repair and improve its structure. A deep plowing or spading in fall will help prevent hardpan from forming.

Jon Grass/Grass Photo Images

Chapter 2
Laying the Groundwork

Fertilizers can be purchased as liquids, granules and stakes. When using granular fertilizers, select products with uniform size for even distribuiton.

Enough of the technical stuff. Now the fun begins—it's time to get dirty!

But where do you start when you visualize a beautiful garden in a spot where there's nothing but grass?

It takes a little imagination and planning and a good strong back. Most family members have fairly specific roles in their gardening projects. One person tends to direct and do the planting, while the other provides the heavy labor.

Since I married a horticulturist, we share these duties—not because we're overly concerned with fairness or traditional roles, but so each of us can stake out our fair share of planting space.

We haven't divided the yard—yet—but each of us usually sneaks in a few of our personal favorites while the other is at work. As we age and our backs and knees creak a bit more, we find we do a much better job of compromising and sharing the load.

Enough about me…you're wondering how can you transform your bare areas into beautiful flower-filled beds.

Best-Laid Plans

FIRST, sketch out a landscape plan that shows the approximate size and shape of your new garden. Then grab a tape measure and garden hose. Use the tape measure to ensure that what you think is 10 feet really is 10, and not 6 or 15 feet. Garden spaces tend to expand out of control, despite the best-laid plans.

Once you've measured the space for your garden, use the hose to create curves and graceful angles in the bed. Leave it in place while you do a little work in another part of the yard, then come back an hour

or so later for a fresh look. It's much easier to move the hose than it is to redig a garden border.

When you're satisfied with the layout, use small stakes and twine or a little landscape paint to mark the border outlined by the hose. Now get out the shovel—it's time for the strongest and most energetic person in your family to begin the grunt work.

Once you've drawn straws, use a sharp spade or mechanical edger to define the garden edge. This is just a rough cut to delineate the garden from the lawn. We'll dress up the edge a little later.

Dig down at least 6 inches, cutting through the grass roots and rhizomes. This makes it easier to kill the grass within the garden while keeping the existing lawn out.

Removing the Grass

This step is a little more time-consuming. You can remove grass with tools and heavy equipment, black plastic, chemicals or by other means.

The fastest method is to cut the sod. You can rent a sod cutter or hire a professional for this. Sod cutting machines slice into the soil under the grass, removing strips of lawn, like sod rolls, with roots intact. Use this sod to repair bare spots in the lawn or add it to the compost pile, grass side down.

Stronger gardeners looking for a workout can use a hand-held sod cutter. This long-handled tool has a sharp round edge that allows you to slice through the grass roots. Get a friend to help. Start at one side of the bed and work your way across it. While you undercut the sod, have your friend roll it back out of the way. Continue cutting and rolling until the piece of sod reaches the maximum manageable size. Move the roll out of the way and start on another piece. Continue until all the sod is removed.

A shovel works, too, but it's tedious and results in smaller chunks rather than rolls of sod. These pieces are best recycled in the compost pile.

Another option is starving the grass with black plastic. This method takes more time, but involves much less work.

Remember the time you left your child's swimming pool on the grass a little too long? When you finally emptied and moved it, the grass had yellowed underneath. Your grass probably recovered after that short period of darkness. But with the black plastic method, we're hoping it won't.

The dark plastic blocks out light, killing the plants underneath. Cover the garden area with black plastic and anchor it with stakes or stones. Be sure to edge the garden first—otherwise, the grass and weeds will draw energy from the roots and rhizomes of surrounding plants.

Leave the plastic in place for several months, over the winter or for a whole year. The longer you leave the plastic in place, the better results you'll get.

The black plastic method also provides some weed control for your new garden. As the sun shines on the plastic, it warms the soil below. The trapped heat raises the soil temperature and "cooks" many of the dormant roots, rhizomes and weed seeds.

Use a garden hose to help create the shape of a new planting bed. Then run the mower, engine off, along the hose to make sure your curves are not too tight.

Although slow, a shovel is an effective way to edge a new planting bed. It can also be used to remove the grass—and you'll burn 480 calories per hour.

Weeding It Out

I try to use as few chemicals as possible in my landscape. But I've found that eliminating existing grass and weeds before planting saves a great deal of work and minimizes the amount of chemicals I need to use later.

A total vegetation killer like Roundup or Finale will kill the leaves and roots of grass and weeds. Apply these to actively growing grass and remember: They can kill anything green they touch.

For safe application of any chemical, read all the label directions first and use only the recommended mixing rate. This will ensure your own safety, protect the environment and provide the best control. Wear gloves, long sleeves, long pants and closed-toe shoes.

Choose a still day with little or no wind so chemical drift doesn't damage desirable plants. Work backward, walking away from sprayed areas and not into them. If the chemicals stick to your shoes, you'll end up with footprints of dead grass on your lawn.

After applying, wait 4 to 14 days before working the area. (Check the label—wait times vary.) Break up the dead grass with a shovel or tiller. Leave smaller pieces in the soil, where they'll eventually break down, adding organic matter and nutrients. I rake out the larger pieces and add them to my compost pile.

From Grass to Garden Bed

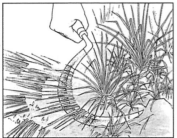

1. Cut down tall weeds and fork them out.

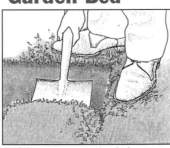

2. If the area was previously lawn, skim off the sod.

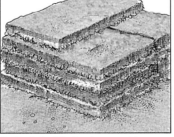

3. Stack the lifted sod, grass side down, to decompose.

4. Dig the area, turning the soil a full spade depth.

As some of the chemicals go to work, you'll see another reason why it's important to edge the border. When the chemicals are absorbed, they spread to the plants' rhizomes and roots, killing not only what you spray, but any surrounding grass and plants that are attached by underground stems. This can give the garden a feathery look if you don't edge it first.

My friend Mike uses this to his advantage. He's always trying to expand his gardening space, but his wife, Becky, wants to maintain more of their lawn. Any time Mike creates a new bed, he sprays the area without edging it. When Becky complains about the uneven edge, he offers to clean it up—by applying Roundup to even out the border.

This goes on until he gets the larger bed he wants. I'm sure Becky has figured out his trick. She just wants to make him work a little harder if he's going to get that larger planting bed!

Raised Beds

Many gardeners with poor soil decide to create a raised bed over the existing soil. Start by marking the garden boundaries. Decide if you want to use building materials to contain the garden or just mound the soil. Timbers, blocks and other materials can be used. Look for long-lasting items that complement your landscape design.

Cut the existing grass and weeds as short as your lawn mower will allow and cover with several lay-

ers of newspaper. (I find an extra set of hands comes in handy for this job. The wind always seems to pick up when I try to lay newspaper.) Fill the area with at least 6 inches of topsoil. Twelve inches or more is even better. Allow for 20% soil settling, or about 2-1/2 inches for every foot of soil.

You can remove the existing grass, but I find the newspaper method works just fine. It helps kill the grass and weeds so they don't grow into your new garden area. Over time, the newspaper, covered grass and weeds decompose, providing nutrients and organic matter.

Areas with good soil that have long been covered with turf and very few weeds may need very little work. In these cases, just edge the new bed, cut the grass as short as possible and cover with newspaper and wood chips.

You can dig holes and plant right through the mulch, although this is such hard work that I do it only when I'm planting a few larger plants like trees and shrubs. Otherwise, I wait a season for the newspaper and covered turf to decompose, which makes planting much easier. I simply move the wood chips aside and plant my flowers or groundcovers in the new bed. Then I move the wood chips back in place to serve as a mulch, reducing future weed problems.

Raised gardens create better growing conditions in naturally poor soils. Create pathways between and within gardens for easy access.

Beefing Up the Soil

NOW WE'RE READY to use the information you collected from your soil test (Chapter 1). But how do we translate the science of soil testing to the reality of a healthy, attractive garden?

Soil tests often cloak the answers in scientific terms that are clear to soil scientists and horticulturists but confusing to gardeners. Ever since I worked as an Extension agent, I've been a big believer in soil testing. Yet I cringed whenever a gardener called about the results of a soil test. I knew they were frustrated and overwhelmed by the math and science of it all. But using this information is easier than you think.

Hidden in the middle of your soil test facts and figures are recommendations based on your soil and the plants you're trying to grow. These will tell you how much fertilizer to add and what type to use. They'll also tell you whether you need to add lime to raise the pH or sulfur to lower it. The physical analysis will indicate whether your soil is high in sand, silt or clay.

We'll start with the physical analysis, because the solution for most soils is the same—add organic matter. This amazing soil amendment improves drainage in heavy clay soils and increases water-holding ability in rocky and sandy soils. Most soils benefit from a 2- to 4-inch layer of organic matter worked into the top 6 to 12 inches of soil. Use the larger amounts on soils with a high percentage of clay or sand.

Peat moss, manure and compost are available at your local garden center or topsoil supplier. (See the chart on page 29 for suggestions on other soil amendments.) Or, make your own organic matter from plant debris you may now be bagging up and throwing away. Chapter 3 offers simple ideas on how to recycle leaves, weeds and other plant debris into some of the best organic matter available—compost.

Golf courses have long used mineral materials to improve drainage. These highly fired calcine clay materials create air spaces, improving drainage in clay soil. They can provide quick and fairly long-lasting results, but I would still use organic matter for all the other good things it provides.

New soil amendments are always being introduced to the market, including shredded tires and other recycled items. I like to wait until someone else takes the risk before introducing something new to my landscape soil. If you like to be on the leading edge, try new materials in only one small bed first.

Working the Soil

Now that the grass is gone, you're ready to work the soil, which takes a little time and strength and a lot of sweat. I like to think of it as working off a few of the extra pounds I always seem to acquire over winter.

The simple act of turning the soil loosens and aerates it so roots are established more easily. It also allows you to add organic matter and to work in fertilizer and amendments where the roots can use them. (For specific instructions on what and how much to add, check out the charts on pages 32-34.)

You should prepare the top 6 to 12 inches of soil before planting. This is the area of the greatest root growth and nutrient absorption.

Double-digging (see illustrations at far top right) works the soil deeply, 12 or more inches, and requires more time and effort. Some gardeners feel this is essential for good root development and plant growth.

Call Before You Dig!

IF YOU'VE SEEN commercials about mishaps caused by digging into an underground gas, electric or cable line, you may think they're overly dramatic. Unfortunately, they're true!

Hitting one of these lines with a shovel or garden tool can cost money or even your life.

So take the time to pick up the phone and call your local utility locating service 3 to 5 business days before you intend to dig. You'll find it listed in the phone book with the major utilities in your area.

To locate them on the internet, just type "utilities locating service" into your search engine. This free service will mark the underground utilities in your yard so you know exactly where *not* to dig.

Doing the Double-Dig

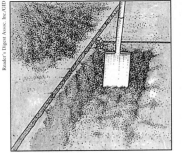

Others worry it brings more of the bad subsoil and weeds to the surface. Let your growing conditions and gardening style be your guide. Just remember, the more effort you invest now, the less you'll expend later on.

Spading the Garden

Start at one end of your garden and work to the opposite side. Place the shovel in the soil and turn it over in place. Set the shovel in the unturned area adjacent to the turned soil. When you've finished that section, start another row, moving from front to back. Continue to turn the soil from front to back and side to side until all of it is turned. The soil surface will be rough and uneven.

Spread amendments and fertilizer over the soil surface. Turn the soil one more time to work them into the top 6 to 8 inches. It will be much easier to work now, and the soil will break apart into smaller clumps.

Rake smooth and allow the soil to settle. This takes about a week, unless the garden gets a light sprinkling or a gentle rain. If you're impatient and you plant immediately, before the soil settles, plant roots may end up exposed.

On existing or fall-prepared beds, you can skip this first spading.

Double-Digging

This is spading at its extreme. Double-digging amends the top 12 to 18 inches of soil, which improves drainage and water-holding capacity in even the worst soils. It's a great way to prepare soil for permanent plantings of perennials, roses and mixed borders.

Start by placing a tarp next to the edge of the garden. Dig and remove the soil, one spade deep, in a 2-foot strip running the length or width of the garden. Place this soil on the tarp. Now dig another spade depth into the trench. Add compost, peat moss or other organic matter to this soil. You may need a garden fork or pickax to loosen heavy clay or rocky soils.

Now dig a trench next to the first one. Take the top layer, one spade deep, and place it over the amended subsoil in the first trench. Add 2 to 4 inches of compost to this soil.

Turn over the bottom of the second trench, adding organic matter to the subsoil. Continue digging and backfilling your way across the garden. The final trench will be filled with the soil dug from the top of the first trench. Amend the removed soil with organic matter before filling in the trench.

1. *Pile soil from first trench on a tarp at the edge of the garden.*

2. *Use a fork to break up the trench bottom and work in some humus.*

3. *Dig a second 2-foot trench, turning the soil upside down into the first.*

4. *Use the pile of soil from the first trench to fill the second trench.*

If you have a tiller, you can do this much faster. Remove the top layer of the first trench and amend the bottom area with organic matter. Dig the top layer from the next trench and place it over the amended subsoil in the first trench. Continue digging as described earlier, but amend only the bottom layer.

Once the bed is dug, spread a 2- to 4-inch layer of organic matter over the soil surface and till it into the top layer. This produces the same results as the first method, with much less work.

Tilling Away the Hardpan

A rototiller can help you create the best possible garden bed, and it makes your task much easier, since it does the hard work of turning the soil.

After you've amended the soil, run the tiller over the garden. Move slowly over the surface to allow the tines to reach deep into the soil. Try to vary tilling depth to avoid creating a hardpan layer.

Hardpan develops whenever the soil is tilled at a

A rototiller is an easy way to turn the soil. Work the soil when it is moist, not wet. Vary depth each year to avoid creating a hardpan layer.

After you've prepared the soil and added edging, rake the bed smooth. A slight crown will prevent water from settling in the garden.

consistent depth, and the soil beneath is compacted by the weight of the machine and action of the tines. This hard layer prevents water from draining through to the soil below, leading to root rot and even plant death. Use a spade or garden fork to break up hardpan layers. Be forewarned, this is much easier said than done!

Experienced farmers learned long ago that a deep plowing in the fall helps to break up hardpan. As the large furrows freeze and thaw throughout the winter, they break apart. Farmers vary tilling depths every spring to avoid creating a hardpan layer. You can do the same with your tiller.

The Finishing Touch

Make a final inventory of your new garden bed, cleaning up any ragged edges or installing edging materials. I prefer to leave my gardens with a nat-

Taking time to properly install edging material will help keep it from heaving out of the ground in winter.

ural edge, using the shovel or edger to dig straight down 4 to 6 inches. This keeps the surrounding grass out and defines my beds.

Many gardeners prefer to use metal, rubber and plastic edging to define the bed. Edging materials are slid into a 4- to 6-inch trench between the bed and the grass. Follow the manufacturer's guidelines for installing the material you select.

Northern gardeners may have problems with edging materials heaving out of the soil over winter. A little spring touch-up may help keep them in line, in the ground and out of the way of the mower.

Pavers, stone and brick also can be used to create an edge around your new garden. Keep maintenance in mind when making your selection. Pavers

laid flush with the soil can create a mowing edge that makes maintenance easier. Run one of the mower tires over the brick edge, and you won't need to hand-trim. Fieldstone edges make a nice natural edge, but you'll have to hand-trim around them.

To make maintenance easier, consider creating a mowing strip—a narrow band of wood chips or pavers flush to the ground—around whatever border you select. A messy border can detract from your beautiful garden.

Rake It Smooth

Once the soil is prepared and the edging is in place, it's time to rake the garden smooth. Create a slight elevation in the center of your garden. Crowning the bed helps create greater visual appeal, keep soil in the bed and out of the lawn and, most importantly, prevent water from settling in the planting bed.

Wait a week to plant your new garden. Remember, the fluffed and amended soil will settle, and planting too soon can result in exposed roots. You can lightly sprinkle the new planting bed with water to speed up settling.

Save Your Back— Safe Shoveling Strategies

- Keep your back as straight as possible.
- Bend your knees, not your back, when filling the shovel.
- Straighten knees to lift the load.
- Keep the loaded shovel as close to your body as possible.
- Turn your whole body—don't twist at the waist to move the load.
- Place the load in a cart or wheelbarrow to transport it long distances.

Selecting Fertilizer And Amendments

BEFORE PREPARING your soil, you'll need to shop for amendments and fertilizer. Just get out your soil test and head for your favorite garden center—and don't panic.

Shopping for these items can be intimidating because there are so many choices. I've seen perplexed looks on the faces of many gardeners trying to select the right fertilizer. Let your soil test results, gardening style and information on the fertilizer bag make the selection process easier.

Reading the Fertilizer Bag

All fertilizers contain the same basic information. Once you know what you're looking for, the task becomes less overwhelming.

The front of every bag contains three numbers, such as 10-10-10 or 10-15-10 or 6-3-0. These represent the percentage of nitrogen, or N (first number), phosphorous in the form of phosphate, or P (middle number) and potassium in the form of potash, or K (last number). Plants need all three elements in relatively large amounts.

It's important to again turn to your soil test recommendations when choosing fertilizer, because too much of any one nutrient can be harmful. What's more, excess levels of one nutrient can interfere with the uptake of others.

Too much nitrogen can result in lush plants with no flowers, brown or "burned" leaves or even death. Years of using complete fertilizers such as 10-10-10 or 12-12-12 also result in high levels of phosphate and potash. You can't take these out of the soil, but you can decrease the problem by adding only the nutrients your soil and plants need.

A 100-pound bag of 5-10-10 contains 5% (5 pounds) of nitrogen, 10% (10 pounds) of phosphate and 10% (10 pounds) of potash. The other 75 pounds is filler that dilutes the fertilizer, making it easier to apply. It also reduces danger of fertilizer burn.

Other Amendments

IT TAKES 100 years for Mother Nature to create an inch of topsoil. Don't destroy her hard work with improper care. Some of these amendments require special caution.

- **Wood ash** is a fine-textured material that does little to improve soil structure. It is alkaline and should be used only in acid soils or compost piles.
- **Sawdust and wood chips** break down slowly, temporarily tying up soil nitrogen. Add supplemental nitrogen whenever incorporating these into the soil. They're better used as mulch around trees, shrubs and pathways.
- **Black walnut and butternut** contain juglone, which is toxic to many plants. Use these chips and leaves only on resistant plants or in compost. Once fully decomposed, they're safe to use as mulch or to amend the soil.
- **Gypsum** supplies calcium and is often used to improve drainage in sodium-rich soils. Make sure your soils need additional calcium or are sodium-rich before applying.
- **Pine needles** improve the soil without making it too acidic. They make an attractive and effective garden mulch, but break down slowly.
- **Oak leaves** are a great source of organic matter and do not make the soil toxic or too acid. Shred them with the mower to speed up decomposition.
- **Sand** is needed in such large amounts that it's not practical for most landscape situations. For every inch of soil amended, you need to add an inch of sand. Use less, and your soil will feel and drain like concrete.
- **Vermiculite and perlite** are great for containers and houseplants, but not garden soil. These materials are crushed and lose their aeration value when walked upon, tilled or highly cultivated.

Many fertilizers will be labeled as fast- or slow-release, indicating how quickly the nutrients are available to the plant.

Fast-release fertilizers dissolve in water and are readily available. They're fast-acting and less expensive, but pose a greater risk of fertilizer burn and groundwater pollution if misapplied.

Slow-release fertilizers release small amounts of nutrients for plant use over time. They have a lower burn potential and require fewer applications, but usually cost more.

The release of the nutrients in slow-release fertilizer is controlled by the nutrient formulation, by microorganisms acting on the fertilizer or by a physical coating on the granule. Weather, temperature and moisture can all affect their release.

To get the results you need, you may want to adjust your application or use a combination of materials. For example, I use mostly compost and organic fertilizers in my yard. A few years ago, we had a cool spring and the nutrients were not available to the plants. I supplemented with a little quick-release fertilizer to give the plants a boost until the soils warmed and the slow-release nutrients became available to them.

Should You Go Organic?

Organic fertilizers improve the soil and have a low burn potential, and some—like manure—are even free. But they're bulkier and harder to handle, their composition may vary and they break down slowly, especially in cold soil.

Inorganic fertilizer is less bulky and easier to apply, and the nutrients are in a simple form more readily available to plants. They also offer a wide variety of nutrient formulations, so you can choose just what your plants need. Just be careful not to use too much. Overfertilizing can damage the environment—and your plants.

How Much Do You Need?

Fertilizer needs are based on the nutrients in your soil, the plants you're growing and the area you're fertilizing. If you haven't tested your soil, you should (see Chapter 1). In the meantime, contact your local county Extension service and use the general guidelines on the fertilizer bag. Recommendations are often given in terms of pounds of the actual nutrient needed. See the Common Fertilizers chart on page 34 for help determining how much fertilizer you should apply to meet your soil's nutrient needs.

First, you'll need to determine the square footage of the lawn or garden to be fertilized. Don't get tense—we'll keep it simple. But we will need to break out a few simple math skills.

For square or rectangular areas, multiply the length in feet by the width in feet. Triangular beds use a different formula: Multiply the height of the triangle by the length of the base, then divide by 2. For circular beds, measure the diameter of the circle, then divide that in half to get the radius. Multiply this number by itself and then by Pi (3.14).

Determining the square footage of irregular beds requires a little creativity. Look at the overall shape. Is it closest to a rectangle, triangle or circle? Estimate using the appropriate formula, or break it down into smaller subsets. Perhaps it looks like a rectangle with a circle on the end. Calculate the square footage of both, then add those figures together.

Doing the Math

Once you've figured out the square footage of your garden, you're ready to calculate how much fertilizer you need. Here's how.

Divide 100 by the *percentage of the nutrient in the fertilizer*. Multiply this figure by *the amount of actual*

Fertilizer Terms

● **Balanced.** These fertilizers have equal percentages of N-P-K, such as 10-10-10 or 12-12-12.

● **Chelated.** Nutrients are in a form that prevents them from binding with the soil so they're available to the plant.

● **Complete.** Fertilizers that contain N, P and K.

● **Incomplete.** These fertilizers contain one or two of the three major fertilizer elements.

● **Fertilizer ratio.** The relative amounts of N, P and K in a fertilizer. For example, a 5-15-10 fertilizer has a 1-3-2 ratio, with three times more P than N and two times more K than N.

● **Grade or analysis.** The guaranteed amount of N, P and K in the fertilizer.

● **Straight.** These fertilizers contain only one of the three elements, such as triple superphosphate (1-46-0) and ammonium nitrate (33-0-0).

nutrient needed. This equals the number of *pounds of fertilizer* you should apply.

For example, let's say you need 1 pound of actual nitrogen per 1,000 square feet. You decide to use ammonium sulfate (33-0-0). Divide 100 by 33; multiply by 1. The answer is 3, so you need 3 pounds of ammonium sulfate to provide 1 pound of actual nitrogen per 1,000 square feet.

Let's try the same thing with Milorganite (6-3-0). Divide 100 by 6. Multiply this figure by 1. The answer is 16.7—the number of pounds of Milorganite needed to provide 1 pound of actual nitrogen per 1,000 square feet.

How to Apply Fertilizer

Now that you've selected a fertilizer, what's the best way to get it into the soil and make it available to the plant? The fertilizer bag usually provides directions for application. Here are some general application techniques.

● **Broadcasting.** In this method, fertilizer is sprinkled over the soil surface and worked in by tilling, cultivating, watering or rain. You can use a hand-held or push spreader for large areas or shake the fertilizer on by hand.

Broadcasting is an easy way to incorporate fertilizer before planting. In existing gardens, broadcast when the plants are dry. Brush off any granules that land on the leaves. Lightly cultivate, water or wait for rain to move the fertilizer into the soil.

● **Topdressing.** This is applying a ring of fertilizer around individual plants. With this technique, you can apply fertilizer only to plants that need it.

● **Sidedressing.** Use this technique for gardens where plants are growing in rows. Spread fertilizer in a continuous strip alongside the plants.

● **Banding.** This is similar to sidedressing, but it's used when seeding flowers or vegetables in a row. Place the fertilizer in a shallow trench at least 2 inches away from, and 1 inch deeper than, the seeds you're planting.

● **Root plug feeding.** This method is for feeding trees and shrubs. Dig narrow, evenly spaced holes 1 foot deep throughout the area under the tree or shrub's drip line. Divide the fertilizer equally and mix it with soil or compost to fill the holes. This gets the fertilizer below the grass roots, so all of it is available to the tree or shrub. As an added benefit, this aerates the soil, too.

● **Lance feeding.** Special equipment is used to inject a liquid fertilizer solution into the soil surrounding the tree. Keep in mind that most of the tree's feeder roots are in the top 12 inches of the soil. To deep-feed your trees, make sure you don't put the fertilizer below the level where it can be absorbed.

● **Spikes and tablets.** Fertilizer spikes and tablets are placed in the soil around plants. You will pay a little more for this convenience. Some plants may experience burn from the concentrated fertilizer in the root zone.

● **Foliar application.** A dilute solution of liquid fertilizer is applied to the leaves until all the foliage is wet. Nutrients are absorbed through the leaves instead of the roots. This is not practical for most home landscapes, since the plants can absorb and use only a small amount of the fertilizer. Foliar feeding is commonly used for applying micronutrients and for testing nutrient deficiencies.

● **Fertilizing containers.** Add a slow-release fertilizer such as Osmocote to your soil mix before planting your container. Every time you water, a little fertilizer is released. This gives plants a small, steady flow of nutrients and eliminates the sometimes messy job—at least for me—of mixing fertilizer with water.

How Much Is a Pound of Fertilizer?

ONE of my professors used to say, "A pint's a pound the world around", and for most commercial-grade fertilizers, this is true. For other formulations, the figures vary a bit. This chart will help:

● **Mixed fertilizers**: 1 pound equals 1 pint, or 2 cups.

● **Composted manures, sewage sludge** and **urea** (45-0-0) and **ammonium nitrate** (33-0-0): 1 pound equals 1-1/3 pints, or 2-2/3 cups.

● **Ammonium sulfate** (21-0-0): 1 pound equals 1-1/3 pints, or cups.

● **Potassium sulfate** (0-0-50) and **ground dolomitic limestone**: 1 pound equals 3/4 pint, or 1-1/2 cups.

For smaller quantities, remember: 1 pound equals 1 pint, 2 cups, 32 tablespoons or 96 teaspoons.

Tools to Use

Drop and broadcast spreaders can be used to apply granular fertilizer to large areas, such as established lawns, or before planting large lawns, landscape beds and gardens.

Hand-held spreaders are used for applying granular fertilizer to small or medium-sized gardens.

You can make your own spreader by punching holes in the bottom of a coffee can. Make sure an

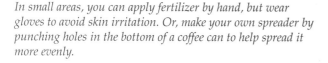
In small areas, you can apply fertilizer by hand, but wear gloves to avoid skin irritation. Or, make your own spreader by punching holes in the bottom of a coffee can to help spread it more evenly.

even flow of fertilizer can be applied. For small areas, hand applications are fine.

Hose-end applicators mix liquid or water-soluble fertilizer with water, allowing you to fertilize large areas of lawn, shrubs, trees and flowers.

General Guidelines

If your soil test results haven't arrived yet, follow these general guidelines on what to apply to various plantings and when.

Annual flowers should be fertilized before planting with a low-nitrogen formula. Use 2 to 3 pounds per 100 square feet per season. You can apply it all with one application of slow-release fertilizer, or make three 1-pound applications spread throughout the growing season.

Ground covers should be fertilized with nitrogen in spring to provide 1 pound of actual nitrogen per 1,000 square feet. Fertilize once a year or every other year.

Perennials should be fertilized in spring with compost or aged manure. Apply 2 inches every 2 to 3 years, using additional fertilizer as needed.

Trees and shrubs can be fertilized every 3 to 5 years as needed in fall after a hard freeze, or in the spring before growth begins. Apply enough nitrogen fertilizer to provide 2 pounds of actual nitrogen per 1,000 square feet. For new plantings, wait a year before adding fertilizer.

Changing Soil pH

I frequently talk with gardeners who want to buy a bag of lime "because Grandma always did and her garden looked great". What they forget is that Grandma lived in an area where the soils were acid. Now they're probably gardening in an area with alkaline clay. The *last* thing they need to do is add lime and make it even more alkaline.

Yes, I know. You're already tired of me telling you to test the soil first. But this is especially important when trying to change the soil pH. Adding lime to sweeten acid soils by raising the pH can have long-lasting effects. Adding too much sulfur to lower the pH can damage plants. Either way, doing it wrong is a mistake you'll be correcting for years to come.

Lime and sulfur are applied just like fertilizers—mixed into the top 6 inches of soil in new gardens or spread directly on the soil and cultivated in existing ones.

It's easier to select plants suited to your soil than trying to change pH. Most plants tolerate a pH range of 6.5 to 7.5. Beyond this neutral range, we're more limited in terms of plants that will thrive in the existing pH. (See charts on pages 32-33.) For a more detailed discussion of pH, see Chapter 1.

Raising Soil pH

You do want to reach for that bag of lime if your soil is acid and your plants' growth and health are

being affected. The amount you'll need depends on the existing pH, the level you want and the soil type. It takes more lime to adjust pH in clay soils than in sandy loam. Follow your soil test report for best results. (See the Liming Chart on page 32 for general guidelines.)

You'll find agricultural or ground limestone in both dolomitic and calcitic forms. The dolomitic type contains 5% to 13% magnesium, while the calcitic contains less than 5% magnesium and 30% to 40% calcium.

Hydrated lime, sold as builders' lime or calcium hydroxide, will work faster but has a greater risk of overliming the soil and damaging plants. It can be difficult to spread and can burn your skin or the plants' leaves if misapplied. Apply it during cool weather, when foliage is dry, and use the recommended amount. A better choice would be to stick with agricultural or ground limestone.

Pelletized lime, which was designed to make application easier and cleaner, is compressed into pellets or granules. Make sure the pellets break down when they become moist or watered in. Otherwise they won't do much to change the pH.

Lowering Soil pH

This is more difficult. Most alkaline soils get that way from naturally occurring lime from limestone bedrock, marl (calcium carbonate-rich clay) or seashells. So, every time you try to lower the pH, there's an endless supply of lime to neutralize your efforts. Alkaline conditions also occur near new masonry buildings, where excess concrete and mortar fell and were mixed into the surrounding soil.

The easiest way to maintain the existing pH or lower it slightly over a longer period is to use acidifying fertilizers like ammonium nitrate, ammonium sulfate and sulfur-coated urea. Aluminum sulfate is often recommended for quick results, but you'll need large amounts to change pH, and you can end up with aluminum toxicity, which will injure your plants.

Regular applications of organic matter, especially acidic peat moss, will help some plants overcome the negative effects of high pH. Yearly or semi-yearly applications are needed. If you're already adding organic matter anyway, this is just another benefit.

Elemental sulfur also can help lower pH. As the soil bacteria act on the sulfur, they transform it into sulfuric acid and neutralize the soil. Be patient—this can take years. Since there's an endless supply of "lime", the sulfuric acid is eventually used up and the pH begins to rise.

You may need to make future applications of elemental sulfur to maintain the lower pH—but, again, be careful. Too much sulfur added all at once can injure or kill the plants.

A single application should never exceed 20 pounds per 1,000 square feet in new gardens, or 5 pounds per 1,000 feet in existing plantings. If you need more, divide the applications over several seasons and retest the soil before each application.

Apply sulfur just as you would lime or fertilizer. Mix it into the top 6 inches of soil in new gardens, or spread it on the soil surface of existing gardens and lightly cultivate.

Use caution when adding lime to soil. If you add too much, you'll be correcting the mistake for years to come.

Garden centers have lots of products to help fortify your flower beds. Take a look at the label for the percent of Water Insoluble Nitrogen (WIN) or Water Soluble Nitrogen (WSN). The higher the percent of WIN, the more nitrogen that will be released slowly. Select a formula that matches your gardening style and soil test recommendations.

How Much Do I Use?

Jerry Howard/Positive Images

Sulfur Chart

Pounds of elemental sulfur needed to lower pH
1 unit in the listed soil types

Sand	Loam	Clay
.8 lbs. per 100 sq. ft. 8 lbs. per 1000 sq. ft.	2.4 lbs. per 100 sq. ft. 24 lbs. per 1000 sq. ft.	3.6 lbs. per 100 sq. ft. 36 lbs. per 1000 sq. ft.

Liming Chart

Pounds of dolomitic or calcitic lime needed to raise pH to 6.5

Current soil pH	Sand	Loam	Clay
6.0	2 lbs. per 100 sq. ft. 20 lbs. per 1000 sq. ft.	3.5 lbs. per 100 sq. ft. 35 lbs. per 1000 sq. ft.	5 lbs. per 100 sq. ft. 50 lbs. per 1000 sq. ft.
5.5	4.5 lbs. per 100 sq. ft. 45 lbs. per 1000 sq. ft.	7.5 lbs. per 100 sq. ft. 75 lbs. per 1000 sq. ft.	10 lbs. per 1000 sq. ft. 100 lbs. per 1000 sq. ft.
5.0	6.5 lbs. per 100 sq. ft. 65 lbs. per 1000 sq. ft.	10 lbs. per 100 sq. ft. 100 lbs. per 1000 sq. ft.	15 lbs. per 100 sq. ft. 150 lbs. per 1000 sq. ft.

NOTE: Never apply more than 150 pounds of lime per 1,000 square feet in one season.

SIGNS OF NUTRIENT DEFICIENCIES

Deficient nutrient	What to look for
Nitrogen	Pale green or yellowish lower leaves; slow growth.
Potassium	Older leaf edges are yellow or brown. May be chlorotic, curl or have spots.
Phosphorus	Stunted, extremely dark-green leaves. Purplish to reddish veins, leaves or stems. Flowers and fruits late.
Calcium	Deformed or failed terminal buds and root tips. Results in blossom end rot in tomatoes and peppers.
Magnesium	Yellow in area between veins and may show mottling of older leaves.
Sulfur	Entire plant is light green; chlorotic younger leaves.
Iron	Upper leaves are yellow between veins and eventually look bleached. New leaves may be yellowish white.
Manganese	Yellow leaves between veins followed by spots that occur on middle leaves first.

Source: North Central Regional Extension Publication No. 356—Fertilizing Garden and Landscape Plants and Lawns.

OPTIMAL pH LEVELS TO MAKE YOUR PLANTS THRIVE AND FLOWERS BLOOM

NOTE: *Plants growing outside their optimal range need to be monitored for nutrient deficiencies.*

Ornamental plants	Best pH level	Ornamental plants	Best pH level
Aconite (*Aconitum*)	5-6	Impatiens (*Impatiens*)	5.5-6.5
Ageratum (*Ageratum*)	6-7.5	Iris (*Iris*)	5-7
Amaranthus (*Amaranthus*)	6-6.5	Ivy (*Hedera*)	6-8
Aster (*Aster*)	6-7	Lilac (*Syringa*)	6-7.5
Boxwood (*Buxus*)	6-7.5	Lily (*Lilium*)	5-6
Buttercup (*Ranunculus*)	6-8	Lily-of-the-valley (*Convallaria*)	4.5-6
Calceolaria (*Calceolaria*)	6-7	Magnolia (*Magnolia*)	5-6
Calendula (*Calendula officinalis*)	6.5-7.5	Maidenhair fern (*Adiantum*)	5-6
Campanula (*Campanula*)	5.5-7	Marigold (*Tagetes*)	5.5-7
Canna (*Canna*)	6-8	Mock orange (*Philadelphus*)	6-8
China aster (*Callistephus*)	6-8	Narcissus (*Narcissus*)	5.5-7.5
Christmas rose (*Helleborus niger*)	6-8	Nasturtium (*Tropaeolum majus*)	5.5-7.5
Chysanthemum (*Chysanthemum*)	6-7.5	Nicotiana (*Nicotiana*)	5.5-6.5
Clematis (*Clematis*)	5.5-7	Oenothera (*Oenothera*)	6-8
Coleus (*Coleus*)	6-7	Oleander (*Nerium*)	6-7.5
Columbine (*Aquilegia*)	6-7	Pansy (*Viola*)	5.5-6.5
Coralbells (*Heuchera*)	5-7	Peony (*Paeonia*)	6-7.5
Cotoneaster (*Cotoneaster*)	6-8	Petunia (*Petunia*)	6-7.5
Crocus (*Crocus*)	6-8	Phlox (*Phlox*)	6-8
Cyclamen (*Cyclamen*)	6-7	Poppy (*Papaver*)	6-8
Dahila (*Dahlia*)	6-7.5	Primrose (*Primula*)	5-7
Daphne (*Daphne*)	6-7	Privet (*Ligustrum*)	6-7
Daylily (*Hemerocallis*)	6-7	Rhododendron (*Rhododendron*)	4.5-6
Deutzia (*Deutzia*)	6-7.5	Rose (*Rosa*)	5.5-7.5
Dianthus (*Dianthus*)	6-7.5	Saxifrage (*Saxifraga*)	6-8
Dicentra (*Dicentra*)	5-6	Scotch heather (*Calluna*)	4-6
Elder (*Sambucus*)	6-8	Snapdragon (*Antirrhinum*)	6-7.5
Filbert (*Corylus*)	6-7	Sneezeweed (*Helenium*)	5-7.5
Forget-me-not (*Myosotis*)	6-8	Spirea (*Spiraea*)	6-7.5
Forsythia (*Forsythia*)	6-8	Spring adonis (*Adonis vernalis*)	6-8
Foxglove (*Digitalis purpurea*)	6-7.5	Stock (*Matthiola*)	6-7.5
Fuchsia (*Fuchsia*)	5.5-6.5	Sunflower (*Helianthus*)	5-7
Gentian (*Gentiana*)	5-7	Sweet pea (*Lathyrus odoratus*)	6-7.5
Gladiolus (*Gladiolus*)	6-7	Tamarix (*Tamarix*)	6.5-8
Goldenrod (*Solidago*)	5-6	Trollius (*Trollius*)	5.5-6.5
Hawthorn (*Crataegus*)	6-7.5	Tulip (*Tulipa*)	6-7
Heath (*Erica*)	4-4.5	Veronica (*Veronica*)	5-6
Hepatica (*Hepatica*)	6-8	Viburnum (*Viburnum*)	5-7
Holly (*Ilex*)	4.5-6	Wax begonia (*Begonia semperflorens*)	5-7
Honeysuckle (*Lonicera*)	6-8	Witch hazel (*Hamamelis*)	6-7
Hydrangea (*Hydrangea*)	4-6.5	Zinnia (*Zinnia*)	5.5-7.5

Common Fertilizers

Fertilizer needed to apply 1 pound of actual nitrogen

Fertilizer grade	lbs. of fertilizer	lbs. P provided	lbs. K provided
45-0-0 (urea)	2.2	0	0
33-0-0 (ammonium nitrate)	3.0	0	0
27-7-7	3.7	.26	.26
24-8-16	4.2	.34	.67
21-0-0 (ammonium sulfate)	4.8	0	0
20-20-20	5.0	1	1
20-10-5	5.	.5	.25
20-5-5	5.	.25	.25
18-6-12	5.6	.34	.67
12-12-12	8.3	1	1
12-6-6	8.3	.5	.5
10-10-10	10	1	1
6-12-12	16.7	2	2
5-10-10	20	2	2
5-10-5	20	2	1
Cow manure .5-.3-.5	200	6	1
Milorganite 6-3-0	16.7	5	0
Kelp and seaweed 1-.5-9	100	5	9
Grass clippings* 1-.3-2	100	3	2
Dried blood 13-11.5-.6	7.7	9	.05

*Don't use clippings treated with pesticides.

Fertilizer needed to apply 1 pound of phosphorous

Fertilizer grade	lbs. of fertilizer	lbs. N provided	lbs. K provided
0-45-0 (triple superphosphate)	2.2	0	0
2-27-0 (steamed bone meal)	3.7	.07	0
0-2-6 (wood ash)*	50	0	3

Fertilizer needed to apply 1 pound of potassium

Fertilizer grade	lbs. of fertilizer	lbs. N provided	lbs. P provided
0-0-60 (muriate of potash)	1.7	0	0
0-0-50 (sulfate of potash)	2	0	0
1-.5-9 (kelp and seaweed)	11	.1	.05
0-2-6 (wood ash)*	16.7	0	.33

* Alkaline material. Use only in acid soils.

The *Plant Doctor* is in

Q: *I have a steeply sloped area in my landscape that I'm tired of mowing. I want to convert this area from lawn to ground covers, flowers or shrubs. How can I get rid of the grass and replant without losing the soil to erosion?*

A: Good planning on your part. Most people realize soil erosion will be a problem only after removing the grass, when the soil begins washing down the hillside.

If you don't mind using herbicides, kill the grass with a total vegetation killer such as Roundup or Finale.

Leave the dead grass in place to help hold the soil in place while your new plantings get established. Cut through the turf to plant, then mulch with shredded bark or wood chips. The dead grass will eventually decompose, adding organic matter and nutrients to the soil.

To accomplish the same thing without using herbicides, cut the grass very short and cover with several layers of newspaper. Top this off with wood chips or shredded bark.

Plant your trees, shrubs and flowers through this mulch. The newspaper and wood chips eventually kill the grass. In the interim, the grass's root system holds the soil while the new plants take over, stabilizing the bank.

Q: *I've heard about gardeners using green manure crops to improve their soil. What are these and how do they work?*

A: Green manure crops are a great way of growing your own organic matter. Quick-growing crops such as annual and winter rye, buckwheat and clover are planted in spring, summer or fall. Prepare the soil as if you were planting a flower or vegetable garden. Seed your crop and water as needed. Mow the green manure crop before turning it into the top 6 inches of soil. Winter crops are tilled under in spring, and summer crops in fall.

Q: *I have an established perennial garden. How do I add organic matter and fertilizer to improve the soil without redoing the garden?*

A: I hear this question a lot. If the soil was properly prepared, you only need maintenance upkeep. Spread a 1- to 2-inch layer of compost over the soil surface every other year. Recent research shows this also fulfills the fertilizer needs for most perennials. Use organic mulches such as shredded leaves, cocoa bean shells and pine needles. As the mulch breaks down, earthworms and insects move the organic matter into the root zone.

Struggling perennials growing in poor soil may benefit from a total overhaul. Dig out the perennials, kill weeds and prepare the soil. It sounds like a lot of work, but it will save you time and headaches in the long run.

Q: *My soil test recommends adding fertilizer to my shrub plantings. The area is covered with a 3-inch layer of wood chips. Do I need to remove the chips before applying fertilizer?*

A: Good news! You don't have to remove the mulch. Spread the granular fertilizer over the mulch. Lightly rake to help get the fertilizer through the mulch and to the soil surface. Irrigation, through sprinkling and rainfall, will help move the nutrients into the soil. Liquid fertilizers also can be applied over the mulch.

Q: *I have old fertilizer that has been stored in my shed. Is it still good?*

A: Your storage area determines the shelf life and effectiveness of fertilizer. Store granular fertilizers in a cool, dry place. Once they become wet, the particles clump together, making them hard to spread and distribute the nutrients evenly. Use damaged fertilizers in your compost bin.

Liquid fertilizers should be kept in a place that's dark and cool, but not freezing. Exposure to light and freezing temperatures can diminish effectiveness. Use questionable products at the recommended rate. You may need to make additional applications. Let your plants be the guide. It's always easier to add more fertilizer than to replace damaged plants.

Chapter 3
Get Rich with Compost

Let's start this chapter off with a green-thumb riddle: What kind of gold grows on trees, is buried in many backyards, won't be found in a bank vault and eventually disappears? You got it if you said "gardener's gold" or "black gold", also known as compost.

This valuable natural resource can be found in just about any backyard. It's simply leaves, stems, branches and other plant parts that have decomposed into a brown crumbly material rich in nutrients.

Many gardeners avoid composting because they feel it's too difficult or just too time-consuming. As you'll see, composting is not only easy, it's one of the best ways to keep your gardens producing beautiful flowers and tasty vegetables.

And, if you're a "casual composter" like me, all you'll have to do is leave your yard waste in a heap and wait for Mother Nature to break it down. I find composting is actually a time-saver because I don't waste time hauling away weeds or grass clippings, or having to buy peat moss and other amendments for my garden soil.

Composting 101

COMPOSTING is as simple as combining your "green garbage"—plant and vegetable debris—with a little soil and fertilizer or manure. It's the perfect recipe for making a conditioner that's good for any garden soil.

This rich organic matter adds nutrients, improves drainage, increases water-holding capacity and buffers the pH.

Many skeptical gardeners ask me, "How can one soil additive do all this—and how can it improve drainage while increasing water-holding capacity?"

It all comes down to the raw materials and composting process. The plant debris serves as a food source for microorganisms (bacteria and fungi), worms and insects. They feed on and digest the plant matter, turning the leaves, stems and clippings into rich soil nutrients. In other words, it's microscopic manure!

The digestive process creates glue-like substances, which help bind sand and organic particles together into larger clumps. These clumps are more effective at holding water on their surfaces, where the plants can retrieve it.

Compost, what we commonly call the final result of the broken-down plant debris, holds up to 10 times more water than poor soils. This means less watering for you.

Sandy and rocky soils treated with compost will hold moisture near plant roots longer than untreated soils. And improved soils will need less attention during periods of drought.

My friend Jerry Nelson does an excellent job amending soils with compost. During a June drought, his established perennial gardens in Racine, Wisconsin outgrew the competing weeds, even with only 1/4 inch of rainfall for the month!

Keeps on Working

Soil improvement continues even after the compost is added to a garden. As worms and insects seek out and digest the organic matter they find in the compost, their travels create natural airways through the soil, improving drainage and creating a better environment for roots to grow.

They also mix the compost throughout the soil,

improving areas where garden tools can't reach. It sure makes our "job" as gardeners easier.

The great thing is, you don't even have to worry about buying worms or calling them over from a neighbor's yard. By adding compost, you're sending out an invitation for nature's recyclers: worms, insects, fungi and bacteria. They'll somehow find the compost on their own and, to thank you, they'll keep improving the soil long after you spaded it in.

Composting also neutralizes the raw plant materials used to create it and the soils where it is added. This increases nutrient availability to plants, because they grow best in neutral soils where the pH isn't too low (acidic or sour) or too high (alkaline, limey or sweet). (See page 15 for more information on pH.)

The all-important micro-organisms that make compost are on the plant debris and soil-covered roots you add to the pile.

Putting It to Work

There are many uses for compost. Use it to improve existing plantings, or till a 2- to 4-inch layer of compost into the soil when planting new gardens. By starting out with the right foundation—rich soil—you're laying the groundwork for years of attractive and healthy gardens.

I recommend adding compost yearly to annual vegetable and flower gardens. Spade an inch or 2 of compost into the soil in fall as you put your garden to bed for winter, or do it in early spring before the growing season begins.

Lots of gardeners ask me, "Won't my garden soon reach my waist if I keep adding compost each year?"

Don't worry. Each 100 pounds of organic matter breaks down into 10 pounds the first year, and then decreases to 1 pound by the second year.

That usually leads to the question, "So why should I bother?"

For one good reason: It's the process of making and breaking down the compost, not just the organic matter itself, that improves the soil.

Topping It Off

When adding compost to your existing perenni-

al gardens, simply spread an inch or 2 around the base of established plants. This process is called "topdressing".

Topdressing adds small amounts of nutrients and organic matter to the soil. Earthworms and insects will move the compost through the soil to plant roots, where it's needed most. Digging into the soil with tools to add compost could damage the roots, so in this case, the easy way is the best way.

Recent research has found that topdressing with compost provides sufficient fertilization for most perennials. That's good news for busy gardeners who just don't have time to regularly fertilize their plants.

It's a good idea to use a shovelful of compost whenever you divide or transplant perennials, too. This is the only chance you'll have to improve the soil until the plant needs to be divided again—which might not be for 3, 5 or even 10 years.

It's easy to do. Just lift the perennial, spread compost over the new and old planting space, and mix it into the top 12 inches of soil before replanting the divisions.

I even use compost as a potting mix. When I dig up plants and seedlings to share with friends and neighbors, I place these starts in a small container of compost.

Compost can be added whenever you work in the garden soil. Adding it in fall helps the soil drain better. Therefore, it warms faster in spring.

"Cook away" many of the weed seeds and disease organisms by heating compost to 160° for 30 minutes.

Some gardeners sterilize their compost with their grill, oven or microwave, and use it in potting mixes for houseplants and seedlings. The grill is probably the best method, unless you're home alone. Many gardeners have told me their families weren't too pleased with the "earthy aroma" of baking soil.

Planning for Perfect Compost

UNLIKE SAUSAGE, compost is easy to watch as it's made. Don't let the process scare you off.

I remember when yard waste regulations became reality in my home state of Ohio. My father called me to ask if I had any information on composting.

I had to chuckle. He's the one who taught me to compost years ago when I was growing up. We just never called the pile of grass clippings and leaves in the backyard our "compost pile".

So relax—there's a composting method that fits your gardening style, even if you don't have one. If you just throw your yard waste in a pile, it will eventually rot into useful compost, with or without your help. There's only one thing your time and effort can accomplish—and that's to speed things up.

I recommend you first check with your local municipality, neighborhood association or condominium board for regulations related to composting. Some communities restrict the size, location or content of the compost pile, so save yourself some frustration and wasted effort by asking first.

Getting Started

Take a walk around your yard and look for a place suitable for making compost. Consider both aesthetics and function as you look around.

The compost area should be convenient for adding raw materials and removing the finished product—otherwise, you won't use it. But you don't want it to detract from the beauty of your landscape. (Be mindful of your neighbor's view as well.)

You may even want to have several compost locations in your yard if your landscape produces plenty of green debris and you use lots of compost.

Many gardeners make it as easy as possible, composting in the middle or at the back of their gardens. When the process is finished, the bin can be removed and most of the compost can be spread right into the surrounding area.

One additional thought: Make sure your pile is within reach of your garden hose. You may need to moisten the pile during hot, dry periods, and that's much easier if you don't have to string lengths of hose together or carry buckets of water to the far reaches of your landscape.

Compost bins should be located in a convenient place in your backyard. Multiple collection bins allow you to have more than one pile of compost at one time. A hose nearby is helpful—a compost pile should be as moist as a damp sponge.

Use climbing vines and trellises help hide compost bins. Grapevines surround this well-hidden compost room (above).

Hidden from View

There are many effective ways to camouflage your working compost bin. I've stumbled upon them below grape arbors, tucked between a garden shed and a neighbor's hedge or hidden in the middle of a tomato patch.

Some gardeners use decorative fencing or compost structures to separate and hide the process. I extended my lattice fence along the garage to hide my pile from the neighbor's view.

One creative gardener solved this dilemma by using her children's old play structure as a large trellis and covering it with ornamental vines. Behind it, hidden from view, was the compost bin. Traditional plant-covered trellises, ornamental hedges or tall plantings also make attractive screens.

Let the Sun Shine in

Composting works in both sun and shade, but warm sunlight certainly helps speed up the process.

The sun also may dry out your pile, so you may need to moisten a compost pile in a sunny location more often than one in the shade. If this is a concern, just place your bin in a partially shaded spot to get the best of both worlds.

Drainage is just as important. Poorly drained sites result in waterlogged piles that decompose slowly and tend to smell bad.

One of the easiest ways to improve drainage is to build your pile on top of a screen-covered wood pallet. You also can dig a shallow hole and lay wood or metal supports across it to hold screening. Then set the pile on top of the screen.

Another option is to run a few drain tiles under the pile to help move away excess moisture.

Recipe for Award-Winning Compost

EVERYTHING will rot given time and exposure to the elements. Composting is our way of speeding up the process.

Plant debris, moisture and oxygen are essential to the organisms that change our green garbage into useful compost. Maximize these resources in the proper proportion and you'll get faster results.

The good news is you can't do it wrong. A mistake can always be corrected, and it will only delay the composting process, not ruin it. All it takes to create the ultimate compost pile is a little planning and knowledge.

To get your crop "cooking", select one of these methods to best fit your time schedule and gardening style. No matter which one you use, the results are the same—rich, crumbly compost that's sure to make your gardens grow.

Layering Method

One of the best techniques that has been used by gardeners for years is the layering method (below). The idea behind it is combining various materials to help create ideal conditions for materials to decompose—thus, speeding up the process.

Building a Compost Pile

Place coarse materials at the bottom and center of the pile, where the higher temperatures will help speed decomposition. As you turn the pile, move less decomposed matter to the center.

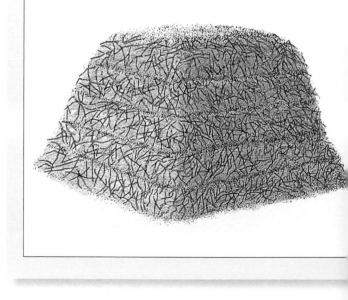

It takes a little more work, but gives you faster results. To do this, you may have to collect different types of plant debris and keep it in a "holding area" until you are ready to construct the pile.

Start by making sure the base of your pile has plenty of air circulation. I highly recommend placing your bin on a pallet covered in hardware cloth.

At the bottom of the bin, place a layer of branches or twigs. This allows air to reach the bottom of the pile, and helps drain excess moisture.

The next layer should be a 10- to 12-inch layer of equal parts green and brown plant material (see the list of greens and browns on page 45). Green debris—"fresh material", like grass clippings—is high in nitrogen and moisture. Brown debris—"weathered" or "coarse material" like fall leaves, corncobs, sawdust and straw—is higher in carbon and more absorbent.

Turbo Boost

To really get the pile going, add a little fertilizer or manure with each layer of vegetation. This provides an added source of food for the microorganisms as they break down the compost.

Cover each layer with a thin layer of soil or finished compost. These ingredients contain the bacteria, fungi, insects and worms that will do the work.

Continue layering vegetation, manure and soil until the pile is *at least* 3 feet tall and wide. This provides the minimum volume needed for efficient results. Smaller piles will break down; it just takes longer.

Be careful not to make the pile too large. Tall piles may topple, and wider piles may be hard to turn and maneuver.

Sprinkle the pile with water to moisten the layers so they're the consistency of a damp sponge. The pile should be damp, not wet—excess moisture limits the amount of oxygen available to the decomposing organisms. A soggy pile also smells bad and decomposes slowly.

If you get carried away with the water, add some compost, dry leaves, peat moss or other absorbent material. During rainy periods, protect the pile by covering it with plastic. Remove the plastic as the weather and pile begins to dry.

The Nose Knows

Now that the pile is complete, use a broomstick, crowbar or pipe to punch holes into it. This creates airways in the center of the pile, which will speed up decomposition.

Your nose will be the first to let you know if your compost pile is properly vented. A poorly aerated pile decomposes slowly and gives off an odor you won't soon forget. Eliminate the smell by turning the pile. This adds more oxygen.

Perforated PVC pipes, cylinders of wire mesh or bundles of twigs placed throughout the compost pile also will help by creating airways, allowing oxygen to reach all parts of the pile. Just remember that a well-aerated pile tends to dry out more quickly.

You also can improve oxygen circulation with a compost aerator, available from garden centers and catalogs. This 2- to 3-foot pole has a collapsible appendage at one end, which you punch into the pile. The appendage opens as you pull back, creating airways in the pile.

Warming up the air surrounding the compost pile also speeds up decomposition. Just cover your pile or bin with clear plastic. As the sun's rays move through the plastic, they warm the air beneath, just as they do inside your car on a cold but sunny day. The heat is trapped, the pile is warmed and the organisms can get to work more efficiently, breaking down the green debris.

Compost Containers

A removable or hinged front gives easy access. In three-part box, compost being used is in the left section, decomposing compost is in the middle and the right section is being filled by layers of raw materials.

Reader's Digest Assoc. Inc/GHD

To Bin,
Or Not
To Bin...

Compost bins come in a variety of shapes and sizes (above). Good bins allow for air circulation and easy access.

OVER THE YEARS, I've learned bins are not necessary for creating quality compost. In fact, some bins can actually get in the way of loading, turning and harvesting compost, making the process more difficult.

But compost bins can be useful and more attractive than a simple mound. They come in many shapes, sizes, styles and configurations. You can make your own or you can buy one from a garden center, catalog or Web site.

A good compost system should fit the space available and match your gardening style and budget. Here are some of the things you should consider before deciding on a compost bin:

● **Select a bin appropriate for your backyard.** Some bins may only be sufficient for small city lots or gardens, while others will handle everything on the "back forty" and then some.

If your property produces lots of yard waste, I recommend using several bins scattered throughout the yard, or one large one with several compartments. When one bin or compartment fills up, just start another.

● **Decide if you want to "turn" the pile.** One of the fastest ways to produce compost is to routinely rotate or mix the materials. A bin that allows you to do this quickly and easily will produce more compost than one left to break down material on its own.

Some bins have movable dividers to help. Other structures with more permanent sides require some elbow grease—you may need to lift the material up and out of the bin and mix it before refilling. To tell you the truth, both methods are too much work for a casual composter like me. I rely on time to break down my materials.

● **Consider a cover.** If you live in the Pacific Northwest or other rainy areas, cover your bin to keep excess moisture from your pile. A clear sheet of plastic draped over the top works well. When the weather improves, remove the cover to improve air circulation.

● **Looks are everything.** If your compost is in a highly visible location, you can purchase a bin designed to blend into the landscape or, if you're handy, build your own. We recycled old pallets to create the outer walls of our compost bin. We covered it with a lattice that blends in with our fence, then planted ornamental grasses around it to "soften the edges".

● **Mounds work great.** The easiest way to compost is by just maintaining a pile of yard debris. To speed up the process, simply turn the materials on occasion. If you're too busy to turn the pile—or just not very motivated—don't worry. Nature will take over for you.

Tumblers (center) make turning yard debris a cinch and speed the compost-making process. The results are the same with a simple heap (above). It just takes longer.

It takes time for yard debris to break down, but as you can see by the sequence of photos above, raw plant debris will eventually reduce itself to a pile of rich, crumbly earth. Amazing!

The Waiting Game

It's time to wait. As the various organisms start breaking down the plant debris, the temperatures within the pile starts to rise.

A perfectly constructed pile will reach temperatures of 160° in the center for several days. These high temperatures help destroy some of the unwanted disease organisms and weeds. If the pile is not "heating up", add more nitrogen-rich green debris (see list on page 45).

It's good to have a nice, long compost thermometer (right) to monitor the temperature of the pile's center. As the temperature begins to drop, turn the pile.

To do this, simply move the less decomposed materials from the sides and top of the pile into the center. Rotate the composted materials from the center to the sides and top. Shifting the material reactivates the pile, and you'll see another slight rise in temperature.

I like to use a garden fork or shovel when turning my compost. It is a great workout—no need to visit the gym on those days.

Other Effective Methods

Another way to compost is in long, narrow windrows at least 5 feet long and 3 feet wide. This method is especially easy if you use a rototiller to turn the pile.

One pass down the middle moves the center to the outside. Another pass on each side mixes the materials and moves the outer material toward the center. A quick touch-up with the rake, and the heating process begins again.

Another easy method that saves your back is using a compost tumbler or rolling compost bags and cubes. You can purchase these, or make your own from a 50-gallon barrel.

These containers take the sometimes backbreaking work out of turning compost. Just roll the bin to mix the materials inside. Many people mount them at a convenient level for loading debris and unloading finished compost.

I was raised on another easy system—the trenching method. After dinner every night, my parents would assign one of us kids to take any rinds, peelings and vegetable scraps to the garden, throw the debris in a hole and cover it with soil. I never figured out if it was because of the trench composting or all the manure we hauled in from Dad's family's farm, but both probably helped him grow the best tomatoes on the block.

Longer trenches in the back of the garden or between rows can provide endless composting space. You can pre-dig the trenches and fill them in as you go. By the next spring, most of the green debris will be composted. The garden can be tilled and the soil will be improved and ready for planting.

Looking for an even easier method? Take your cue from nature. Composting occurs all the time, without any help from us. Look at the forest floor, natural areas and even your mulched garden. As old vegetation drops to the ground, the fungi, bacteria, insects and earthworms move in and start converting it to rich soil.

You can do the same thing in your garden with "sheet composting", putting noninvasive weeds, excess seedlings and leaves right back on top of the soil. As I pull weeds and surplus seedlings, I place them between the rows and around the desirable plants. (One word of warning—don't do this with invasive weeds like quack grass or bindweed or any weeds with seeds.)

These garden discards act as mulch, conserving moisture, reducing future weed problems and returning nutrients to the soil. In fall, I shred leaves with my mower and spread them around perennials, shrubs and other plants. Composting doesn't get much easier than that.

Decision Time

Regardless of which method you choose, after about two turns of the pile, you'll need to make a choice. You can add fresh material and keep the process going, or start a second pile with fresh material and let the first pile finish composting. The second method gives you faster results, while allowing you to continually compost your green debris.

Avid composters usually have several piles going at once. They may use one area or bin as a holding area, storing green debris until they're ready to create another pile.

They'll also have a fresh pile that has recently been constructed and is actively decomposing. The remaining piles are in various states of decomposition.

Ready to Harvest

Compost is "ripe" when it's brown and crumbly and looks like rich soil. Some gardeners use a wide mesh screen to filter out twigs, stems and other larger materials that have not fully decomposed. This is a good practice if you're using compost for potting and seed starting.

Even compost that is only about 50% decomposed can be used in the garden. Dig it in or spread it over the surface as mulch. It will continue to decompose and eventually move through the soil, with the help of earthworms and insects.

Composting Your Lawn

You can give your lawn an added boost by recycling its clippings, too, with no additional work.

By mowing frequently, using a mulching mower or making several passes over the grass, your nitrogen-rich clippings stay on the lawn and break down within a few days, increasing the organic matter in your soil. This adds as much as 3 pounds of actual nitrogen per 1,000 square feet—equal to 30 pounds of a 10-10-10 fertilizer!

You can apply the same technique in fall. Rather than using a rake to gather and bag leaves, simply use your mower to chop leaves into fine pieces. As long as you can see blades of grass beneath the leaf debris, your lawn will be fine.

So there you go—composting isn't as hard as it sounds. And instead of buying soil additives at the garden center, loading them into the car, hauling them home and into the garden, you're creating rich organic nutrients just a few steps from where you'll use them.

What a great way to save money and natural resources. No wonder compost is "gardener's gold"!

Wear gloves, ear plugs and safety goggles when using chipper-shredders. Don't wear loose clothing that could get caught in the machine.

Do You Need a Chipper-Shredder?

YARD WASTE, no matter how large, will eventually decompose, so a chipper or shredder isn't absolutely necessary. But smaller pieces do break down faster, ensuring quicker compost.

Commercial shredders and chippers are available at garden centers and equipment stores, but they can be pricey. Before you invest in one, find out which type works best for the yard waste you generate. Certain shredders work best on leaves and small brush, while others will handle twigs 1 to 2 inches in diameter. Some models may clog when shredding fresh or wet materials, so be sure to investigate your options before buying.

I recommend renting shredders first. This way you can try several different models and find one that works best for you. No matter how good a piece of equipment looks in the garden center or catalog, if it doesn't fit your needs, you won't use it.

If you decide to buy equipment, consider splitting the cost with several friends or relatives. (Just make sure your relationship can withstand the test of sharing!)

Several Master Gardeners I know earn a little extra income by shredding other gardeners' yard waste for a minimal fee. I couldn't convince my husband we needed a chipper-shredder, but he's happy to hire a friend to help us with our large debris.

The Compost Mantra

"EQUAL PARTS of green and brown help to break the compost down"—is a good guide for creating fast compost. But don't let the science get in your way. Just adjust the mix if the pile isn't decomposing fast enough, or if it starts to smell bad.

If your compost has an ammonia odor, you need more carbon-rich brown debris. To turn up the "heat", you can add more nitrogen-rich green debris.

Here are a few common sources of green and brown debris:

GREENS

Fruit wastes
Garden weeds
Grass clippings
Manure
Seaweed and kelp
Vegetable clippings

BROWNS

Cornstalks and cobs
Evergreen needles
Paper
Sawdust and
 wood chips
Straw and hay
Most tree leaves

Jerry Howard/Positive Images

What Not to Compost

- **Disease and insect-infested plants.** Most compost piles do not heat up enough to kill these harmful organisms.

- **Charcoal ashes.** The ashes contain materials that may be toxic to plants.

- **Fabric.** Most contain synthetics that don't decompose.

- **Grass clippings treated with weed killer.** Leave these clippings on the lawn until you've cut the grass four to six times.

- **Meat, fish and fats.** These attract animals and rodents.

- **Pet, bird and human waste.** These can contain diseases.

- **Weeds gone to seed.** Seeds survive temperatures of most compost piles. Using compost containing these seeds will reintroduce weeds to your garden.

- **Invasive weeds.** Weeds like bindweed and quack grass can survive the composting process.

Q: I have tried composting several times. Each time it starts out fine, but the pile eventually ends up smelling bad. What am I doing wrong?

A: Smelly compost means too much water.

Keep the pile moist, about the consistency of a wrung-out sponge, but not soggy and wet. Cover it with plastic during prolonged rainy periods, or add a cover to your bin if you live in a wet region of the country.

Adding oxygen helps dry the contents and dissipate the smell. Punch holes in the pile with a crowbar, pipe, aerator or similar tool.

You may need to turn extremely wet, smelly piles with a shovel or garden fork—and keep doing so for several days if it's waterlogged. Add leaves, straw, sawdust or other absorbing materials as you turn the pile.

Fork it over! Turning your compost pile helps aerate the material and keeps moisture levels in proper balance.

Q: I live in an urban area and am worried about attracting rats and other rodents to my yard by composting. What do you think?

A: Proper composting will not attract rodents. The important rule to remember is that you can't use meat, fat or other animal products in your compost. Also avoid moistening the pile with dishwater—it may contain grease and other food wastes that can attract animals.

Some municipalities require trench composting of any food waste. Check with your local Health Department or Extension service for tips on composting in your city.

Q: How do I know when my compost is ready to use? Will it hurt to add unfinished compost to my garden?

A: Remember, everything breaks down eventually, whether it's in the compost bin or garden, so there's no danger in using unfinished compost.

Use finished compost—it's brown and crumbly and looks like rich soil—in potting mixes or anywhere soil needs to be improved.

Partially decomposed compost still resembles some of the original materials. Spade it into the garden in fall or early spring so it can finish decomposing before planting, or spread it over the soil and use it as mulch. In time it will break down, and earthworms and insects will move the compost through the soil.

Q: I'm a working parent and barely have time to garden, let alone do all the work involved in composting. How can I compost with limited time?

A: I can relate to your dilemma. Each spring I'm filled with good intentions, but family and work commitments quickly bring me back to reality. In my garden, if it isn't quick and easy, it doesn't get done.

I use a combination of composting techniques. First, I have a compost heap. I add garden waste to the pile as it appears. I occasionally turn the pile, usually when I need to vent some frustration or burn off calories. It takes a year or more to fully decompose, but I can harvest some great compost from

Karen Bussolini/Positive Images

Compost bins don't have to be unsightly to you or your neighbors. Clever gardeners can camouflage their bins with some attractive plantings, as shown by the shrubbery above. The wooden slats, which provide a decorative face, can be removed for easy access.

the bottom of the pile each spring and summer.

I also compost in place. That means I use most of the annual weeds (no seeds, of course) and excess seedlings from my gardens as mulch. Most of my leaves are shredded and left on the lawn, and the rest are used as mulch or dug into my small vegetable garden. Look at composting as a way to actually cut down on garden chores—you may find you'll save time and money.

Q: My neighbors have very tidy landscapes. I am worried they will be upset with having a compost pile next door.

A: A friend once said, "We all found places for our garbage cans. We certainly can find an acceptable space for composting." I think he was right.

Your compost pile should be on a level, well-draining spot near a water source, and located where you can easily work the pile.

Now consider the aesthetics, for both yourself and your neighbors. Try hiding the pile with a screen of plants, decorative fencing or a garden structure. Or select a bin that's decorative as well as functional.

Who knows? When your gardens look the best in the neighborhood because of your effective composting methods, your neighbors just may follow your lead.

Q: My old knees and bad back are making it harder and harder to turn my compost pile. I hate to give it up. Do you have any ideas for me?

A: Survey your neighborhood for willing apprentices. You'd be surprised how willing children are to help compost. Kids I've never seen in our neighborhood turn up to help turn my compost pile. It sometimes takes a little longer as we look for worms and insects, but I figure I'm training future gardeners and getting help along the way.

Also, new gardeners may be willing to help in exchange for some of your gardening know-how. See if they'd be willing to "work for compost" to use in their gardens. If you have friends in apartments or condos, they may even volunteer to lend a hand if they miss working the soil.

Otherwise, you may want to consider some of the tumbler or rolling compost bins, which make less work out of turning the pile.

Basic Gardening Techniques

Photo: SuperStock

Chapter 4
Perfect Planting

You can buy them by the six-pack, gallon or container. No, we're not talking about soda pop or milk—I'm talking plants.

The wide variety of plants and the ways they're sold can be overwhelming…especially in spring when nurseries are overrun by eager gardeners. Price, plant size and your gardening style will help determine which ones are best for you.

If you're like me, you'll start with small plants and watch them grow. It's not only more fun, but small plants recover from transplanting faster. And by starting small, you'll also stretch the gardening budget a little farther.

But, if you want quicker results, go ahead and spend a little extra for that early burst of color.

Proper planting starts with making the right selections, which means picking plants suited for the growing conditions of your region and landscape. Too often, we're lured into buying beautiful plants advertised as specimens that will "grow well in every garden", only to find they're suited for every garden but ours.

So before you purchase any new plants, take a little time to do some investigation. Read the tags and talk with other gardeners in your neighborhood. My rule of green thumb is, "Any plant that sounds too good to be true probably is."

Getting into the Zones

SINCE my garden is in Wisconsin, I always look at a plant's hardiness to cold first. Likewise, my Southern gardening friends are particularly concerned with heat hardiness. Fortunately, there's help for all of us—heat and cold hardiness maps to help with making plant selections (see pages 52 and 53).

Cold hardiness ratings are based on the average minimum winter temperature in an area. The USDA Cold Hardiness Map is the most commonly accepted and the one pictured in each issue of *Birds & Blooms*.

The American Horticultural Society more recently developed the Plant Heat-Zone Map (see page 53). This rating reflects the duration and extremes of heat in each region. It's based on the average number of 86° or hotter days per year from 1974 to 1995. The 86° mark is where heat starts damaging plants.

On both maps, you'll notice small islands of warmer or colder areas surrounded by other zones. This is typically where elevation differences, bodies of water or urban areas create different growing conditions in a particular zone.

Your own landscape may have such islands, too. Fencing, stonework, construction materials and existing plants may block cold winds, reflect heat, cast cooling shade or create sheltered beds. These can be one whole growing zone warmer! Luckily for you, these microclimates can stretch your planting palette beyond what's recommended for your area.

To get a better idea of the microclimates in your backyard, conduct a hardiness rating of your own. Just monitor temperatures in different areas and record your planting successes and failures. Soon you'll have a personalized hardiness map customized to your yard.

Finding the Perfect Match

Temperature is just one factor influencing plant survival. Soil type, pH and drainage also play important roles. Soggy or droughty winter soils can kill even the hardiest plants, so it's vital to select ones

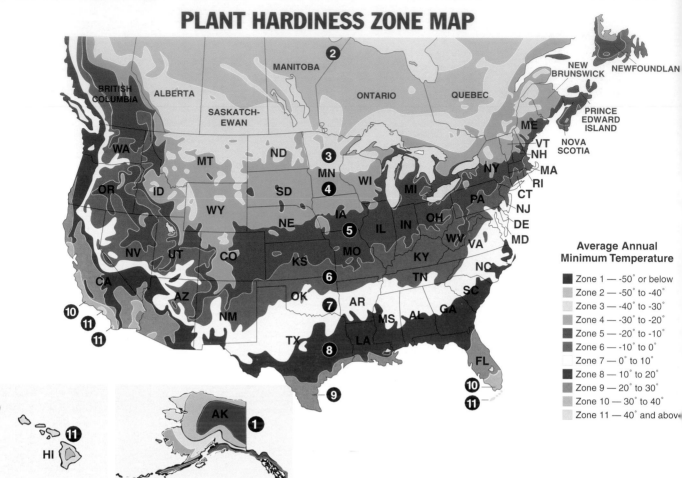

PLANT HARDINESS ZONE MAP

Average Annual Minimum Temperature

- Zone 1 — -50° or below
- Zone 2 — -50° to -40°
- Zone 3 — -40° to -30°
- Zone 4 — -30° to -20°
- Zone 5 — -20° to -10°
- Zone 6 — -10° to 0°
- Zone 7 — 0° to 10°
- Zone 8 — 10° to 20°
- Zone 9 — 20° to 30°
- Zone 10 — 30° to 40°
- Zone 11 — 40° and above

best suited to your soil conditions. (Refer to Chapter 1 for details on amending and improving your soil for gardening success.)

Moisture is essential to plant health. Sure, we can give nature a hand through regular watering, but it's less work and better for our environment if we choose plants that do well in our existing conditions. (We'll discuss how to get the most out of your watering efforts in the next chapter.)

If rainfall and water supplies are limited, select plants that are better adapted to hot, dry locations. Use moisture-tolerant tropical plants in areas with lots of rain.

During the growing season, blustery winds can stress plants, tatter large leaves and topple tall perennials. Simply choose low-growing plants with smaller leaves for these areas.

Winter winds can be drying, especially for evergreens, causing needles to brown.

Environmental factors like pollution, deicing salts and ocean spray can stress or kill plants. In these areas, take extra time to look for plants that will tolerate your unique conditions.

And last, but just as important, select a plant that will fit its location when mature. It's hard to imagine that cute little evergreen tree in the 1-gallon pot will soon grow into a towering giant in your front yard, but it will.

Make sure there's plenty of room for your plant to reach its full potential. That means looking up as well as around. The electric company won't like pruning your trees around the utility lines any more than you'll like the finished result.

Leave sufficient space between the plants and your home, walkway, drive and other permanent plantings. If you have questions, refer to plant tags, talk to qualified nursery personnel or call your local county Extension service.

Once you've narrowed down your choices, remember that aesthetics is the overall goal in gardening. Maximize your planting efforts by placing tall plants in back of shorter ones you want to view. I have a small yard with several narrow paths and plants of various sizes. Some are hidden from the road by their taller neighbors, but all are visible as you stroll along the inside paths.

PLANT HEAT-ZONE MAP

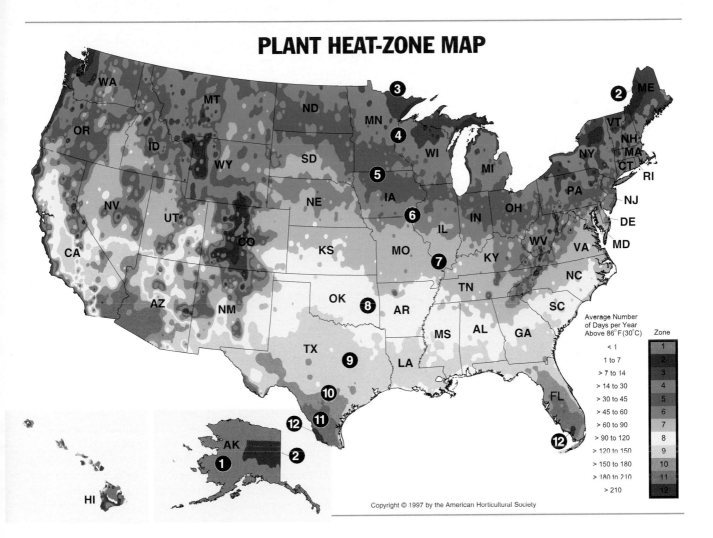

Average Number of Days per Year Above 86°F (30°C)	Zone
< 1	1
1 to 7	2
> 7 to 14	3
> 14 to 30	4
> 30 to 45	5
> 45 to 60	6
> 60 to 90	7
> 90 to 120	8
> 120 to 150	9
> 150 to 180	10
> 180 to 210	11
> 210	12

And don't forget to add plants that provide several seasons of interest. Fall color, eye-catching texture, winter interest or a unique form can give your garden year-round appeal. I like to include a few plants, accents or combinations that create the "aah factor"—something that makes passers-by stop and say, "Aah, what a great idea!"

Starting Your Own Plants From Seeds

YOU CAN EXTEND the planting season and your gardening space by starting seeds indoors. It's lots of fun, and there's a great sense of accomplishment seeing tiny seeds develop into beautiful flowering plants. This is often the only way to get the latest and more unusual varieties that aren't yet available at the garden center.

The downside is that this takes lots of patience, time, daily attention and plenty of space. Right now, I'm lacking all four. So I start a few plants here and there, but I'm waiting until I retire to empty a cor-

ner in the basement so I can go into this full swing.

Before you start planting seeds, take a look at your lifestyle and see if you have the desire to take on this task. If you do, you'll need just a few supplies to start—good-quality seeds, sterile planting mix, sufficient light and clean containers.

Top-Quality Seeds Are Top Priority

For the best results, *always* invest in top-quality seeds. Don't get lured into those in-store specials that seem too good to be true. (Remember my green-thumb rule in my introduction on page 51?) Read each seed packet before buying—this will help you determine the quality of the seeds inside and help predict your success later.

Buy seeds that were packaged for the current growing season or tested within the past 6 months. If you can't find this information on the packet, don't buy them. Simply look for a brand that includes this information.

Another important piece of information is the germination percentage. The higher the number, the more seeds are likely to sprout.

The backs of quality seed packages include lots of useful information, such as starting dates, growing conditions and germination times. Don't forget to compare package weights rather than their overall physical size.

Setting Down Roots

You can start your seeds in purchased or recycled containers, flats or cell packs. Recycled containers and flats should be cleaned first with a solution of one part bleach to nine parts water to destroy any disease organisms that could contaminate the planting mix and kill your seedlings.

A convenient method is to plant in peat pots or compressed peat disks that expand into planting pots when wet. When you start seeds in these, you can transplant the entire container into the garden. This reduces your workload and transplant shock.

To save money and help the environment, consider recycling household containers for starting seeds. All you'll need to do is punch holes in the bottom of these containers for drainage.

Reusing things you'd otherwise discard, such as yogurt containers, pudding and applesauce cups or paper and Styrofoam drinking cups, makes the job more fun and teaches young gardeners about recycling at the same time.

Covered fast-food salad containers make great mini greenhouses. Cut the tops off plastic soda pop bottles for instant seed pots. Egg cartons work well, too, and so do gallon milk jugs.

You can even cut rings from the middle of soda bottles and use them to line flats. This keeps the soil in place. When it's time to transplant, remove the plant with minimal disturbance to the roots.

Inventory your current planting supplies before shopping or ordering more. The money saved can be used for purchasing more seeds.

Regardless of the pots you choose, it's important to fill them with a sterile seed-starter mix from your local garden center. Most of these are a combination of peat moss and vermiculite, which provide good moisture retention and drainage at the same time.

The Perfect Setup

If you wish to grow your own seedlings, start by cleaning out an area in the basement, spare room or other location to create your propagation space. It's difficult to grow compact, healthy transplants with natural light, so you should consider investing in artificial lights.

All you need is a fluorescent light fixture and bulbs. Use a combination of cool and warm fluorescent bulbs or the more expensive "grow lights" to provide the spectrum of light your seedlings will need.

Hang light fixtures over a table or from a shelf, sus-

Peat pellets (below left) expand into planting pots when moistened. Recycle cups (below center), egg shells, cartons (below right) and other household items into pots. Make sure to provide drainage holes as needed.

pending them from chains or a pulley system so you can raise and lower them easily.

Paint the shelf or table white, or cover it with a mirror, aluminum foil or other reflective surface to increase the amount of light reaching the plants.

You can make your own system, convince a handy friend to help you build one or simply buy one of the systems found in garden supply catalogs.

Planting the Seeds

Now you're ready to start planting. Fill your clean containers with sterile seed-starting mix. Leave about a 1/2 inch between the lip of the container and the top of the soil.

Check each seed package for planting details. It will tell you when to plant seeds indoors based on your last spring frost. (If you don't know the date of the last spring frost in your area, contact your county Extension office.)

Most seeds come ready to plant, but check the label to be sure. Some seeds have a hard covering and need to be nicked, scratched or soaked overnight to help them sprout. Others need a cold treatment before they'll start growing. This may be more critical if you've collected your own seeds from the garden to start indoors. (See Chapter 6 for tips on propagation.)

Don't be too eager to start your seeds. Patience, as always, is important to success. If you plant them too early, you'll end up with leggy transplants that suffer more transplant shock than those started at the proper time.

Place two seeds in each container, just in case one doesn't sprout. For larger containers, broadcast seeds randomly over the soil surface before covering with more starter mix or plant them in rows. As the seedlings grow, transplant them into larger individual pots.

Whatever technique you choose, planting depth remains the same—sink each seed into the soil to a depth about twice the diameter of the seed. Fine seeds, like begonias, or those that need light, like browallia, should be sprinkled onto the

Start a few seeds in each container, just in case one doesn't sprout. Be sure to use sterile seed-starting mix.

Making Your Own Potting Mix

SOME GARDENERS prefer to make their own potting mix. Homemade compost mixed with vermiculite or perlite works just fine, but you'll need to sterilize the compost first to kill harmful bacteria and fungi.

The easiest way is to heat the compost in a microwave oven. It only takes about 90 seconds on full power to pasteurize a quart of soil.

You can also "cook away" harmful organisms in a conventional oven by heating the soil or compost to 160° for 30 minutes. (Don't "overcook" the soil, or you can create harmful toxins.)

Fill an oven-safe container—you may want to use something disposable—with no more than 4 inches of moist soil or compost. Cover with foil and cook until the soil reaches and maintains a temperature of 160° for 30 minutes. Cooking soil in a 200° oven for about 1 hour is usually sufficient.

You can use a meat thermometer to monitor the soil temperature, but the potato technique is more fun. Place a small baking potato in the container and cover with soil. When the potato is done, compost it—your soil is now pasteurized.

A word to the wary—this process does fill your home with an earthy aroma that some family members may dislike. I'll only do this on days when I plan to grill supper outdoors.

Once your soil is pasteurized, cover it until you're ready to use it.

soil surface. Just water to settle the seeds in place and ensure good soil-to-seed contact.

Water the planted containers with a gentle spray. Keep the soil moist by watering new plantings daily or as needed. Many gardeners cover their pots with a sheet of plastic, a plastic bag or a plastic lid to conserve moisture. You won't need lights at this point. Most seeds germinate best in the dark. For those that do need light to sprout, normal room light is sufficient.

Keep the soil warm to improve germination. Most seeds sprout best when soil temperatures are between 65° and 70°. Place flats on heating ducts, atop the refrigerator or in a warm location to speed up germination. You can also purchase heating mats and coils designed for this purpose.

Make sure to use only approved products and follow label directions. I've met a few gardeners who melted their flats and almost burned down their homes by not following this advice.

Let There Be Light

Move the seedlings under lights at the first sign of green. At this time you should also vent or remove plastic covers to avoid excess condensation, which can lead to disease. Some gardeners cover their whole light stand with plastic, which increases humidity to a more desirable level.

The lights should be about 4 inches above the tops of the seedlings. Raise the lights or lower the seedlings as the plants grow. Keep an eye on them—if the plants are leggy, move your lights closer, and if they're compact, move the lights away.

Your growing lights should be on for 14 to 16 hours a day. More than this won't hurt the plants, but it will waste energy—and money you could be spending on more seeds and plants. To make this job easier, I use a simple timer. That way you won't have to wake up in the middle of the night to check if you turned the lights off—or worry at work that you did not turn them back on.

Give Them a Name

It's important to label the containers and seed trays when you plant. This saves a lot of effort trying to identify the young seedlings once they sprout. You can buy labels or make your own.

My friend Clyde Wallenfang, a Master Gardener from Greenfield, Wisconsin, was the first to show me the "mini-blind technique". He cuts the slats from

Water seedlings with a gentle spray. Be sure to keep the soil moist, but make sure they're not sitting in excess water.

old window blinds into label-sized pieces and writes all the information on them with permanent ink.

Another friend, neighbor Cindy Coe Hartl, saves Popsicle sticks year-round for this purpose. They're the perfect size for small containers and flats.

Once the plants are in the garden, you might want to try this trick from my friend Jerry Nelson of Raymond, Wisconsin. He saves the tops from orange juice cans and uses a label maker to make raised-letter stickers for the metal disks. He mounts these on a wire cut from a discarded hanger and tucks them neatly into the garden.

Thinning and Transplanting

Once your seedlings have two sets of true leaves —they look like the mature plant's leaves—it's time to give them more space to grow.

In containers, make sure you have only one seed per cell pack, pot or container. Cut, don't pull, the weaker seedling off at ground level so you don't disturb the roots of the remaining plant.

Broadcast or densely planted rows will need to be thinned. Use a spoon, wooden stick or your fingers to gently lift seedlings out of the tray. Carefully pull them apart. Place one seedling in a container filled with sterile planting mix. Use a pencil or your finger to make a planting hole. Cover the roots with soil and water to ensure good root-soil contact. Move newly transplanted seedlings back under the lights.

Gently hold the seedling by the leaves, not the stem, when transplanting.

Fertilizing

Most seed-starting and planting mixes are made of peat moss mixed with vermiculite or perlite. This mixture retains moisture, provides adequate drainage and reduces disease problems, but it does not provide nutrients. You'll need to do that yourself.

Use a diluted solution of any fertilizer that is labled as "complete" or for flowering houseplants. Check the label for guidelines. It's easier to add more of the diluted solution than to rinse out excess fertilizer. Some growers use a highly diluted solution every time they water, some fertilize once a week and others use a slightly more concentrated mix every 2 weeks.

To save yourself the hassle of mixing and measuring, you may want to incorporate a complete slow-release fertilizer into the potting mix at planting time. This way, a little fertilizer is released every time you water. Pick the method that best suits you and the plants you're growing.

Moving Outdoors

As the plants grow and develop, they'll need more room. They may even outgrow the space you have available for them indoors.

Before you run into this problem, consider adding a cold frame to your outdoor gardening space. It provides extra growing space early in the season by protecting tender seedlings from cold temperatures and frost. They can also be used to acclimate seedlings to the harsher growing conditions outdoors. (See Chapter 13 for details on weather and Chapter 17 for more information on short seasons.)

With or without a cold frame, you need to gradually introduce your tender seedlings to the more intense light, lower humidity and other harsher conditions of the outdoor garden.

Think of the shock your body had the last time you visited another part of the country. Northerners are famous for overdoing the sunshine on their winter visits to the South. Their sun-deprived skin suddenly exposed to 8 hours of sunshine burns. The same happens to your seedlings.

First, stop fertilizing and cut back on watering 1 to 2 weeks before you plan to move the plants into the garden. Set the transplants, still in their containers, in a shaded location outdoors. Gradually expose them to direct sunlight, starting with an hour or 2 and then increasing the time a bit every day after.

At night, be sure to cover the plants or move them back indoors or into the garage or garden shed when temperatures drop.

Sowing Seeds Outdoors

As the air and soil start to warm, my favorite activity of the year comes—planting seeds directly outdoors. Quality seed packets should provide all the information you need to do this, including timing, spacing and depth.

But, before you can sow the seeds, you must prepare the planting bed. So go back and review Chapters 1 and 2 if you skipped ahead. Yes, I know the preparations described in these chapters can be tedious, but once you dig and plant in properly prepared soil, you'll see why you'll never want to skip this step.

What's so much fun about sowing seeds directly outdoors is that you start with a blank canvas just waiting for you to fill it with color. There are several ways to do this:

Cold frames can extend your propagation space and growing season. Be sure to vent the frame on warm and sunny days and close at night to maintain the desired temperature.

• Broadcast seeds throughout the garden and cover them with the recommended amount of soil.

• Mix the seeds with garden soil and spread the seed-soil mixture throughout the planting bed. Water the garden to ensure good seed-soil contact.

• Organize your seeds in neat rows or patches.

Broadcasting and seed mixes result in an informal look, much like a natural meadow. The drawback is it makes weeding and thinning a bit more challenging because it's hard to tell weeds and flowers apart until one or the other has overrun the place.

Row planting is easy. Just dig a shallow trench at the depth recommended on the seed packet (I use the handle of my shovel or hoe). Place the seeds in the trench at the recommended spacing, and cover with soil by carefully hoeing the disturbed soil back into the trench.

Gently tamp the row with the back of your hoe and be careful not to walk over seeded rows, especially in heavy soils. Applying too much weight to the furrow can compact the soil and reduce your success. Then water the freshly planted seeds with a gentle spray.

Planting mats and planting patches provide all you need in one package, although you'll pay extra for this convenience. The seeds are embedded in straw, cellulose or other mulch material. You roll out the mat or sprinkle the patch over the prepared soil, water it and you're finished.

No matter which technique you use, just remember to keep the top few inches of soil moist until the seedlings start to grow. When they sprout, cut back on watering frequency, but start watering more deeply as the seedlings develop.

Select Picks

Thin seeded areas when the young plants have at least two sets of true leaves. Most plants start with a set of seed leaves, but soon develop their actual leaves in a few days. It's a bit of a chore, but well worth the effort. Thinning reduces pest problems and improves the appearance of individual plants and, eventually, the overall look of your garden.

The remaining plants should now be at

Speaking of Seeds...
Planting Fine Seeds

FINE SEEDS, like those for begonias and impatiens, are small and hard to handle. Whether you start your seeds indoors or out, these tips can make the task a little easier.

• **Mix seeds with sand or vermiculite** before planting.

• **Buy pelletized seeds.** The fine seeds are covered with a thick coating to make planting easier.

• **Use seed tapes**—long, narrow strips of paper embedded with seeds. Roll out the tape, cover with soil and you're ready to grow.

• **Sprinkle fine seeds in a row**. Moisten soil and cover with lath—a thin, narrow wood strip used in construction—to conserve moisture and hold the seeds in place. Remove it as soon as the seeds sprout.

• **Purchase one of the commercially available seeders** designed to improve seeding success.

• **Make your own seeding machine**. My friend Ray created one with an electric razor and an index card that he cut and folded into a spout. He taped the card to the razor and filled the trough with seeds. Then he plugged in the razor and let the gentle vibrations shake the tiny seeds off the card one at a time.

Are Your Seeds Still Good?

SAVED SEEDS can last for 1, 2 or more years, depending on the variety and storage conditions. Here's one way to check the germination rate of any seeds you've saved.

Place 10 seeds on a moist paper towel. Fold the towel to cover the seeds. Place the towel in a plastic bag and store in a warm location. Check in 5, 7, 10 and 14 days to see how many seeds have sprouted. If half the seeds sprout, you have 50% germination and should plant these seeds twice as thickly as you normally would.

Recycle colorful seed packets as labels for your garden. Or, place them in your garden journal for future reference.

Thinning reduces pest problems and improves the appearance of individual plants and, eventually, the overall look of your garden.

their final spacing, with plenty of room to grow to their mature size. After thinning, don't forget to water the planting area to help settle the soil and any disturbed roots.

Thrifty gardeners will move excess seedlings to other garden areas, put them in containers or trade them with friends and relatives. If you don't plan to save them, you can speed up the thinning process by cultivating or cutting excess plants out of the row and placing them in the compost bin. This is the preferred method for gardeners like me who are less patient or too busy.

Now relax and enjoy your hard work. Keep after the weeds, monitor for pests and don't forget to water and fertilize as needed. Until we get to the maintenance phase, you'll have a little time to admire your planting efforts.

Buying Plants from a Nursury

IF YOU'RE buying plants from a garden center or nursery, make a plan and a shopping list first. This will reduce the temptation of impulse buying.

If you do succumb—and we all do—you'll still buy fewer plants than if you didn't have a list. And that minimizes your need to expand garden beds, crowd plants or hide that extra purchase from your gardening companion.

As you shop, remember that it's worthwhile to pay more for better plants. I consider it an investment. After all, an attractive landscape can add 15% or more to the value of your home. We all gamble on sale plants and sometimes end up with a cheap but attractive tree. But like most gambles, the odds are against us.

A discount plant may not have been handled properly during growing, digging, shipping or holding, and the stress often shows up *after* you place it in the ground. So select better-quality plants that cost a little more. The extra money spent now may save years of lost time trying to salvage a bad purchase, and money if you end up having to replace it.

When choosing your plants:

• **Avoid those that show signs of stress and pests.** Why pay for the additional challenge? The leaves should be of normal size and color for that variety. Leaves with brown edges, holes, speckling or spots have suffered from neglect, insects or disease.

• **Choose trees and shrubs that are well shaped.** Trees should have straight trunks with properly spaced branches or the right shape for that variety. Shrubs should have several stems with leaves from top to bottom.

• **Perennials and annuals should have stout, compact stems.** Where appropriate, they should be well branched or have multiple crowns.

• **All plants should show signs of new growth.**

Bringing It All Home
Once you've selected your plants, you want to keep your investment safe—and your car clean—for the ride home. Most nurseries will have plastic, twine and some other transporting materials you can use, but it's best to come prepared.

Smaller plants are usually not a problem. Most

A plant list can save you time and money when visiting the garden center. List the number and types of plants needed or space available for planting.

Transporting plants from a garden center to your backyard can be tricky. Bring containers or plastic to reduce the mess and prevent damage.

stores provide cardboard boxes or sheets of plastic to help keep your car clean. I always have old blankets in my car to cover the seats and stabilize the plants.

One of my horticulture students uses a hard plastic child's pool that fits perfectly in the back of her car, keeping her upholstery clean and her plants contained. It also makes a great weed receptacle when she's working in the garden.

Here are some more pointers when traveling with plants:

• **Avoid excess heat.** Don't leave plants in the car with the windows up for long periods during hot weather. Extreme heat can stress, damage and even kill them.

• **Protect trees and shrubs.** Make sure your vehicle is large enough to hold the plants without damaging them. Wrap tree trunks with cardboard, carpeting or fabric to prevent bark damage on the ride home. Anchor trees to the sides of the trailer or trunk to minimize movement and rubbing of the bark.

• **Watch out for wind damage.** I cringe every time I see newly purchased tree or shrub standing upright in the back of a truck or trailer traveling at 65 mph, with the wind ripping through the delicate leaves. Lay large trees on their sides in the bed of your truck or trailer and wrap leafy branches with a tarp, blanket or plastic to protect them from the wind. Many nurseries will lend a hand.

• **Move trees by the root ball.** Too many gardeners use the trunk as a handle, damaging the roots as they move the tree. You paid extra for that large root ball. Don't damage it before it gets into the ground.

• **Consider delivery.** Many nurseries will deliver larger plants and big orders. If you're buying trees or shrubs, dig the hole and have the nursery employees deliver it to the hole so you can finish planting.

In some cases, it may be worth the extra expense to have the nursery do the whole job—delivery, digging, planting and mulching. They have equipment and trained staff to do the job efficiently.

If your gardening ego gets in the way of asking for help, let me share my planting story. When I bought a candymint crabapple for my husband's birthday, a former horticulture student gave me a great deal—the biggest, best-shaped tree available.

As horticulture professionals, my husband and I have transported and planted many trees and shrubs in our career—but this was bigger than we could handle. We needed one more set of strong hands and one less boss.

If anyone had seen us planting this huge tree, we both would've had to turn in our shovels for good. The moral: Don't be afraid to ask for help or to pay a little extra for delivery.

Planting in the Garden

PLANTING times vary depending on the type of plant you select, its overall health and your weather. Whether you grow your own plants from seed or buy them from a nursery, it's important to harden them off before planting them outdoors.

Many garden centers and greenhouses do this for you, but it's best to check if you're not sure.

There are three different types of annuals—hardy, half-hardy and tropicals.

• **Hardy annuals** are the first to get planted in the North and brighten the winter gardens of the South. Pansies, snapdragons, lettuce and broccoli can tolerate cool soils and light frost.

• **Half-hardy annuals** like cleome, sunflowers and ageratum shouldn't be planted until the danger of frost has passed.

• **Tropical plants** like impatiens, caladiums, elephant's ear and peppers prefer warm soil and air.

There are also a number of different types of perennials:

• **Dormant perennials** can be purchased at the nursery or through mail-order catalogs, and can be planted whenever the soil is ready. Buying them is truly an act of faith, so use a reliable supplier.

My friend Mary bought quite a few dormant perennials from my horticulture students at their plant sale. Her husband was skeptical about her spending so much money on "bare sticks in a pot", but they all grew and flourished.

• **Greenhouse-forced perennials** need some help making the transition to your landscape. Harden them off just as you would annuals. The gradual introduction to outdoor growing conditions reduces transplant shock and plant damage.

● **Field-grown and container perennials.** Because they're grown outdoors, they're ready to plant when you buy them.

Moving Day

Your plants are ready to move to the garden, and you're eager to get them there. If your beds are prepared (refer to Chapters 1 and 2 for guidance), it's time for planting.

Early on moving day (or the night before), water your annuals or perennials so the soil is moist but not wet.

Gently squeeze small containers or roll larger ones on the ground to loosen roots from the pot. Then tip the container and slide out the plant.

I usually place my hand over the soil to guide the plant. Do not pull on the stem. This damages the valuable roots you spent so much time growing—or money to buy.

Gently loosen tightly wound roots or use a sharp knife to make shallow cuts from top to bottom in

Roll large container plants on the ground to loosen roots from the pot. Tip container and gently slide out.

several places on the sides of the root ball. This loosens girdling roots, encouraging them to forge into the surrounding soil.

I often see gardeners shudder as I describe this process, so I've started telling them to "lightly massage the roots". This makes it sound less stressful for the plants.

Whatever you call it, this step is important. I've seen too many failed gardens caused by pot-bound girdling roots. By mid-season, the tops and bottoms of these plants are the same size as when they were

Use a sharp knife to slice through pot-bound plants that have circling roots. This encourages roots to grow into surrounding soil instead of girdling the plant.

planted. The lack of root growth limits water and nutrient uptake and plant growth. So gently massage those roots to encourage them to spread into the surrounding soil.

For each transplant, dig a hole larger than the root ball. Loosening the surrounding soil also encourages root growth.

Place the plant so its base is no deeper than it was in its container. Fill the hole with soil and gently tamp.

Make a small "planting dish" of soil around each plant to help capture and direct water to the roots. This is especially helpful on slopes where water may run away from the roots.

Space plants according to the directions on the seed packet or plant tag. It's tempting to put little transplants closer together for a quicker display, but they'll quickly outgrow their space.

Now comes the hard part—remove the flowers. Yes, you read correctly—remove the flowers. You want your new plants to put their energy into forming roots, not into the flowers and seeds.

Removing the flowers will encourage branching and better root development. It may be painful for you, but in the long run, you'll have an attractive, deeply rooted plant that produces many blooms.

If you can't give up *all* the flowers, try this trick used by many of my professional colleagues. Remove the flowers on every other plant or every other row of plants. The following week, take off the other flowers. This gives you some "instant bloom" while still encouraging healthy growth.

Keep some materials on hand to protect the plants from cold weather, just in case you have an unseasonable frost. Average frost-free dates are just that. Most of us have lost a few plants to cold well after the last "average" spring frost.

My grandma, who was always busy doing something in the garden, used to cover new transplants with scraps of cardboard or newspaper. She would make little tents and anchor them with soil. She believed a couple extra days of shade helped her transplants adjust to their outdoor location by reducing moisture loss.

Bare-Root Transplants

Mail-order perennials, roses, fruit trees and berry bushes are often sold and shipped bare-root. These plants are grown at the nursery, and when they're dug up, the soil is removed from the roots, which

Mail-order plants are usually sold and shipped bare-root. Remove them from the container and plant immediately or store in a cool, damp place to plant later.

makes it easier and cheaper to ship. Then the plants are placed in cold storage and shipped to you at planting time.

Ornamental trees and shrubs are sometimes sold bare-root, too. These cost less, but usually have a lower survival rate, and you only have a short time to get them in the ground.

For the best results, plant bare-root trees, shrubs, roses and perennials as soon as possible. It's easy to do. Just soak the roots several hours or overnight be-

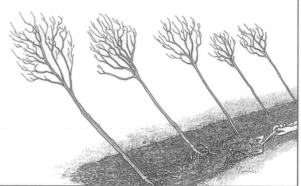

Heeling plants in a trench is a great way to store bare-root plants until you're ready to move them to their permanent location. Cover the roots with soil. Water to keep the soil and roots slightly moist.

fore planting. This helps the roots start absorbing moisture.

Before planting, be sure to prune any damaged or girdling roots. Dig a hole wide enough to accommodate the remaining roots. Don't skimp—cramming long roots into a small planting hole can lead to a number of problems. It may even kill the plant. Dig a shallow hole so the root flare rests at or slightly above the soil surface. A deep hole allows settling and can lead to root and crown rot.

When planting these types of plants, I find it helpful to create a mound of soil in the middle of the hole so I can rest the trunk or stem on this mound and drape the roots down the sides. Then I just backfill the hole with existing soil, making sure the crown—where the stems join the root—is even with the soil surface.

If you're buying bare-root plants from a catalog, the company will try to ship at your region's "normal" planting time. This usually works, but sometimes the plants arrive before you (or your garden) are ready. And many times the weather isn't suitable for planting. That's when it gets tricky.

If the timing isn't right, store the plants in a cool, frost-free location like a spare refrigerator (for small plants), garage or shed. Pack the roots in sawdust or peat moss and keep moist. Wrap the tops of smaller plants in moist paper or loose plastic to prevent them from drying.

You can also try heeling them into the ground (see illustration above). Just dig a trench in a vacant garden area. Place the bare-root plants in the trench and cover the roots with soil. Don't worry about spacing, since this is only a temporary location. Water often enough to keep the soil surrounding the roots moist.

A more challenging situation occurs when your bare-root perennials have already started to grow, and it's too cold to plant. Like other plants, such as annuals, the young tender growth needs to be hardened off before planting outdoors.

Pot these plants and grow them indoors under lights or outside in the protection of a cold frame until cold weather passes.

For trees and shrubs, pot them and place in a protected porch or the garage. Water thoroughly—enough to see the excess water seep from the bottom of the pot—whenever the soil is dry. Cold weather may damage the new growth, but with any luck, the plant will have enough energy to replace the leaves and keep developing new roots.

Giving Perennials the Right Start

1. *Properly space out plants.*

2. *Use a trowel to dig planting holes large enough for the roots.*

3. *Loosen the plant's roots and place in hole.*

4. *Place plant so the crown is even with the soil surface.*

Larger root plants need a larger hole. Dig with a shovel.

Get added value from large root clumps by dividing them into smaller plants. Plant divisions immediately so they don't dry out.

Growing Bulbs

The word "bulb" may conjure up visions of daffodils, tulips and hyacinths. But many people, myself included, use the word for many more plants, such as crocus, tuberous begonias, caladiums, cannas and any plant that starts from a bulb-like structure. Hardy and tropical plants grown from true bulbs, tubers, tuberous roots, rhizomes and corms are often lumped into this general category called "bulbs".

Northern gardeners are always trying to cheat the cold, while those in the South need to beat the heat. The same applies to bulbs.

Many North American gardens get too cold to leave cannas, calla lilies and caladiums in the ground for winter. To get a jump on the blooming season, start these non-hardy bulbs indoors. Planting directly outdoors will work, but it will take much of the growing season to get them to bloom.

Tropical bulbs can be grown indoors about 2 to 3 months before you plan to plant them outdoors. Start them in a flat with equal parts of peat and perlite or vermiculite. If you have just a few, plant them in a larger container where they can stay until the weather is good enough to plant them outdoors. Here's a quick guide for starting some of the most common tropical bulbs:

• **Tuberous begonias** should be sunk into the potting mix with their concave side up.

• **Canna rhizomes** should be laid on their sides and covered at least halfway with potting mix.

• **Dahlia roots** must be covered, with the eye (growing point) just below the surface.

Once growth begins, you can move the bulbs started in flats to larger containers filled with a well-drained potting mix. Plant tuberous begonias just below the soil surface and canna rhizomes several inches deep. For dahlias, keep the roots buried when moving them to new containers.

Treat these young plants just like the seedlings you're growing indoors. Provide adequate light and enough water to keep the soil moist. Use a diluted solution of any flowering or complete fertilizer labeled for indoor use. Harden the plants off before planting them outdoors.

Directly Planting Bulbs Outdoors

Tropical bulbs can be planted directly outdoors. Cannas and gladiolus can be planted

as soon as the danger of hard frost has passed. For tuberous begonias, callas and caladiums, you'll have to wait until the soil starts to warm. For other tropical bulbs, you'll have to check their tags or labels for more specifics on timing, planting depth and spacing.

Here's a quick guide for the common bulbs:

• **Gladiolus corms** should be planted directly in the garden starting in mid-spring and continuing through early summer. Stagger the plantings every 2 weeks—this will lengthen bloom time. Place corms 3 to 6 inches deep and 6 to 9 inches apart.

• **Cannas** have beautiful foliage that provides a nice backdrop for other flowers while you wait for the cannas themselves to bloom. When planting outdoors, place the rhizomes 4 to 5 inches deep for stability because their large leaves act like sails in gusty winds.

• **Dahlias** require a bit more work. Dig a hole 4 inches deep and place the tuberous root on its side. Some gardeners add an inch of soil every week as the plant grows, but I'm usually not that patient. I simply place a stake next to the tuberous root and cover with soil. Staking at that time avoids spearing a buried tuber.

• **Caladiums and tuberous begonias** should stay near the soil surface, covered with an inch of soil and planted 1 foot apart. Calla lilies can go a bit deeper, to a depth of 3 to 4 inches, and should be 12 to 18 inches apart.

Hardy Bulbs

Fall is planting time for most hardy bulbs. This means they need a cold period to set flowers and put on their beautiful spring or summer display. The best part is they can stay outside all winter in the North, without any extra fussing.

Southern gardeners, however, need to select species that are adapted to their short, mild winters. Another option is buying pre-cooled bulbs,

In colder areas, dahlias' tuberous roots must be lifted and stored for winter.

Tulips and other hardy bulbs need an extended cold treatment to rebloom. Mix with smaller bulbs like squills and grape hyacinths for a double feature.

where the grower does the work of nature by chilling the bulbs before selling them.

Unfortunately, they'll only bloom once without another artificial cold treatment, so consider them annuals and enjoy their one-time show.

Plant hardy bulbs in fall as temperatures cool. Planting too early can result in tender fall growth that can be damaged over winter. So hold off planting until the ground freezes. I'm often trying to get my last few bulbs in the ground as the snow flies. I've known a few fellow gardeners (procrastinators who will remain nameless) who have used blowtorches to thaw the soil or pickaxes to break through the frozen surface.

One of my students dubbed the latter the "manhole planting technique". And it works quite well. Just wait until the ground lightly freezes, then break out the pickax or shovel to break through the frost. Lift the plate of frozen soil and plant the bulbs in the non-frozen ground below. Water and replace the frozen "cover". Your bulbs will be safely tucked in for winter, protected from pesky critters.

Whenever you prefer to plant hardy bulbs, they should be placed at a depth that's 2 to 3 times their vertical diameter. This insulates them from cold and heat.

Spacing between bulbs should be about 3 to 4 times their diameter. Check the bulbs' tags for more specific planting and spacing information.

And don't forget to plant them right-side up. This is easy with daffodils and tulips—the pointed side faces up. It gets more difficult with ranunculus and other bulbs, where it's hard to tell the top from the bottom.

Don't worry if you make a mistake. These plants find their way to the surface—it just takes a little more energy and time when they're upside-down.

Water newly planted bulbs as needed until the ground freezes. During this time, the bulbs are busy putting down roots and need moist soil for best results. Keeping the soil moist for the bulbs is usually not a major task, since fall showers and cooler weather often does the watering for you.

After the ground freezes, winter mulch will help reduce the risk of early sprouting, frost heaves and other weather-related problems. (See Chapter 5 for more ideas on winter care.)

Planting the BIG Stuff

TREES, shrubs and roses are available as bare-root, container, potted or balled-and-burlapped plants. These larger plants present a bit of a challenge because of their size, weight and other handling issues.

Soil preparation is also different because of their larger root system. Their roots could extend 2 to 5 times the height of the tree, so it's next to impossible to amend the entire root zone.

And you *don't* want to amend the soil in the planting hole for bigger items. This creates more problems than it solves.

Adding lots of peat moss and compost creates a wonderful growing environment that the roots will never leave. When the roots hit the heavy clay or dry sand outside the planting hole, they turn and stay within the highly amended planting hole. This leads to girdling roots and early death.

Your primary focus for trees and shrubs is making sure the hole is the proper size. There's an old horticultural saying, "It's better to place a $50 tree in a $100 hole than a $100 tree in a $10 hole." Take time to dig a proper hole for your investment. Trust me—I've seen many gardeners waste time and money replacing failed plants just because they skimped on the planting hole.

Be sure to dig a hole at least 2 times wider than the diameter of the root ball on shrubs, and 2 to 4 times wider than the diameter of the root ball of trees.

But don't dig deeper than the height of the root system. Otherwise, your heavy plant will sink. Sunken planting holes collect water, and the plant's health may decline.

Before placing your large plant, scratch the sides of the planting hole with your shovel to make it easier for roots to penetrate the surrounding soil.

Then place your plant centered in your hole and backfill with the existing soil.

Shrubs should be at the same depth they were growing in the container. On trees, look for the root flare—the area where the trunk widens into roots. (You may have to gently dig through the soil around the trunk to find it.) Keep the root flare at or slightly above the soil surface. Burying the flare leads to trunk decay, root rot, early decline or death.

Potted Plants

Potted plants are a cross between container-grown and bare-root plants. Garden centers and nurseries pot bare-root plants in early spring and get them growing in their nursery or greenhouse. When the planting season arrives, the potted plants have already started to root and grow. This extends the planting time and makes it easier to care for them before transplanting.

On the down side, the immature root system may fall apart during transplanting. I found this out the hard way when a friend gave me a wonderful potted shrub rose. I assumed it had a well-developed root ball, but I was wrong. I took it out of the pot and watched the root ball fall apart before I could get it into the hole, leaving me with a fully leafed bare-root plant. It didn't make it, and I never made that mistake again.

Now I always check plants before taking them out of the pot. If the container is pliable and the soil crumbles, the plant is probably potted and needs extra care. If the container feels solid and it's hard to push a finger through the root ball, the roots are well established. If in doubt, ask. The grower should be able to give you a little history on the plant you plan to buy.

Potted plants need a little extra care at planting time. After preparing the hole, move the pot close to the planting area and cut off the bottom of the container. Set the pot in the hole, making sure it's at the same depth as in the container.

Slice through the side of the pot

Before planting, tilt the tree to remove any broken branches. They're easier to reach this way.

to remove it and backfill with existing soil. Gently tamp to remove air pockets and water. Mulch to conserve moisture, reduce weeds and moderate the soil temperature.

Container-Grown Plants

Container-grown trees and shrubs have an established root system. They cost more than bare-root plants, are more readily available, can be planted throughout the season and have a greater survival rate.

One problem often seen in these plants, however, is girdling roots. As the roots grow, they start to encircle the pot and begin constricting each other. When moved into the landscape, the roots continue this growth pattern, eventually strangling the trunk and preventing water and nutrients from moving between the roots and leaves.

To prevent this, do a little root pruning at planting time. Start by carefully removing the plant from the container. Set the plant in the hole, or use the same technique as for potted plants. Some gardeners and professionals cut away the pot on all container-grown plants to avoid damage.

With a sharp knife, make several cuts from top to bottom on the sides of the root ball. This encourages roots to grow out and away from the trunk.

Decomposing Pots

Horticulturists, like gardeners, are always looking for better, easier ways to grow plants. Paper and other decomposing pots are one such innovation.

The idea is to minimize transplant shock by growing, selling and planting trees and shrubs in the same container where they were raised. Over time, the pot should decompose, allowing the roots to grow and fully develop. Unfortunately, it doesn't always work.

When I worked as an Extension horticulture agent, a distraught homeowner brought in pictures of his dead junipers. The shrubs had been planted 4 years

A little root pruning at planting time is a good step to take to prevent girdling, which could eventually kill the plant.

earlier, and had done well until then. Since the junipers were dead, I asked him to dig one up and bring it in. As it turned out, the plant was in a "decomposing" pot—but the pot hadn't decomposed. It looked as good as the day he'd planted it. Needless to say, the plants were pot-bound and unable to

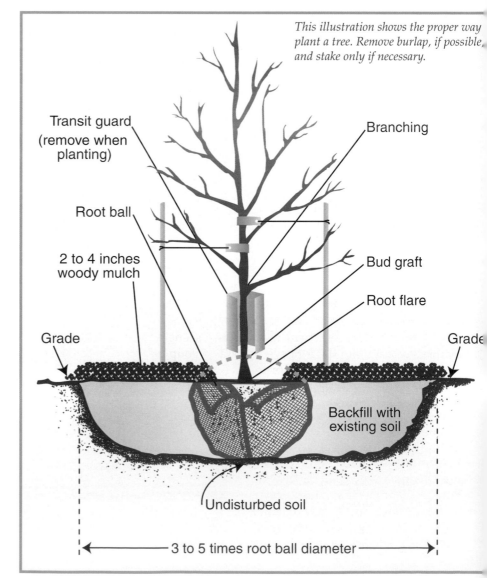

This illustration shows the proper way plant a tree. Remove burlap, if possible, and stake only if necessary.

Transit guard (remove when planting)

Root ball

2 to 4 inches woody mulch

Grade

Branching

Bud graft

Root flare

Grade

Backfill with existing soil

Undisturbed soil

3 to 5 times root ball diameter

absorb enough water and nutrients.

If you decide to use these pots in the ground, slice through the sides to allow roots to grow through the container. Also remove the lip so it doesn't extend above the soil. Exposed paper pots act like a wick, pulling moisture away from the roots.

Balled-and-Burlapped Plants

These plants are grown in the ground at a nursery and are dug up when dormant. The root ball is wrapped in burlap and sometimes placed in a wire basket to hold it together for shipping, storage and planting.

But there's a debate about how to plant them. Some nursery people prefer to leave the burlap and wire baskets in place so the root ball stays intact during planting. Arborists, tree-care professionals, suggest removing them. I fall in the latter group—I've seen too many mature trees girdled and killed by these materials.

If you're in doubt, check with your nursery. Many larger plants carry a warranty, but may require specific planting techniques. You'll have to weigh the pros and cons for yourself. No matter which method you select, it's best to leave everything intact until the tree or shrub is placed in the hole.

Before you dig the hole, locate the root flare and measure the distance from it to the bottom of root ball. This will give you the proper hole depth.

Loosen the twine around the trunk and place the tree in the hole. You'll need a bolt cutter to remove the wire baskets. Then cut the twine from around the trunk and peel back the burlap.

I recommend removing or cutting away all the burlap. If this isn't possible, at least remove half of it or slice through the fabric in several places to allow the roots to penetrate.

Prune off only the damaged and broken branches. The more top growth you leave on the tree, the more leaves there are to create and absorb the energy needed to rebuild the root system. Wait a couple of years after planting to start pruning.

Fertilization can wait, too. Let the tree get established first. Fertilizers can damage tender roots and interfere with establishment. If you feel you *must* fertilize, use a low-nitrogen, slow-release fertilizer at planting time. Better yet, apply the first dose of fertilizer the following season. Remember that you have a whole lifetime to fertilize.

If you already have trees that are planted too deeply or have burlap still on their roots, don't dig them up. The damage you'll cause will far outweigh any potential benefits. Instead, remove any twine around trunk and any exposed burlap…and hope for the best.

Preparing for a Stake-Out

Recent research has shown that staking trees can be detrimental to their growth and development. Staked trees are not allowed to move and flex in the wind, which helps the trunk grow larger in diameter. When the stakes are removed, the upper portion of the trunk is often larger than the lower portion and the plant can't support itself. Trees that aren't staked develop larger trunks and can better withstand adverse weather.

Of course, there's an exception to every rule. Bare-root trees should be staked, because their root system is small and lightweight compared to their top growth. Plants with large canopies and small roots, and those in extremely windy locations, need support, too.

If staking is needed, install them at planting time. For the best results, use two stakes placed in line with your tree. Make sure they're anchored in undisturbed soil for better stability. Use a wide cloth strap to secure the stakes to the tree. This distributes the pressure over a larger area and prevents po-

The proper way to stake a tree is with two wide cloth straps (above), each extending from a stake placed on opposite sides. Thin straps, wire or rope (at top) will damage the trunk, as will having more than one strap from a stake.

After planting, it's important to water thoroughly.

tential damage to the tree's trunk.

If you use wire to help anchor the tree, loop it through a rivet on the strap and back to the stake. Allow some slack so the tree can move in the wind.

Don't try the old wire-in-a-garden-hose trick—it doesn't work. All the weight is still on the wire, and that can damage the tree. Remove stakes after the first year.

Finishing Touches

Once your plant is in the ground, water it thoroughly. This settles the soil, ensures root-soil contact and encourages root development. Add enough water to moisten the top 6 to 12 inches of soil and water often, keeping the root zone moist but not soggy. Overwatering new plants can be detrimental, too, so don't be overly generous.

Check new plantings frequently. Annuals and perennials will need to be watered every couple of days in the first few weeks. Once the transplants begin to root into the surrounding soil, you can water less often. Moisten the top 4 to 6 inches of soil whenever the top few inches begin to dry. It should feel slightly moist but crumbly to the touch.

Trees and shrubs need thorough but less frequent watering. Check newly planted trees growing in sandy soils or hot regions twice a week. Those in clay soils or cooler regions should be checked every 7 to 10 days. Moisten the top 12 inches of soil in and around the planting hole whenever the top 4 to 6 inches start to dry.

There's one exception—container-grown trees and shrubs growing in soilless potting mix. This medium dries out faster than the surrounding natural soils, so you'll need to water more frequently.

Keep the root ball moist, watering several times a week, while keeping the surrounding soil moist, but not wet, with less frequent watering. Once the plant roots extend beyond the planting hole into the surrounding soil, it will be fine. Be patient—this can take up to two or three growing seasons.

Apply a layer of mulch around new plantings, but be careful not to pile it around the trunks of trees or over the crowns of plants. Mulching helps conserve moisture, moderate soil temperatures and keep mowers and weed cutters away from the plants.

If your soil is too difficult to plant in, consider adding a raised bed to your backyard.

Planting in Difficult Sites

MOST GARDENERS have less than ideal soil. In fact, many of us are growing in the subsoil excavated from the lot when our basements were built. Here are some things you can do to improve your planting success:

• **Create berms and raised planting beds** from existing soil. The mere act of raising the soil improves drainage.

• **Bring in topsoil** to create berms and planting beds.

• **Amend soil in large planting beds** to accommodate a number of plants and roots.

• **Install drain tiles** in problem planting holes to move water away from the roots.

The *Plant Doctor* is in

Q: *I have started plants from seeds for the past few years. Each year, the seedlings start to grow but suddenly fall over and die. Please help.*

A: "Damping off" is a fungus disease that causes the dieback you described. Start with new or sanitized pots and a sterile planting mix. This is usually sufficient to prevent the problem. If the disease invades your plantings, you need to act quickly. Apply a fungicide, labeled for this purpose, as a soil drench to the remaining seedlings as a preventative. Be sure to read and follow all label directions carefully.

Q: *I have leftover seeds every year. Can I save them for next year's garden?*

A: Store leftover seeds in their original packet, so you have the needed plant information, or a labeled envelope. Place in an airtight jar and store in the refrigerator. Keeping the seeds in a consistently cool, dark location will increase their life span. Most seeds last a year or more. (See "Are Your Seeds Still Good?" on page 58 to evaluate your success.)

Q: *I moved down South and miss my tulips and daffodils. Are there any I can grow?*

A: I have great news—you can purchase pre-cooled bulbs for winter planting. These will bloom in early spring. Allow the foliage to fade naturally, then dig up the bulbs and store them in your refrigerator until next winter. Replant firm, healthy bulbs and keep your fingers crossed. They should bloom again. Or, treat them as annuals and try new pre-cooled bulbs each season. (You also can chill bulbs yourself—just put them in the fridge for 12 to 15 weeks.) Some daffodil varieties can tolerate heat, and some will even bloom the following season in your growing region. Visit *www.bulb.com* for more details on growing bulbs in Texas and other regions.

Q: *I want to plant flowers under my tree, but the roots make it difficult to plant. How much topsoil do I need to grow flowers?*

A: None. Adding as little as an inch of soil around trees can kill some, although the damage doesn't show up for 5 to 10 years. Declining trees turn color early in fall and lose their leaves prematurely. Branches and, eventually, the whole tree can die.

Try growing perennials and ground covers around trees and shrubs. The digging will be difficult, but you only have to do it once.

You can also brighten up the area with pots filled with annuals, or set pots amid ground covers for a different look. Or, sink some old nursery pots in the ground. Then plant your annuals in a smaller container, set it in the sunken pot, and you have an instant floral display.

Q: *I have trouble growing trees and shrubs in my landscape. They start out fine, but by the end of the season they start to wilt. I water them every day.*

A: Too much water can be just as detrimental as not enough. Water new plantings thoroughly so you moisten the top 12 inches of soil. Wait until the top 4 to 6 inches of soil feels moist but crumbly before watering again. Watering frequency will vary based upon weather and soil. Clay soils and cooler weather mean less frequent watering. Plants in sandy soils or hot environments need to be watered more often.

Q: *Every spring, the leaves of my newly planted annuals develop white blotches. The plants seem stunted for the first few weeks. Eventually they seem to outgrow the problem. How can I prevent this?*

A: Sounds like your plants are getting sunburned. They need time to adjust to the brighter sun and drier conditions of the garden. Allow 1 to 2 weeks between purchase and planting to harden off the plants.

Chapter 5
Maintaining Paradise

Many gardeners ask me to recommend the perfect no-maintenance plant—a long-lived plant that blooms all season, requires no maintenance and is very inexpensive, or, better yet, free.

So far, I haven't found a plant that fills this bill, but my sister-in-law Cindy has some pretty convincing silk gladiolus, geraniums and other garden plants that even fooled me from a distance.

If you're not ready to toss in the trowel and opt for silk plants, then you may want to learn a little more about how to properly care for real live plants.

Providing the right amount of water, using the proper pruning and training techniques, and knowing how and when to move a plant to a better growing location will help keep your garden treasures healthy and looking good.

Water It Right

THE MOST DIFFICULT QUESTION I'm asked about gardening is, "How often should I water?"

Most gardeners don't like my steadfast answer: "It depends".

But it really does. Plants are living organisms growing in a changing environment, and nature always seems to give us either too much water or not enough. This makes it impossible to set a watering schedule based on the calendar.

Instead, I like to suggest watering based on your plants' needs and their environment. This way, you can make the most of what nature provides and maximize the impact of how you supplement it.

Gardeners naturally always try to do what's best for our plants. But sometimes our efforts do more harm than good. Watering is a perfect example.

As I drive through neighborhoods, I'm struck by the prevalence of what I call the "soda-can watering technique". A gardener arrives home from work, opens a cool drink and waters the entire landscape—grass, flower beds and vegetable garden—in the time it takes to finish a can of pop. The homeowner feels good about accomplishing the task, yet the water has barely penetrated the soil. This only encourages roots to develop near the surface.

And once you start watering your plants every day, there's no turning back. You must keep doing it throughout the season. A few days missed for vacation or illness can stress or even kill these plants. This type of watering is way too much work and responsibility for me.

Next time you reach for the hose, think *thorough but less frequent watering*. Thorough watering encourages roots to grow deeper. This gives them a larger area to draw moisture and limits the number of surface roots that draw moisture only from the top few inches of soil—the first area to dry out.

Rule No. 1: Apply enough water to thoroughly moisten the root zone of your plants. This is at least the top 4 to 6 inches for lawns, flowers and vegetables. Water a little deeper, 9 to 12 inches, for trees and shrubs. Applying an inch of water per week usually can do this.

When the top few inches of soil begins to dry (when it's slightly moist but crumbles in your hand), it's time to water again. For trees and shrubs, wait until the top 4 to 6 inches begin to dry.

The more experience you have, the easier this task gets. Soon you'll be able to tell whether your plants need water just by looking at them. Leaves that turn gray-green or a slightly "off" color, containers that feel lighter and lawns with visible footprints are all reliable signs that your plants need a drink.

But a few plants can fool you. After I recommended flowering tobacco (*Nicotiana*) for my mom's front garden, for example, she told me she liked the plants, but was tired of watering them every day. She said the plants always wilted in late afternoon.

I suggested Mom ignore the wilting and check on the plants later in the day, as the temperature cooled. Sure enough, they were fine.

Plants like this have a natural drought defense system—it's a way of reducing moisture loss.

If your plants wilt, check the soil before reaching for the hose.

Watering Tools

Many of us grew up using the old thumb-over-the-end-of-the-hose technique when watering. My,

Watering wands make reaching hanging baskets an easier and drier task.

have times changed. Now there are many watering devices that can be used to improve your efficiency in the garden.

Standard hose nozzles are great for creating a strong blast to knock pests like mites and aphids off plants. But they're a bit too rough on plants.

I prefer to use watering wands or nozzles designed specifically for gardening. The nozzles ap-

Select the watering can that best fits the job. A large reservoir may be heavier, but you won't have to fill it as often. And long spouts extend your reach.

ply a gentle but directed spray. And many have long handle extensions that allow me to water directly at the base of the plant.

They're also perfect for watering containers or spot-watering new plantings or moisture-lovers. Some even have bent handles for watering hanging baskets.

The only drawback is that these wands aren't the best for deeply watering established plants. Most of us don't have the patience or time to stand near a plant and apply enough water.

So my choice for deep watering is soaker hoses. If you've never seen these hoses, they have small holes or are made of porous materials. Because the water is slowly released, it's fully absorbed by the soil rather than running off. And you're free to tend to more important garden chores.

Sprinklers are another good tool for large areas. They apply a gentle flow of water for as long as you need. The down side is, sprinklers water the leaves as well as the soil, which can sometimes lead to some plant diseases.

Oscillating sprinklers are among the most common. Use these to deliver even coverage for large rectangular areas, like lawns. A model with multiple settings allows you to direct the water where it's needed, instead of on the sidewalk and driveway.

I have several different sprinklers for my small landscape. I use an oscillating sprinkler when watering my small patch of grass or major areas of my garden.

My rotating sprinkler has several nozzles on arms for watering circular areas. The arms are attached to a spinning pivot turned by the force of the water. The nozzles can be mounted at ground level for watering lawns, or raised on long stems to use as perennials grow. The raised nozzles clear the taller plants, getting water to all parts of the garden.

Pulsating sprinklers (also known as pulse-jet sprinklers) deliver water in a circular pattern, shooting out bursts as the single jet rotates. They can be mounted at ground level or raised on stakes.

Some new products on the market are even better at getting water where it's needed. The Noodlehead sprinkler has individual nozzles mounted on flexible stems, so you can position the nozzles to reach all parts of a garden, regardless of shape.

Decorative copper-sculpture sprinklers combine function and beauty. If you use them as a primary water source, treat them like any other sprinkler, monitoring the water they deliver.

Like all garden tools, watering devices should be clean and in good condition. Check for clogs, irregular discharge patterns and leaky washers. Monitor soil moisture throughout the area to detect problems, or place some cans in the areas you're sprinkling and make sure they're all receiving the same amount of water. You may need to clean or replace the sprinkler, adjust watering patterns or hand-water some areas to compensate for uneven delivery.

Handling Garden Hoses

Hoses seem to gain a life of their own as soon as you unwind them. I often feel like I'm wrestling a snake as I try to maneuver my hose through the packed landscape.

To make the job less frustrating, place hose guides at corners and other places where your hose often gets caught. These will help protect your plantings.

To make things easier, I like to walk out the full length of my hose, as far as it will stretch, before I start watering. Then I backtrack to individual plantings around corners. This way, I'm maneuvering as little hose as possible.

Reeling in your hose correctly can also save frustration and time. Consider investing in a hose reel to store it neatly.

My friend Sande Carne of Greenfield, Wisconsin is very good at managing such tasks. She plans her watering so she finishes with the hose stretched to its farthest point, preferably on a downward slope so it drains as she rolls it up.

If there's no slope, she drains the hose herself. She starts at one end and moves the length of the hose, lifting it over her head to drain the water. Then she coils the hose, secures the ends and neatly binds it with an easy-release tie before storing it for the next use.

Commercial hose reels, or a simple homemade device like this, help you keep hoses neatly coiled.

The new flat and self-coiling hoses are designed to minimize this struggle. The only drawback I see is that you need to fully unwind the flat hose before turning on the water.

How Much Water is Enough?

I AGREE—it's unrealistic to expect gardeners to dig down 4 to 6 inches to see if they've adequately moistened the root zone each time they water. So here's a trick to make this task easier, especially when using a sprinkler.

Set out shallow, straight-sided cans in the area you're watering. When the water in the cans measures an inch, it's time move your sprinkler to the next area.

Note the setting of your faucet and sprinkler, and the time it takes to provide the needed moisture. Repeat this every time you water, and you'll be assured that you've given the proper amount of moisture.

The same process can be used with soaker hoses. Monitor the time and faucet setting to apply the needed water. You now know the formula for perfect watering.

Use a rain gauge or straight-sided can to monitor rainfall and irrigation. Adjust the watering schedule based on water collected.

Irrigation Systems

Many gardeners save time and conserve water by installing an irrigation system. But like any tool, this can be misused, resulting in waterlogged soil.

It's easy to forget to calculate recent rains into your watering formula, and the system must be designed to allow for many plants' needs. Good design by an irrigation professional should help.

If you're willing to make the investment, make sure you choose a system that can be adjusted to compensate for changes in the weather and plants' needs. Use various nozzles to apply different volumes of water in time, or set up separate watering zones to accommodate the differences in plants' needs.

Soil-Wetting Gels

In the past few decades, several new polymers have been introduced to help reduce watering. These crystals absorb up to 200 times their weight in water, holding moisture in the soil for plant roots to use.

I've heard mixed reviews from gardeners and professionals alike. Many feel they make a difference, especially with new plantings and in containers. Others weren't as impressed.

Timers and various nozzles help irrigation systems apply different volumes of water, depending on need.

I think they're worth a try if you need something to help extend your watering efforts. Be sure to read and follow label directions carefully.

Getting the Timing Right

Often I'm asked when is the best time to water. This time I have a direct answer—early morning. When you water early in the day, less water is lost to evaporation, so more of it reaches the plant's roots.

Late afternoon is the next best time to water. This allows enough time for the leaves to dry before nightfall. Wet leaves after dark can encourage disease.

If you can't water at the best times, then water whenever you can. Watering at less than ideal times beats letting your plants die from drought stress.

Make Your Own Irrigation System

GARDENERS are resourceful, and many have increased their watering efficiency by recycling household items into chore savers. They may not be pretty enough for the front flower bed, but work fine for new plantings or in the vegetable garden. Here are a few of my favorites:

- **Gallon milk jugs or old buckets** can be used for drip irrigation (top left). Punch holes in the bottom of the jug and place it next to large plants or between several smaller ones. Fill with water and leave uncapped. The water will drain slowly into the soil.

- **Coffee cans** with the tops and bottoms removed create water-retaining collars around transplants. The collar directs the water to the plant's root zone where it is needed.

- **Twine or nylon stockings and a bucket** make perfect wick systems for potted plants (bottom left). Run cotton twine or nylon stockings from a container and into a flowerpot. The water moves through the wick into the dry soil, directing it to the plant's roots. This can be useful for managing containers when you're on vacation.

Water-Wise Xeriscaping

NO MATTER where you live, conserving water helps you, the plants and our environment, too.

There are many things gardeners can do to conserve water. One that tops my list is to use plants that minimize water use. This is called "Xeriscaping". Here's how:

- **Look for plants that survive on your average local rainfall**. You may have to water during unusually dry periods, but they won't need constant watering if Mother Nature cooperates.

- **Let nature be your guide**. Select native plants that are suitable for your growing conditions.

- **Group plants by water needs.** This saves time and water, concentrating your efforts to specific areas rather than individual plants scattered throughout the yard.

- **Limit moisture-loving plants to high-visibility areas.** This gives you the greatest impact for the water and effort.

- **Improve your soil!** (Thought you'd escape that advice this chapter? Not a chance.) Add compost and other organic material to improve water-holding capacity.

- **Design landscapes that conserve water rather than waste it.** Create windbreaks and shade structures that help reduce water loss.

- **Mulch plantings with organic materials**. This conserves moisture and reduces erosion.

- **Let your lawn grow to its the tallest recommended height**. Tall grass forms deeper roots and tolerates drought better.

- **Let grass go dormant during drought.** Believe it or not, it will bounce back once the rains come.

- **Recycle water from downspouts and other areas**. Many new water-collecting systems are designed to store water but keep out mosquitoes. Check with your municipality for any local restrictions.

Margaret Hensel/Positive Images

Mulching It Over

WHEN YOU SAY the word "mulch", what comes to mind? Do you see a beautiful garden growing in a rich soil covered with shredded leaves? Or do you see an expanse of red wood chips or white stone surrounding a few forlorn trees?

My friend Carol Bangs, a designer and native plant expert, says we should consider both aesthetics and function before selecting mulch.

I'm always looking for material that will improve the health and vigor of my plants. I also tend to be more informal, so fading wood chips, shredded leaves and other natural materials fit into my garden design.

But for those who like a more formal look, you may prefer stone or other alternatives.

There are many different mulches to choose, but for simplicity, they can be divided into two broad categories—organic and inorganic.

Organic mulches moderate soil temperatures throughout the day and year-round. They keep the soils cooler in summer, warmer in winter and minimize the difference between daytime and nighttime temperatures.

These materials conserve soil moisture (so you need to water less), block light to reduce weed seed germination and protect the soil from pounding rains that lead to compaction and erosion. Best of all, as these materials break down, they add organic matter and nutrients to the soil. Over time, the earthworms, ground beetles and other insects move these goodies to the roots of flowers, trees and shrubs.

I know some of you are shaking your heads and muttering, "But what about the slugs, beetles and other insects?"

Organic mulches do create a cool, dark environment that slugs like. But I'd rather deal with slugs than pull weeds and water. You have to make your own choice.

Other insects found in mulch are ground beetles, sow bugs and a number of other members of nature's recycling team. They feed on the mulch, helping it break down and decompose. These insects won't harm you or your plants. In fact, they actually help them.

Inorganic mulches work just the opposite. They tend to keep soils warmer in summer and cooler in winter. Soil covered with stone mulch tends to have greater temperature changes from day to night. These mulches can help reduce weeds, but they don't improve the soil. Most inorganic mulches are used for aesthetic value.

For flower and vegetable gardens, stick with organic mulch. The yearly soil preparation in annual gardens and the regular digging and dividing of perennials make it important to use mulch that will break down when worked into the soil. I prefer leaves, cocoa beans, pine needles and other materials that break down quickly and don't tie up the soil nitrogen.

How to Apply Mulch

It's easy to make mulching a part of your planting process. Spread a layer over the soil surface, but keep it away from tree trunks, shrub stems and the crowns of annuals and perennials. Northern gardeners may want to wait until the soil warms before applying mulch to annuals and vegetables, as the mulch will keep the soil cool and slow down new growth. One of my colleagues follows this rule: It's safe to mulch when the soil is warm enough to walk through barefoot.

It's never too late to mulch new plantings or existing beds. Remove all weeds first—otherwise you're just helping them grow. I often use pulled weeds as mulch in the back of beds, under shrubs and in other less visible locations. But don't use weeds that are aggressive or have gone to seed.

Spruce up existing tree and shrub beds as time allows. Some landscapers prefer to do this in spring so the mulch is fresh throughout the summer. Others make it an off-season project when they have more time. One nice thing about mulching is that you have a long window of opportunity.

A spaded edge or edging material helps keep wood chips and other mulches in the planting bed and out of the lawn.

Watch Out for Weed Barriers

As far as I'm concerned, no discussion of mulch is complete without addressing my concerns about weed barriers. These spun-fabric mulches allow air and water through, but block sunlight to prevent weed seed germination. In theory, this sounds great—but in most landscapes, it doesn't work because the barriers aren't installed properly.

I've spent most of my career removing or recommending the removal of weed barriers. Many landscapers and gardeners put them on planting beds, then mulch with wood chips. This works fine for several years, until the chips start breaking down and more are added. Eventually, gardeners end up with a 6- to 12-inch layer of compost trapped above the soil.

Weed seeds blow in, grass creeps in from the side, and soon the planting bed is filled with weeds, grass and even shrubs rooted through the chips and into the fabric.

What's more, as the plants grow, the barrier does not move. If a gardener isn't vigilant, the barrier can girdle trees.

Sometimes people buy homes with beds like these and simply plant in the compost, unaware the soil lies beneath a weed barrier. The plants are drought-stressed and stunted, because compost alone does not hold water and nutrients the same as topsoil.

The best solution for the plants is to redo the bed. Rake off any wood chips, move the decomposed chips aside and remove the weed barrier. Then work that wonderful compost into the planting bed, add a little fertilizer if lots of chips are present and replant. It's a lot of work, but you'll have a better garden in the long run.

This was not the plot hatched by your landscapers or the weed barrier's manufacturers. The consequences weren't clearly understood before the test of time. Now I'm doing my part to change that. Every semester that I teach maintenance classes, we spend 2 hours removing the weed barrier that seems to cover our campus. My goal is to get rid of all of it (I'll be 90 by then) and teach future landscapers about the long-term problems it causes.

All that said, there is a use for weed barrier fabrics—they work fine under stone mulches. The barrier helps suppress weeds so you need less mulch, and it also keeps the stones out of the soil. If you try to reclaim a stone-mulched garden that didn't have a weed barrier, you'll be digging stones out of the top 12 inches of dirt.

Master Gardener Lowell Kendall also used a weed barrier in his vegetable garden. He'd prepare the soil,

Cocoa bean shells work well in both formal and informal gardens. Use a 1-inch layer for best results.

roll out the weed barrier and plant peppers, tomatoes and vine crops through the fabric. It worked great at suppressing weeds—so well, in fact, that another Master Gardener who tried it complained that she didn't have enough to do in the garden anymore.

At the end of the season, Lowell would remove the barrier to store it for winter. This allowed him to get more use from the barrier and amend the soil below. He even took the barrier to the local coin-operated laundry to clean it first—imagine the poor person who'd use the washing machine next!

I'd skip that step, opting to just shake off the excess soil before storing.

How Much is Enough?

We seem to be a society of excess. If a little is good, than twice as much must be better. But if we take this approach with mulching, we can actually harm our gardens.

Thick layers of grass clippings can smell bad, get moldy and mat down so that water can't penetrate it. Excess wood chips can lead to nutrient deficiencies and increase problems with sour mulch (see the box on page 79).

Here's a simple green-thumb rule to help out—the finer the mulch, the thinner you should layer it. One inch of cocoa bean shells, grass clippings and pine needles are more than enough. Wood chips and other coarse materials should be 2 to 3 inches thick.

Organic mulches need to be replenished every couple of years to maintain the recommended depth. Many gardeners like to add new mulch annually to keep it looking fresh. Add only enough to replace what has decomposed. Otherwise, you'll soon be tripping over your mulch rings and digging out buried perennials and evergreens.

To save time, some of my landscaping friends cover newly planted annuals and perennials with overturned containers before applying mulch. When you remove the pots, you have a neat, professional-looking ring around your plants, and you won't have to uncover smaller plants.

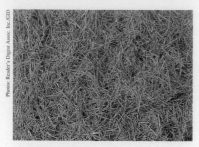
Grass clippings

Shredded bark

Wood chips

Cocoa hulls

Pine needles

Organic Mulches

- **Cocoa bean shells** are a by-product of the chocolate industry. Use a thin (1-inch) layer to suppress weeds. This mulch smells wonderful—but you may crave a candy bar each time you visit the garden.
- **Cocoa bean shells mixed with rice hulls.** This is an attractive combination. The rice hulls aerate the cocoa beans, reducing the risk of slime mold.
- **Enviromulch and other recycled wood products.** Pallets and other wood waste products are shredded and dyed to make colorful mulch. They tend to last a little longer than other shredded wood or wood chips.
- **Eucalyptus.** This long-lasting wood mulch gained its popularity in the West, where eucalyptus trees are abundant. It can hold its color and last for several years.
- **Pecan and almond shells.** Another case where a by-product of one industry becomes a resource for another. Use a thin (1-inch) layer for best results.
- **Pine straw.** In the South, pine needles are harvested, baled and sold to gardeners for mulch. All evergreen needles make excellent mulch. Rake the excess from beneath your trees and move it into the garden. Use a 1- to 2-inch layer.
- **Oyster shells.** These are ground and used as a soil amendment, with larger pieces used for mulch. They're most readily available in coastal areas.
- **Shredded leaves.** Fall leaves shredded with a mower make suitable mulch for all plants. They break down quickly, so use a 2- to 3-inch layer.
- **Wood chips** are made from trees and shrubs. Many types and varieties are available. Some are free from your local municipality or utility company, but you'll have to pay for those of finer quality or longer-lasting wood. Maintain a 3-inch layer for weed control.
- **Twice-shredded wood chips and pine bark** tend to break down faster than regular wood chips. But their fibrous nature also makes them hold together and stay in place better than wood chips.

Inorganic Mulches

- **Stone.** This is usually selected for its aesthetic value. A wide variety of types, sizes and colors are available. Use a weed barrier beneath the stone.
- **Rubber mats.** This new, porous product made from recycled tires is said to provide good weed control.
- **Shredded rubber** from old tires is dyed for aesthetics. This soft, pliable mulch is long-lasting and suited to paths and play areas. For garden use, experiment on a limited basis.
- **Weed barriers** are spun fabrics that let air and water through to the soil below; they're best used beneath inorganic mulches. This looks better and lasts longer than an exposed barrier that breaks down in sunlight, and prolongs the barrier's life by protecting it from sunlight.
- **Plastic.** These products don't let air and water through to the soil, although some of the newer products are woven or perforated. Gardeners have reported problems with torn or exposed plastic mulch.

Sour Mulch Syndrome

IMPROPERLY MANAGED wood mulches can emit toxic substances that cause leaf edges to yellow and brown, make leaves drop and even kill plants.

Avoid this problem by selecting properly handled wood mulch that has a woody smell. Improperly handled mulch has a sour or vinegary odor.

Once toxic mulch has been applied, and the plants are damaged, there's nothing you can do. Leave the mulch in place, let the toxins dissipate and wait for the plants to recover.

Mulching Tips

WHENEVER YOU MULCH your garden, trees and shrubs, keep these guidelines in mind.

• Keep mulch away from tree trunks. "Mulch volcanoes" piled around trunks can lead to rot, decline and early death.

• Limit use of wood chips and sawdust to paths, trees and shrubs. Wood breaks down slowly and temporarily ties up soil nitrogen.

• Avoid using black walnut leaves, chips and nuts. They all contain juglone, which is toxic to many plants.

• Place a layer of newspaper under organic mulch to work as a weed barrier. As the paper breaks down, it also improves the soil.

• Pine and spruce needles and oak and maple leaves make great mulches and won't harm your other plants or the soil.

Ben Phill ps/Positive Images

Stone and gravel

Straw

Compost

Autumn leaves

Sawdust

79

Support Sytems

EVERYONE can use a little support now and then, plants included. But some plants always need a little help keeping their stems held high. I'm not referring to vines—I'm talking about asters, delphiniums, snapdragons and other plants that like to lie around the garden unless you give them a backbone of support.

Staking 'Em Out

Reduce the need to stake by selecting dwarf or self-supporting varieties. These plants have been bred to stand up straight and tall without any additional support.

Peonies are a perfect example. Who hasn't seen a blooming peony nearly flattened by the weight of the flowers or a heavy rain? I recommend visiting a botanical garden after a rainstorm to help select your next peony. That's when it's easy to spot the self-supporting varieties.

Another alternative: Surround these leaning giants with medium-sized plants that help support them. Ever notice how the asters growing along the freeway do fine without help? Look closer at those highway asters and you'll see their neighbors are holding them upright.

Try pruning back asters, mums, Shasta daisies and other floppy perennials early in the season. This encourages shorter, more compact growth without interfering with blossoming. Use garden snips to make the cut above a healthy leaf.

Some gardeners use a layered approach, pruning the plant's outer stems and leaving the center intact. The inner stems will grow taller and bloom earlier than the supportive outer stems. This reduces maintenance and extends the floral display.

Dividing perennials every 3 or 4 years also helps keep some plants more compact and eliminates the need to stake. So follow this simple rule—when the plants begin to flop, it's time to dig and divide.

Choosing a Structure

When plants need support, select a structure that's appropriate for their size and weight—preferably one that's invisible to the viewer or complements the landscape design.

This is where you can be creative in the garden. You're limited only by your imagination. Check garden centers and catalogs—there are many new prod-

Place stakes on the windward side (above) to avoid plant damage. Use prunings from trees and shrubs to create attractive plant supports like the one below.

ucts on the market, and there's one for just about every situation.

Bamboo stakes and twine have long been used, although they're difficult to hide. To best hide your supports, select a stake that's about two-thirds the height of the plant.

For single-stemmed plants, sink one stake into the ground near the plant. Be careful not to injure the roots. Tie the plant to the stake by making a loop around the stem and then one around the stake with twine or plastic ties.

For multi-stemmed plants, use several stakes around the outer edge. Try to camouflage them with the plant's leaves. Loop the twine around one stake, then the next and so on until you have created a ring around the plant. Place twine on stakes at two positions—at one-third and again at two-thirds of the plant's height.

Gardeners—particularly the British and the Hmong—have long recycled twigs and branches for use as stakes. Today, more and more gardeners are creating attractive supports from twigs and branches, including tepees and fences.

Plant rings—metal circles supported by several legs—work, too. Whether it's a tomato tower, peony

Plant rings, placed over young plants, become hidden as the plants grow.

ring or other circular support, the concept is the same. These are placed over young plants so they grow up and through the ring.

Grow-through stakes take this idea a bit further. The metal circle is filled with a crosshatching of metal wire, and the individual stems grow up and through the holes for a look that's a bit more natural.

Want to make your own grow-through system? I heard of a gardener who used a piece of white lattice mounted on stakes so it was parallel to the ground. Gladiolus grew through the lattice and held their blooms high above it.

For a no-assembly-required version, place a piece of wide-mesh plastic netting or chicken wire over the emerging plant. As the plant grows, the stems will grow through the mesh and lift it. The mesh holds the clump together so the plant stems support each other. And without stakes, the plant can move, giving it a more natural appearance.

Tip for Success

PLACE STAKES, rings and other supports in the garden at planting time or as soon as the plants emerge in spring. It may be a little unsightly early in the season, but the plant will quickly grow up and through the supports.

Trimming, Pinching and Pruning

ONCE OUR PLANTS are growing upright, we want to do everything possible to keep them looking good. Deadheading, dead-leafing, pinching and disbudding can improve appearance and extend bloom time.

Deadheading sounds gruesome, but it's simply removing flowers as they begin to fade. This creates a neater appearance and is often critical in getting plants to bloom again.

You see, a plant's goal in life is to re-create. Once it flowers and sets seed, its work is done and it stops producing blossoms. Pinching off spent flowers before they go to seed encourages the plant to produce new ones.

Use garden snips or your finger and thumb to remove faded flowers, or prune a stem back to the first set of leaves. Be careful not to remove any flowering side shoots.

If the plant produces several individual flowers in one cluster, as daylilies and balloon flowers do, you have two choices. You can remove the faded flowers one at a time, then remove the whole stem when all the flowers have faded. The other option is to wait until most of the flowers have faded and remove the flowering stem.

Gardeners with mass plantings and limited time may want to break out the hedge clippers. Let perennials go through their first and secondary set of flowers, then clip off the faded stems. Many gardeners prune plants back halfway to encourage stouter growth and a possible second flush of flowers.

Pinching back encourages compact growth, as mentioned earlier, but also increases fullness and flowering. Remove tender stems by cutting them off with garden snips or breaking them off between finger and thumb. I find it is faster for me and better for the plant to use garden snips or a pruner, which result in cleaner cuts and smaller wounds.

Disbudding is used to remove some or all of the flower buds. Peonies, dahlias and mums are often disbudded. Side buds are removed from the stems, leaving the terminal bud—the one at the end of the stem—intact. This results in fewer but larger flowers. Some gardeners prefer to have more flowers, even if they're smaller. In these cases, they remove the terminal bud and leave all the side buds intact.

Removing all the flower buds is a common practice on coleus and other plants grown for their foliage rather than their flowers. If these plants are allowed to flower, their foliage begins to decline. Remove all buds or flowers as soon you spot them for a more compact, beautiful plant.

Dead-leafing is removing old, faded or discolored leaves. Removing diseased leaves is a must, but dead-leafing is also done for aesthetics. Removing weather-worn foliage in late summer improves a plant's appearance for the rest of the season.

Pruning

Before you break out the pruning equipment, make sure you have a purpose in mind. You see, many people prune because it's spring, or because their neighbor is pruning or—if you're like my Aunt Mary—for stress relief. She always felt better when she finished pruning. My cousins, however, were always worried there'd be no trees or shrubs left in the yard.

Prune trees and shrubs to establish a strong framework, improve their growth, remove branches that are diseased, dead or damaged and improve branch color, flowering and fruit production.

When to Prune

The old saying that you can prune "anytime the saw is sharp" is basically true, with a few exceptions we'll discuss later.

I prefer late winter for most of my pruning chores. It's easier to see the structure of the tree, so you can decide what needs to stay and what should be removed.

There's also less going on in the backyard then, so it's the perfect thing for those who can't wait to do something in their little plot of paradise. In most of the country, pruning is about the only garden chore that can be done in late winter.

Plants pruned in late winter generally recover faster. As they start to grow, the wounds close quickly, keeping disease and insects at bay.

Dormant-season pruning is a must for certain disease-susceptible trees like oaks and honey locusts. Oaks can succumb to oak wilt and honey locusts are prone to developing nectria canker.

But when pruned in winter, the disease-carrying insects, fungal spores and bacteria that find their way into these plants through open wounds are inactive. This decreases the risk of infection.

Summer-flowering shrubs should also be pruned

For spring bloomers, prune after flowering so you can enjoy a colorful display.

during the dormant season, in late winter or early spring. This encourages more growth, which means more flowers for the summer garden.

When it comes to safety, it's best to remove hazardous or damaged branches as soon as possible, regardless of season. Making a proper cut and repairing damage allows the tree to recover quickly and minimize exposure to insects, disease and rot.

Pruning Exceptions

Lilacs, bridal wreath spireas, forsythias and other spring-flowering shrubs flower on the previous season's growth and should be pruned as soon as possible *after flowering*. Pruning at any other time, including the dormant season, can eliminate the spring flower display. And without their beautiful blossoms, they'll just look like any other green shrub.

Another group requiring special pruning attention is the blue, pink and lacecap hydrangeas (*Hydrangea macrophylla*). They flower on shoots that arise from the previous season's growth. If you prune them back to the ground—or the cold winter does it for you—you'll have no flowers. Remove only dead, weak and wayward stems. On established plants, remove 3- and 4-year-old stems. Leave most of the growth intact for a better flower display.

There are two times to avoid pruning altogether—in spring when the leaves expand and late in the growing season. In spring, stray cuts, leaning ladders and improper climbing may damage bark. Pruning in late summer can encourage late-season growth that may not have time to harden off for winter.

Pruning Shrubs

The best way to minimize pruning is to plant shrubs that are the right size for their location and are properly spaced. Gardeners are notorious for squeezing in that extra plant or two, or underestimating how big a plant will be at maturity. Then we try to give nature a hand by keeping plants confined to the space available.

If you followed the planting directions, you'll have less pruning to do, but most plants will eventually need stray growth or damaged branches removed.

Occasional pruning is necessary to improve ornamental features, too. Remember, timing is critical—make decisions on when to prune based on when a plant blooms and if certain pests are a problem (see "When to Prune" on page 82).

Newly planted shrubs need very little pruning. Recent research has shown that the more top growth a plant has, the more energy it produces to grow new roots. Remove only damaged and crossed branches. Do the major pruning and shaping in a year or 2.

Once a plant is established, the variety and your landscape style will help determine your pruning schedule. Sheared shrubs need to be pruned once, twice, maybe even three times a season. More naturally shaped plants need minimal pruning. Overgrown plants will need major attention.

Making the Cut

When you make a cut, it's best to prune above a healthy bud or where one branch joins another. For suckering-type shrubs (shrubs that have new growth stemming from the ground), it's best to prune back to ground level. All these cuts close quickly and stimulate natural growth where you want it.

Always make cuts on a slight angle just above single buds. Make sure the bud is pointed away from the center of the plant, in the direction you want the new growth. That bud will develop into a stem, so making the right choice now can save you additional pruning work in the long run.

Make a straight cut slightly above double and whorled buds. All these buds will develop into stems. Select buds pointed in directions where there's room for new growth.

Use something called a heading cut to reduce the size of the plant by removing stems back to a shorter side shoot or a healthy bud. This method controls those few branches that outgrow the rest of the plant.

Use thinning cuts to renew shrubs on a regular basis. The more vigorous the plant, the more often you need to prune. Remove older stems to ground level or to the main stem. Thinning opens up the plant, increasing airflow and light penetration, which improves flowering and discourages diseases.

In a Pinch

I'M OFTEN ASKED what gardeners mean when they talk about "pinching back", or the difference between a "hard pinch" and a "soft pinch". Here are some general guidelines.

- **Pinch back.** This is removing the growing tip—the youngest leaf that's just starting to unfurl or has just expanded. Removing the tip encourages branches to form along the stem.
- **Soft pinch.** This removes just the tender new growth, usually the top few inches of the stem. This reduces height and encourages branching.
- **Hard pinch.** This cuts back further into older, tougher portions of the stem. A hard pinch helps encourage bottom growth on top-heavy plants.

Shearing Your Shrubs

SHEARING creates a neat, formal look in the landscape. It's easy for gardeners since it can be done quickly and requires few decisions. But it's hard on the plants.

When shearing, cuts are made anywhere along the stem, usually leaving stubs that provide entryways for insects and disease. Shearing also promotes dense tip growth, discouraging leaf development at the bottom and in the center of the plant. This means fewer leaves to produce energy to support the plants.

Most sheared plants must be pruned several times, in early spring, midsummer and again at the end of the season. The last pruning should be light to avoid stimulating late-season growth that can die off over winter.

Prune so the bottom of the plant is slightly wider than the top. This allows light to reach all parts of the plant, encouraging leaf growth at the base as well as the top.

Use renewal and rejuvenation pruning to manage overgrown or top-heavy hedges, preferably in late winter or early spring so they have time to recover.

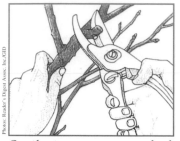

Photos: Reader's Digest Assoc. Inc./GID

On the top, remove any dead stumps by cutting flush with the branch bark collar.

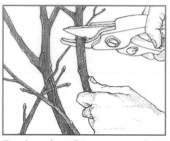

Don't make arbitrary cuts along the stem (above). Instead, cut above a healthy bud.

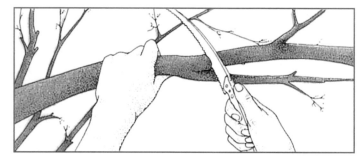

Prune longer branches back to a shorter side shoot, so that you can maintain the plant's natural form while reducing the plant's overall size.

Renewal pruning uses thinning cuts to remove older growth, which is more susceptible to insects and disease. Remove one-third of the stems, starting with the oldest, each year for 3 years. The height also can be reduced by a third at this time.

After 3 years, your plant will be shorter, leafed from top to bottom and producing more flowers and fruit than before.

Rejuvenation pruning is used on overgrown plants or vigorous growers like spirea, potentilla and butterfly bush, and on plants that die back in cold northern climates, like hydrangea. This technique is best used in late winter or early spring so the plant has a full season to recover.

For rejuvenation pruning, cut all the stems back to 4 to 8 inches above ground level. This drastic pruning is only for vigorous shrubs and hearty pruners. If you're not sure how the plant—or you—will respond to this technique, try renewal pruning instead.

To renew shrubs like spireas and potentillas, cut all the stems back halfway. Then cut half of what's left back to ground level. Stagger the cuts so you have a mix of high and ground-level stems. The older growth will provide added support and reduce the floppiness that often occurs after these shrubs are rejuvenated.

Pruning and Training Young Trees

With young trees, your goal is to establish a strong framework for its long life. Proper pruning will get them off to a healthy start. Pruning early on and throughout the tree's development lessens the risk of storm damage. What's more, you'll need to make fewer cuts on larger branches when the tree is more mature.

To establish the proper framework, you must know the tree's natural shape. This will help you decide which branches should be removed.

Most trees have a central leader, a single trunk that grows straight and tall. When side branches bend skyward, they try to compete with the main leader. This can result in multiple leaders and a weak structure prone to wind, ice and snow damage. Try to maintain the central leaders by pruning back and removing competitors.

Once you know the desired shape, you're ready to start pruning. Making the first cut is the hardest part.

Most gardeners new to pruning suffer from "pruning paranoia", making lots of little cuts before working up the courage to cut off a whole limb—which would've accomplished the same goal with much less effort. Don't be afraid to make the needed cuts. Just keep stepping back and looking at the total picture throughout the process.

I like to start with the broken and damaged branches. Because they have to go anyway, why not get them out of the way and see what's left?

If the tree has just been planted, that's all the pruning you should do. Wait until your tree has been in the ground 2 or 3 years before doing more.

For established trees, identify the major branches that will create the framework. Look for branches with wide crotch angles (the angle between the trunk and side branches). The wider this angle, the stronger the branch and the less likely it will be damaged in a storm.

Look at the oaks growing in your area. Despite their size, these long-lived giants have wide crotch angles and suffer less wind and storm damage than other trees. Now look at the elms and eucalyptus, which have narrow crotch angles. Their branches are often lost in high winds and snowstorms.

Select branches so they're evenly spaced in a spiral pattern along the trunk. Avoid leaving branches that are directly across from each other, which creates a weak point, or parallel—these will eventually grow into each other, causing damage.

Once the framework's established, we need to remove anything that gets in its way. Step back and get a good look at what remains. Remove any branches that are crossing and rubbing the main branches that create your framework. Prune off branches growing toward the center of the tree, water sprouts growing straight up from major branches and any weak drooping branches.

Leave the Collar

Where you make your cut is just as important as what you prune. Prune back small branches just above a healthy bud or where a branch joins another branch. Prune larger branches back to the branch bark collar, the area where the trunk and bark tissue meets.

Most of us have seen branch bark collars—we just didn't know what they were called. Think about your last walk through the park or woods. Picture that old tree with one dead branch. A swollen area encircled the base of the branch like a doughnut. This is a branch bark collar, which provides the callus tissue to close and cover the wound.

This piece of advice may take a while to get used to. For years, experts have told you to cut flush to the trunk of the tree. The concern was that stubs made perfect entryways for insects and disease. We still don't want to leave stubs, but we do want to leave the branch bark collar. Once you learn to identify it and see the positive results, it'll become second nature.

Use the Three-Step Cut

To remove large-diameter (2 inches or more) branches, use a three-step pruning cut to prevent the branch from breaking off and tearing the bark below it.

Make the first cut about 1 foot from the trunk. Cut from the bottom of the branch upward and one-fourth of the way through. Your next cut will be about 1 inch away in either direction. Prune from the top to the bottom of the branch until it breaks away.

Make the final cut flush with the branch bark collar.

After pruning, don't use pruning paints to seal cuts. Recent research has shown that these materials trap moisture and disease inside the plants, rather than keeping them out. The exception—you know there's always one—is when pruning certain disease-susceptible plants, like oaks, during the growing season. If it must be done, a pruning paint will help reduce the risk of oak wilt or other fatal diseases.

Make Pruning Routine

After the framework is established, you'll need to do only minimal pruning. Here's a quick list to help:

- Remove diseased, damaged or hazardous branches as they appear.
- Watch and prune off crossing and parallel branches.
- Eliminate water sprouts. Pruning a few off each year is easier for you and better for the tree,

Leave It to the Pros

WHEN I GIVE pruning advice, I always caution gardeners to save big jobs for professionals. It's better to hire a certified arborist than to risk injury by tackling a job you don't have the equipment, experience and knowledge to do safely.

Check the yellow pages for tree-care professionals, visit the International Society of Arboriculture Web site at *www.isa-arbor.com* or ask friends for recommendations. Before hiring someone, ask if they're certified—this is a voluntary program through the International Society of Arboriculture—and whether they're members of any professional organizations. Ask about staff training, too, and make sure they're insured.

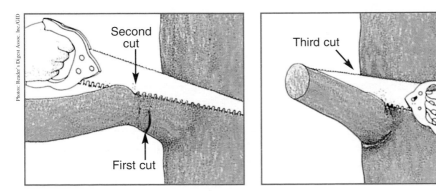

Use the three-step pruning technique to avoid ripping bark or damaging the trunk of the tree. Make the first cut from under the stem, about 12 inches from the trunk. Make the second cut (left) just beyond the first cut (right). The final cut should be flush with the branch bark collar.

too. Pruning off lots of them in one season can lead to even more the next year. Sprout-preventing products seem to discourage sprouting at the pruning site. However, most arborists and gardeners find that after using these products, more sprouts pop up in other areas.

• Remove suckers—shoots that arise from the ground near the trunk—every spring. Cut or pull

Remove suckers to maintain an attractive tree and to prevent suckers from the rootstock of grafted plants from outgrowing the desirable plant.

Photos: Reader's Digest Assoc. Inc./GID

them off below ground to reduce the risk of re-sprouting. If left to grow, these stems can interfere with the growth and beauty of your tree.

Pruning Vines

Whether trained on a trellis, crawling up a wall or covering an arbor, vines need some pruning to keep them looking good.

As with shrubs, flowering time influences pruning time. Prune spring-flowering vines like five-leaf akebia right after they bloom. Summer- and fall-blooming vines can be pruned anytime during the dormant season. Some, like wisteria, may need some summer pruning to keep them in line.

Start pruning at the time of planting. Tip-prune small plants and cut back long, leggy vines to encourage more branching at the base of the plant. Train the vine on a structure.

Once established, slower-growing vines like climbing hydrangea need minimal pruning. Remove dead and damaged branches in spring. Head back stems to encourage denser, more compact growth.

Vigorous vines like honeysuckle need yearly attention. Prune out overly long branches and shorten branches that are near their desired size.

Aggressive vines like bittersweet and wisteria need more severe pruning. Cut these way back each year to keep them in check.

Most overgrown vines can be renovated in late winter or early spring. Prune the plant back to 12 to 24 inches above the ground. You might feel reluctant about doing this the first time, but once you see the positive results it gets much easier.

Keeping Evergreens Shipshape

Most broadleaf evergreens are managed like other shrubs, as described earlier. But needled evergreens need a different approach when it comes to pruning.

Hemlocks, arborvitaes, yews, junipers and chamaecyparis should be pruned in early spring, before growth begins, or in summer, after the new growth has expanded. Fall pruning should be limited to areas where winters are mild and plants are less subject to injury from cold.

Arborvitaes, hemlocks and yews will tolerate more severe pruning, since they can produce new needles on older wood. They're some of the few evergreens that will even handle shearing.

When pruning by hand, make heading cuts to remove branches injured in winter and to help control size. Pruning cuts made in spring will be hidden by new growth. Thin damaged or overcrowded stems back to the main trunk.

Junipers and chamaecyparis need little pruning. Remove overgrown, diseased and damaged growth back to a side branch. This hides the cut and maintains the plant's normal growth habit. Do not shear or severely prune these evergreens back to old, leafless growth. It takes years for new growth to mask the old wood.

Pines, spruces, firs, Douglas firs and cedars need minimal pruning. Prune pines to develop a dense, compact plant. Cut the candles (expanded buds) by one-half or two-thirds in spring, before the needles expand.

Prune spruces, firs, Douglas firs and cedars above a healthy bud in spring before growth begins. Remove dead or damaged branches back to a healthy side branch or back to the trunk and flush with the branch bark collar. Don't prune back to old wood—these trees won't produce new growth from needleless branches.

No Need to "Limb Up"

WHILE many people do this, there's no benefit to the plant when we "limb up", or cut off the lower branches of our spruce, firs and pines. The more branches a tree has, the more needles there are to produce energy to support it.

Gardeners often remove healthy lower branches so they can grow grass below their pines, extend a view or change the look of the landscape. Keep in mind this is strictly for aesthetic reasons and isn't necessary for the health of the tree.

Be Persnickety When You Prune

CLEANLINESS COUNTS, especially when you prune. Disinfecting pruning tools will help prevent the spread of disease. Just dip them in a solution of 1 part bleach to 9 parts water, or clean or spray the cutting blades with rubbing alcohol.

Always disinfect tools between pruning plants. Better yet, disinfect them between each cut.

At the end of the day, clean your tools by wiping off any plant sap with an oily rag or steel wool. Then lightly oil the blade to prevent rust.

Don't forget to routinely sharpen the blades to make better cuts with less effort. Replace all bent or damaged blades as soon as possible.

These basic tools, a pruning saw, loppers and a pair of hand pruners with a sheath, should take care of most pruning needs.

Tools of the Pruning Trade

Choosing and using the right tool is important for both you and your plants.

Reduce muscle strain by selecting tools that fit your physical build. For hand tools, look for those that fit comfortably in your grip. Larger tools should not be too heavy—make sure you can easily lift them over an extended period of time and that they are not too difficult for you to operate.

Many new ergonomic tools are designed to help you avoid injury, maximize your strength and allow you to work longer.

Shop around and try different tools before investing in new ones. You may want to add a few of the better-quality and ergonomically improved tools to your birthday or holiday gift list. I've told my husband never to buy me another appliance, but he knows garden tools are always welcome.

Here are some of the basics:

• **Garden snips or scissors** are used for deadheading, clipping back tender new growth and harvesting flowers. Some are designed to cut and hold the stem for easy harvesting.

• **Hand pruners** are a better choice for heavier jobs. Use them to cut woody stems up to 1/2 inch in diameter and larger tender shoots.

• **Bypass pruners** have two sharp blades and cut like scissors. They slice through the stem and leave a clean cut that closes quickly.

• **Anvil pruners** have one flat and one sharp blade. You must keep them sharp to minimize crushing of the stem. If you aren't willing to do that —and most of us aren't—avoid using this tool, or limit its use to removing dead wood.

• **Loppers** are long-handled pruners that provide greater leverage and reach. Use these on hard-to-reach stems or woody stems up to 1 inch thick.

• **Pruning saws** should be used for any branch or stem larger than 1 inch in diameter. They come in several designs and blade lengths. I use my small foldable saw for lots of yard work like pruning shrubs. They're especially handy for getting into tight places. My larger curved or straight-bladed saws are stronger and more suited for trees and larger work.

• **Pole pruners** are long handles with a pruner or saw attached. Use these sparingly. The extra-long pole extends your reach, but it's difficult to make a proper cut when guiding the tool with a 10-foot handle.

Additional Features to Consider

• Select pruning tools with removable blades for easy cleaning and sharpening.

• Make sure hand pruners have a safety latch to lock the blades when not in use. Folding saws should have the same feature.

• Look for loppers and hand pruners with ratchet systems if you have limited strength or endurance.

• Buy tools with bright handles or paint them yourself. This makes it easier to find them in the garden.

• Invest in a pouch, gardener's tool belt or tool bag. This makes it easier to tote your tools around the yard. You're also more likely to use the right tool if it's handy, and less likely to lose it if there's a place to store it.

Transplanting

THE BEST-LAID PLANS—and that includes landscapes—don't always turn out as expected. Maybe the design was not right or the spacing wasn't sufficient. Perhaps a road is widened or your house is remodeled. Even when your garden works out exactly as planned, your plants may need to move for other reasons. That's where transplanting comes in.

Digging, Dividing and Moving Perennials

Perennials need regular digging, dividing and transplanting to maintain healthy, attractive growth. When the middle of a plant dies out or looks like a doughnut, or if plants start to flop, fail to bloom or outgrow their location, they need to be divided.

Division is a good way to create new plants for yourself or to share with friends. Some fast growers are so productive you may need to toss the surplus in the compost bin.

How do you know when to divide? A good starting point is to follow this old saying: "Divide spring bloomers in fall, fall bloomers in spring and summer bloomers in either fall or spring."

I'm always pushing the limits. Sometimes I do this as an experiment, but usually it's because my schedule does not mesh with what the plants need.

You can stretch the transplanting guideline with most perennials as long as you provide proper care afterward.

Digging In

When moving perennials, dig around the outside edge of the plant, undercut the roots and lift the plant out of the ground.

Some gardeners use two garden forks or shovels, back to back, to divide the clump of roots. I prefer a sharp linoleum knife. The curved blade and sturdy handle make cutting easy. I even have friends who prefer a chopping block and machete for tough perennials.

Each plant can be divided into halves, fourths or eighths, depending on its original size and how many divisions you want.

Another way to divide a plant is to soak or gently wash off the excess soil to expose the roots and crowns. Cut or pull individual plants apart, then follow the guidelines for bare-root planting described in Chapter 4, pages 62-63.

Amend the soil where the original plant was growing, and where the new divisions are to be placed. This is one of your only chances to deeply amend the garden soil around perennial plants.

Replant divisions at the same depth they were growing. You may want to put one of the divisions back in the original location. But don't replant the center of the plant if it's dried out or dead. That is better suited for composting.

To divide perennials, dig the entire plant with a fork or shovel.

Use two forks or shovels to divide the plant.

Add fertilizer and organic matter to the planting sites.

Spade in amendments.

Replant divisions at proper spacing.

Separate and replant individual bulbs at proper spacing.

Rejuvenating Bulbs

Many people replace bulbs rather than move them. But if you don't like to waste anything, or have a sentimental attachment to your bulbs, you can dig, divide and move them at their normal planting time.

The only problem—there are no leaves to help you find them.

Mapping and labeling your garden helps. When you know what's planted where, it's easier to plan new additions and find where other bulbs are located.

Plant labels at garden centers contain lots of useful information, but can be a little distracting in the garden. Someone once said gardens filled with these looked like a plant graveyard.

I use dowel rods to mark my bulbs. I paint the tips orange or pink and sink them level with the ground. Brent Heath of Brent and Becky's Bulbs in Gloucester, Virginia recommends using long-stemmed colored golf tees to mark your bulbs. This is a good idea—and the way I play golf—a much better use for my tees.

Several of my students use cheap chopsticks, which are less obtrusive than labels and longer than tees. The extra length prevents them from being heaved out by frost or accidentally knocked out of their location.

If you can't move the bulbs at normal planting time, the next best time is when the foliage starts to fade and the bulbs begin their dormant stage. The leaves are the most accurate marker, so it's easiest to find them when they're still attached.

I have even moved bulbs in full bloom. It's definitely not the best solution, but it can be done when it's your only option.

When transplanting bulbs, heel them in (see pages 62-63) or store dormant bulbs in a cool, dark place until their normal planting time. Just remember where you stored them. I've found a few stragglers tucked away in my basement long after the ground was frozen.

Trees on the Move

Trees and shrubs are more challenging to move because of their weight and extensive root system. Don't be afraid to ask for help. And save large trees—anything over 2 inches in diameter—for professionals with heavy equipment to do the job right.

The best time to move trees and shrubs is before growth begins in spring or after the leaves drop in fall. Northern gardeners will have better luck with spring transplanting. Southern gardeners may want to stick with moving plants in fall to avoid the summer heat.

It's important to wait until the soil is moist before starting. A moist root ball will hold together better than one dug from dry soil.

Loosely tie the branches of shrubs with twine or cloth strips. This keeps them out of your way and protects them during the move.

Dig a root ball 12 to 16 inches in diameter and 9 to 12 inches deep for shrubs. Trees will need a larger root system—14 to 28 inches wide and 11 to 19 inches deep. The bigger the plant, the larger the root ball you need. But remember, it must be manageable. A large root ball is no good if it's dropped and broken into pieces.

Use your shovel to undercut the root ball. A lopper will be a helpful tool as well, cutting through the roots your shovel can't handle.

At this point, you'll probably need an extra set of hands. Each person should grab one side of a piece of burlap or canvas and slide it under the root ball. Then lift the canvas, using it as a sling to move the plant to its new location. To save your back, use a wheelbarrow or garden cart.

Take extra care when moving plants in light, crumbly soils. Wrap the root ball with the burlap or canvas before lifting and moving it out of the hole. You may need to temporarily tie it in place to help keep the roots intact throughout the move.

Place the plant in a properly prepared hole (see guidelines for planting trees in Chapter 4, page 65). Cut or slide away the canvas and finish planting.

After all this, you may decide you're better off removing the old plant and buying a new one. They often catch up and surpass the larger transplants.

Use a shovel to lift plants so a burlap sling can be slipped under the root ball for safer moving.

Winter Care

IF YOU'RE a Southern gardener, you may want to read this chapter in July or August. It may make your summer heat more bearable to know that you don't have to worry about babying your plants through a harsh winter.

For Northern gardeners, tucking your plants in for the winter can mean the difference between spring cleanup and spring replacement.

As always, proper plant selection and placement are important. It's not just the cold weather that kills our plants. It's also poorly drained soils, drying winter winds and sun.

One of my students found this out firsthand. She designed a landscape with boxwoods at the front entrance. It seemed like a good idea, until she learned boxwood shouldn't be planted on the south side of a building exposed to drying winter sun. Too late—guess where she planted them?

She went back to the nursery that had recommended the plants. "No problem," they said. "We sell green burlap. Wrap them and they'll be fine."

I don't know about you, but a shrub wrapped with burlap is not my idea of winter interest.

A real solution would be to plant them in an east location, try a more winter-hardy cultivar or use something better suited to the site.

Lo and behold, there are two extremes to looking at winter protection. There's the "If it can't make it on its own, then it doesn't belong in my garden" approach. The other camp will do nearly anything to help every plant survive. Most of us are somewhere in between.

No matter which winter protection strategy you prefer, you can help your plants by watering them well before the ground freezes. Mulching also helps conserve moisture as well as moderate temperature extremes.

Winter Mulching

Mulch will help protect tender late plantings, expensive perennials and bulbs. The goal is to keep the soil frozen throughout winter and early spring, rather than fluctuating between freezing and thawing. This causes frost heaving, damages roots and can actually push some plants and bulbs out of the ground.

Snow is nature's mulch, and as usual, nature only uses the best. If you live in a snowy climate, feel lucky that your gardens are set for winter—a blanket of snow is the best protection for your plants. The rest of us may want to winter mulch if we can't rely on continuous snow cover.

Wait until the ground freezes (the surface should be solid or at least crunchy) to apply a 4- to 6-inch layer of straw, marsh hay or evergreen branches. If there's already snow on the ground, keep some mulch ready for when it melts later in the season.

Patience is important. If you mulch too soon, the plants may start to grow and are susceptible to disease. Or, once the ground freezes, the mulch will become a bed-and-breakfast for wild animals. The breakfast will be your covered plants.

One way to wait long enough for the ground to freeze is to wait to mulch until you're ready to recycle your Christmas tree.

I prune off the branches and use them as winter cover. In fact, I help my neighbors and the environment by collecting all their discarded trees, which are headed for the dump. My teenage daughter, how-

Here's a simple way to winter protect tender evergreens. Surround them with chicken wire and fill with straw.

ever, does ask me to wait until dark or at least until she's out of sight, before I drag them home.

Broadleaf Evergreens

Rhododendron, boxwoods, holly and other broadleaf evergreens are subject to drying from winter wind and sun. The large leaf surfaces still lose moisture even when the soil is frozen and roots can't absorb moisture.

Plants growing in locations protected from winter winds and sun will probably survive. Proper fall watering and mulch will help, too.

Grow holly in a protected location where no covering is needed, so you can enjoy the winter show.

You may need to create your own windbreaks and winter shade for plants growing in less-than-ideal conditions. Discarded holiday trees can be placed in snowbanks or propped in the landscape to cut the wind, cast some shade and make a welcome shelter for birds.

For more traditional shelters, surround tender plantings with three or four stakes and wrap them with burlap or weed barrier.

Smaller plants or those subject to animal damage can be surrounded with hardware cloth. Be sure to sink it several inches in the ground before the soil freezes. Once the soil is frozen, cover the plant by filling the cylinder with straw or evergreen branches.

If winter damage is an annual problem, consider adding a decorative screen or living windbreak to provide shelter. It'll mean less work, and probably a better looking winter landscape.

Other Evergreens

Winter wind and sun also can also damage dwarf Alberta spruce, arborvitae and new evergreen plantings. Provide screening the first few years to mini-

mize damage. Consider a more permanent solution for the more susceptible evergreens or those growing in extremely harsh conditions.

Prevent snow and ice damage on upright arborvitaes, junipers and yews. Loosely tie the stems with twine or cotton strips in fall before it snows. This holds the stems together to help prevent splitting, bending and disfiguring.

If such damage occurs anyway, be patient. Nature will repair it. As the snow melts, the plants will start straightening themselves. They'll usually recover after one or maybe even two episodes, but more can cause permanent damage. Mark your calendar now, so you remember to prevent the problem next season.

Deciduous Trees

Do not wrap tree trunks with burlap, paper, plastic guards or other tree-wrap materials. Recent research has shown that they don't help prevent winter damage, sunscald or frost cracking. And if you think they keep out the animals, look closely—you may find tooth marks and missing wrap.

If you feel you *must* wrap the tree, wait until late fall. Remove the wrap in spring, so the bark has an opportunity to toughen up during the growing season. Do not wrap trunks for more than two winters.

Increase winter survival by thoroughly watering all new plantings and evergreens before the ground freezes.

Compost, topsoil or wood chips mounded over the base of hybrid tea roses can help protect the graft from winterkill.

Rose Protection

Hybrid tea roses and winter protection go hand in hand in the North. I love hybrid teas, but hate telling people why theirs died and how much work it takes to protect them.

Some rosarians have suggested growing them as annuals in the North. If they survive the winter, it's a bonus. If not, look at it as an opportunity to plant something new. I find very few gardeners like this approach.

I choose shrub roses and other hardy roses that require no special care. This is one instance where I prefer plants that can "make it on their own".

See Chapter 7 for details on growing, maintaining and protecting roses.

Managing Snow and Ice

Our attempts to manage snow and ice often cause more damage than the elements themselves. Next time the snow starts to fall, reach for your shovel, not the bag of deicing salt. Shovel first to remove the bulk of the snow. Salt only the areas where ice poses safety concerns.

I live at the bottom of a hill, so all the snow melts during the day, runs down the hill and seems to freeze in front of my house. This forces me to use some deicing compounds, but I select more environmentally friendly prod-

ucts like magnesium chloride and calcium acetate. These are more expensive than rock salt, but easier on the plants and environment. Sand is used in many communities. Just avoid using it near sewers and drains, where it can cause problems.

Create barriers to keep salt spray from roads off your plants. Select salt-tolerant plants like Austrian pine, put up decorative fencing or use screens, burlap and weed barrier to keep road salt off more sensitive plants.

Spring rains wash the deicing salts through the soil and beneath the plant roots. If it's a dry spring, you'll need to thoroughly water salt-exposed areas several times.

Areas subject to heavy salt use may need a bit of redesign. Would a wider path, stone edge or salt-tolerant ground cover be a better alternative?

When I was landscape operations manager for the City of Milwaukee, we replaced salt-damaged grass along many of the police stations' sidewalks each spring. These walks were salted heavily to prevent slips and falls. To protect the grass, we edged the sidewalks with brick pavers that matched the bricks in the buildings, keeping the salty runoff from reaching the grass.

If you have snow and ice on your trees and shrubs, I recommend letting them fend for themselves. Shaking trunks and pounding branches can cause more damage than it prevents.

If you want to help, gently brush snow off the

Burlap and stakes are one way to protect shrubs from winter sun and wind damage.

branches with a broom before it freezes, but this usually isn't practical. Sometimes it's better to stay inside, make some hot chocolate and enjoy the winter scene.

Container Gardens

Trees, shrubs, roses and perennials growing in pots need extra protection for winter. These containers don't provide enough insulation to protect the roots from below-freezing temperatures. See the section on container gardening in Chapter 7 for tips on getting them through winter.

Moving Plants Indoors

Some annuals, tropicals and miniature roses can be moved indoors for winter. Make sure you have enough space, a good source of light and time for their care (especially during the busy holidays). Otherwise your early efforts might be wasted. It may be better to let the plants die quickly from frost than slowly from neglect.

Like most gardeners, I always have to bring "just a few" indoors. The best strategy is to overwinter them in a sunny window or under artificial lights, and care for them like your houseplants.

Start by gradually introducing these plants indoors. Move them to a screened porch or spare room. Keep them isolated for 2 to 4 weeks while you watch for signs of insects. Treat infested plants before mixing them with your indoor plant collection—or, better yet, just keep them isolated throughout the winter.

Control insects with one of the more environmentally friendly products like insecticidal soap; neem, a plant-derived insecticide; or a conventional insecticide labeled for use on indoor plants. Make sure there's good ventilation, or move the plants outdoors before spraying.

The leaves will often yellow and drop as these plants adjust to the low light indoors. Be patient—new leaves should start to appear. Continue to water as needed, but don't fertilize until the plants show signs of active growth.

Move these plants back outdoors in spring, after the danger of frost has passed. Harden them off just as you would annuals or other plants that need to adjust to a drastic change in environment.

Another option worth considering is taking cuttings of geraniums, coleus and other annuals and moving them indoors. This reduces the risk of bringing unwanted pests inside, and the smaller plants require less growing space. Find out how to start plants from cuttings in Chapter 6.

Storing Dormant Geraniums

Some gardeners store geraniums indoors as dormant plants over the winter. The key to success is a cool, dark, damp storage space like a root cellar. Basements in most new homes are too warm and dry for this method.

Is it worth a try? You have nothing to lose but your time. Just dig the plants in fall before frost kills the tops, remove the soil and store them.

Container plants can be left intact and moved indoors as well. Leave the tops intact as they dry and wither. Some gardeners moisten the roots once a month, while others do nothing. This depends on your storage location, so you may have to experiment to see which works best.

Bring the plants out of storage in spring, about 1 to 10 weeks before the last spring frost. Pot up bare-root plants and cut the tops back to 4 inches on all plants. Move to a sunny window or under artificial lights. Water thoroughly as often as needed. Wait until new growth begins before feeding with a diluted flowering or complete fertilizer.

With some luck, you'll have some good-sized geraniums to add to your garden next spring.

Moving annuals indoors is one way to extend the garden season. Many plants like geraniums, annual vinca and coleus can add color in to a long, dreary winter.

The *Plant Doctor* is in

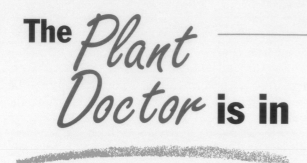

Q: My mums and asters start out looking good but soon become floppy and aren't very attractive by the time they start to bloom. Any suggestions?

A: You can improve appearance and bloom with minimal effort. Pinch back the growing tips, keeping these plants 4 to 6 inches tall through late spring and early summer. This will give you shorter plants with lots of flowering stems. Stop pinching at least 6 weeks before their normal flowering time. Pinching later than this can delay or eliminate fall bloom. This is especially important in the North, where snow may be flying before the delayed flower buds start to open.

Q: When and how should I prune my clematis?

A: That depends on when it flowers. Spring-flowering clematis bloom on last season's growth. Wait until after it blooms to prune. Remove dead and damaged stems and prune back remaining stems to reduce the size of your plant.

Late-spring flowering clematis bloom on shoots produced on old growth. Remove dead and damaged stems before growth begins. Trim remaining stems back to healthy buds. This is the framework for the flowering shoots.

Summer- and fall-blooming clematis bloom on new growth and can be pruned anytime during the dormant season. Cut these plants back to 6 to 12 inches above ground level.

Prune clematis based on bloom time.

Q: I have some major construction occurring around my house and need to move a lot of plants. I want to replant them in the same location when the work is complete. Please advise.

A: Dig up the plants and pot them in containers. Store in a partially shaded location, at least until they recover from transplant shock. Water thoroughly, until the water runs out the bottom, and as often as needed. Mulch the containers with wood chips, especially in hot dry regions, to keep them cool and moist. Once construction is complete, you can replant them. Be sure to prepare soil that may have been damaged during construction.

In colder regions of the country, sink the containers in the ground if they need to be stored over winter. This insulates the roots, preventing damage caused by freezing temperatures. Another alternative is following the instructions for heeling in bare-root plants, described in Chapter 4.

Q: There is yellowish brown-beige stuff on my wood chip mulch. It looks like my neighbor's dog got sick in my garden. Will this hurt my plants?

A: It's not surprising this common slime mold is often called "dog vomit fungus". This is frequently seen on wood chip, cocoa bean and a few other organic mulches during wet weather.

The fungus feeds on the organic matter in the mulch. It looks disgusting, but it won't hurt your plants. As the weather dries, it will dry up and disappear. To prevent this, lightly rake mulched areas during wet weather. I like to mix rice hulls with my cocoa bean shells. They lift and separate the bean shells and help eliminate the problem.

Q: My flowers and vegetables are pale and stunted. Someone told me the wood chip mulch was stealing nitrogen from my plants. Is this true?

A: Wood chips, sawdust and other wood mulches break down slowly. The microorganisms helping them decompose use soil nitrogen as an energy source. This indeed ties up nitrogen the plants would like to use and can lead to the yellow, stunted plants you are seeing.

Once the chips have decomposed, that nitrogen and more will be available for the plants to use. This is not a problem for most large-root plants like trees and shrubs. For smaller plants, I recommend adding a little supplemental nitrogen to compensate.

Avoid tilling wood mulches into the soil at the end of the season, or limit their use to paths and areas around trees and shrubs.

Q: I read about a spray you could put on your mulch to keep it looking fresh. Is it safe?

A: These food coloring-based dyes are usually mixed with water and sprayed on or applied with a spray attachment for your garden hose. They reportedly have no adverse environmental effects, and I haven't seen or heard of any problems with plants exposed to them. But be careful in applying them—over spraying stains sidewalks, driveways and buildings.

Q: My shrubs are blocking the view through my bay window. How much can I prune off without hurting the plants?

A: This will vary with species of shrub. Honeysuckle, spirea and other vigorous growers can be pruned back to several inches above ground level without harming the plant. A safer, more conservative alternative for most other shrubs is to reduce their height by one-third.

Q: There are hundreds of miniature plum trees sprouting in the grass around my big tree. Is there an easy way to kill these?

A: Ornamental plums and cherries, crabapples and a few other landscape plants are notorious for producing these sprouts. The shoots arise from the root system, making them hard to pull and impossible to kill without injuring the parent plant. Anything applied to the sprouts will be absorbed by the roots, injuring or even killing the parent tree. Many gardeners just mow them down and live with the inconvenience. Others cut them off below ground to keep them from resprouting.

Q: The top of my spruce was damaged in a snowstorm. Now I have a bunch of shoots growing straight up at the top of my tree. Can this be fixed?

A: Yes. Select one of the upright stems and train it into a new leader. Remove the rest of the shoots back to the trunk. With the competition gone, this stem will take over as the central leader. If this happens again, you can get started sooner. Prune back the broken leader so you have a 1-1/2-inch stub. Select one of the small side shoots to be your new leader. Carefully bend the stem so it points upward. Tie it to the stub. Just prune off any side shoots that try to compete for the job.

Q: Should I cut my perennials and ornamental grasses back in fall or spring?

A: This is a matter of personal preference. I like to leave mine standing for winter interest and to attract birds to my backyard. I have more time to sit and look out my window in winter, and the seed heads, pods and grasses add color and motion to my winter garden.

And by leaving them until spring, this is one less fall chore you'll need to worry about. By late winter, most of us are eager to start working in the garden again.

Do cut back and destroy pest-infested leaves and stems in fall to reduce future problems, and consider cutting them back before winter if voles (meadow mice) have caused damage to your gardens and yard in the past.

Loppers extend your reach, making it easier to reach into shrubs for renewal pruning.

Q: My lilac has lots of leaves at top, but only bare stems at bottom. How do I correct this?

A: This is a common sight on lilacs, older hedges and many other shrubs. Renewal pruning will help stimulate new growth at the base of the plant, while reducing its size and improving its overall health.

Remove one-third of the stems at ground level when it finishes blooming, and reduce the height by about one-third. Repeat this for the next two seasons. You'll be amazed at the transformation.

rooting
powder
No.1

Chapter 6
Propagation Made Easy

No matter how many times I watch seeds sprout, bulbs burst open or plant cuttings take root, I'm amazed. Plants are able to re-create themselves in so many ways, and one of the fun things about gardening is to help them do just that. Collecting seeds, taking cuttings, layering or experimenting with grafting can result in successful propagation of new plants…or the opportunity to give it another try. However it turns out, it's always a fun challenge.

You can't talk about propagation without a discussion of the birds and the bees. Actually, we'll start with the flower parts that most interest the birds and bees.

Flower Parts

YOU MAY REMEMBER learning about a flower's composition in your grade-school science classes. If you've forgotten, here's a quick refresher course.

Flowers share some common parts, but vary in overall makeup. A "complete flower" (illustrated below) contains all the possible parts of a flower. Its petals are usually the most colorful and attractive

parts to birds, bees and other pollinators. The protective sepals may be strictly functional or as pretty as the petals.

The male reproductive parts, contained in the stamen, produce the pollen needed for pollination, fertilization (where pollen meets egg) and seed formation. The pollen in the anther is held in position by filaments to allow wind, insects or other pollinators to reach and transfer it.

The female reproductive parts make up the pistil. The pollen enters the stigma and travels down the style to fertilize the eggs held in the ovules. Once fertilization occurs, seeds start to develop.

A perfect flower contains both the male and female reproductive parts, but may be missing other features, such as petals or sepals. A staminate flower only contains the male reproductive parts. Pistillate flowers contain reproductive parts that are female only, plus various other flower parts. Some plants have both male and female flowers (*monoecious*), while others have them on separate male and female plants (*dioecious*).

Corn is one example of a species that both male and female flowers growing on a single plant. Bittersweet and holly, meanwhile, have separate male and female plants.

A good understanding of these functions will help you grow plants for seed and fruit production.

Pollination

The source of the pollen and eggs determines the look and vigor of the offspring. Self-pollinating plants produce and use their own pollen to fertilize their flowers (eggs). This results in a fairly consistent look from parent to offspring. Cross-pollination depends on wind, birds, bees and other means to transfer pollen from one plant to another. In these cases, offspring can look different from the parent

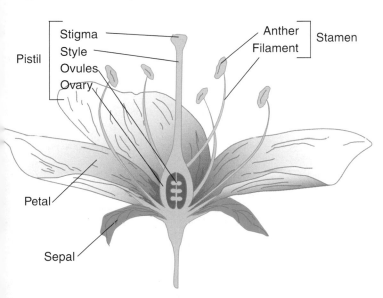

Pistil
Stigma
Style
Ovules
Ovary

Anther
Filament
Stamen

Petal

Sepal

plant and from each other.

Open-pollinated plants receive pollen from other plants of the same species via wind, birds or bees. This results in a genetically rich makeup and variability in size, color and shape. Seed-saving gardeners often isolate these plants from other varieties to prevent cross-pollination and loss of desired characteristics.

Hybrids are created when man gets involved and plays the part of the bee. The pollen of one plant is purposely crossed with the eggs of another to get an offspring with a certain color, flower, fruit shape, vegetable flavor or other characteristic. Seeds saved from hybrids can give the gardener a bit of a surprise. The offspring may look like one or the other parent or be utterly unique.

Saving the Seeds

Collecting, storing and starting seeds can add a new dimension to your gardening. Many seed-savers pass them down through generations, like any other family heirloom. Some gardeners want to preserve old varieties, while others simply try their hand at saving seed for next year's crop. Whatever your reason, start with the end result in mind.

Select seeds from healthy plants that have the color, size or fragrance you want. A good basis of desired characteristics will increase your chances for desirable offspring. Keep in mind that only self-pollinated plants will "come true" from seed with offspring that look like the parent. But even then a few surprises can be fun, and may result in something better than expected—or at least a topic for conversation.

My favorite cross-pollinating plants are squash. When I worked for the Extension service, every fall my office was filled with squashes of unusual shapes and colors. Gardeners would bring them in to be identified and ask if they were safe to eat. I remember a white acorn squash, a green zucchini with yellow spots and many other interesting mixes.

I explained to the puzzled gardeners that the seed they saved from last year's crop had been pollinated by another variety. The offspring kept a few characteristics from each parent, producing a unique

Collection Tips

EXTEND your seed collection time and increase your success with these simple techniques:

● Place a paper or cloth bag over the seed head as it nears maturity. This will reduce the number of seeds lost to birds, squirrels and gravity, as they may drop to the ground before you have time to harvest them.

● Cut the stems, bundling them together, and cover seed heads with a paper bag. Use a rubber band or string to secure the bag and trap the seeds inside.

● Pour the seeds out of the bag and continue with the cleaning and drying process.

Reader's Digest Assoc. Inc./GID

squash. I assured them that these unusual vegetables were safe to eat, and then we had some fun making up names for them.

Collecting Seed

Collect seeds once the fruit matures or the seed-pods dry on the plant. Timing is important, because collecting seeds before they ripen can result in poor germination or none at all.

Seeds in fleshy fruits like berries, tomatoes and crabapples are best harvested when the seed is fully ripe or slightly overripe. Scoop out the seeds and eat or compost the rest of the fruit. Place the seeds, pulp and water in a bowl or jar of water. Set the mix aside to ferment for several days.

The pulp and bad seeds will float to the top. Scrape this away, pour off the water and save the larger seeds in the bottom. Rinse, then spread those seeds on newspaper to dry for several days.

You can also try picking out the seeds with a fork. Rinse off the fleshy pulp and then dry the seeds.

✔ *Melinda's Tips*

WRITE IT DOWN! Seems that the older I get, the harder it is to remember details. Record seed-collecting information such as the seed source, dates, cleaning procedure, storage treatment, germination success and other related information. These records will help you repeat your successes and avoid duplicating your failures.

Collect dry seeds from plants like coneflowers, and those in pods like yucca, after the pods or seeds dry. That's about a month after the flowers fade. Cut off the flower heads and move indoors to clean them. Loosen dried seeds from the stem. Break pods apart to release the seeds inside. Remove any debris or poorly developed seeds. The seeds may look dry, but give them a few more days to dry thoroughly before you pack them away for winter.

Place dried seeds in an envelope, label the contents and place them in a dry, airtight jar in the refrigerator. This will keep the temperature consistent and the seeds dry. Wet seeds may begin to sprout in the fridge instead of your garden.

Seed Treatment

Some seeds need special treatment to germinate. Many perennials, trees and shrubs native to colder climates need a cold treatment known as "stratification". Storing seeds in the refrigerator for several months will do the trick. Leave them in cold storage until you're ready to plant.

Some seeds, especially from nut trees, need moist stratification. Pack them in peat moss or plant them in containers filled with any well-drained potting mix. Keep the medium moist and cool for several months.

"Scarification" is used on seeds with hard coverings or seed coats. This is done just before planting. Rub the seeds on sandpaper or nick the hard coat with a file so the seeds can absorb moisture and start to grow. Do not, however, cut through the seed coat and expose the inner seed. You want to scratch the surface only enough to dull the covering, but do not crack the surface.

Some gardeners prefer to soak these seeds overnight before planting to soften the coat further. A hot-water bath works for most seeds, though several conifers, such as Monterey pine and Douglas fir, prefer a cold-water treatment.

Seeds can also be soaked overnight to speed germination. It works fine for a handful of seeds that you'll be planting in the garden. But some gardeners have tried this when reseeding their lawns. Yes, they've seen professionals do this—but the pros have years of experience and the materials to do it successfully.

When homeowners try this, most of them end up with a big glob of seed they can't spread. The key to success is finding a dry material such as peat, sand or vermiculite that will separate the wet seed for spreading. Most gardeners have better luck skipping the pre-germination step, spreading their seed dry and waiting a little longer for the grass to sprout.

Plant treated seeds immediately. Most seeds won't last in storage once they've been soaked. Handle seeds with care and plant indoors or out as explained in Chapter 4.

Asexual Reproduction

PICTURE THIS. You have a clump of salvia in your hands. Cut it in half, and you have two. Cut these in half, and you have four. Cut them all in half again, and you have eight new plants where there once was one. It's like magic!

Many plants can be divided like this, or will reproduce identical plants if you remove small pieces of leaves, stems and roots and replant them.

This is asexual propagation, and it allows you to start new plants from old while maintaining all the characteristics—good and bad—of the parents. It's often quicker and easier than starting plants from seeds. Select a method that fits the plant, your skill and gardening style.

Save only the best seeds. This will increase the germination percentage and growing success. Remove undersized, damaged or malformed seeds.

Photos: Graham Rice/GardenPhotos.com

1. To take a cutting, use bypass (scissor-like) pruning shears for a clean cut.

2. Remove lower leaves on portion of stem to be buried.

3. Dip cuttings in root hormone powder to discourage rot and encourage rooting.

4. Gently water until the root medium is moist.

5. Loosely cover the pot in plastic for humidity.

Leaf-Stem Cuttings

My grandmother always had a piece of some plant rooting in a glass in her kitchen. Everything seemed to grow for her, and I think grandparents just have the magic touch. Whether you do or not, you can try this to increase your plant collection, expand your propagation knowledge and improve your gardening skills.

Before you begin, gather all the necessary materials so you can get the cutting planted quickly. This will minimize drying and mishandling, which can lead to failure. You'll need:

- **A sharp knife or garden scissors** for taking cuttings.
- **Rooting hormone**, available at most garden centers. This contains hormones that encourage rooting and chemicals that discourage rot.
- **Rooting media** like sand, perlite, vermiculite, a mix of peat and vermiculite or a sterile, well-draining potting mix.
- **Plastic** to create a mini greenhouse or a plant mister to increase humidity.

Start with a healthy stem, free of insects and disease. Remove a piece 3 to 5 inches long. Cut just below a node, the point where leaves and buds emerge. I like to clean up the parent plant after all the cuttings are made. Trim stubs back to just above a healthy leaf. It will look better, and the wound will close faster, keeping insects and diseases away.

Remove any flowers or buds from the cutting. We want all the energy to go into the formation of roots, not flowers. Cut the bottom of the stem on a slant to ensure it's planted right side up. It won't root if planted upside down.

Don't try to rush the process by taking longer cuttings. Longer stems have more leaves, which means more moisture loss, which impedes root development. You *can* take a longer cutting and divide it into smaller sections, though. Be sure to cut the bottom of each piece on a slant or somehow mark it for proper planting.

Remove the lower leaf or two. Then dip the cut end in a rooting hormone if desired. Place the cutting in the rooting medium deep enough to cover the bottom nodes. This is where the new roots will start to form.

Place the cutting in a bright location, but out of direct sun. Increase humidity by covering it with a loose bag, misting several times a day or setting it under the canopy of a shade tree.

You can also put the cutting on a humidity tray. Set the pot atop a saucer filled with pebbles and water. The pot should sit on the pebbles, but out of the water. As the water evaporates, it increases humidity around the plant.

Depending on the plant, it will root in 1 to 4 weeks. You will know it's rooted when you feel resistance as you gently tug on the stem. Then the cutting can be moved directly into the garden. If you want it larger before you move it to the garden, put it in a container filled with well-drained potting mix and let it grow a bit first.

Trees and shrubs add a bit of a challenge, and timing and technique are more critical to success. Professional propagators have spent years studying, training, sharing information and recording data to become successful.

As a kid in high school, I tried propagating lilacs from the plant growing outside my bedroom window. I thought I did everything right. After the cuttings failed to root, I discovered my timing was off. I should have taken cuttings right after flowering.

Try a few different techniques. Good record keeping of successes and failures will help.

Hardwood Cuttings

Cuttings of forsythia, privet, olive, wisteria, spirea, juniper, hemlock and many other deciduous and needled trees and shrubs should be made during the dormant season, using the previous season's growth. Take 4- to 8-inch cuttings with at least two nodes. (Professionals use longer cuttings for special grafting and training techniques.) Cut the bottom on a slant.

Take a few extra cuttings, since trees and shrubs are more difficult to root than cuttings from flowers and houseplants. If you're lucky enough to have 100% success, you'll have plenty of new plants to fill your yard or share with friends.

To increase your chances of success, you can try several different types of cuttings.

A straight-stem cutting contains only the previous season's growth. A heeled cutting has a small piece of 2-year-old stem tissue at its base. A mallet cutting

Make forsythia cuttings in the dormant season.

Root cuttings outdoors in a narrow trench.

In a year or 2, your cuttings will be ready for transplanting.

has a section of 2-year-old stem. Some plants root best with one type of cutting, while others root from any type. You may want to try a few of each for insurance, and note which worked best for each plant.

Store cuttings in a cool (above-freezing), moist location for the winter. Northern gardeners will probably need a root cellar, spare refrigerator or other frost-free location.

If your area has mild winters, you can store cuttings outdoors. Bundle the cuttings, lay them on their sides and bury them in sandy soil, sand or sawdust.

Plant the stored cuttings in spring, slanted end down, in a large, deep flat or container filled with sand or vermiculite, or a mix of peat and perlite or vermiculite. Once the cuttings root, treat them like bare-root plants and move them into the garden.

You also can transplant the rooted cuttings into a larger container filled with well-drained potting mix. This gives you more control over the environment and lets the plants establish a larger root system before they're moved to the garden.

In areas with mild winters, you can combine the storage and rooting phases by rooting cuttings outside in fall. Dig a trench. Place the cuttings 3 to 4 inches apart, and plant deeply enough to cover all but the uppermost bud. Fill the trench with soil, and then water. Keep the soil moist to encourage root development. By the following spring, your cuttings will be rooted and ready to transplant.

Semi-Hardwood Cuttings

These cuttings are made in summer, when new growth has started to mature. Pittosporum, holly, azaleas, euonymus, citrus, olive and other broadleaf evergreen and deciduous trees and shrubs are often propagated with this method.

Take cuttings in the morning, when the leaves are firm and full of moisture. Cut pieces into 3- to 6-inch lengths for rooting. Remember to cut the bottom of the stem on a slant. Remove the lower leaves. If the remaining leaves are large, cut them in half to minimize moisture loss.

Root semi-hardwood cuttings in a shaded location with high humidity. Professionals have special propagation beds with built-in misting systems, but a shady spot under a tree often provides enough light and humidity.

For extra insurance, loosely cover the rooting bed with plastic. Remember, though, you want to capture the humidity without cooking the plants. Monitor temperatures regularly and vent the covering as needed.

Softwood Cuttings

As the name implies, these cuttings are made from tender new growth. Lilacs, forsythia, magnolias, weigela, spireas, fruits and other trees and shrubs are often propagated this way.

Softwood cuttings usually root quickly and easily, but must be handled with care. Take 3- to 5-inch cuttings early in the day. Remove any flowers, flower buds or seed heads. Plant the cuttings immediately for best results. If some must be stored for later planting, wrap them in moist paper, burlap or plastic and keep them out of direct sunlight to prevent drying.

Keep the rooting medium moist, the humidity high and the soil warm for best results. These cuttings root in 2 to 4 weeks.

Other Stem Cuttings

Some plant stems look more like roots and bulbs. In fact, bulbs, corms, rhizomes and stolons are all modified stems and can be propagated with stem-cutting techniques.

Rhizomes and stolons are stems that grow horizontally. The rhizome grows underground, while the stolon grows along the soil surface. Both develop roots and shoots. You'll need a sharp knife or pruner and a shovel to cut them.

Bearded iris, cannas and peonies are perfect examples of rhizomatous plants. Dig them to fully expose the rhizome and roots. Use your knife to cut the rhizomes into smaller sections. Make sure you have at least one to three eyes (growing points) per section. Replant the rhizome at the same depth it was growing before—usually in the top few inches of soil.

Suckering shrubs also fit into this category. Use a sharp shovel, knife or pruner to cut through the rhizome or stolon. Dig out the small plants that have developed along the rhizome, and you have a rooted shrub ready for transplanting.

Tubers are swollen stems. Irish potatoes are the most common example, though tuberous begonias and caladiums fall into this category, too. We've all grown new plants from tubers, sometimes unintentionally—like the potato left in the pantry a little too long that started to grow. This is a great opportunity to learn from your mistakes.

1. *Take softwood cuttings from tender new growth early in the season.*

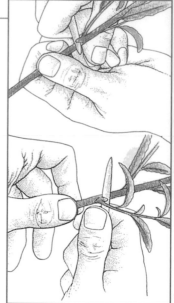

2. *Make heel cuttings by removing a stem and a piece of last year's wood. Make a slant cutting into the main stem below the joint. Now make a slant cutting on the opposite side.*

Rooting for Success

SOME GARDENERS seem able to make any seed sprout or cause any cutting to root. Don't be discouraged if your green thumb seems brown when it comes to propagation. Just keep these key things in mind:

• Use rooting hormone, even if your green-thumbed buddies don't. Such products may give you the edge you need.

• Use vermiculite, perlite, peat or other sterile media to root your cuttings. Replace or sterilize before using it again.

• Bury at least one node—the point where leaves and buds grow on the stem—when placing cuttings in the ground.

• Use small cuttings to minimize moisture loss and increase rooting success.

• Work in the shade and keep the cuttings cool and damp to minimize moisture loss.

• Maximize humidity by placing cuttings with other plants, setting them on a gravel tray filled with pebbles and water or covering them with a plastic bag.

• Root your cuttings in warm (65° to 75°) soil to speed root development. Select a warm location, create a mini greenhouse or place rooting trays on heating pads designed for this purpose.

The eyes on potatoes and other tubers are the growing points, or nodes. To propagate, just cut them into smaller pieces containing at least one or two eyes. Plant the tuber, cover it with soil and wait for the eyes to sprout and stems to appear. Now you've got a new plant.

Dividing Bulbs

True bulbs, such as tulips and daffodils, and corms, which include crocus and gladiolus, develop new bulbs (bulblets) and corms (cormels) next to the old. These can be lifted, divided and replanted to help expand your plant collection.

Dig and separate the bulbs as foliage starts to decline. Plant some of the bulbs back in the original location and use others for new plantings or to trade with friends and neighbors. Water new plantings to help settle the soil and encourage root development.

Smaller bulbs may not bloom until the second or third year. You'll see leaves the following season, but will have to wait for the flowers. Full-sized bulbs should flower the first season after division. For tropical (non-hardy) bulbs and corms like gladiolus, just separate them before placing all the bulbs in winter storage.

Scaly bulbs such as lilies and fritillaries (crown imperials) can be propagated by scaling. Dig and clean scaly bulbs in late summer or early fall. Remove a few scales and replant the bulb so it can continue to grow and flower. Or, sacrifice the bulb and use all the scales to propagate even more new plants. Make sure a piece of the basal plate (flat portion at the base of the bulb) is attached to each scale.

Now the process moves indoors. Place the scales in a sealed bag filled with a mixture of peat and perlite. Keep it in a warm, dark location for about 3 months. Then move it to a cool (above-freezing) location like the refrigerator for 6 to 8 weeks to encourage bulblet development. Once the bulblets form, move them (with the scales attached) to a container or an area of the garden that's protected from late-summer heat. Plant so the top of the scale is just below the soil surface. Cover with winter mulch or a cold frame for the winter.

Next spring, they'll be ready to dig and move into a permanent location. You'll have to wait a couple of years before they bloom.

Lilies also produce vegetative growths, called bulbils, at the base of their leaves. Harvest these when they turn black and can easily be removed. Place them in the garden in rows about an inch deep. Next fall, dig and replant them. They should reach flowering size in 2 or 3 years.

An easier method is to let nature handle the job. My husband sprinkled a few bulbils from his parents' garden alongside our house. In just a few years, thanks to the natural proliferation of bulbils and bulblets, we had quite the collection of tiger lilies.

Dividing Tuberous Rooted Plants

Dahlias and sweet potatoes have large, fleshy tuberous roots. The growing point is at the top of the tuberous root. Divide these plants in spring as growth begins.

Start by moving the tuberous roots out of storage. The eyes should have started to swell, which makes division much easier. Use a sharp knife to divide the plant into sections, with at least one eye (swollen bud) or shoot per tuberous root.

Start these indoors for an earlier bloom during the growing season, or plant them directly outdoors once the soil has warmed and there's no danger of frost.

Leaf Cuttings

Some plants can be propagated from only a leaf. This technique takes a little longer and often has a lower success rate than leaf-stem cuttings. Professionals do this when they have a limited number of plants available for propagation. Gardeners do it for the challenge and fun of trying something new.

Try this method with jade plants, begonias, sansevieria (snake plant) and other tropicals, cacti and

Some plants, like strawberries, spider plants and this Episcia, can be started from plantlets called runners.

Begonias can be propagated from seed or asexually from stem or leaf cuttings.

succulents. If you've ever grown jade, you've probably found fallen leaves that have rooted in the pot without your help.

As with stem cuttings, there are several variations for this technique.

Leaf cuttings with the leaf stem (petiole) intact are often used with African violets, peperomias and other tropical plants. Remove a leaf from the parent plant. Bury the petiole in sand, vermiculite or a well-drained potting mix. Keep the planted cutting in a bright location out of direct light. Water it often enough to keep the rooting medium moist…and wait. A new plant will develop at the base of the leaf in 4 to 8 weeks.

Kalanchoe and begonia leaves are treated a bit differently. Lay these on the soil surface, using small stones or hairpins to hold them in place. Slice the veins of the begonia and other thin tropical leaves.

New plants will form on the edges of the kalanchoe plant and at the cut veins of the begonia. The original leaf eventually disintegrates, but you end up with many new plants.

With some plants, the leaves will form roots, but no new plant. Make sure to take a bud along with the leaf to start new plants from jade, rhododendron, lemon, camellia, blackberry and other tropical and herbaceous plants.

Place the leaf-bud cutting in sand, vermiculite or a perlite-peat mix so the bud is about half an inch below the soil surface. Keep the soil warm and moist for best results.

You can even use pieces of leaves to start new plants. The snake plant is commonly started this way. Cut a leaf into several pieces about 3 to 4 inch-

es long. Cut the bottom of the leaf on a slant. This end must be placed in the soil for rooting to occur.

Bury the bottom half of the leaf cutting in a moist rooting medium. A new plant will begin to grow in 1 to 2 months. This is fun and gives you a real sense of accomplishment. I use this method when showing teachers and children various propagation techniques. Once I ran into a teacher years after he'd attended one of those workshops, and he proudly took me into his sunroom to show me how much success he'd had with this technique.

Root Cuttings

Cuttings from tuberous and fleshy roots can be used to start new plants. Poppies, trumpet vine, phlox and silk tree are a few of the plants that can be propagated this way.

Make 2- to 4-inch root cuttings in late winter or early spring. For Oriental poppies, wait until midsummer. Cut the bottom of the root—the part farthest from the stem—at a slant. Plant the cuttings vertically, with the top just below the soil surface. Keep soil warm and moist.

How to Make a Mini Propagator

YOU CAN MAKE your own propagation chamber with materials from your home or garden center. Find a clean 6- or 8-inch pot. Place a small clay pot, with the drainage hole plugged, in the center to act as a water reservoir. Fill the space around the small pot with rooting medium, nestling the little pot so its lip is even with the soil surface.

Place cuttings in the rooting medium surrounding the small pot. Fill the small pot with water and cover everything, plants and all, with plastic. Some gardeners bend wires to make a frame to keep the plastic off the plants. Move your propagator to a bright location out of direct light.

Add more water to the small pot as it dries up. Vent the plastic if condensation or temperatures build. Once the cuttings are rooted, transplant them to their own containers

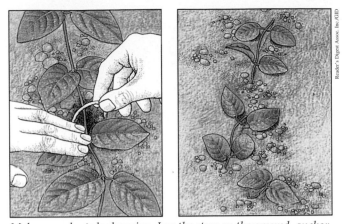

Make new plants by layering. Lay the stem on the ground, anchor it in a hole and cover a node where the leaves were removed. Repeat all along the stem, leaving at least two leaves above the ground between the buried portions of the stem.

Layering

As you work in your garden, you may find nature is already propagating some new plants. Shrub stems and vines lying on the ground often develop roots and start new plants. Take your cue from nature and use this method yourself to propagate vines, perennials, shrubs with pliable branches and some tropical plants.

Layering allows you to start a new plant while it's still attached to the parent plant. This "umbilical cord" sends water and nutrients from the established root system to the rooting stem.

Start by selecting a healthy stem on the outer edge of the plant. Make a cut halfway through the stem about 9 to 12 inches below the tip. Remove nearby leaves. Treat the cut with rooting hormone to encourage root development. Carefully bend the stem to the ground, bury the cut portion and leave the top 6 inches above the ground.

The plant will develop its root system over the summer. At the end of the season, you'll have a rooted stem ready to grow on its own. Gardeners in mild climates can "cut the cord" where the stem enters the soil and move the newly rooted plant to a new location. Northern gardeners may want to wait until late winter to make the move with minimal transplant shock.

Variations

Many gardeners layer successfully without cutting the stem or using a rooting hormone. These steps just encourage the plant to form roots. Experiment to find out which method works best for you and the plants you're propagating.

Some gardeners just anchor the stem on top of the ground. Use a wire hook, stone or other object to keep the stem in contact with the soil. The roots will develop on the underside of the stem. You'll know if your plant is suited for this if it's already rooting like this without your help.

Another option is to bury the cut stem in a pot of soil instead of the ground. Once the plant roots, cut it off and you have a potted plant ready to move to any location. It makes everything much easier and reduces the risk of transplant shock.

Air Layering

Try this method on shrubs with stiff upright stems, houseplants and tropicals. The concept is the same as layering—it's just done above the ground instead of under it.

Make a cut halfway through the stem. Do so anywhere along the stem, as long as the top growth isn't too long or heavy to support itself. Most gardeners make the cut below the leafiest portion of the stem.

Wedge the cut open with a toothpick or wooden matchstick. Sprinkle with rooting hormone to encourage rooting and discourage rot.

Cover with moist sphagnum moss and plastic. Tie the plastic at the top and bottom to secure the moss. You may need to use a stake to support top-heavy stems so they don't break.

In 1 to 2 months, you'll see roots peeking through the moss. Cut the stem below the plastic, remove the plastic and let the moss fall away. Now you have a bare-root plant ready to place in a container or a new spot in the garden.

Ferns

Ferns can be propagated by sexual or asexual means. Divide large plants with a sharp knife to increase your collection. If your ferns send out stems complete with leaves and roots attached, you can treat them like rooted cuttings or layer them to start new plants while they're still attached to the parent.

Spores are the "seeds" of the fern. But they differ from true seeds and require different care. You'll usually find them on the undersides of the leaves. Some gardeners have mistaken the sori that hold these spores for scale insects. But those pests aren't as neat and orderly as the sori lined up on the undersides of fronds.

Collect spores when they're mature. You should be able to see, with the help of a magnifying glass, small, dark, swollen spore cases around the edge of the sori. Cut a frond and lay it between the folds of a piece of white paper overnight. The mature spores will drop onto the paper. If nothing happens, wait a few days, pick another frond and try again.

Gently tap the paper on the folded edge to knock the spores into the fold. Now sprinkle the spores over a container filled with moist, sterile potting mix.

Carl Taylor, curator of botany for the Milwaukee Public Museum, recommends using compressed peat pellets and a glass jar to make a germination chamber. Pour boiling water over the peat pots to sterilize. Let it cool, then fill with sterile potting mix. Sprinkle the spores over the soil and mist gently. Cover with a clean glass jar, or place several pots in a clear plastic shoe box and cover with the lid.

Place the germination chambers in a bright location. In a few weeks, you'll see a moss-like growth. Keep watching, and soon you'll see small ferns appear. Transplant these into individual containers as soon as they're 1 inch tall, and place them in larger containers, such as a clear plastic shoe box with a lid.

Growing ferns from spores can be a fun family activity or science project—or just a great way to try something new.

Grafting

Grafting unites two plants to create one with better hardiness, flowers or growth habit. The root system of one plant, called the "understock" or "rootstock", is united with a bud or stem from another plant, called "budwood" or "scion". Bud grafting is common in roses for increased root hardiness.

Fruit trees are often grafted on dwarfing rootstocks to create small, productive trees. And many shade trees and ornamental cultivars are grafted onto seedling rootstock to speed up the propagation process.

Grafting is one of the more difficult propagation techniques. It requires careful attention to detail, years of practice and some luck.

The scion and rootstock must be compatible for grafting to be a success. The two pieces must make and maintain solid contact, and the cambium—the living tissue beneath the bark—must line up on the scion and understock. Other than that, it's not too difficult.

Giving It a Try

You'll need a sharp knife; wire brads, grafting bands or tape; grafting wax; and a source of roots and buds or stems. Cut the rootstock off just above the point where you want the grafting to occur. Roses are grafted just above the roots, but other plants are grafted higher on the stem. Some gardeners try grafting several varieties of apples onto one tree. In this case, the graft union will occur on the branches.

Collect several pieces of scion wood 4 to 6 inches long. Cut the bottom of each to form a wedge. Cut the branch or stem back to just above the point where the graft will be made.

Now make a cut in the rootstock. It should start at the edge and run 1-1/2 to 2 inches down the stem and 1/4 to 1/2 inch wide. Peel the bark back and

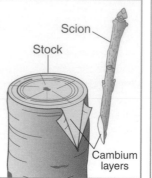 

1. *If you want to try grafting, make a 1-1/2- to 2-inch slit down the rootstock.*

2. *Peel the bark back, and slide the scion under the bark and tack down.*

slide the wedged end of the scion wood under the bark. Try to match up the cambium layers. Secure with wire brads, grafting tape or bands to hold the graft union in place. Seal with wax to prevent drying.

Bud grafts are handled a little differently. Take a small shield-shaped chip of wood, with bud intact, off the desired plant. Make a T-shaped cut into the rootstock at the graft union. Slide the bud chip into the T slice and beneath the bark. Use bud bands to anchor the budwood in place.

Next season, if the graft has taken, prune out the rootstock growing above the graft. This will allow the budded growth to take over.

Bridge Grafting

This is the grafting technique I recommend most often to gardeners. It's used to save fruit trees and other woody plants girdled by animals. It doesn't always work, but sometimes it's the only hope for damaged plants.

Gather scion wood from the stems and branches of the damaged plant, or one that's related to it. You'll need 6 pieces for larger trunks that are completely girdled. Cut the pieces slightly longer than needed to bridge the damaged area. Wedge *both ends* of the scion. Mark the bottom to maintain proper orientation during the grafting process.

Trim away the ragged edges of the damaged area. Cut several slots into the tree trunk across from each other, above and below the damage. The top and bottom of the scion will slide into these slots. Make sure the top of the scion is lined up with the top of the tree. Leave a slight bow in the scion to allow for normal tree movement.

Use power staples or wire brads to secure the scion wood. Cover the graft with grafting wax or grafting paint to prevent drying. With some luck, the graft will take and your tree will survive the damage.

The *Plant Doctor* is in

Q: I collected seeds from a wonderful apple tree in my backyard. What do I need to do to make sure they sprout?

A: I always look to nature first for my information. Seeds of plants native to colder regions, like your apple, often require stratification to ensure seed germination. Store collected seeds in an envelope in the refrigerator in an airtight jar for 3 months. Remove the seeds from cold storage and start them indoors, like other seedlings.

And remember, most apples are hybrids or open-pollinated varieties. This means the apples you grow from the collected seed will not necessarily look or taste like those from the wonderful tree in your backyard.

Q: My tulips produced seeds for the first time this season. Can I start new plants from these?

A: Bulbs can be grown from seed. It just takes a lot longer—often 5 years—for the plant to reach flowering size. Offspring of hybrid tulips will vary in size and color. Species tulips come true from seed, and do so in nature.

In the future, you may want to remove the fading flowers from your hybrid bulbs. This will elimi-nate seed formation but allow the plant to put energy back into the bulb for next season's bloom.

Q: I divided my peony last fall and it did not bloom this spring. Did I do something wrong?

A: No. Fall is the best time to dig and divide peonies, as the foliage begins to decline. It's common for them to produce only foliage the following spring. You should see flowers next season. If not, you need to examine the plant and growing conditions. Peonies won't flower if they're overfertilized, or if they're planted too deeply or in too much shade. Correct the problem, and you'll have beautiful blossoms in the future.

Q: My bittersweet does not produce fruit. Do you have any suggestions?

A: Bittersweet, holly and kiwi produce both male and female plants. You need at least one male plant for every four to five females to grow fruit. These plants are often sold with a male and a female in one container. If one of the sexes dies over time, the plants can't produce fruit. Check the blossoms in spring to see which plant survived. The diagram on page 97 will help you identify the sex. Or, plant another male and female just to be sure.

Q: I took a leaf cutting from my variegated snake plant. I was able to grow a new plant, but its leaves were solid green, not variegated like the parent plant. Can you tell me what happened?

A: The gene that controls the variegation in this plant is in the rhizome, not the leaf. You must divide these plants, cutting the rhizome into several smaller pieces, to maintain the variegation.

Q: When should I divide my dahlias and cannas?

A: I prefer to divide these and other non-hardy bulbs in spring. Remove the stored tuberous roots, rhizomes and other bulb-like structures. As the eyes begin to sprout, it's easy to see where you can cut and divide. Plus, as the plant begins its spring growth, the wounds will close quickly, minimizing the risk of insects and disease.

Tulip bulbs can be grown from seed, but it can take as long as 5 years for plants to reach flowering size.

Chapter 7
Specialty Gardens

SuperStock; opposite page: Faith Bemiss

A garden isn't complete until it has a few specialty plants, and a yard isn't complete without a specialty garden or two. All the general techniques of soil preparation, planting and pruning apply for these special additions, but you'll need a few different strategies for success.

Before you decide to dig a hole to build a water garden or add a hybrid tea rose bed, plan ahead for the work involved in installing, planting and caring for your special garden.

Bird and Butterfly Gardens

NO *BIRDS & BLOOMS* book would be complete without a discussion on how to attract these "flying flowers" to your garden. Just adding flowering and fruiting plants will increase the number of these colorful visitors, but with a bit more work, you can help extend their visits and increase the variety of visitors.

This is a great way to get children interested in gardening. I hate to admit that birds, butterflies, caterpillars, bugs and worms are much more exciting to kids than flowers. But once the children are in the garden, you may be able to get them excited about plants, too.

In a bird garden, it's nature—and not me—that refills and renews the feeders. If I plan my garden right, I can provide birds a variety of food throughout the year. Plus, many birds will eat the insects that often damage my plants.

When you're attracting birds and butterflies, you need to learn to live with caterpillars and their feeding—after all, many will soon transform into beautiful butterflies.

Let the birds and beneficial insects take care of

bothersome bugs. Trap, handpick, remove and destroy those that are out of control. If you must treat your plants, stick to wildlife-friendly products, and spot-treat to minimize chemical use.

To get started, look for ways to increase food, shelter and water for your flying visitors. Massing plants makes for a more appealing buffet and a better display in the yard. Make sure it's in a location you can enjoy, near the kitchen window or a garden bench.

My first butterfly garden was missing this element. I married a horticulturist, and we have a small yard. That can mean "turf wars" over planting space! When I suggested a butterfly garden, Wes pictured an informal garden filled with plants that weren't on his "top 10" list. I lost that debate, and my garden was relegated to the planting area next to the alley.

I filled it with a butterfly bush, purple coneflowers, creeping phlox and other butterfly-attracting plants. The butterflies came, but this wasn't the best place to sit and watch them. The neighborhood kids passing by enjoyed the butterflies, though, and it was more fun to weed than other areas in my yard.

Ironically, the front garden Wes and I planted with garden phlox, coreopsis, veronica and other perennials attracted just as many butterflies. We just chose flowers we liked, and the butterflies liked them, too. I found myself sitting on the front steps, watching my daughter and the butterflies play.

Attracting Butterflies

We all like pretty butterflies, and to see more, we need to attract the caterpillars they come from. So it's important to include food sources for both.

Colorful flowers such as phlox, coneflowers, marigolds and zinnias make attractive additions to

the garden and great food sources for the adult butterflies. For added protein, place some rotten fruit in a small container.

For the larvae (caterpillars), add some butterfly weed, parsley, licorice vine and dill. Use a variety of plants, so that while the caterpillars are eating one plant, the neighboring plants will mask the damage until they're finished eating.

Include several plants of each so you have plenty of food for unexpected guests. My friend Arlene Kaufman, Master Gardener and butterfly garden expert, was overwhelmed by a large number of swallowtail butterflies one season. Once the swallowtails devoured her parsley, she bought several bunches of it to supplement their diet. This usually isn't necessary, but those butterflies seemed to know Arlene would take care of them all.

Butterflies prefer a sunny location out of the wind. Include a few stepping-stones or warming stones, too. The butterflies like to spread their wings and warm their bodies. It's good for them and fun to watch.

Trees and shrubs should be planned into your butterfly garden, because they can provide shelter, nectar for butterflies, food for the larvae and egg-laying and pupating sites.

And don't forget the water! You've probably come across butterfly drinking parties called "puddling". You can build your own puddle with a bucket, sand and water. Bury the bucket in the ground. Fill with sand, then fill with water. Some gardeners put a few stones in the middle.

Once your butterfly garden is established, don't be too quick to tidy up the place. Eggs and cocoons are often hidden on branches and stems. A thorough garden cleanup may eliminate the butterflies you're trying to attract.

For the Birds

As with butterflies, you need to provide food, water and shelter to attract and keep birds in your landscape. Trees, shrubs and evergreens make good nesting areas for many different species. My neighbor has a huge white spruce tree in front of her house. Every morning I hear the cardinals sing as I sit at my computer to write. It makes it much easier to crawl out of bed at the crack of dawn knowing I have company waiting for me.

I recycle my Christmas tree. I use it as mulch or leave it intact for a windbreak. It also provides shelter for birds during the cold winter months.

Many trees and shrubs provide food for birds as well. You'll find birds feeding on crabapples, serviceberries (Juneberries), hawthorns, elderberries and many others. American robins line up on our fence every June to feast on my Juneberries.

Perennials also offer a source of food. Hosta seeds attract juncos, while coneflowers and rudbeckia bring in the finches. This adds needed color and interest to the winter landscape.

Hummingbirds feed on the nectar of various flowers. They usually prefer brightly colored trumpet-shaped flowers such as fuchsias and trumpet vines. Some gardeners add a hummingbird feeder to guide the birds to the nectar-rich flowers in their gardens.

Add a birdbath or water feature for the birds. Every gardener with a fountain or pond raves about

Hummingbird Feeders

Shelby Carter

MANY GARDENERS supplement their natural hummingbird feeder—their gardens—with a commercial one. Mix 1 part sugar into 4 parts boiling water. Do not use honey, as it spoils easily. Cool the solution and fill the feeder. Replace it after 2 days to prevent fungus from forming. Soak the feeder in a diluted bleach solution, rinse, dry and refill.

all the birds it attracts. Make sure the water feature and visiting birds can be seen from inside the house and the sitting areas in the garden. Watching the birds while doing household chores makes those tasks more bearable.

Standing dead trees and fallen logs make excellent nesting and feeding sites. Consider leaving them in the landscape as long as they don't create a hazard. If you don't have this natural nesting habitat, add a birdhouse and give nature a hand.

You might also want to supplement your landscape buffet with a few feeders. I was always reluctant to do this—as I told my daughter, I'm not responsible enough to fill it every day. But George Harrison, *Birds & Blooms* bird expert, assured me the birds would survive even if I missed filling it on occasion.

George says birds get less than 25% of their food from feeders, so they have alternative sources to meet their daily needs. We added a few feeders and have enjoyed the increased number and diversity of birds that visit. Once you start feeding and enjoying the birds, you'll find it hard to forget to fill the feeders.

Plants That Attract Birds and Butterflies

Bird (B)   **Hummingbird (HB)**   **Butterfly (BT)**   **Butterfly Larvae (L)**

Trees

Beech (*Fagus*)	B
Birch (*Betula*)	BT, L
Black cherry (*Prunus serotina*)	B, L
Black gum (*Nyssa sylvatica*)	B
Crabapple (*Malus*)	B, L
Dogwood (*Cornus*)	B
Elm (*Ulmus*)	L
Fir (*Abies*)	B
Hawthorn (*Crataegus*)	B, L
Hickory (*Carya*)	B, L
Holly (*Ilex*)	B
Mulberry (*Morus*)	B
Willow (*Salix species*)	L

Shrubs

Azalea (*Rhododendron species*)	HB, BT
Blueberry (*Vaccinium*)	B
Blue mist spirea (*Caryopteris*)	HB, BT
Butterfly bush (*Buddleja species*)	HB, BT
Firethorn (*Pyracantha*)	B
Holly (*Ilex*)	B
Juniper (*Juniperus*)	B, L
Lilac (*Syringa species*)	BT
Mock orange (*Philadelphus*)	BT
Serviceberry (*Amelanchier*)	B
Spicebush (*Lindera*)	B
Spirea (*Spiraea*)	BT
Sumac (*Rhus*)	B
Viburnum (*Viburnum*)	B, BT
Weigela (*Weigela*)	HB, BT

Vines

American bittersweet (*Celastrus scandens*)	B
Grape (*Vitis*)	B
Honeysuckle vines (*Lonicera*)	B, HB, BT
Trumpet vine (*Campsis radicans*)	B, HB, BT
Virginia creeper (*Parthenocissus quinquefolia*)	B

Perennials

Aster (*Aster*)	HB, BT
Bee balm (*Monarda*)	HB, BT
Butterfly weed (*Asclepias tuberosa*)	BT, L
Cardinal flower (*Lobelia cardinalis*)	HB, BT
Columbine (*Aquilegia*)	HB, BT
Coneflower (*Echinacea*)	B, HB, BT
Delphinium (*Delphinium*)	HB, BT
Lupine (*Lupinus*)	HB, BT
Penstemon (*Penstemon*)	HB, BT
Phlox (*Phlox*)	HB, BT
Salvia (*Salvia*)	HB, BT

Annuals

Cosmos (*Cosmos*)	BT
Dill (*Anethum*)	L
Fuchsia (*Fuchsia species*)	HB, BT
Licorice vine (*Helichrysum petiolare*)	L
Lobelia (*Lobelia species*)	HB, BT
Marigold (*Tagetes species*)	BT
Parsley (*Petroselinum*)	L
Pot marigold (*Calendula officinalis*)	BT, L
Salvia (*Salvia*)	HB, BT
Snapdragon (*Antirrhinum*)	BT, L
Stock (*Matthiola*)	BT
Sunflower (*Helianthus annuus*)	B, HB, BT
Verbena (*Verbena bonariensis*)	HB, BT
Zinnia (*Zinnia species*)	BT

Bees—They're Keepers

YOU'VE TAKEN CARE of the birds, now don't forget the bees! They're important pollinators in your garden and pretty docile companions. Attracting bees to your garden will increase seed and fruit production. That's important for fruit, vegetable and herb gardens, and for gardeners who want to collect and save seed.

If you have some untreated scrap lumber, turn it into a bee house. Use a piece at least 3 to 5 inches thick. Drill holes 1/8 to 5/16 inch in diameter, going 90% of the way into the wood. Space the holes 1/2 to 3/4 inch apart. Add a roof if you like, and hang the bee house in a protected site out of direct sun and rain.

Specialty Gardens

Container Gardening

WHETHER YOU LACK GARDENING SPACE, have excess plants or just need a little color in a spot where there's no soil, container gardens can help. These mini gardens allow us to do more than just add plants to the landscape—they can help us extend the gardening season. You can move these "portable gardens" in and out of cold and heat extremes.

Selecting Containers

Choose containers that fit your garden design and the plants you want to grow. Since my plant palette changes every year, I use adaptable planters that complement a variety of plants. Don't worry about using pots that all look alike. A variety of containers is just as interesting as a variety of flowers in your garden. Many gardeners visit rummage sales and antique stores to find something just right.

Buy containers large enough to support the plant, but not so large that they overwhelm it or steal the show. Keep in mind, the larger the container, the more soil and moisture it will hold. This means less watering and fertilizing.

When planning, remember that wet soil and mature plants can be quite heavy. This will be a concern if you need to move your planters or are gardening on a balcony. In those situations, consider lightweight containers and soil mixes. Make sure your container has drainage holes. It's almost impossible

Add herbs and colorful vegetables, like the leaf lettuce above, for an edible addition to your container garden.

to judge exactly how much water to add so your plants receive enough water without overdoing it. Plus, nature doesn't always provide the right amount of moisture for our gardens, let alone our planters. Select containers made from the following materials that match your plants' needs and your gardening style:

• **Porous containers** like clay pots dry out faster. They're good for wet areas or for gardeners who like to water. They're also heavy and less likely to tumble in a windstorm or when filled with taller plants.

• **Plastic materials** hold moisture longer, but don't always meet the aesthetic standards of some gardens. One of my friends uses old black nursery pots. He feels the black color is neutral and not easily noticed. Plus, he spends most of his money on beautiful, unique plants, and the last thing he wants is for the container to steal the limelight. You may need to add a stone to the bottom of a plastic pot if you plan to fill it with top-heavy plantings. The lighter weight is no benefit if the planter topples or takes flight in a windstorm.

• **Fiberglass** adds some new choices to container gardening. This lightweight material is strong, durable and can be molded and finished to look like stone or other materials.

• **Concrete** is the man-made substitute for stone. It's long-lasting but very heavy, so make sure your planting location can bear the weight. You may want to try making your own concrete trough garden. They're quite the rage and seem to work in a variety of garden styles.

• **Wood** is another material that blends with a variety of plants and gardens. If you're just picturing a whiskey barrel, think again—tubs, window boxes and other attractive wooden planters are available.

Select one made from naturally long-lasting materials or one treated with plant-friendly products. (The lumber industry is voluntarily abandoning materials that contain arsenic.) Paint or seal containers that contain any questionable preservatives.

Use outdoor shelves, old crates and other furniture (above) to display your collection of pots. They create a nice backdrop, add interest and allow you to better show off each container by varying the height.

Tips for Containers

TRY THESE TIPS to increase the fun and success of container gardening:

• Fill the bottoms of large containers with Styrofoam packing peanuts, cans or other material. Cover with weed barrier and fill with soil. This reduces the planter's weight and the cost of filling the whole thing with soil.

• Use the double-pot method for containers without drainage holes. Plant your flowers in a cheap plastic container (with drainage holes) that's slightly smaller and shorter than the decorative pot. Place stones in the bottom of the decorative pot. Set the plastic pot on the pebbles. Cover the inner pot with moss or mulch. Pour off excess water as it begins to fill the bottom of the larger pot.

• Buy or make feet for your pots. Use small flat stones, pieces of wood or other material to elevate the container off the ground. This allows excess water to flow freely through the container and out the drainage holes.

• Use a rope-and-pulley system for hanging baskets so you can raise and lower the pots as maintenance is needed. The easier it is to do a job, the more likely it is to get done!

Sizing Up Your Containers

Select a container that complements the plants and accommodates their needs. The "one-third guide-

line" is a good starting point. The pot height should be about one-third the total height of the planting—pot, plants and all.

With small containers, you'll need to do a little more work. These dry out faster, so that means more watering and fertilizing. I like to use the largest pot possible, as long as it's in scale, to minimize maintenance.

Creative Containers

Your imagination is your only limit. Look at everything as a potential container. Here are just a few ideas:

• Convert an old chair with a broken seat into a planter. Replace the seat with a container full of flowers and vines.

• Use an old bike (above) as a plant stand. Line the baskets with peat moss, coconut fiber or containers, fill with a potting mix and plant.

• Update the familiar old boot planter to grow hens and chicks. How about converting one of your kids' old brightly colored rain boots, or your old golf or bowling shoes?

• Use leftover rain gutters for small planters. Mount them on the wall or hang with chains at a convenient, attractive height.

• Build a vertical planter with 2x4s. Create a frame of wood, back the planting area with plywood and front it with plastic covered with chicken wire or lattice to hold the soil in place. Cut small planting holes in the plastic and chicken wire. Fill it with impatiens, colorful lettuce or other plants to create a garden in even the smallest space.

• **Metal pots** can add a different look and feel. Paint to deter rust and soften the metallic glow. Visit your local craft store for materials and ideas.

The latest hanging basket trend is the metal frame with a fibrous mat or peat moss liner. These provide a softer, more natural look. Soak the container so the mat is thoroughly moistened for best results.

Selecting a Potting Mix

Selecting the right potting mix can guarantee success or lead to failure. You'll probably need to experiment to find out which mixture works best for you and your gardening style.

Most plants purchased in containers are grown in soilless mixes of peat moss, vermiculite and perlite. Such mixes dry out faster. I find these mixes just don't work with my "benign neglect" style of care.

Other gardeners consider them the perfect solution. If you like to give that extra care, need a lightweight material or want something that's ready to use, give these a try.

If you don't want to spend a lot of time caring for your potted plants, start with the old standard mix. Combine equal parts of peat moss or compost with vermiculite or perlite and topsoil. You may need to adjust the mix to find what works best for you.

I've tried several variations, depending on what was available at planting time. I've used a mix of mushroom compost and topsoil, composted yard waste and topsoil or purchased potting mix and variations in between. Keep track of what works so you can use the recipe next season.

Consider starting with fresh soil each season. It reduces the risk of disease and insects overwintering in the pot. I recycle soil from the containers in the compost pile at the end of each season. This helps speed up the compost process, and I eventually get the potting mix back as compost to use in my other gardens.

Incorporate a slow-release fertilizer into the soil mix. It's much easier, and less messy, than mixing the fertilizer with water. Again, if it isn't easy, it isn't going to get done—at least in my garden.

Some gardeners also incorporate wetting gels—polymers designed to trap water. I've heard mixed reports on these. Some gardeners and professionals feel it helps, but others see no benefit. You may want to try it and see what you think.

Plant Selection

Just about any plant that will grow in the ground can be grown in a pot. Start with drought-tolerant annuals if you feel hesitant. Gazania, moss rose, wave petunias and zinnias are almost guaranteed to provide a colorful show in the sun. Impatiens, coleus and begonias are surefire winners for shade. Add a spike (*Dracaena*), ornamental grass, dill or fennel for vertical interest. Include vinca vine, licorice vine or other trailing plants to soften the edge.

The standard Midwest planter holds a combination of geraniums, dusty miller, sweet alyssum and vinca vine with a spike in the middle. People like the look and find it easy to manage. Try updating the design by substituting new varieties and tropicals. Consider training vines on a decorative trellis for vertical accents.

Perennials, trees and shrubs can be grown in containers, too. Northern gardeners will need to provide special winter care, while Southern gardeners may need to do some root pruning or transplanting as these larger plants outgrow their containers.

I use perennials in containers for one growing season, then plant them in my garden to expand my collection. Double-pot the perennials as described on page 113, placing the nursery pot inside a decorative container. In fall, remove the inner pot and sink it in-

Tall plants, such as the ornamental corn above, provide vertical interest and keep plantings in scale with the container.

to the garden. This insulates the roots and helps get your plant through winter. In spring, just lift the container, divide the plant and repot if needed, and repeat-plant it for another season of enjoyment.

This sounds like a lot of work, but it's worth the effort. I've grown climbing hydrangea, five-leaf akebia and porcelain vines in pots for several years. You see, containers allow me to have large plants where there is no soil, only concrete. The vines and other plants help soften the look of brick and concrete in my small backyard. I plant them in the yard and garden every few years—about the time my husband threatens to stop helping me wrestle the big planters. Then I start over with smaller plants in my containers.

Larger planters can be moved to an unheated garage for winter. Water the soil whenever it's thawed and dry. The goal is to keep the plants dormant but protected from temperature extremes. Heated garages are usually too warm—the plants will begin to grow. You'll need to provide light and water more often to keep these plants alive.

Planters also can be moved to a protected location outdoors for winter. Insulate the roots by grouping planters together and placing bales of hay around the pots. Water whenever the soil is thawed and dry.

For trees and shrubs, increase your chance of success by selecting plants at least one zone hardier than your growing location. This may give you the added hardiness needed to carry them through winter.

You can create container gardens in several different ways. Grow one type of plant in each container, and group them for a mass display. This gives you great flexibility in mixing and matching plants, creating seasonal change and covering mistakes and pest-damaged plants.

Or, buy large planters and create a miniature garden in one pot. Use a variety of plants, but be sure they all require the same amount of water, light and fertilizer.

Don't forget to add a pot or two where you need

a splash of color or greenery. Consider using potted plants under trees and shrubs. The height of the container can add to the dramatic effect and prevent damage to tree and shrub roots.

Some gardeners sink old plastic pots in the ground under their trees, then pot annuals in slightly smaller containers. The smaller pots are placed in the buried ones, eliminating the need to dig new planting holes each season. It's much easier on your back and on the tree. This is especially effective for adding some color to a bed of ground cover.

Watering

Check containers once or twice a day. The hotter the weather, the smaller the pot and the more plants you have in it, the more often you'll need to water. Thoroughly moisten the soil until the excess water runs out the bottom. Pour off the excess so the container doesn't sit in the water, which can lead to root rot. I even remove the saucers from my hanging baskets to avoid this problem.

Allow the soil to dry just slightly between waterings. When the top few inches are moist and crumbly, it's time to water again. Use the soil moisture, not the clock and calendar, as your guide.

Consider investing in self-watering pots and systems. These use reservoirs and wicks to minimize the need to water. Check out your local garden center or garden supply catalog for ideas. Some gardeners use 5-gallon buckets of water with cotton strips or old nylon stockings as wicks (see page 74). It may not be pretty, but it's sure useful for watering planters while you're on vacation.

Fertilizing

With a small reservoir of soil and frequent watering, nutrients move quickly through the root zone and out the bottom of the pot. Add to this the low or nonexistent nutrient-holding capacity of most potting mixes, and you'll probably need to fertilize throughout the growing season.

Two methods work for me. Using compost as part of my mix provides some nutrients to the plants in the early part of the season. Incorporating a slow-release fertilizer like Osmocote into the soil at planting should provide enough nutrients for most or even all of the growing season. These products release small amounts of nutrients into the soil every time you water. Check the label for specifics.

Some gardeners use manure and compost tea or worm castings as a natural source of nutrients. I avoid fish emulsion. The scent often attracts unwanted wildlife and stray cats.

Green pathways of grass set off the colorful flower display. Create "grassways" with gentle curves that are wide enough to accommodate a mower.

How to Grow a Lush Lawn

A BEAUTIFUL CARPET of green grass can provide the perfect backdrop for your flower gardens, trees and shrubs. Some gardeners like it as a focal point, while others—like my husband—view it as a way to keep their feet from getting muddy when it rains. In either case, proper care can give you a good-looking lawn with minimal care.

Proper care involves watering, fertilizing and mowing. Do these things right and you can decrease your weed, insect and disease problems.

Start with a soil test. See Chapter 1 for details on taking and interpreting your results. Check Chapter 2 for tips on amending and preparing your soil for planting.

Seeding Your Lawn

First, you should select a grass suited to your growing conditions. The major cool-season grasses grown in the northern states and Canada include bluegrass, fescue and rye. These are often mixed together to create an adaptable lawn seed suitable to a variety of conditions.

Warm-weather grasses include Bermuda, carpetgrass, centipede, St. Augustine and Zoysia. Gardeners growing lawns in the transition zone—all of Tennessee, central and northern North Carolina, northernmost South Carolina, Georgia, Alabama, Louisiana, Arkansas, Oklahoma and Texas—can grow both types.

All these grasses can be started from seed. Prepare the soil as described in Chapter 1. Soil preparation is just as important when sodding or seeding a lawn as it is when starting it from sprigs and plugs. Rake the amended soil smooth, removing any rocks and

debris. Wait a week or water to help settle the soil. Make sure the lawn slopes away from the foundation of your home, and the final grade is 1 inch lower than adjacent sidewalks and driveways.

Seed cool-season lawns in spring or fall, when air temperatures are cool. Late August through September is the best time. The soil is warm but the air is cool—perfect grass-growing conditions. Plus, there are usually fewer thunderstorms and heavy rains to damage freshly seeded lawns.

Wait until the soil temperatures warm, near 70°, before planting warm-season grass. These plants will germinate and grow faster with warm soil and air temperatures.

Spread the grass seed at the rate recommended on the label. Apply half the recommended amount in one direction. Apply the rest at right angles to the first pass to ensure even coverage. Use a drop or rotary spreader to cover large areas or a handheld spreader for smaller spaces.

Lightly rake the seed into the soil surface and roll to ensure seed-soil contact. Use an empty roller on heavy soils to avoid compaction. Add water as needed on lighter soils with a high sand content.

Mulch your newly seeded lawn with straw or marsh hay to help keep the soil moist and improve germination. You may want to try some of the new materials on the market, like compressed cellulose pellets. Just spread the pellets over the lawn, water and watch the mulch appear. Or, try some of the row-cover fabrics such as Grass Fast. These products allow light, water and air through, but warm

Select a grass seed that matches the light (sun or shade) and soil conditions.

the soil to speed seed germination.

Keep the surface of the soil moist until the grass seed sprouts. You may need to water once or twice a day depending on the weather. Remove any excess straw or mulch fabric as the grass becomes established. Start watering more deeply but less frequently to encourage deep rooting and a healthier, more drought-tolerant lawn.

Sprigs, Plugs and Sod

You can also grow grass from sprigs, plugs or sod, although their availability may be limited in certain regions.

Some warm-season grasses can be started with sprigs. These are pieces of stems or runners with several nodes (growing points). You can buy them, or make your own from sod or an existing lawn area.

Place the sprigs 6 to 12 inches apart and 1 to 2 inches deep. The closer they're planted, the faster the lawn will fill. Or, spread the sprigs over the soil surface. Cover them with topsoil, leaving about one-fourth of the sprig exposed. Water whenever the soil surface starts to dry.

Plugs are another popular method for starting warm-season lawns. These are just small pieces of sod cut into circles or squares 2 to 4 inches across. They contain the grass plant, soil and roots. You usually have to make your own plugs from sod. Starting a lawn from plugs takes less sod, but requires more time to establish. Plant plugs 6 to 12 inches apart at the same depth they were originally growing. Water often enough to keep the soil moist.

Sod is commonly used for starting all grasses. The grass is grown in large fields, harvested with roots attached and sold for immediate installation. Sodding is the most expensive method but results in an instant lawn.

Start laying the sod adjacent to a drive or walk. Butt the sod ends to allow for shrinkage. Stagger seams, as if you were laying brick. Keep the sod and the soil below moist.

Once the sod, springs or plugs begin to root and grow, reduce the watering frequency and increase the amount applied. Make your first cutting when the grass has reached regular mowing height.

Established lawns generally need 1 inch of water per week. See the watering section in Chapter 5 for watering tips.

Minimizing Drought Stress

BROWN LAWNS are a common sight during hot, dry weather. Some gardeners choose to water their lawns in an attempt to keep them green and more competitive with weeds. Others allow the grass to go dormant. Here are ways to help your lawn through drought:

- Select the most drought-tolerant grass varieties available.
- Raise your mowing height. Taller grass grows deeper roots and is more drought tolerant.
- Don't fertilize or use weed killers on lawns during drought. The fertilizer can damage tender roots and shoots, while helping drought-tolerant weeds take over.

Mowing

Neatly trimmed lawns were once a sign of wealth. The more money you had, the more sheep you owned and the more grass was "mowed". Though we've exchanged our sheep for mowers, we still seem to like neat and tidy lawns.

Let the grass grow to its preferred height (see chart on page 119). Taller grass can keep weeds at bay, and is more resistant to insects and disease. Set the mower at the desired height and cut the grass. Now measure the cut grass to see if you got the results you wanted. Adjust the mower height as needed.

Cut the grass often enough so you're removing no more than one-third the total height at a time. If you want your final cut to be 2 inches, cut the grass when it's about 3 inches tall.

This is less stressful on the plant and less work for you. I know what you're thinking: "I'll need to cut the grass twice a week during the active growing periods." Yes, you will—but you can leave the short clippings on the lawn instead of raking or bagging them. Even the best mulching mowers tend to jam up with those extra-long, moisture-rich clippings. And in the long run, you'll have fewer problems to repair.

Keeping your mower blade sharp will reduce your fuel use by as much as 20%. It also will make mowing easier on you and less stressful for the grass. A clean cut seals quickly, keeping moisture in and pests out.

What About Thatch?

Thatch is old grass stems and leaf blades that have not fully decomposed—and it's developed a bad reputation. As with many things, a little thatch is good, but twice as much is bad. A thin layer of thatch—half an inch or less—acts as a mulch, conserving moisture and providing a cushion for foot traffic, equipment and heavy rains that can wear on your lawn.

Dense and heavily fertilized lawns tend to build up thick layers of thatch. The old plants die, but can't reach the soil surface because the grass is so dense. These decompose partially and start building into an impenetrable layer. A thick layer of thatch prevents water and nutrients from reaching the soil. The lawn starts to thin, insects and disease move in, and your once-lush lawn becomes an eyesore.

Dethatching is stressful for the lawn and should be done only when grass is actively growing. Don't make this a regular part of your lawn care program.

Vertical mowers (dethatching machines) use knives or tines to slice through and pull out the thatch. If you use one, prepare yourself for a shock—the lawn will look worse right after you finish. Rake off and compost the thatch. Consider overseeding right away to start rebuilding the lawn.

I prefer core aeration. This method removes plugs from the soil, opening up the lawn. It allows the thatch to decompose, and water and fertilizer to reach the grass roots. Use a machine that grinds and spreads the plugs over the soil surface. The added organic matter will speed up the breakdown of the thatch. This technique also helps improve drainage in heavy and compacted soils.

Fertilizing the Lawn

Your soil test results will tell you how much fertilizer to add, and which kind. The chart on page 119 shows the range of fertilizer needed to maintain specific types of grass. Use your soil test and observations to develop a fertilizer program that best suits the grass and the time you have available for lawn care.

Fertilizer is generally applied during major periods of growth. That's in fall for cool-weather grasses (lightly in spring) and spring and summer for

Preventing Thatch

STOP THATCH from becoming a problem in your yard—and work less, too!

- Avoid overfertilizing and overwatering.
- Mulch or rake and compost excessively long clippings (more than 2 or 3 inches).
- Eliminate or minimize pesticide use, which can disrupt beneficial insects and nature's aerating machine—the earthworm.

warm-season ones. Avoid using fertilizers during hot, dry periods unless you're able to water. Otherwise, put away the fertilizer and let the grass growth slow down until cooler weather and rains return.

Winterizing fertilizers are used to encourage root development and winter hardiness. Many are high in phosphorous (for the roots) and potassium (for hardiness). Make sure your lawn needs these extra doses of P and K before applying. If your lawn already has too much, why spend the time and money adding more?

Use a broadcast or drop spreader to fertilize large areas. A handheld spreader will work for smaller areas. Apply half the fertilizer in one direction and the rest in a pattern perpendicular to the first. This helps avoid dark and light streaks that can occur with misapplication.

Try to fertilize when you're feeling fresh and have some time. Rushing can result in an inconsistent application or missed areas. Avoid chatting with friends and neighbors. I've often seen dead patches caused by people stopping to chat and forgetting to close the spreader.

To reduce your fertilizer bill and save yourself some work, leave grass clippings on the lawn. Short clippings, 1 to 2 inches long, will break down in several days. They add moisture, organic matter and nutrients to the soil. You may be able to reduce your fertilizer needs by as much as 25% to 40% just by leaving your grass clippings on the lawn. This is a good reason to put away the rake and bagger until fall.

Rent a core aerator or hire a professional. Make sure the machine breaks through the thatch and removes plugs that are at least 2 to 3 inches long.

These are applied when the lawn is actively growing. Treating a dormant or drought-stressed lawn can damage the grass. It also leaves open areas for new weeds to grow before the grass breaks dormancy and fills in the newly created bare spot.

Weed-and-feed products combine fertilizer with weed killer. The idea is, you make only one application to put fertilizer and herbicide on the lawn. Sounds good, but there are drawbacks. The best times to fertilize and apply weed killers don't always coincide. And the application rate for each may not be appropriate for your lawn.

Consider spot treating problem areas with a weed killer. This minimizes the chemical exposure for you and your pets, and for the birds and wildlife you'd like to attract. If you only have a few weeds, consider digging. You may remember digging dandelions for a penny apiece when you were a kid, although I think the rate has increased. It gave you good memories and something to complain about when you returned to school. Or, have a weeding contest to see who can pull the most weeds. Maybe the winner gets to skip the next weeding contest.

Grass weeds are more difficult to control. Anything that kills them will also kill your lawn grass. Annuals can be treated with pre-emergent weed killers. But quack and other perennial grasses must be dug out or spot treated with a total vegetation killer. Reseed bare areas to prevent new weeds from moving in.

If more than half of your lawn is filled with weeds, you may want to start over. You'll probably use fewer chemicals and less time in the long run. Kill the grass and weeds, prepare the soil and then add seed or sod.

Dealing with Weeds

A healthy lawn is your best defense against weeds. Use weed problems as a diagnostic tool to improve the health and vigor of your grass. These unwelcome plants take over when our grass is stressed. For example, knotweed grows well in compacted and salt-laden soils, while moss indicates excess moisture, shade or poor drainage. Eliminate the cause and you'll reduce future problems. See Chapter 9 for more details on weed control.

In general, there are two times to control weeds: before they sprout, and after they start growing. Use a pre-emergent weed killer to prevent weed seeds from sprouting. These prevent your grass seed from sprouting as well, so watch the timing on weed control and seeding of the lawn.

Existing weeds are controlled with post-emergent weed killers. These herbicides are absorbed through the leaves or roots and kill the plant. Broadleaf weed killers will destroy dandelions, clover, plantain and other broadleaf plants without harming the grass.

Cool-Season Grasses Grown in the South

Grass	Uses	Planting Method	Mowing Height	Fertilizer (lbs. N/1000 sq. ft. per year)
Kentucky bluegrass	Sunny areas	Seed and sod (March, April, late September-October)	2-1/2 to 4 inches	1 to 3 pounds (March, October)
Fescue, tall	Tough play lawn	Seed and sod (March, April, late September-October)	2 to 3 inches	1 to 3 pounds (March, October)

Cool-Season Grasses

Grass	Uses	Planting Method	Mowing Height	Fertilizer (lbs. N/1000 sq. ft. per year)
Kentucky bluegrass	Sunny areas	Seed (April-May, late August-September); or sod when available	2-1/2 to 4 inches	2-4 pounds (May or June, September, late October or early November)
Fescue, fine	Shade- and drought-tolerant	Seed (April-May, late August-September)	2 to 4 inches	1-2 pounds (May or June, September, late October or early November)
Fescue, tall	Tough play lawn	Seed or sod (May-June)	2 to 4 inches	1-2 pounds (May or June, September, late October or early November)
Rye, annual	Not recommended	Often found as part of seed mixes	2 to 4 inches	*
Rye, perennial turf types	All purpose	Seed (April-May and late August-September)	2 to 4 inches	*

* Most lawns are a mixture of bluegrass and fescue. Start with 2 to 3 pounds and adjust based on grass performance.

Warm-Season Grasses

Grass	Uses	Planting Method	Mowing Height	Fertilizer (lbs. N/1000 sq. ft. per year)
Bermuda grass	Play lawn	Seed, sprigs, plugs, sod (April-June)	1/2 to 2 inches	1 to 3 pounds (April, June, August)
Carpetgrass	Low-maintenance; moist and acidic soils	Seed, sprigs, plugs, sod (March-May)	1 to 2 inches	1 to 3 pounds (April, June, August)
Centipede	Low-maintenance; slow-growing	Seed, sprigs, plugs, sod (April-June)	1 to 2 inches	1/2 to 2 pounds (April, June)
St. Augustine	Shade-tolerant	Seed, sprigs, plugs, sod (April-June)	2 to 4 inches	1 to 3 pounds (April, June, August)
Zoysia	Slow-growing; heat-tolerant	Seed, sprigs, plugs, sod (April-June)	3/4 to 1-1/2 inches	1 to 3 pounds (April, June, August)

Stop to Smell the Roses

THE ROSE has captured the hearts of many gardeners—and many cultures. Its fragrance has scented soaps and perfumes, its image has decorated pictures, dishes and clothing, and the plants themselves have been included in gardens for more than 2,000 years.

You may want to include just a few, or a garden full of these beauties. Consider the space available, your design goals and how much time to you have to devote to them before adding roses to your yard.

I love the look and scent of hybrid tea roses. And, like most people, I like receiving a bouquet of roses for Valentine's Day, my birthday or for no reason at all. But I always cringe when gardeners want to add them to their landscape. As the "Plant Doctor"—a title bestowed upon me by the radio programs I've appeared on—I've spent more than 20 years diagnosing sick plants and telling people why their roses died.

Diseases such as black spot, insects such as cane borers and leafhoppers and extremely cold winters can hinder growth and even kill plants. Fortunately, shrub roses are back in favor, and they provide many of the positive qualities we attribute to roses, with fewer problems. Some of the shrub roses popular today are old varieties, but many of the new

Roses are available in a wide range of colors, sizes and shapes.

ones are more pest resistant and winter hardy.

I've added four roses to my small landscape. My Fairy rose gives me a season of small pink flowers with minimal deadheading and no need for winter protection. My Floral Carpet rose made it on the second try. It fills the front of my alley garden with blooms and glossy foliage all summer long. The Knock-out rose, bred by a friend, William Radler, even impressed my teenage daughter with its raspberry-red flowers. And my latest addition is William Baffin, one of the Canadian Explorer series. This large shrub rose is being trained up my fence and over my neighbor's garage to keep out uninvited guests.

Whether planting one rose or a whole bed, soil

Bourbon   *Climbing rose*

Types of Roses

ROSES COMPRISE a large group of plants. Here are a few popular categories.

• **Old roses.** Varieties introduced before 1867. This group includes Gallica, Damask, Bourbon, Tea and others. Most are hardy and require little care.

• **Hybrid tea roses.** The most popular rose around the world. They grow to 2-1/2 to 3 feet tall. These grafted plants need protection when winter temperatures drop below 10°.

• **Polyantha.** Low-growing roses that can be massed or used as low hedges. They produce lots of flowers.

• **Floribundas.** These are a cross between hybrid teas and polyanthas. They grow 2 to 3 feet tall and produce flowers in clusters. Most are grafted.

• **Grandiflora.** A hybrid of the floribunda and hybrid tea rose, it's hardier than its parents. Grows 3 to 6 feet tall and has flowers similar to the hybrid tea. Always grafted.

• **Miniature roses.** Ranging from 6 to 18 inches tall,

these are perfect for containers, small gardens, edging or the indoor garden.

• **Shrub roses.** Large, dense plants that can be wild species, hybrids or cultivars. They're hardy throughout the United States and traditionally have less showy flowers but attractive fruit.

• **Climbers.** These produce long canes that need support. They can be trained up a trellis, over an arbor or against a wall. Some are grafted.

• **Ramblers.** Climbing roses that bloom once a year and are very hardy.

• **Tree roses.** These are hybrid teas, grandifloras, floribundas or miniature roses that have been grafted and trained into a tree form. A straight stem is grafted to a hardy rootstock, and the desired rose is grafted to the top of the trunk.

preparation and proper planting are keys to success. Review Chapter 1 for tips on soil preparation and Chapter 4 for tips on planting bare-root and potted plants. Select a location with at least 6 and preferably 8 hours of direct sun. An east-facing location is perfect. The early morning sun will dry the foliage and help reduce the risk of disease.

Roses do have an added feature to consider at planting: many are grafted, with a small bud placed on a hardy rootstock. To find it, look for the swollen area on the stem. Plant the graft 2 inches above the soil surface in areas with warm (above 10°) winters. If your winter temperatures drop below 10°, plant the graft at the soil surface. In even colder climates, put the graft 2 inches below the soil surface to insulate it.

Caring for Roses

Many of the basic maintenance techniques covered in Chapter 5 apply to roses, but there are a few exceptions and variations.

Water roses long enough to moisten the top 6 to 8 inches of soil. Water again when the top few inches of soil feel moist but crumble in your hand. Use a watering wand or soaker hose to direct the water to the roots and away from the foliage. Keeping the leaves dry discourages disease problems.

Hybrid teas are heavy feeders and like to receive nutrients three or four times during the growing season. Start fertilizing just after new growth appears, and repeat every 6 to 8 weeks. Stop fertilizing at least 6 weeks before the first expected frost if your winter temperatures drop below 10°. Later fertilizations may stimulate late-season growth that can die over winter.

Shrub, floribundas, climbers and old roses need much less fertilizer. Feed in early spring as the buds begin to swell. Give repeat bloomers a second shot of fertilizer once they finish their first bloom.

Pruning roses requires some special equipment. Long sleeves and sturdy gloves are at the top of my list. Get out the hand pruners, loppers and saw as well.

In spring, before growth begins, cut out all the dead wood. This is usually discolored, and the pith (center of the stem) is dark instead of white.

For modern roses, the way you prune will affect the bloom. Heavily pruned roses produce fewer but very showy flowers. Leave three or four canes and cut them back to 6 to 10 inches if this is your goal. For Northern gardeners, this may be all that's left alive after a hard winter. For a nice-sized plant with a good flower display, try moderate pruning, cutting five to 12 canes back to 18 to 24 inches.

Light pruning is usually done on floribundas, grandifloras, newly planted hybrid teas and species roses. Remove less than one-third of the plant to produce a large plant with lots of flowers on short stems.

Shrub roses and climbers need different treatment. For shrub roses, prune out old, dead and diseased canes. Next, remove any spindly and weak growth. Prune these back to ground level or the bud union, whichever applies. Thin out the plant and reduce the height as needed.

Don't prune climbing roses until their second or third year in the garden. This gives them a chance to root and grow mature flowering canes.

Prune ramblers and one-time bloomers after flowering. Repeat bloomers can be pruned in early spring before growth begins. Removing old, dead and diseased canes and suckers may be all the pruning you need. Shape vigorous climbers by cutting back the lateral shoots—the ones that flower—to four or five buds.

Treat the tree rose much like the shrub roses. Remove dead and damaged canes. Thin the crown and reduce its size by about one-third. Remove any suckers that form at the base of the plant.

Avoid leaving stubs (above) that create perfect entryways for insects and disease.

Harvesting Roses

Roses are wonderful additions to the garden, but even more fun to bring indoors. Select a rosebud that's just about to open. Cut the stem back to a five-leaflet leaf. Make sure at least two five-leaflet leaves remain on the stem left behind. The new growth will be thick and sturdy.

Use the same strategy when deadheading roses. Northern gardeners should stop cutting roses after the last flush of flowers. Allow the plant to form rose hips. These provide food for the birds and winter interest in the garden, and signal the plant to harden off for winter.

A fellow garden writer, Jim Fizzell of Park Ridge, Illinois, uses a sharp knife to harvest and deadhead his roses, with a nifty twist: a safe thumb protector. He simply slips an old piece of garden hose over his thumb, slices through the rose stem and holds onto the stem until it reaches the bucket of water or compost container.

There are also new hand pruners that cut and grip. These flower-gathering snips are designed to grip the flower stem after it's cut. This saves a lot of scratched arms, so you don't have to reach in with both hands, as well as time spent picking up the dropped stems. You may want to add these to your wish list.

Winter Protection

Winters with temperatures below 10° can be hard on hybrid teas and other grafted roses, but there are several options for winter protection. No matter which technique you use, timing is key. Wait until the ground lightly freezes to start covering your less-than-hardy roses.

Now select the method that works best for you. Judging by the winter landscape throughout the

Soil, compost or wood chips (above) will help insulate cold-tender grafts.

North, rose cones seem to be the most popular choice. But I see many dead roses that were overwintered with this method. People cover the roses too early, leave the cones on too long and cook the plants on sunny winter days.

Here's how to increase your success rate with this method. After a week of freezing temperatures, prune back the roses just enough to fit under the

cone. Mound soil over the base to protect the graft—the portion that produces your desired plant. Cover with the rose cone. You may want to put some additional soil around the base of the cone. When this freezes, it will help keep the cone in place and rodents out. Place a stone or brick on top of the cone to anchor it.

Check the cones on sunny winter days and open the vents. Or, cut a vent into the side, away from the prevailing winds. This will allow the hot air to escape while protecting the tender graft.

Remove cones in late winter or early spring when the temperatures start hovering around freezing. Allow the soil to gradually wash away with the spring rains. This gives the plant a chance to adjust to the unprotected climate.

The soil mound method is very similar. Loosely tie the rose canes or surround them with hardware cloth. Mound 8 to 10 inches of soil over the base of the plant. Once this freezes, use straw, hay or evergreen branches to cover the rest of the plant.

Boerner Botanical Gardens in Hales Corners, Wisconsin has had good success using leaves as winter mulch. A rose bed is surrounded by hardware cloth. The bottom few inches are sunken into the ground, and the top remains 3 to 4 feet above ground. Once the ground freezes, the roses are cut back to 18 inches. Dry leaves are packed around the roses and stacked 3 feet high. Plastic can be placed over the leaves to keep them dry.

The fencing is removed and rolled up for storage in the spring, when temperatures remain near freezing. The leaves are carefully removed and used as mulch or added to the compost pile. The roses need minimal pruning and they're ready to grow.

In Minnesota, gardeners bury their roses. They dig trenches in fall next to all the roses that need protection. Then they cut through the roots on one side of the plant, tip it over into the trench and cover it with soil for the winter. After the ground freezes, evergreen branches or straw can be added for additional insulation. Tree roses and climbers also can be protected with this method.

Container roses can be wintered by sinking the container in the ground and protecting with one of the methods described above, or by moving them to an unheated garage. Miniature roses are small enough to move indoors and grow under artificial lights.

If all this seems like too much work, but you still want roses, treat them like annuals. If they survive the winter, it's a bonus. If they die, you have a chance to try a new variety.

The color and texture of leaf lettuce creates an attractive display in any garden.

Kitchen Gardens

NOTHING BEATS THE FLAVOR of fresh-from-the-garden vegetables. Even if you're not an enthusiastic cook, home-grown veggies can improve the flavor of your meals.

Kitchen gardens have traditionally been right outside the back door, filled with vegetables, herbs and even some flowers. Fruit trees, berries and medicinal plants were also found in the kitchen gardens of Colonial times.

For a while, vegetables and fruits were relegated to the far corners of the landscape where they wouldn't be seen. Now, many of these plants are making their way into flower beds and containers.

If you've ever visited Alaska, you know how attractive huge cabbages can be when mixed with flowers. One of my favorite gardens was designed and planted by my friend Maryann Ricker of Stoughton, Wisconsin. She planted her front entrance with Swiss chard, brussels sprouts, parsley, flowering tobacco, salvia and alyssum. It was fun to harvest dinner and flowers for the table from Maryann's front flower bed.

My city lot is too small to grow every vegetable my family enjoys. Since I can't grow all I need, I include the main ingredients for my favorite recipes—tomatoes, peppers, eggplant, basil and parsley. I may grow a few squash in a container, too.

Try creating your own kitchen garden. Grow vegetables in wide rows to save space and create a more attractive presentation. Use decorative stakes and trellises as opposed to the vegetable-garden variety. Functional doesn't have to mean ugly. Or use some of the dwarf plant varieties that need little or no staking.

Select cultivars with colorful leaves, fruit and flowers. I like purple peppers, rainbow Swiss chard, red sails lettuce and delicata squash. They all add color and eye appeal when placed in a prominent location.

Mix a few flowers in for color and interest. I like to border my little garden with alyssum and parsley for a fragrant, edible edge. Or, follow *Birds & Blooms* founder Roy Reiman's lead, and plant every fourth row in flowers. This adds color, attracts the pollinating bees and provides fresh flowers for the table.

Grow fruits, vegetables and herbs in full sun. Root crops like beets and radishes can tolerate partial shade. Leafy crops like lettuce and spinach can get by with as little as 4 hours of direct sunlight.

Once you find the perfect location, you need to plan for the harvest. Visit your garden several times a week so you can gather vegetables as soon as they ripen. This will give you the best flavor, longer storage life and a continuous harvest. The more you pick, the more the plants produce.

Make plans to fill the void left by short-season crops like lettuce and radishes. Replant the area with another short-season crop, or let the larger, longer-season vegetables like tomatoes and peppers take up that space.

Use pole beans, squash and melons to mask your chain-link fence, compost area or other space you want to screen. Sunflowers, corn and dwarf fruit trees can provide a living fence. And can you think of any better barrier plant than raspberries? Those thorny stems are sure to direct traffic around that part of your landscape.

Don't forget the herbs. Their color, fragrance and texture make them a good addition to containers, flower beds and vegetable gardens. I always mix a few in with my perennials. Purple ruffle basil adds a nice dark foliage that complements yellow marigolds and classic zinnias. I used tricolor sage in a container filled with Persian shield, heliotrope and blackie sweet-potato vine.

I grow so many herbs that a former neighbor thought I must be quite the cook. I told her I didn't use them all for cooking, but liked the way they looked in the garden. I shared my harvest to ease my guilt.

Water Gardens

A DISCUSSION of specialty gardens wouldn't be complete without a water feature. The sound of water can soothe your nerves, muffle traffic sounds and attract birds. It can be a small fountain, a water-filled container or a pond as large as you want.

As always, planning is the key to success. The more time you spend planning, designing and buying the right equipment, the less time you'll spend maintaining the garden, so you'll have more time to enjoy it.

Check Local Ordinances

Start with a call to your local municipality. Rules and regulations for water depths and fencing vary from one community to the next. It's much easier to adjust your design on paper than to backfill or add fencing later.

Consider the human traffic in and around your landscape, too. A water feature doesn't provide much relaxation if you're worried about unwanted visitors. I live in a very urban area with lots of unattended children roaming through my gardens on their way to the park. I worried that if I added a water garden, I'd find children wading through the water lilies—or, worse yet, facedown in the pool. Now that we've fenced our backyard, I can finally add one.

If you can't wait or don't want to install a fence, try building in a safety net. Cover a wood support with 2- to 3-inch black plastic netting. Place this over the pond, resting on a shallow shelf created along the pond's edge. Use stones or bricks to support the center of the structure. The water plants will grow through the mesh, providing support for plant stems, while keeping children out of the water and hungry birds and wildlife at bay.

Location, Location, Location

Location is as important in placing your water feature as in buying a home. The right location will increase enjoyment, maximize function and decrease maintenance.

Start with the view. Consider all the places you want a vantage point of the water—next to the pond, from other places in the yard and from inside the house.

Before my friend Judy Gleason of Lake Forest, Illinois added three water features to her landscape, she checked the views from her bedroom, kitchen, dining area and living room. A helper outside marked the spots she indicated. Now she can see the water

Not sure if you want a water garden? Try a "pint-sized" water garden first.

✔ Melinda's Tips

CONSIDER CREATING a water garden in a pot if space and time are in short supply. A small decorative ceramic pot, whiskey barrel with plastic liner or similar container filled with water and one or two plants can be the perfect way to start water gardening. Add a small fountain, oxygenating plants or fresh water to keep the system in balance.

features—and the birds that visit them—as she washes dishes, eats dinner or relaxes at the end of a busy day.

Find or create a level spot for your garden. Sloped areas can reveal the liner or other unsightly features on the low side. Water also will spill over, making the ground soggy and hampering growth of plants bordering that side of the pond.

Avoid low areas that collect runoff from the driveway, lawn and other areas. This water contains nutrients that can increase problems with algae, and may contain pesticides harmful to the plants and fish.

Look for a spot that receives at least 6 hours of sunlight. This will give you the best growing conditions for water lilies, lotus and most other water plants. Keep the garden away from trees to minimize debris—it causes algae problems and adds to your cleanup chores.

Make sure the site is near a source of water and electricity. Plan an area in and near your pond to hide the mechanics—pump, filter and such. Nothing ruins a view like a pipe, pump or other piece of equipment sticking out the side.

If you need ideas, many Web sites and water garden experts can help with design, installation and maintenance.

Choosing the Right Equipment

Before you start digging, make sure to select a pump and filter system that fit into your plan. Some systems are external and require a housing unit near the pond. Others are submersible and need space and proper depth to be hidden within the water feature.

Choose a pump that's strong enough to handle the volume of water in your pond. Calculate the volume of a square or rectangular pool by multiplying the length in feet by the width in feet. Multiply this figure by the depth in feet, and then multiply this number by 7.5 gallons.

A circular pond's volume is calculated by multiplying the diameter times the diameter times the depth, then multiplying that figure by 5.9 gallons. For oval gardens, multiply length by width by depth by 6.7 gallons.

Use either a free-standing or submersible pump. Free-standing pumps sit outside the water in a housing unit. Submersible pumps are easier to install and generally more quiet. They should be set on stones or bricks in the pond bottom. Make sure the pond is deep enough to cover the pump.

If your pond is deep enough to support your plants and fish, and you're using the proper plantings, you won't need a filter. But if your area is subject to temperature extremes or long periods of bright sun—or if your pond doesn't have the right number of plants or fish—a filter system will help pull out the impurities, keeping the water clear and the fish healthy.

Mechanical filters use screens, charcoal or other means to remove algae and other particles. You need to remove, clean or replace the filters several times during the season, so make sure they're in a convenient place. Many designers hide these and other mechanics with fake rocks, decking or other decorative screens.

Biological filters are placed over the intake pipe of the pump. Beneficial bacteria develop on these filters and convert toxic materials into food for the plants. It takes several weeks for the bacteria to reach sufficient numbers so they can manage the waste.

Before you start, call your municipality to check on any building codes and needed permits. Consult a licensed electrician for wiring and specialized installations. Use only UL-certified and grounded

✔ Melinda's Tips

SOMETIMES the best location for a water feature is in the shade of your favorite tree. Reduce cleanup by covering the pond with black netting (sold by most pond supply companies) in fall. As the netting fills with leaves, you can quickly lift it and empty the leaves into the compost pile. Replace the cover and repeat as needed.

equipment. Underwater lights, pumps and equipment must have ground fault interrupters.

Installing a Prefabricated Pond

Growing interest in water features has increased the variety and availability of materials. Product quality and ease of installation has improved, too. Prefabricated liners are easiest for beginners.

Place the liner upside down in the desired location and mark the location with a garden hose, rope or spray paint. Dig a hole as deep as the liner. Place a 2x4 across the edges of the hole and use a yardstick to measure the depth from the bottom of the hole and planting ledges to the board.

Remove any debris and level the hole. Add 2 inches of sand to the bottom to cushion the pond, preventing punctures. This also sets the pond 1 to 2 inches above the surrounding surface to keep landscape runoff out of the water.

Place the liner in the hole and make sure all sides are level. Add 4 to 6 inches of water to hold the pond in place. Now backfill with sand and add more water. When you're done, you can use stones or plants to disguise the edge of the pond. You'll find more landscaping suggestions at the end of this section.

Creating Your Own

Flexible liners allow you to create a water garden of any size or shape. Consider the plants, fish and equipment needs when planning the depth.

The center of the garden must be 18 to 30 inches deep to support plants and keep the pond healthy. Make it deeper, at least 2-1/2 feet, to insulate fish and plants from freezing in Northern gardens and extreme heat in the South.

Think about which plants you want to grow be-

fore you start digging. You can make the garden all one depth, or create ledges to accommodate various plants.

Some water plants float on the surface, others grow at depths of 10 to 32 inches and oxygenators stay submerged. You can vary planting depths by using bricks or overturned pots to boost plants. For larger, more permanent variations in planting depths, add planting shelves to the sides of your pond. These also make nice "steps" into and out of the garden for easier maintenance and cleaning.

Create planting shelves to accommodate individual plant needs. Marginal plants like sweet flags and rushes grow at the edge, in shallower water. Make them a shelf 9 to 12 inches deep and 9 to 12 inches wide. A few gardeners create a second shelf of the same width, but 6 to 9 inches deeper, to accommodate lotus and other aquatics that prefer deeper planting.

Consider hiring a professional with earth-moving equipment for large excavations. Or, invite a few strong friends over to lend a hand. Just remember, you'll owe them big-time when the project is complete. Pace yourself to avoid overexertion. This should be fun, not one of those nightmare projects that never gets finished.

Start digging from the edge of the pond, working your way to the deepest area in the center. Place excess soil on a tarp or in a wheelbarrow for easy removal. Use the excess to create a new raised garden, add it to the compost pile or donate it to a neighbor. Save enough for leveling the pond, masking the edges of the liner and creating planting beds around the perimeter.

Make sure the sides are vertical, and the planting shelves and bottom are level. You may want a shallow slope in one area to encourage birds to gather at the water's edge. Remove any stones and debris from the hole. Fill the bottom with an inch of sand and work it into any crevices on the sides. Put in a liner pad to prevent punctures from sticks, rocks and other sharp

Jerry McCallister of Huntington, West Virginia (top) used bricks to mark the edge of his water garden. After planning, digging and planting, he has a beautiful addition to his landscape (above).

objects that may eventually work their way to the soil surface.

Invest in the best quality liner you can afford. You'd hate to spend all this time digging, preparing and planting, only to remove it all to replace a torn plastic liner. Select one of the high-quality black flexible liners designed to last for many years.

The rubber-based EPDM (45 mil) liners and PVC (at least 20 mil) liners are durable, flexible and readily available. The rubber liner is heavier, making it a bit harder to maneuver. The PVC is ultraviolet sensitive, so all parts must be covered with water, stone, soil or plants. New products are on the market, too. Compare them to the rubber and PVC products for durability, flexibility and longevity.

Make sure to buy a liner large enough to cover the pond's bottom and sides. Here's how: Multiply the maximum depth of your pond by two. Add this number to the maximum length of the pond, and add 2 feet for edging. This figure is the length of liner. To determine its width, use the same equation, but plug in the maximum width and add a foot.

Have I lost you yet? Let's try an example. Say your garden is 2-1/2 feet deep. The greatest length is 8 feet, and it's 5 feet wide. Two times 2.5 is 5 feet. Add this to the length (8 feet), add another 2 feet for edging and your liner should be at least 15 feet long. The width would be 12 feet—5 (the depth, doubled) plus 5 (width) plus 2 (edging).

Try installing the liner on a warm, sunny day—the sun will warm the liner, making it more flexible and easy to manage. Drape the liner into the hole and anchor the edges with a few large rocks. Begin filling the liner with water. The weight of the water will push the liner into its final position. Readjust rocks as needed and keep filling until the water is near its desired depth. Backfill with soil as needed to create a level bank.

Allow the pond to sit overnight. Make final adjustments and trim away any excess liner, leaving at least 6 inches beyond the water's height. This will be hidden with stones, soil and plants.

Adding Plants

Once the pond is filled, you must treat the water to eliminate chlorine, which is harmful to plants and fish. Many water-clarifying (dechlorinator) products are available. Follow label directions. After you've added the clarifier, most products recommend a waiting period before putting in plants and fish.

The water, plants and fish form their own ecosystem. Consider everything that's added to the contained system—plants, fish waste, plant debris—and all the materials that need to be removed by filters or oxygenating plants or recirculated by the pump.

When all is working well, the fish and plants will be healthy and the water will be clear. If the pond has too much of any one thing, it'll be out of balance, and adjustments may be needed to restore harmony in the mini ecosystem.

Plants are the main focus of this ecosystem. Cover one-third but no more than one-half of the water surface with plants. Most gardeners grow water plants in containers submerged in the pools.

As with terrestrial gardening, you may be tempted to overplant—but don't. Like other perennials, water plants look small when purchased in spring, but soon grow and fill the garden. Most water lilies need 10 square feet of space, and even dwarf ones require 2 square feet. Most catalogs will tell you a plant's size and preferred planting depth.

Plant lilies in containers filled with a loamy topsoil or aquatic plant soil mix. Plastic pots are lightweight and easy to use. Some have lattice sides and use a permeable liner to allow air exchange while keeping the soil intact.

Whatever pot you select, make sure it's plant, fish and water friendly. Select a size that fits the vigor of the plant. Pygmy lilies can be grown in pots 8 to 12 inches in diameter. Larger lilies need pots at least 15 inches in diameter and 7 to 9 inches deep.

Don't use potting mixes formulated for terrestrial gardens and planters. Their organic matter and lightweight additives can float away and cloud the water. Buy potting mixes specially formulated for water gardens or mix your own from a good clay-loam topsoil, or a mix of 3 parts topsoil and 1 part sand.

Plant hardy lilies with the rhizome at a 45-degree angle, with the crown just below the soil, near the side of the pot. Tropical lilies should be in the center of the pot, with the crown just above the soil. Follow any special directions provided by the grower.

Firm soil around the plant to eliminate air pockets, then add a slow-release fertilizer formulated for water gardens. Remove any dead or dying leaves. Cover the surface with an inch of pea gravel to keep fish from digging and disturbing the roots.

Set the plants in the water away from pumps, waterfalls and moving water. For a pot without a gravel covering, tip it on its side and submerge slowly, keeping the pot at a slight angle. This allows water to move in and fill the air spaces so the soil doesn't float out. Pots covered with pea gravel can be lowered directly into the water.

Position plants so their leaves are just below the water surface. If you submerge small plants at the recommended depth right away, they'll use lots of energy just to get the leaves to the water surface, where they can grow efficiently and produce energy.

As the leaves begin to grow, continue lowering pots until they reach their final depth. Use bricks or blocks to adjust pot depth.

Include a few oxygenators to help keep the water clear. These are often sold as cuttings, and the directions recommend tossing them in the water, but you'll have better results if you plant them in containers. Cuttings are often bundled and tied to a weight. Stick these in a container of the same planting mix used for lilies. A 12-inch-diameter pot can hold 5 or 6 bundles. Scatter these pots throughout the garden. Use about one bunch of oxygenating plants for every 2 square feet of garden.

Tropical lilies typically hold their flowers above the water, while most hardy lily flowers (below) rest on the water's surface.

Floaters live on the water surface, with their roots dangling below. Toss these on the surface and let them grow until they cover one-third to one-half the water surface. Net off excess plants to keep their population under control. These plants spend the winter as buds or spores in the mud and debris on the pool bottom. If you scrub or vigorously clean pools in winter and spring, you'll need to replace them each season.

Marginals—plants growing on shallow shelves at the pond's edge—are managed much like water lilies. Plant them in containers on shallow ledges, or directly in soil if you have shallow planting beds. Containers should fit the plant and water depth, and offer wind stability. Many taller marginals are susceptible to wind damage. A slightly larger pot or strategically placed stone will provide added weight to prevent this.

Dave Alexander of Zanesville, Ohio used stone to create a waterfall and mask the mechanics of his water garden.

the pond to the surrounding landscape.

Add boulders and stones to anchor and hide the liner and pond edge. Include creeping plants and spreading shrubs to soften the stones and create a more natural feel. Some of the best water features I've seen look like they were placed by nature, with the landscape built around them.

Maintenance

Care of your water garden will vary depending on its size and inhabitants and your climate. These basics will get you started:

● **Spring.** As air and water temperature rise, you can increase water circulation. Begin feeding the fish when the water temperature reaches 50°. Remove any accumulated leaves and debris. Start digging and dividing existing plants. Most water plants need to be divided every 2 to 5 years.

Some gardeners leave the existing water in place, adding fresh water to fill it. Use water clarifiers if you add large amounts of tap water.

Others prefer to empty the pond, clean out the garden and start with fresh water. The water must be pumped into a large container to hold the fish and any plants overwintered in the pond.

Remove debris and sludge from the bottom, but don't scrub the surface. The velvety algae lining the bottom is beneficial and may contain oxygenator spores and buds. Refill the pond, add a water clarifier, and follow label recommendations for reintroducing fish and plants.

Introduce new hardy plants when the water reaches about 60°. Wait until water and air temperatures reach 70° before introducing tropical plants. Get a jump on the season by starting these plants indoors. Pot mail-order plants or overwintered lilies in 4-inch containers. Southern gardeners can start planting indoors in early March. Northern garden-

Judy Gleason's water garden in Lake Forest, Illinois (above) creates the perfect resting spot in her landscape.

Landscaping Around the Pond

Landscaping around a water feature is just as important as the water garden itself. Too often, I've seen beautiful water gardens plunked in the middle of the lawn without flowers, shrubs or structures to blend in with the rest of the landscape. These gardens are pretty, but look out of place. Landscaping makes them more attractive and inviting.

A garden around the pond also attracts wildlife. Include a few shrubs for year-round structure, color and bird shelter. Ornamental grasses add color and winter interest as well as motion and sound. The addition of a few annuals and perennials will tie

ers need to wait 4 to 6 weeks longer.

Grow these plants in a trough or aquarium. Keep them in a bright window or under artificial lights, covered with 2 inches of water. Transplant into larger containers before planting outdoors.

• **Summer.** Remove dead leaves and flowers as needed. This organic matter can upset the water garden's balance. Fish, frogs and toads will do a nice job of keeping insects, including mosquitoes, under control. Use a strong blast of water to dislodge aphids and other insects. Handpick and destroy caterpillars and other insects. Avoid using pesticides—they can harm the fish and disrupt the pond's balance. Patience is usually the best control. In time, weather or natural predators like ladybugs and dragonflies will move in to give the fish and toads a hand.

Diseases are seldom a problem in water gardens, especially if you plant properly and use disease-free plants. If you do spot signs of disease, remove infected leaves immediately. If spotting continues, lift and isolate the infected plant so it doesn't pass a disease to its neighbors.

Fertilize plants only as needed. Overfertilizing increases problems with troublesome algae. Many of the slow-release formulations used at planting provide several needed nutrients. Add more fertilizer when these are depleted and normal plant growth slows.

Add water as needed to replace what's lost through evaporation. Monitor pH, algae and water clarity. Adjust plant cover (no more than 50%), cleanup strategies and algae controls to keep water clear and the garden in balance.

• **Fall.** Southern gardeners should continue summer maintenance throughout fall, but Northern gardeners should start preparing for winter. As water temperature drops, so does the appetite of your fish. Cut back on feeding when the water drops to 60°. Stop feeding at 50°.

Fish and hardy water plants can be left in outdoor gardens where the water does not freeze solid.

Keep your garden beautiful with proper care throughout the year. Fine plastic netting (above) keeps leaves out in the fall.

Some gardeners use heaters or aerators to prevent freezing. Others create solar covers of plastic or fiberglass. Air spaces keep the air above the pond warm and prevent ice from forming. In deeper ponds that don't freeze solid, fish and plants can overwinter below the ice. Move all hardy plants to the deep, ice-free sections or move them indoors for winter.

Store hardy lilies in a cool, dark location in the basement. Leave them in their containers and keep the soil moist. You can place them in a black plastic bag or cover the pots with a damp cloth.

Tropical lilies are only hardy to zone 10, and just a few survive mild winters in zone 9. You can treat these like annuals and replace them each spring, or overwinter their tubers as you would callas, cannas and other non-hardy bulbs.

After the first frost, or as the floating leaves decline, remove tropical lilies from the water. Carefully lift the tubers out of the soil and rinse them with water. Pack in moist sand and store in a cool (55° to 65°), dark location. Check bulbs occasionally for excess moisture, rotting or drying, and adjust storage conditions accordingly. These will stay in storage until spring, when they can be started indoors for larger, earlier-blooming plants.

• **Winter.** Southern gardeners can prepare their gardens for winter by using the autumn methods described above for Northern gardeners.

In colder climates, gardeners should provide extra protection for fish and plants left in the pond. In shallow ponds, the water should be kept open with a heater or circulating pump. On deeper ponds, allow a layer of ice to form—the plants and fish will be fine as long as the pool doesn't freeze solid.

If the ice freezes, make sure there's space between it and the water below to prevent the buildup of toxic gases. To do this, use boiling water to melt an air hole. Do not forcibly punch a hole—this stresses the fish and can damage the liner. The air passage lets toxic gases escape and oxygen enter the water.

The *Plant Doctor* is in

Q: *I heard there is good algae I should leave in my water garden and bad algae that needs to be removed. How do I tell the difference and what should I do to get rid of the bad stuff?*

A: There are three general categories of algae. The free-floating algae makes the water green, and means you have too much carbon dioxide, excess nutrients or insufficient oxygen. Keep the water garden free of debris like fallen leaves, reduce nearby lawn fertilization, avoid overfeeding your fish and reduce the number of fish in the pond if necessary.

Hair algae is long and stringy, and forms in all types of ponds, even those in balance. Physically remove the algae and clean out any plant debris that has collected in the pond.

Green slime is found on the sides and bottoms of ponds. This is actually a good part of the pond's ecosystem, providing as much as 60% of the oxygen in the water. Avoid scrubbing off the slime during spring and fall cleanup.

Chemical and biological algae-control products are also available. Use these only as a short-term solution for an out-of-balance pond. Create a balanced growing system, and you'll have few problems with algae and little need for these types of control.

Q: *I want to add a water garden to my landscape, but I'm worried that I'll be overrun with mosquitoes. Do you have any suggestions?*

A: Mosquitoes are usually a problem in standing, stagnant water. This is not the case with most water gardens. Growing plants, swimming fish and water pumps circulate the water and prevent mosquitoes from breeding in your pond. Minimizing algae growth, using oxygenating plants and keeping your pond in balance also reduces the risk of mosquitoes.

If mosquitoes do become a problem, use *Bacillus thuringiensis* 'Israelensis'. This naturally occurring bacteria kills mosquito larvae but won't harm other insects, fish, birds or people. It's sold under several brand names, including Mosquito Dunks, at garden centers and in catalogs.

Q: *Quite a few of my plants are being devastated by mites. I don't want to use pesticides, since I plant flowers to attract birds and butterflies.*

A: Try spraying the plants with a strong blast of water. Repeat a couple of times a week. This is often enough to slow down their eating and mating. If it doesn't work, you may want to try insecticidal soap. It's effective at killing mites, aphids and other soft-bodied insects but safe for birds, butterflies and the environment. Treat the upper and lower leaf surfaces of infested plants. You may need several applications to get the mites under control.

Fountains help aerate water gardens and reduce unwanted algae growth.

Avoid spraying caterpillars. The soap may be irritating to them. But since this is a contact insecticide, it won't harm caterpillars that eat the treated leaves.

Q: Can I grow tulips and daffodils in containers? Do they need special care?

A: Tulips and daffodils need a cold period to initiate flowering but cannot survive temperatures much below freezing. Southern gardeners will need to buy pre-cooled bulbs or chill them in their fridge. Precooled bulbs can be purchased and planted directly in the planter. Untreated bulbs need a little more work. Pot them in a container smaller than their final destination. Water the soil and place in cold storage for 12 to 15 weeks.

Northern gardeners can do the same or take advantage of nature. Sink the potted bulbs in a vacant spot in the garden, an empty water garden mulched with leaves, or packed in a Styrofoam cooler in an unheated garage. Place the chilled bulbs in the planter once temperatures near freezing. Camouflage the pots with wood chips or moss, and your friends and neighbors will never know your secret.

Q: I am tired of hand-trimming around flower beds, trees and shrubs. Do you have any suggestions?

A: Try installing a mowing strip around your gardens. Place bricks, pavers or similar materials around the garden, flush with the soil. You can run one mower tire on this strip, eliminating the need to hand-trim. Consider mulching around trees and shrubs. Better yet, combine individual plants into larger beds. This creates better growing conditions for the plants and less work for you. I just mulch the edge of the bed with wood chips and use that as my mowing strip.

Q: I have lots of bare spots in my lawn. How can I repair these without starting over?

A: Remove any dead grass from the area. Loosen the soil surface and add organic matter to the top 4 to 6 inches if needed. Spread grass seed over the soil surface, then rake, mulch and water. Lawn patching kits provide the seed and mulch in one package. Prepare

Black spot is a common disease of hybrid tea roses.

the soil and follow label directions.

My friend Al Nees shared this technique. Mix a handful of grass seed into a bucket of topsoil. Sprinkle the mix over the roughened soil surface. Water, mulch, if the spots are large, and wait for the seed to sprout. His technique ensures good seed-soil contact while eliminating a few steps.

Q: Someone told me I do not need to stake my tomatoes. Is this true?

A: Tomatoes are vines that can be tied to a stake, supported by wire cages or left to sprawl on the ground. Sprawling tomatoes produce the most fruit. Unfortunately, some of it is lost to soilborne pests and gardeners' big feet. Mulch the soil with straw, leaves or other material to reduce pest problems. Staking tomatoes requires pruning and tying the two main stems to a post. You'll have less fruit, but you'll get it earlier. This is also a great way to increase air circulation and reduce disease problems. I usually cage my tomatoes. It's not much work, and I get a good harvest with fewer pest problems.

Q: My roses start out looking good each spring. Then the lower leaves get black spot, turn yellow and fall off. I have tried spraying but had no luck.

A: Black spot is a common disease on hybrid tea roses. This fungal disease overwinters on leaf litter near the plant. Once a bed is infested, it's almost impossible to clean out the disease. Start treating roses with a fungicide just prior to the time you usually see this disease.

Use several different products throughout the season, so the plant doesn't develop a resistance to them. You might want to try some of the new plant-derived fungicides. Check the label to make sure whatever you choose is labeled for controlling black spot on roses. Spray weekly throughout the growing season. Fall cleanup will help reduce, though not eliminate, the problem next year.

Consider replacing these roses with more disease-resistant shrub roses. You'll be pleasantly surprised with the change.

Garden Problems

Photos: Karen Bussolini; insets (from top, left to right)—Albert Squillace/Positive Images. John Bokin/Dembinsky Photo Assoc. Pam Spaulding/Positive Images; Alan and Linda Detrick (bottom row).

Chapter 8
Plant Problem Primer

Brown Spots . . . creepy crawling things on stems …holes in the leaves…dead plants. Sound familiar?

All gardens—even those of green-thumb gardeners—experience problems with pests and disease. Proper diagnosis can help you manage these problems and minimize their recurrence.

Diagnosing plant problems is what I've done for the past 20 years. I spend so much of my time giving advice for curing what ails plants that many people know me as The "Plant Doctor". This has been fun, rewarding and provided great stories to share.

Once, when I attended a wedding, the photographer took a picture at our table, then came over and said, "Aren't you Melinda Myers? I heard you were going to be here. I have a sick barberry in my car. Could you take a look and give me some advice?" I was a bit surprised, but followed him to the parking lot to look at his plant.

I don't mind being asked such questions, even at a wedding. And I hope the tips I share in this chapter will help give you a start in identifying some basic problems.

Others may require some help from your local Extension service or landscape professional—but if you do the groundwork for the pros, you'll get quicker and better results. It's worth trying to become your own plant doctor—or at least a diagnostician of sorts.

deners often bring me "problems" that turn out to be normal plant parts. The woody cone like structures on alders or pollen sacs on pines are often mistaken for egg cases, cocoons or growths caused by pests. These are normal parts and not harmful to the plants' well-being.

Keep in mind that plant varieties may exhibit characteristics much different than related species. Take the Sunburst honeylocust. Its new growth emerges bright yellow and gradually changes to green. This can be quite alarming if you don't realize it's a desirable trait, not a nutritional- or moisture-induced symptom.

Hair, waxy coverings and other features are normal on some plants and absent on others, and can vary with the time of year and the plant's age. Knowing the changes your plants experience will help you differentiate between what is normal and what's a problem.

Find out all you can about the plant's preferred growing conditions. As gardeners, we often push the envelope and grow plants in less-than-ideal situations. Sometimes this works. Other times, the plants suffer. Compare your growing conditions with those the plant prefers. Sometimes correcting maintenance practices or moving the plant is all that's needed.

Start by Knowing Your Plants

LEARN THE NAMES of the plants you're growing and what is "normal" for them. Some plant parts can be mistaken for insects, webbing and disease. Gar-

Consider checking several sources. Plant labels, catalogs, garden books, botanical gardens and your local Extension service provide information on plants growing in your area. Many gardeners, however, get

Common Symptoms

WHEN YOU READ BOOKS or discuss plant problems with experts, you'll be exposed to many new terms. Knowing their meanings can help you better understand what you're seeing, and what might be the cause.

Blight is the sudden death of flowers, leaves and twigs.

Cankers appear as sunken, swollen and often discolored areas on plant stems and bark.

Chlorosis is the yellowing of leaves.

Spots are circular or irregular discolorations on leaves, stems and other aboveground plant parts.

Galls are abnormal growths, lumps, bumps and swellings that can appear on leaves, stems and roots.

Necrosis is the death of plant tissue.

Necrotic lesions are spots of dead tissue.

Rot is the breakdown and decomposition of plant tissue.

Signs are the actual organisms, such as insects, mites, viruses and fungi, that are doing damage to the plant.

Symptoms are the visible changes in plant growth caused by insects, disease or environmental factors.

information from friends and relatives. Often this information becomes distorted or presented out of context as it's passed from one generation or friend to the next.

Yvonne Jensen, who worked with me at the Milwaukee County Extension office, had the perfect example. A man called our horticulture hotline and asked why his young horse chestnut tree wasn't growing any taller. Yvonne asked the gentleman lots of questions and found he was doing everything right in terms of water, mulch and location. After 10 minutes of exploring possibilities, the caller said, "I keep pulling off all the leaves and it still won't grow tall."

There was the problem. Plants need their leaves to produce energy and grow. Without them, the tree was lucky to be alive. Somewhere along the way, this caller received some misinterpreted information tak-

en out of context. Once he stopped pulling off the leaves, the tree began to grow and thrive.

Weather Factors

Evaluate recent weather patterns. Drought, temperature extremes and other drastic weather can cause immediate problems—or gradual decline that's not noticed right away.

Frost is an easy example. The first exposure to freezing temperatures kills coleus, impatiens and other frost-sensitive plants. The effect of sudden cold snaps on hardy plants may not be as obvious.

One fall, the Milwaukee area experienced very mild weather throughout October and into early November. Then one day, the temperatures dropped from 40° to –4°. Many trees and shrubs were fully leafed and not hardened off for winter. The result was an unusually large amount of winter kill the following spring. By then, many people had forgotten that cold snap and wondered what happened to their plants.

Other factors like flood and drought may cause damage that does not appear for a year or more. Like many parts of the country, Wisconsin experienced a severe drought in the late 1980s. Over the next 3 years, many trees declined and died. The stress of the drought weakened them, making them more susceptible to borers and disease.

Think of the last drought or flood your area experienced. Do you remember an unusually large number of sick plants and unexplained decline afterward? It could have been caused by weather. Gardeners are often skeptical when I blame the weather, but if you start tracking it and watching your plants' health, you'll see a definite correlation.

Lack of water due to drought, root damage and vascular disorders can cause brown leaf tops.

More Detective Work

Weather is only one factor in plant health. Look for other factors, such as pollution, pesticides, fertilizers, deicing salts and human and vehicular traffic, to name a few. Look for any change in the environment that seems to correspond to the change in your plant's health.

Now look at what you've done for your plant lately. Did you recently move it, change the soil level, store building materials nearby or run heavy equipment over the roots? These changes can directly or indirectly harm plants by increasing their susceptibility to insect and disease problems.

With so many potential factors, it's difficult to sort out the cause. Take a look at the plants in the garden, landscape and neighborhood to determine how a problem appears and progresses. If symptoms appear suddenly, follow a strong pattern and attack a variety of unrelated plants, it's probably caused by an abiotic (nonliving) factor. These include pesticide damage, fertilizer burn, pollution and frost.

For instance, frost damages a variety of unrelated plants. The leaves and stems are discolored or dead the very next morning. If this damage had been caused by a biotic (living) factor, like insects or disease, the progression and pattern of damage would be much different. A fungal disease like powdery mildew would affect only susceptible plants like phlox and lilac. It would start out as a white substance on the bottom leaves and spread upward through the plant. Over time, the infected leaves would yellow, turn brown and die.

Patterns of damage from abiotic causes are quite distinct. Think of the last time you saw light and dark stripes on a lawn—on your neighbor's, of course, not yours. You could see exactly where the fertilizer was applied and which areas were missed.

My favorite example is the footprints of dead grass cross-

Powdery mildew is a common sight on zinnia, bee balm and phlox. Use resistant varieties, provide proper spacing and sunlight to minimize this problem.

Frost-covered fall leaves signal the end of the growing season is near.

137

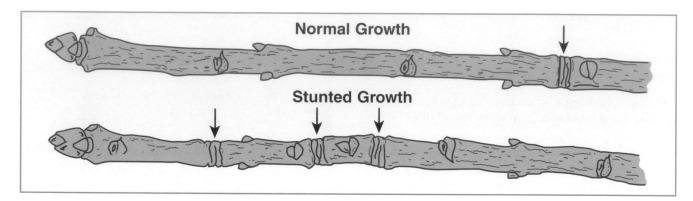

Normal Growth

Stunted Growth

ing a lawn. I visited a landscape where someone used a total vegetation killer to kill grass for a new planting bed. When he finished spraying, he walked through the bed and across the lawn to clean and store the sprayer. His shoes, still wet with herbicide, acted like pesticide applicators, killing the grass wherever they went. There was no doubt about who and what killed the grass.

Look at the growth of the plant over time. On woody plants, each year of growth is marked by a ring of scars left when the terminal bud scales shed in spring. Find these scars and compare the growth rates from each season to what's normal for the plant.

Shorter-than-normal growth may indicate a tree is drought-stressed, recently transplanted or suffering from some type of pest. Normal or longer than normal growth indicates favorable growing conditions and few, if any, pest problems. Continual decline in yearly growth shows the problem is ongoing and not just a one-season occurrence.

The arrows highlight the terminal bud scale scars (rings on the twigs) that mark the plant's yearly growth. The upper twig exhibits normal growth, while the lower twig has stunted growth induced by stress or pest problems.

Interpreting Signs and Symptoms

I always tell people the challenge to diagnosing sick plants is our patients can't talk, and they're already half-buried. But the plants do give us clues. We just need to be good detectives.

Look for symptoms and signs of problems. Symptoms are the visible expression of the disease, like the rash we get with measles. The cause of measles is a virus, but what we see—the symptom—is a rash. The same is often true with plants. Brown spots, yellow leaves and dead branches are symptoms. The real cause may be a fungus, boring insect or moisture stress. As gardeners, we use these symptoms and the plant's history to discover the real cause.

The signs are the causal organisms. It is the Japanese beetle chewing on leaves, the verticillium wilt fungus causing tomato plants to wilt, the bacteria that causes fireblight on crabapples. Finding these will give us a definite answer about what's wrong with the plant—but these signs are often hidden inside the plant, too small to see or safely tucked from view.

Sometimes what we see is not the real cause. Borers are the perfect example. These insects typically attack stressed, unhealthy plants. When we discover bronze birch borer in a paper birch, we're quick

Leaf discoloration and brown spots can be caused by drought, insect feeding, disease or a combination of these.

to blame the insect for the tree's decline. But the real cause is the heat and drought stress that weakened the tree, making it more susceptible to the borer, which just moved in to finish off the tree. The solution is to grow the birch in a more suitable location.

I hope it's getting a bit clearer, but as you can see, we still have a lot of detective work ahead of us.

Patterns of Damage

How symptoms appear on a plant can provide insight into the cause. Note the time frame and progression of symptoms to determine the culprit. There are always exceptions, but these guiding principles will help move you toward discovery.

When the entire aboveground portion of a plant dies, the problem is usually in the roots. A root problem prevents uptake of water and nutrients, resulting in discolored, wilted or dead leaves and, eventually, death.

If the dieback occurs gradually, disease or insects could be causing problems in the roots or vascular system, which moves water and nutrients through the plant.

Sudden plant death is probably caused by a chemical or a drastic change in the environment.

When a single branch or stem dies, the cause is likely above the ground. Dead branches that appear gradually, scattered throughout the plant, are probably caused by insects or disease. If the dead branches appear suddenly and are concentrated on one side, it's an abiotic disorder caused by something like storm damage, chemicals or other environmental factors.

Not sure? Take a closer look at the stem. If there's a sharp line between the healthy and dead tissue, it's most likely an environmental problem. If the line is irregular, it's more likely a biotic cause. Look for cankers (sunken areas), spores, ooze and other pest symptoms and signs.

Disease and insect problems will usually progress unless nature (weather, predators and disease) or man steps in to stop it. Damage from nonliving factors, like frost and pollution, stop as soon as the cause is removed.

Determining the Cause

By now you should have identified the symptoms, examined where they occurred on the plant and established how they developed over time. You should have a preliminary idea of whether the cause is abiotic or biotic, and occurring above or below the ground. Armed with this information, you're ready to start narrowing down the suspects. Let's start with

Crown rot on obedient plant causes sudden wilting and death of the plant. Remove infected plants and improve soil drainage.

the biotic group of problems—insects, disease and wildlife.

First, find out the common pests and environmental problems for the plant, and match up the symptoms and the progression of damage on your plant and when it occurred.

Holes, a clear sticky substance, translucent blotches or serpentine trails in leaves, missing leaf parts or sawdust-like material falling from the stem are just a few symptoms of insect damage.

The pest often can be found by checking along the stem, under the leaves or when digging up the roots. Other times, the insect has done the damage and moved on to the next phase of its life. Again, we rely on the timing and pattern of symptoms to identify this problem. See Chapter 10 for help identifying the top plant insects found in most of the United States and Canada.

Plant disease covers a large category of biotic disorders. Diseases can be caused by fungi, bacteria, viruses and other similar organisms. Symptoms include spots, blotches, canker, chlorosis, wilting and death.

When I see these symptoms or a combination of them, I look for common disease problems affecting the plant I'm diagnosing. See Chapter 12 for more specifics on diagnosing disease.

When large leaves, stems or small plants disappear from my garden overnight, my thought turns to animals and perhaps the exuberant children of my neighborhood. Droppings, teeth marks and eating patterns can often pinpoint which animal is using your landscape as a buffet. Some pointers on identifying and coexisting with wildlife are in Chapter 11.

Once you've managed existing problems, you'll want to prevent them from recurring. Your best defense is a healthy plant. If you've read the other sections of this book, you're already on your way.

Plant Health Care

The strategy of growing healthy plants and minimizing problems with a holistic approach is called Plant Health Care (PHC). The goal is to maintain healthy, vigorous plants by using environmentally safe, cost-effective solutions over the long term.

PHC is an outgrowth of Integrated Pest Management, a program initially used for agricultural crops. PHC, which evolved in the early 1980s, is adapted to meet the needs of plants found in the landscape. First used by landscape professionals, it's now familiar to many homeowners as well.

The first step in PHC is using the plants best suited for your growing conditions. This will eliminate most problems and minimize your maintenance efforts, too.

For example, green ash trees are very tough and tolerant of adverse conditions, but when pushed beyond their tolerances, even they can experience problems like ash borer infestations. That was our experience at the City of Milwaukee Forestry Division. The ash trees planted in sidewalk areas downtown were monitored and treated for borers. But the same type of trees growing in wide, grassy borders on the city's outskirts had no problems. We quit spraying the borer-infested ashes and replaced them with hybrid elms, which were more tolerant of the extreme conditions.

Select disease- and insect-resistant plant varieties whenever possible. If you've grown an old crabapple, you know what I mean. Older varieties like Almey, Hopa and Elyi are very susceptible to apple scab. Their leaves usually develop black spots and drop by midsummer. Newer, disease-resistant cultivars such as Prairifire and Louisa do not succumb to the disease.

Monitoring and Detection

Another important part of PHC is scouting—regularly inspecting all your gardens and plants. Observe any changes and note the impact of weather, pests and maintenance practices on the health and appearance of your landscape.

Even with proper plant selection and care, insects and diseases will invade. Catching them early may mean the difference between picking off a few diseased flowers or spraying the whole planting, as with botrytis blight on begonias.

Check the stems, upper and lower leaf surfaces, fruits and flowers for symptoms or telltale clues that insects and wildlife are present. Again, it helps to know what's normal and what's not. Speckled leaves mean mites and aphids are feeding; yellow leaves indicate root rot, nutrient deficiencies or improper watering; brown spots may be a fungal leaf spot.

Detecting problems early allows you to isolate when the problem began and look for any significant environmental factor that may have caused it. Early detection also helps you follow the progression of the disorder. Most problems that appear "overnight" have often been developing for weeks before we notice them.

Problems found and identified early require less effort to control. One mite can be destroyed, but left unchecked, it can produce 100 offspring in a week… and each of them can produce another 100. Soon you'll have thousands of mites to control.

Large isolated colonies of aphids can often be controlled by simply pruning off and destroying the infested plant part.

Aphids feed on roses and many other plants and come in a variety of colors, including green, peach and black.

Columbine leaf miner is not detrimental to the plant's health. Cut back infested plants after flowering to promote new growth.

Identification and Control

Once you find a pest, identify it and decide which, if any, control to use. Be sure to record the problem in your garden journal and on next year's calendar. (I'll talk more about record keeping a little later.)

We discussed identification strategies earlier in this chapter. Most of the sources you use to identify pests will offer control options as well. But only you can decide whether control is needed.

Look at the plant's overall health and vigor. A healthy plant will tolerate occasional bouts of insects or disease. For instance, honeylocust plant bugs are common pests in late spring. High populations can cause distorted growth and even delay leafing out. A healthy tree can tolerate this with little or no long-term effects, but a stressed tree would be weakened even further by this defoliation and may need treatment.

Know the pest and its severity on the species affected. Paper birches are a good example. These trees have two major insect pests, leaf miner and bronze birch borer. Leaf miners feed between the upper and lower leaf surfaces, causing brown blotches on the leaves. This isn't life threatening, but it's often treated to avoid additional stress on the tree.

Paper birches growing in the southern end of their native range are heat-stressed and susceptible to bronze birch borer. In these areas, trees are treated for the miner to prevent *additional* stress that would invite the life-threatening borer.

Some problems are weather-related and only appear when environmental conditions are right. Cool, wet springs increase the risk of fungal disease, while hot, dry weather means more aphids, mites and other heat-loving insects.

Treatment depends on plant health, the frequency of the weather pattern and past problems. Healthy plants that haven't had problems in the past can usually tolerate an attack. If the plant has suffered from the same problem for several years in a

✔ Melinda's Tips

RECORD significant weather events such as drought, flood, rainfall, frosts and temperature extremes in your garden journal. It helps you track the progress of your plants from one year to the next.

Or, invest in a weather calendar that provides temperatures, rainfall and significant weather information from past years. I buy one written by our local television station and sold as a charity fund-raiser. I've seen similar calendars at botanical gardens, Extension services, nature centers and other locations. You might find it worth the investment. I do.

You may have seen self-proclaimed "garden experts" on TV or heard them on the radio recommending homemade concoctions that include beer, soaps, cleaners and other household items. These "fun" solutions are often perceived as safer than those bought in the garden center. But read the labels. Many are as toxic as those developed for garden use—and sometimes worse. Remember that some of the products that go into these mixtures were formulated for use on floors, appliances and furniture, not plants. I've heard from many gardeners who damaged their garden plants or killed lawns with these concoctions.

Clear cloches protect young plants from frost and hungry wildlife like rabbits, birds and deer.

row, treatment may be a good idea.

Other problems are more of a nuisance than a threat. Remember those honeylocust bugs? They can be a nuisance when honeylocusts are planted over a patio or deck. You and your guests may tire of picking the insects out of your hair, food and drinks. In this case, control is strictly for your comfort, not the health of the tree.

Gypsy moths are more than a nuisance—they can be a health issue for some people. The hairs on the caterpillar enter the air and cause problems for people with asthma and other respiratory illnesses. Controlling these insects minimizes some human health problems, while improving plants' health and beauty.

In some instances, we discover problems too late to control them. The insects may have finished feeding and moved on to the next phase of their lives. Or, a disease may have already infected a plant, and treatment won't reduce its spread.

Revenge spraying—treating after the pest is gone—may make you feel better, but it doesn't help the plant. In fact, it may hurt your plants in the long run. Unnecessary pesticide use increases the risk to beneficial organisms, upsetting the balance of nature—which can result in more pest problems in the future.

Control Options

Once you decide to treat, there are many different control options. I usually start with the most environmentally friendly methods, saving chemicals as a last resort.

The first step is to evaluate the environment and care the plants receive. Sometimes a simple change in the watering, fertilization program or pruning schedule can eliminate pest problems. Watering in the morning, or by drip irrigation rather than overhead, can eliminate many fungal diseases. Applying most of your nitrogen fertilizer to the lawn in fall will encourage dense growth while reducing problems with lawn diseases. Prune oaks during the dormant season, when oak wilt—and the sap beetles that carry this disease—are less active.

If altering a plant's care isn't enough, you may need to look to other means. Sanitation is often my next step. Picking off and destroying insects and disease-infested plant parts can eliminate or contain the problem. Remove nearby weeds that can harbor insects and diseases. Diligent deadheading of petunias, begonias and other susceptible flowers during wet weather is often enough to avoid problems with botrytis blight.

Barriers and traps can be used to keep pests out or catch them for removal—just make sure the traps aren't

Insect traps can help you monitor pest populations to determine if and when control is needed.

Floating row covers or loosely woven fabrics, like the cheesecloth below, let air, light and water through, while keeping insects such as cabbage worms and root maggots out.

harmful to humans, wildlife or beneficial insects. Use season-extending fabrics over cabbage to keep out the worms, netting over grapes and strawberries to discourage birds and fences to exclude the rabbits. Yellow bowls filled with soapy water will attract and kill aphids, and beer-filled cans help control slugs.

If further treatment is needed, consider using one of the more environmentally friendly chemicals. Soaps, vegetable oil-based fungicides, *bacillus thuringiensis*, the plant-derived insecticide "neem" and similar products are effective at controlling certain insects and diseases. Even though they're friendlier to the environment, you must still read and follow all label directions.

Write It Down

Once you've used control measures, continue monitoring. If you need to make adjustments, evaluate their effectiveness and record your successes and failures in your garden journal. The year passes quickly, and we often forget lessons learned the previous season. The next time this pest attacks, you'll be armed with knowledge, experience and an accurate record of past results.

Thomas Jefferson kept a garden journal for more than 50 years. He recorded all the information on plants purchased, care given and the date and time of their deaths. He felt this was a valuable tool in making him a successful gardener. Recording plant, pest and environmental information will help you produce a healthier, more attractive landscape, too.

My friend Phil Pellitteri, the University of Wisconsin Extension's insect diagnostician, suggests making notations on next year's calendar, too. It's a great idea. When you spot pests, note the date and mark the next year's calendar to check for them a week or 2 earlier than that.

Many more environmentally friendly pest controls are now available. Check the label for application and control information.

Chapter 9
Those Nasty Weeds

It starts with one innocent little plant. Next thing you know, they've invited their relatives. Pretty soon, the whole garden is overrun with unwanted plants. Yes, they're weeds—also known as plants out of place. Some start from seeds that have lain dormant in the soil for years. Others move in on the wind, in soil additives or with garden transplants.

Ignoring them won't make them go away. They'll just linger and multiply, stealing water and nutrients from your garden plants, harboring insects and disease and ruining the appearance of your landscape—not to mention irritating your neighbors by spreading into *their* yards.

Don't let weeds take control and ruin your garden enjoyment. A few good pre- and post-planting strategies, combined with a little persistence, will help tame these unwelcome guests.

Understanding the Opposition

A CLOSER LOOK at weed types and their life cycles and habits helps us prevent and manage these plants. Both grasses and broadleaf plants can be weeds. Grasses are monocots, with narrow leaves that have parallel veins. Broadleaf plants like dandelion and clover are called dicots, whose wider leaves have a netted vein pattern.

The internal arrangement of the vascular system—the vessels that carry water and nutrients through the plant—also differs. Monocots have scattered vascular bundles, while the vascular system of broadleaf plants encircles the stem. This is why broadleaf weed killers can kill dandelions without harming your lawn.

Knowing a weed's life cycle also helps us prevent and control it. Annual weeds sprout from a seed, grow, flower, produce seed and die within a year. Spraying these plants after they flower and set seed is just an act of revenge—it won't reduce the problem. Winter annuals sprout from seed in fall or winter and complete their life cycle the following spring or summer. Summer annuals sprout in spring, grow all summer, flower and seed before winter arrives.

Biennials complete their life cycle in 2 years, giving you a little more time to get them under control. Their seeds sprout and grow a short rosette of leaves the first season. The next year, they produce more leaves (often taller and a bit different from the first season), flower, set seed and die. Then the 2-year process starts again. After a few years you'll have seeds sprouting and various weeds blooming and setting seed each season.

Perennials are the long-lived among this group. They sprout and produce a rosette of leaves the first year. In subsequent years, they produce leaves and flower each season. This continues until nature or man steps in to stop the process.

Grasses and broadleaf plants can be annual, biennial or perennial. Once you've identified the life cycle of your weeds, you can select a control method to stop them without harming desirable plants in your yard.

An Ounce of Prevention

A healthy lawn and garden are your best defense against weeds. Thriving plants grown in the proper environment can out-compete most weeds. Unwanted plants get a foothold in thin or bare spots, where grass and garden plants are struggling. The weeds are better adapted to adverse growing conditions and will quickly take over and crowd out the good plants. As their seed and roots spread, the

weeds encroach into other areas.

Evaluate the light, soil and moisture in your landscape. Find out what conditions give the weeds an edge over your garden plants. Correct these problems so your garden can outgrow the weeds. A little effort now can save you a lot of work each year battling weeds and struggling to keep your plants alive.

If drainage, moisture and nutrients are the problem, revisit the first section of this book. Properly amended soil won't eliminate weeds, but it can help good plants thrive despite unwelcome neighbors. I hate to admit that I have observed this firsthand in my own yard.

Some summers, my horticulturist husband and I get so busy advising and tending others' gardens that we run out of time for ours. The areas that can tolerate this neglect are the ones where the soil was properly prepared and managed. Beds that receive less preparation are the first to become overrun with weeds. Pulling weeds sure motivates me to work on the soil.

Shade is a little harder to manage. It's easier to change your planting scheme than move a shade-casting building or a neighbor's tree. Fortunately, many annuals and perennials can tolerate shade. Replace sun lovers with hostas, astilbe, impatiens and other shade-tolerant plants.

If the trees casting shade are your own, thinning out the canopy may provide enough additional light to improve growing conditions. Hire a certified arborist to do this. You'd hate to injure the tree or shorten its life with improper pruning. (For more ideas on shade gardening, see Chapter 14.)

Controlling Weeds Before Planting

REMOVING WEEDS before planting is easier and often more effective than controlling them afterward. A blank planting palette allows you a wider range of control options, since there are no existing plants to avoid or protect. Controlling quack grass, bindweed and other persistent invaders first makes long-term control easier.

Start by edging the bed with a shovel or edger. This separates weeds and grass growing in the garden from the surrounding lawn. Maintaining an edge once the garden is established also helps keep grass and weeds out. Next, decide if you want to use non-chemical or chemical weed-control methods.

Where Weeds Take Root

Weeds are good indicators of problem growing conditions. Correct the problem conditions as your first step in weed control.

Weed	Problem Growing Conditions
Clover	Originally part of grass seed mix; may indicate nitrogen-deficient soil
Equisetum	Moist and wet soils
Ground Ivy/ Creeping Charlie	Shade, though this weed grows everywhere
Knotweed	Compacted, droughty, salt-laden soil
Moss	Shade; compacted, poorly drained soil
Mushrooms	Decaying tree roots or other wood materials in soil
Purslane	Hot, dry areas
Sedge	Wet areas
Spurge	Hot, dry areas

Non-Chemical Controls

Black plastic, clear plastic, newspaper with mulch and cultivation are all non-chemical ways to control weeds. They take more time but are more environmentally friendly.

Black plastic kills existing weeds by preventing light from reaching their leaves. It also can cook some of the weed seeds near the surface. Cover the prepared garden area with black plastic, anchor the edges and wait. The longer you leave the bed covered, the better the results. Many gardeners apply the plastic in fall, leave it on through winter, remove it in late spring, lightly till and plant. Be patient. Looking at black plastic instead of a beautiful garden can be a bit disheartening.

Clear plastic is a better choice for established gardens that need some help with annual weeds. My friend Ray Greiten taught me this simple technique for sprouting weed seeds. Prepare the planting site several weeks in advance. Cover the bed with clear plastic to create a greenhouse effect. The sunlight will warm the soil beneath the plastic, causing weed seeds to sprout. After several weeks, remove the plastic. Cultivate lightly to kill the sprouted weeds without bringing new weed seeds to the surface. You've just controlled the majority of your weeds prior to planting.

Recycling your newspaper in the garden works, too. This technique should be reserved for areas with soil that doesn't need much improvement. Cover the garden area with several layers of newspaper. Anchor it with wood chips or other organic mulch. The grass and weeds under the newspaper eventually die and decompose along with the paper, adding organic matter to the soil. The two layers of mulch block sunlight, preventing most weed seeds from sprouting.

If you want to plant immediately, cut a hole in the mulch. Planting is easier if you wait a few months for the newspaper, weeds and grass to decompose. I like to use this method in fall. By spring, the grass and weeds have started to break down, so planting is easier.

Cultivation can also be used to prepare new gardens. Till the soil once a month for at least one (preferably two) seasons to eliminate quack grass, bindweed and other perennial weeds. The first few tillings actually increase the weed population. Existing quack grass and bindweed plants are chopped into smaller pieces that start growing new plants. In addition, many weed seeds buried deep in the soil are brought to the surface and start to grow. But repeated cultivation removes the energy-producing leaves so the roots eventually die. This method takes patience. If you shorten the process, you may end up with *more* weeds.

Another option is planting a "green manure" crop in winter to crowd out weeds and hold soil in place. Tilling the crop into the soil in spring doubles its value by adding organic matter and nutrients.

Chemical Weed Control

Total vegetation killers like Roundup and Finale give quicker results, but need to fit with your personal philosophy. I use very few chemicals at home. I want a pretty yard that my daughter, her friends, the birds and most other wildlife can safely explore.

I do, however, use total vegetation killers when establishing new gardens. It greatly reduces my workload and future chemical use.

For new beds, edge and apply a total vegetation killer. Treat badly infested areas a second time, after more weed seeds have sprouted or the hard-to-kill weeds recover. It's safe to plant once the waiting period listed on the label has expired. This can be from 4 to 14 days—the time varies depending on the active ingredient and formulation.

Remember, herbicides are designed to kill plants. Misapplication can harm desirable plants and damage the environment. Understanding how these chemicals work will help you avoid problems. As always, read and follow label directions when using these, or any, chemicals.

• **Selective herbicides** are designed to kill certain plants while sparing others. Broadleaf weed killers are a perfect example. They kill dandelions and other broadleaf plants without killing grass. Keep in mind that they can also damage petunias, trees and shrubs if misapplied.

• **Non-selective herbicides** can kill most everything they touch. Roundup, Kleen-up and Finale are common non-selective herbicides used in the home landscape. Spray only the plants you want to control.

• **Pre-emergent herbicides** prevent seeds of a variety of good and bad plants from germinating. Do not use these products before seeding the lawn or your garden. Follow the recommended waiting period between application and seeding.

• **Post-emergent herbicides** are used on existing plants. They do not control weed seeds or seedlings that have not yet emerged.

• **Systemic herbicides** are taken up through the leaves or roots and move through the plant. There are selective and non-selective systemic herbicides.

• **Contact herbicides** damage the parts of the plant they touch. Many of the more environmentally friendly products containing cacodylic acid work this way. They burn the foliage, but do not move

---

✔ *Melinda's Tips*

GARDENERS CONSTANTLY ASK ME for ways to manage weeds in the lawn and garden without using chemicals. I now have an answer—corn gluten. A researcher in Iowa found that corn gluten was effective at suppressing germination of a variety of annual and perennial weeds. Spring and late-summer applications will prevent weed seed germination. The product won't kill existing weeds, it can be pricey and it may take several years to significantly reduce weed populations. But many gardeners are willing to accept those limitations in return for more environmentally friendly weed control.

through the plants to kill the roots. This works for annuals, but repeat applications will be needed for established perennial weeds.

Weeds in Existing Gardens

ELIMINATING WEEDS before you plant won't eliminate weeds forever. It just gives you and your garden plants a competitive edge. Clean and weed gardens throughout the season. Pull offensive plants as soon as they peek through the soil. Young plants have a smaller root system and are easier to yank. Removing them before they can set seed means hundreds of fewer weeds to pull next season.

Some gardeners find weeding a chore, especially when it's hot and humid and the mosquitoes are looking for fresh blood. I find weeding therapeutic. All my frustrations and aggravations seem to fade away with each weed I pull. Many parents claim gardening helps them maintain their sanity.

When the weeds start taking over, break out your favorite weeding tool. If you don't have one, ask a friend or check out the tool rack at the garden center. You can remove weeds efficiently with the old-fashioned hoe or cultivator, as well as many newer weeding devices.

I like the action hoe. It has a movable stirrup-like attachment on the end of the handle and glides through the soil, cutting the weeds as it goes. The only problem is, it moves so well that I've accidentally weeded out some of my flowers and vegetables. The circle hoe is a similar device. I like the short-handled version for small or hard-to-reach weeds.

My husband prefers a one-tine cultivator. This long-handled tool has a single curved metal tine attached at the base. It's great for pulling weeds out of confined areas, like established perennial gardens.

Quick Reference Guide to Weeds

Grass Weeds
Crabgrass—Summer annual
Annual Bluegrass—Winter annual
Quack Grass—Perennial

Summer Annual Broadleaf Weeds
Dodder (Parasitic Plant)
Jimsonweed
Lamb's-Quarters
Morning Glory
Purslane
Ragweed
Speedwell
Prostrate Knotweed
Prostrate Spurge
Thistle
Velvet Leaf

Winter Annual Broadleaf Weeds
Common Chickweed
Henbit
Shepherd's Purse
Speedwell

Biennial Weeds
Bull Thistle
Burdock
Garlic Mustard

Perennial Weeds
Bindweed or Creeping Jenny
Canadian Thistle
Creeping Charlie (Ground Ivy)
Dandelion
Equisetum
  (Horsetail and Scouring Rush)
Mouse-Ear Chickweed
Poison Ivy
Purple Loosestrife
Speedwell
Violet

Avoid hoeing near shallow-rooted plants. It's very easy to damage the roots of good plants while trying to remove the bad ones. I usually hand-pull weeds growing next to my tomatoes, peppers and flowers to avoid this. A knife is good for removing weeds from flower and vegetable seedlings. The small blade allows you to cut away the weed without damaging tender young plants.

Removing quack grass, bindweed and other aggressive weeds from established planting beds can be difficult. You must be thorough and persistent to remove the top *and* all the underground roots and rhizomes to prevent their return. Chemicals used to kill these, such as broadleaf weed killers and total vegetation killers, can harm your flowers and may injure your trees and shrubs.

To spot treat problem weeds with a total vegetation killer, paint or wipe the product on the leaves to avoid touching your garden plants. Or, use a milk jug to create a spray barrier. Remove the bottom of the jug. Place it over the weeds and spray the chemical into the opening. When the plant dries, move the jug to the next location. Several applications may be needed for thistles, bindweed, wild grapes and other difficult weeds. If you have more weeds than perennials, you may want to cover the perennials while spraying the surrounding weeds.

I often cut taller weeds back to the ground before spraying. Remove and properly dispose the top portion. Once the roots resprout, I apply total vegetation killer as described above. This gives me a smaller plant to manage, which reduces the risk of harming my nearby flowers, shrubs and trees.

Preventing New Invasions

Once the garden is planted and weeded, you may want to invest some effort in reducing future infestations. Mulching with leaves, pine needles, herbicide-free grass clippings, wood chips and similar materials conserves moisture and helps prevent weed seeds from sprouting. As the organic mulch breaks down, it also helps improve the soil.

I mentioned this in an earlier chapter, but it bears repeating: Don't use weed barriers (black fabric) under organic mulches. As the mulch decomposes, it creates a suitable growing environment for invading plants and weed seeds.

If the weeds are still winning in your garden, consider using a pre-emergent weed killer. Apply after the garden is planted and before weeds begin to sprout. This herbicide doesn't control weeds that have already begun to grow, but prevents seeds from germinating. Some gardeners find that using a pre-emergent weed killer for one or two seasons breaks the vicious cycle, allowing them to get the weeds under control and return to cultivation and mulching.

Keeping weeds in check will improve the health and beauty of your landscape. And all that bending, pulling and hoeing might even improve your mental and physical well-being.

Common Weeds

THIS SECTION PROFILES some of the more common weeds. Remember, a healthy landscape is your best defense. Start with that and then implement the management strategies described for each weed. For further details on managing lawn weeds, see Chapter 7.

Bindweed or Creeping Jenny

What: Perennial vine with morning glory-type flower.

Where: Throughout the United States in both cultivated and uncultivated areas.

Control strategies: You must be more persistent than bindweed to control this deeply rooted weed by cul-

Bindweed

tivating the garden. Spot treat with a total vegetation killer, protecting your desirable plants. Several applications may be needed.

In the lawn, try spot treating with broadleaf weed killers labeled for controlling this and other difficult weeds. Several applications and a healthy lawn are needed to keep this weed under control.

Burdock

What: Biennial with large rhubarb-like

leaves and burr-covered seedpods.

Where: Throughout most of the U.S. Grows in cultivated fields; moist, rich soils; fence rows; roadsides; waste areas.

Control strategies: Remove from garden in first season. By second year, it develops a deep taproot and seeds. Spot treat with a total vegetation killer if cultivation is unsuccessful. In the lawn, mowing will eventually kill the plant and prevent it from reseeding.

Chickweed (Common and Mouse-Ear)

What: Common chickweed is a winter annual; mouse-ear is a perennial.

Chickweed

Where: Throughout the U.S. and southern Canada. Can tolerate some shade and dry conditions. It's an alternate host for several diseases.

Control strategies: Shallow-rooted and easily pulled

or cultivated in the garden. Remove early to prevent reseeding. Mulch to reduce future sprouting.

Broadleaf herbicides for difficult weeds will control both annual and perennial varieties in the lawn. Pre-emergents like corn gluten can be applied in late summer. Do not use prior to reseeding the lawn.

Crabgrass and Other Annual Grass Weeds
What: Summer annual. Seeds sprout when soil temperatures reach 50°.

Where: Throughout the U.S. Tolerates a wide range of conditions, especially heat and drought.

Crabgrass

Control strategies: A dense, healthy lawn can crowd out crabgrass and other annual weed grasses. Taller grass, mowed at the proper height, will shade the ground, preventing seed germination. Infested areas can be treated with a crabgrass pre-emergent before spring germination; treat infested areas for several feet beyond. For gardens, mulch and cultivation are usually sufficient.

Dandelions
What: Perennial. Early pollen source for bees. Used for making salads and wine.

Where: Throughout North America. Tolerant of a wide range of conditions.

Dandelion

Control strategies: Dig up in the garden, pulling out the whole taproot. Several attempts may be needed to eradicate plants. Mulching will help reduce seed sprouting.

A healthy lawn will contain invading dandelions. Dig or spot treat with a broadleaf weed killer. Fall applications seem to be more effective.

Dodder

Dodder (Parasitic Plant)
What: Annual. Threadlike, leafless yellow or orange vine.

Where: Various species throughout the U.S.

Control strategies: Pull plants from garden before seed sets or use pre-emergent herbicide. Usually not a problem in lawns.

Equisetum (Horsetail and Scouring Rush)
What: Perennial. Used by pioneers to scrub pots and pans.

Where: Throughout U.S. and Canada in wet and poorly drained areas.

Control strategies: In the garden, improve drainage and cultivate. This weed is resistant to most weed killers but does not tolerate regular cultivation. Keep the lawn healthy to keep this weed out. Regular mowing should keep it under control.

Equisetum

Garlic mustard

Garlic Mustard

What: Invasive biennial that is taking over woodlands and crowding out native wildflowers. The round or heart-shaped leaves have jagged edges and smell like garlic when crushed.

Where: From eastern Canada south to Virginia and as far west as Kansas and Nebraska. Adapts to a wide range of conditions, but most often seen in moist, shaded soil of forests, floodplains, woodland edges, roadsides and trails. Disturbed sites are most susceptible to rapid infestation.

Control strategies: Pull 1-year and 2-year plants from the garden before they flower in spring. Tell your neighbors and get everyone to remove these plants before they set seed. Make a long-term commitment to yearly control. Seeds can last for many years in the soil. In the lawn, healthy turf keeps garlic mustard out; frequent mowing prevents reseeding.

Ground ivy

Ground Ivy and Creeping Charlie

What: Perennial that hugs the ground. It has round scalloped leaves with a distinct aroma when crushed. Purple flowers in spring.

Where: Most common in northeastern and north-central U.S., but can be found in the South. Common in shady, damp soils.

Control strategies: Hand-pull from the garden, taking care to remove all roots and stems. If this does not work, spot treat with total vegetation killer.

Treat lawns with traditional broadleaf weed killers in fall after a hard frost, or in spring when plants are in full bloom. It takes several years to control these weeds and all their seeds in the soil.

Henbit

What: Winter annual that resembles ground ivy. Both are low-growing, with round scalloped leaves and purple flowers. Henbit is more upright, and the leaves have no odor when crushed.

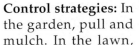

Where: Throughout the U.S., but most common in the East and along the West Coast. Common in lawns and gardens in cool, fertile soils.

Control strategies: In the garden, pull and mulch. In the lawn, healthy turf keeps this
Henbit

weed under control. Seedlings emerge in early spring or fall, so properly timed pre-emergent applications may help. Spot treat badly infested areas with a broadleaf weed killer before seeds form.

Jimsonweed

What: Summer annual. Toxic to livestock and humans.

Where: Throughout most of U.S. except the Northwest and northern Great Plains. Tolerates a wide range of conditions.

Control strategies: Pull plants from the garden as soon as they appear, before they set seed, and mulch. Not a problem in lawns, as it doesn't tolerate mowing. Poisonous.

Jimsonweed

Lamb's-quarters

Lamb's-Quarters

What: Summer annual. White mealy covering on leaves, especially new growth.

Where: Throughout U.S. in farmland, landscapes, gardens and vacant areas.

Control strategies: In gardens, pull and mulch. Healthy turf and regular mowing control emergence in lawns.

Morning glory

Morning Glory

What: Summer annual; reseeds in gardens and lawns.

Where: Most troublesome in southern and central U.S. Less of a problem in colder regions. Adapts to a wide range of conditions.

Control strategies: Mulching and cultivation work in the garden. Not a problem in lawns; mowing and broadleaf weed killers will prevent any strays from taking over. Do not confuse this with perennial bindweed, which looks similar and is a problem in lawns.

Poison ivy

Poison Ivy

What: Perennial, deciduous, woody vine with three-leaflet leaves that turn red in fall; produces white berries. Causes allergic reaction in many people.

Where: Native plant widespread throughout northern, eastern and midwestern U.S., parts of Canada.

Control strategies: Pull young plants in the garden while wearing gloves, pants and long sleeves. Do not burn pulled plants; this can cause an internal allergic reaction. Spot treat older plants with a total vegetation killer. Dead plants can also cause allergic reactions.

In the lawn, healthy turf and mowing keep this weed under control. If problems occur in remote areas or turf edges, use a chemical labeled for controlling poison ivy that will not harm the grass. Follow precautions described above.

Prostrate Knotweed

Prostrate Knotweed

What: Summer annual.

Where: Throughout the U.S. and southern Canada in compacted, salt-laden or other damaged areas.

Control strategies: In the garden, pull weeds as soon as you find them, before they set seed, and mulch. For lawns, eliminate compaction. In spring, water salt-laden soils and use a pre-emergent weed killer when not reseeding the lawn.

Prostrate spurge

Prostrate Spurge

What: Summer annual that lies flat on the ground. Leaves are green with red blotch in center. Stems and leaves exude milky sap.

Where: Throughout the East, Midwest and Pacific Coast in gardens, brick walkways and waste areas.

Control strategies: Pull and mulch in gardens. For lawns, use pre-emergent weed killer in spring; for later treatment, use broadleaf weed killer before seed sets.

Purple Loosestrife

What: Tall perennial with spiky purple flowers. Has escaped cultivation and is invading wetlands, ruining wildlife habitat.

Purple loosestrife

Where: Northeast through Midwest. More than 20 states are implementing control measures. In many states, it's illegal to grow this invasive plant.

Control strategies: Remove plants from the garden. Even sterile cultivars have been found to set seed. Mowing prevents problems in the lawn.

Purslane

Purslane

What: Summer annual with thick, fleshy stems that lie flat on the ground. Can be steamed and eaten as a spinach substitute.

Where: Throughout the world, in new and thin lawns and in gardens. Especially tolerant of hot, dry areas.

Control strategies: In the garden, pull and mulch. For lawns, improve turf health and use a pre-emergent weed killer in spring.

Quack Grass and Other Perennial Grass Weeds

What: Perennial; spreads by seed and rhizome.

Quack grass

Where: Throughout northern U.S. and southern Canada.

Control strategies: Pull from the garden, making sure to remove all roots and rhizomes, and destroy. Do not compost. Spot treat with a total vegetation killer. Healthy lawns help crowd out grass weeds. Kill badly infested areas with a total vegetation killer and reseed.

Speedwell

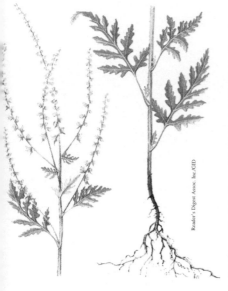

Ragweed
What: Summer annual responsible for hay fever. Common ragweed has deeply lobed, ferny-looking leaves, similar to carrots. Giant ragweed has large three-lobed leaves.

Where: Throughout North America in gardens and vacant lots.

Control strategies: Pull ragweed from the garden as soon as you spot it, before it sets seed, and mulch. Usually not a problem in managed lawns, as it doesn't tolerate mowing.

Where: Lawns and gardens throughout most of North America.

Control strategies: In the garden, pull and mulch. Tall, healthy turf can help crowd out this weed in the lawn. Seeds can sprout in fall, winter or very early spring. Pre-emergent herbicides applied in fall may prevent some seeds from germinating, but not all. Broadleaf weed killers can be applied before seed sets to reduce future infestation.

Thistle

Shepherd's Purse
What: Winter annual with a low rosette of leaves that look like a lacy dandelion. The heart-shaped seedpods are the real ID clue.

Where: Worldwide in gardens, landscapes and vacant areas.

Control strategies: In the garden, pull and mulch. Mowing usually prevents stray plants that enter the lawn from seeding and becoming established.

Speedwell
What: Several species of low-growing summer and winter annuals and perennials that form a dense mat.

Thistle
What: Annual, biennial and perennial species.

Where: Throughout the U.S. and southern Canada.

Control strategies: In the garden, pull weeds, mulch and use a pre-emergent herbicide. Spot treat with a total vegetation killer. For the lawn, use broadleaf herbicides labeled for controlling thistles. Paint total vegetation killer on unresponsive weeds. Several applications may be needed.

Velvet leaf

Control strategies: Pull as soon as you find them, before they set seed, and mulch. Mowing prevents lawn problems.

Violet
What: Perennial spread by roots and seeds that shoot across the landscape when ripe.

Where: Northern, southeast and western U.S.; southern Canada.

Violet

Control strategies: Pull existing plants from gardens and mulch to reduce seeding. Spot treat problem areas with total vegetation killer. For lawns, treat twice in fall, about 6 weeks apart, with a broadleaf weed killer labeled for controlling difficult weeds.

Velvet Leaf
What: Summer annual with large, velvety, heart-shaped leaves and attractive seedpods. Do not let pods dry out and distribute seeds.

Where: Throughout U.S. in farms, gardens, roadsides.

The *Plant Doctor* **is in**

Q: My perennial garden is overrun with weeds. Should I kill everything and start over?

A: If the weeds outnumber the perennials, it may be quicker and easier to start over. Remove and set aside any valuable plants, or those with sentimental value. Be sure to remove any troublesome weeds that may have invaded their roots and crowns. Kill all the weeds, amend the soil and replant.

If you have a lot of good plants, you may want to try to reclaim the garden instead. Cover your perennials with a bucket or gallon milk jug. Spray the weeds with a total vegetation killer. Remove the covers when the weeds are dry. Several applications may be needed. Leave the dead plants in place to serve as a mulch. Cover with leaves, pine straw or other organic mulch to improve appearance and weed control. Spot treat new weeds as needed.

Q: I think I destroyed my landscape. I used a weed killer on the paths and in my flower beds. The plants' leaves curled and many died. What can I do?

A: Broadleaf weed killers should really be called broadleaf plant killers. Most are designed for use in turf grass, which isn't damaged by these products. Never use a broadleaf weed killer in a garden filled with flowers, vegetables and other broadleaf plants.

Instead, spot treat weeds with a total vegetation killer, which kills the tops and roots of treated plants. Once the chemicals hit the soil, they're no longer active, so the roots of other plants don't absorb them. In the meantime, water thoroughly to help dilute and wash the herbicide through the soil. Then wait. It can take up to a full year for this material to dissipate. Always read and follow label directions before buying and using any chemical. This can help you avoid similar problems in the future.

Q: Is it necessary to wear gloves and goggles when mixing and using over-the-counter weed killers?

A: Personal safety equipment is always a good idea. Gloves, goggles, long sleeves and pants can protect your eyes and skin from chemical exposure. This is especially important when handling the concentrated product during the mixing and tank-filling stage. A little discomfort is worth the extra safety.

Chapter 10
Stop Bugging Me

Ladybugs (below) are helpful in a garden, while Japanese beetles (opposite page) are harmful.

"It's a BUG! Kill it, kill it!" If this is your natural response to creepy-crawly things, we have a little work to do. There are about 100,000 species of insects living in North America, and probably 1,000 of them visit your backyard.

Most are welcome guests because they pollinate our flowers, help convert plant debris into compost and eat harmful insects. The few that cause damage—less than 3%—are often controlled by weather, other insects, birds, animals and gardeners.

Insects, both good and bad, are among the oldest and most numerous creatures on Earth. When an area is devastated by toxic material or natural disaster, insects are among the first, if not *the* first, living organisms to move in. Their ability to adapt to environmental change is incredible. So we need to be realistic in our expectations and try to manage insect pests rather than eradicate them.

Eliminating all problem insects would be impossible and unwise. Even pests are beneficial to our environment. It's just hard to remember that when they devour your favorite rose.

I'll give you some pointers on diagnosing insect damage, identifying pests and managing problems using a Plant Health Care approach. This system advocates environmentally friendly methods, using chemicals as a last resort. Pesticides are constantly being removed or added to the list of chemicals that are legal to use. Their label recommendations change and availability varies, too, so I usually won't recommend a specific chemical. I hope you won't need many.

Identifying the Culprit

SPECKLED LEAVES, holes and webbing are often the first things we notice when insects move into our garden. A closer look at the symptom may reveal what's causing the damage. When I teach my students at Milwaukee Area Technical College about pests, we start with the obvious—the damage. Then we review our list of pests that cause that type of damage and look for the guilty party.

Most insect damage is caused by feeding. Chewing insects such as beetles, caterpillars and grubs have mouthparts that allow them to gnaw holes in leaves, roots and stems. Suspect a chewing insect if you see holes in leaves, flowers and fruits, or sawdust spilling from a hole in a woody stem or trunk.

Aphids, mites and leafhoppers are a few of the insects with piercing, sucking mouthparts. These pests use their needle-like mouths to suck plant juices, leaving a tiny pin-sized yellow or brown dot that causes bronzing or speckling. These insects often secrete a clear, sticky substance commonly called honeydew.

Thrips use a file-like mouthpart to scratch the surface of leaves and flowers, releasing plant sap for them to feed on. Damaged plants may have brown streaks or scratched leaves. Flowers may be damaged or fail to open.

White and brown snakelike trails or blotches mean leaf miners are dining on your plants. At the larval stage, this pest feeds between the upper and lower surface of the leaf, creating trails and blotches. The damage is usually only

cosmetic, but it's noticeable.

If your plants are suffering from high populations of insects, particularly mites, aphids and plant bugs, the leaves may yellow, curl and brown. These pests also can stunt or distort plants, resulting in bumps, spindles and growths in which the insect may be hiding.

How Insects Develop

Once the pest is identified, you need to decide if treatment is needed. By the time damage is found, the insect often has moved on to another location or phase of its life, making treatment unnecessary. It might make you feel better, but the damage is already done, and the pest has escaped. Revenge spraying may kill beneficial insects that are keeping problem pests under control.

Understanding insect makeup and development will help you understand why and how to control them.

Most insects are born as eggs, hatch and start an interesting development to adulthood. This process can be simple or complex and take as little as a week or as long as several years. Some insects go through life cycles several times in one season, dining on your plants from spring through fall.

Insects overwinter in different stages. Some spend winters as eggs, others survive as larvae or adults, others head for warmer weather.

The egg stage is often hard to detect and is the least affected by common insecticides. Insects lay eggs under bark, on leaves, in the soil and in other locations protected from weather, predators and gardeners. They can be colorful or dull, round or oblong, solitary or massed.

Eggs can be smashed, removed or treated with a dormant oil (made for plants) to prevent them from hatching. But don't treat unless you know what laid the eggs. Many insect eggs look alike, so it's easy to kill beautiful butterflies or predatory ladybugs by mistake.

In the next phase, different types of development become obvious. Some insects hatch into miniature versions of their adult form, while others start out as something totally dissimilar. The first is called simple or gradual metamorphosis; the latter is complete or complex.

Insects such as aphids, plant bugs and grasshoppers go through simple metamorphosis. The young

Beautiful butterflies, like the tiger swallowtail above, start as plant-eating caterpillars. Grow a variety of plants to provide enough food for the caterpillars, while maintaining an attractive garden. At right, this ladybug larva can consume more aphids than its more recognizable adult form.

insects, called "nymphs", look very much like the adults. The wings may not develop until they're older, and their color may change, but the shape and appearance are recognizable.

As the young insects grow, they must shed their exoskeleton, or outer shell, just like a snake. You may have found the large cast-off exoskeleton of a cicada or the white threadlike exoskeletons of aphids. At the final stage, the fully developed insect mates. The females lay eggs and die, and the process starts all over again.

Beetles, butterflies and sawflies go through a complete metamorphosis. They start as eggs and hatch into a grub, caterpillar, maggot or larva. As the larva eats and grows, it molts several times, shedding the exoskeleton each time. When the larva reaches full size, it pupates. This is the resting and transformation phase. The pupa may be exposed or protected in a cocoon. The pupa emerges in its adult form as a beetle, moth, butterfly or fly. The adults eat and mate, the females lay eggs and the process starts again.

Damage can occur at any stage, depending on the insects. Eggs themselves aren't harmful, but the laying of the egg can cause damage. Treehoppers damage tree trunks to create a safe place for their eggs. Apple maggots cause lumpy fruit when laying their eggs in a developing apple.

Aphids are easy to identify. Look for two tailpipe-like appendages (cornicles) at the bottom of their pear-shaped bodies.

During the immature nymph or larval stage, worm-like caterpillars eat holes in plant leaves, but as adult butterflies and moths, these insects help pollinate and beautify your garden. The cabbage root maggot feeds inside the roots, while the adult fly does not feed on the plant.

In other cases, the adult causes the damage, as with the blister beetle. The larvae actually help gardeners by eating other insects, but the adult chews holes in the leaves of vegetables, flowers, young trees and vines.

Other insects cause damage in both the immature and adult phases of their lives. Aphids feed from the moment they hatch until they die. Most beetles feed throughout their life cycle. The larvae may feed on plant roots, under the bark or in a stem, while adults move to a different plant part to dine.

Understanding an insect's life cycle and knowing when damage occurs will make it easier to find and control it. Most insects are hardest to see but easiest to manage when young. When they reach maturity, you may have fewer control options and pesticides are less effective. So check your garden frequently for clues. Caught early, the population will be smaller, and the insects younger and easier to control.

Garden "Good Guys"

Most of the insects in your garden are helpful. Rove and ground beetles are a few of nature's recyclers, chewing on decaying plant debris and turning it into organic matter that improves the soil. Even slugs and snails help with recycling. Unfortunately, they start the process with leaves that are still on the plant.

Building a Bug House

BUG HUNTS and treasure hunts were favorite activities when I was a kid. When my daughter was young, she and her friends scoured the backyard and garden for interesting twigs, stones and wildlife. Even with the distractions of computer games and in-line skating, I still have neighborhood kids come into my garden looking for worms, butterflies and beetles. These treasures—including the bugs—need a place for safekeeping.

Every gardener or parent should have a bug house, just in case. You can buy one at a nature center or make your own. I like the latter—it brings out the artist, architect and scientist in us all.

Put cocoons, caterpillars or other insects you discover into a plastic jar, coffee can or similar container with their favorite food. Replace the lid with netting or wire mesh and secure with a canning jar ring, wire or rubber bands. Then wait and see what happens. It's a great way to bring science, magic and fun into your home.

Ladybug larvae and adults eat aphids and other insects. Many small wasps lay their eggs on caterpillars. As the eggs hatch, the immature wasps become parasites on the caterpillars. Praying mantids or lacewings can help control pests in your yard, too.

You don't need to buy these good guys to get their help, but you may need to adjust your gardening practices to make them feel welcome. Wait a while before treating problem pests. You need a food source to attract beneficial insects. This is one instance where procrastination pays.

When my daughter was little, we always passed a goldenrod on our way from the garage to the house. One summer it was infested with aphids. Every day for about a week, I said, "I ought to do something about that." Of course, I didn't.

Luckily for me, nature stepped in. The ladybugs started eating the aphids. When I showed my daughter, she was delighted. She took every visitor to see the ladybugs eating aphids. Each summer thereafter, she looked for the "aphid plant" and waited for the lady beetles to arrive.

You also can try cultural controls or other methods that don't harm beneficial insects. A birdhouse or birdbath may entice birds to your lawn for a nice lunch of bugs.

If you must use a chemical, try to use more environmentally friendly products. Spot treat problem plants to limit exposure of other insects and wildlife. Choose "selective" products that kill fewer types of insects rather than broad-spectrum chemicals that kill a wide variety of good *and* bad ones. Be sure to choose a product labeled for the pest you're trying to eliminate and for the plant affected. Always read and follow label directions carefully. Increasing the concentration may kill the plant without improving insect control.

Supertock

Invite insect-eating birds into the landscape by providing shelter and water.

Lacewing

Watch for these beneficial insects in your garden. They eat many pests and save you lots of work. Do not spray insecticides when these insects are present. You'll destroy them and their food sources.

Photos: Liz Ball/Positive Images

Praying mantis

Ladybug

Who's Been Nibbling In My Garden?

CLUES—PLANT DAMAGE	POSSIBLE SUSPECTS—PESTS
Holes in leaves	Beetles, caterpillars, earwigs, sawflies, slugs, snails
Speckled leaves	Aphids, mites, whiteflies, plant bugs, leafhopper, spittlebugs
Blotches/trails on leaves	Leaf miners
Brown leaf tips	Leafhoppers, plant bugs
Scraped leaves/flowers	Thrips
Missing roots	Grubs (immature beetles and weevils)
Distorted growth	Aphids, mites and plant bugs
Clear, sticky substance (honeydew)	Aphids, mites, whiteflies, scales
Sawdust-like substance	Borers
Bumps on leaves/twigs that don't rub off	Gall-forming insects and mites
Bumps on leaves/twigs that can be scraped off	Mealybugs and scales
Soil mounds in lawn/garden	Ants

A Pest by Any Other Name...

SLUGS, SNAILS AND MITES aren't true insects, but I've included them in this chapter because they cause similar damage, and many gardeners lump them into that category. A true insect has three body parts—a head, thorax (chest) and abdomen. Insects have three pairs of legs attached to the thorax. All have antennae, and some have one or two pairs of wings attached to the thorax.

Spiders, often mistakenly called insects, are generally beneficial and eat many other pests. But there's one exception: mites. These spiders do cause plant damage. Mites have two body parts—a fused head and thorax, plus the abdomen. Mites have four pairs of legs, which are attached to the fused head and thorax. Mites have no wings or antennae.

Snail

WHEN YOU SEE a problem, don't panic. Reach for this book before you reach for the spray.

These are some common insects that may cause problems in your garden. I've included a quick "verbal snapshot" of each pest, the damage it causes, other pests it may resemble, damage that may look similar—but have another cause—and management strategies. For easier identification, they're organized by the type of damage they cause.

Chewing Insects

THE PRIMARY SIGN of these insects is holes in leaves. Chewing insects may eat all the leaf tissue except the veins, giving the leaf a lacy appearance.

Caterpillars

Damage: Holes in leaves. Eventually, the whole leaf is devoured.

Time of damage: All season. Various species are active at different times.

The pest: Caterpillars are the worm-like larvae of butterflies and moths. They have segmented bodies with a pair of legs on each of the first three segments. Segments 3, 4, 5 and 6 of the abdomen have false legs known as "prolegs", with little "crochet hooks" at the ends. Caterpillars can be smooth, hairy or spiny, and dull or brightly colored.

Swallowtail caterpillar eating dill plant

Look-alikes: Sawflies.

Plants attacked: Larvae feed on a variety of vegetables, flowers, trees and shrubs.

Management strategies: A few caterpillars can eat a lot of leaves in a short time. Most healthy plants can tolerate the damage and will produce replacement leaves. I leave most caterpillars in my garden, since many of them turn into swallowtails, monarchs or other butterflies. Birds and disease will keep most of these insects under control. Remove unwanted caterpillars or damaging populations by hand. Check under the leaves and along the stem. A flashlight at dusk is helpful for finding them as they feed.

Or, treat infested plants with *Bacillus thuringiensis*, sold as Dipel or Thuricide. This bacteria kills only true caterpillars and won't harm birds, wildlife or people.

Cutworms

Damage: Young transplants are cut off, as with scissors, just above ground level. The top of the plant is left lying intact in the garden.

Time of damage: Spring and early summer (planting time).

The pest: The larval stage (caterpillar) of several species of brown moths.

Look-alikes: Animal damage or vandalism.

Plants attacked: Young plants and transplants.

Management strategies: This is a common problem in gardens that were recently converted from lawn. Cutworms are seldom seen in established planting beds. Protect young transplants with homemade cutworm collars. Remove the top and bottom of a tin can, cut 3-inch sections from paper towel rolls or use similar materials to make a barrier (above). Place the collar around the transplant. Sink the bottom into the soil so at least 1 to 2 inches remain above ground. When the cutworm encounters the barrier, it moves on to another plant.

Cutworms

Earwigs

Damage: Holes in leaves, petals and ripe fruit.

Time of damage: All season.

The pest: Earwigs are reddish brown, narrow insects with pincher-like forceps at the tail end. They feed at night and hide under rocks, boards or other cool, dark places during the day.

Look-alikes: Damage and feeding locations are similar to those of slugs.

Plants attacked: Young earwigs eat holes in the leaves of flower and vegetable plants. Older earwigs eat rose, clematis, dahlia and other blossoms as well as fruit.

Management strategies: Earwigs are predaceous of other insects, but they're a nuisance in the home and

Earwig tail end

a pest in the garden. Try trapping them with a piece of crumpled paper under a flowerpot. Collect earwigs in the morning and drop them into soapy water or crush them. You must be fast, as earwigs flee quickly when disturbed. Some Europeans use earwig houses. They trap the insects in the garden and move them to orchards to eat codling moths and other pests. Insecticides can also be used. Place a granule barrier of insecticide around your house's foundation to keep earwigs out of the home.

Gypsy Moths

Damage: This pest eats holes in leaves until the entire leaf is consumed and the plant is defoliated. One caterpillar can eat all the leaves in a 2-square-yard area. About 17 Eastern and Midwestern states are infested, and the insects are spreading.

Time of damage: Spring through early or midsummer.

The pest: Gypsy moth caterpillars are black with hairs, white stripes and red and blue dots.

Look-alikes: Mourning cloak butterfly (different coloration) and tent caterpillars (form webby nests).

Plants attacked: Gypsy moths prefer oaks, but attack more than 500 different trees and shrubs.

Management strategies: Treat overwintering eggs with a dormant oil spray to prevent hatching. Use a plant-derived oil for a more environmentally friendly option. As many as 1,000 eggs can be clustered in a single beige or yellow hairy egg mass. Check tree trunks, campers, birdbaths, firewood and other areas for egg masses. Trap larvae with sticky bands of paper or burlap hiding bands. Wrap tree trunks with a 2- to 3-foot-wide strip of burlap. Secure in the middle with twine, allowing the top half to drape over the bottom. The larvae will hide in the cloth, and you can remove and drop them in a can of soapy water. *Bacillus thuringiensis*, which kills only true

Gypsy moth caterpillar

caterpillars, can be used to control young larvae. Hire a certified arborist to treat large trees. Check with your local Department of Natural Resources, county forester or Extension service for information about this pest in your area.

Japanese Beetles

Damage: Grubs (larvae) feed on grass roots, resulting in a wilted, stunted and stressed lawn. A gentle tug reveals the roots have been eaten. Skunks and raccoons often dig up lawns to look for the tasty grubs. Adult beetles skeletonize leaves, eating all the green tissue, leaving just the veins.

Time of damage: Grubs feed on grass roots underground in late spring and early fall. Adults feed on leaves of various plants in midsummer.

The pest: Adult is a metallic greenish-brown beetle with white tufts along the abdomen. The larva is a

Japanese beetles on hydrangea

white grub that curls into a "C" when disturbed. Japanese beetles are currently found in much of the eastern half of the United States.

Look-alikes: Other grubs like June beetles and billbugs, which cannot be controlled by milky spore bacteria (see "Management strategies" below). Grub damage also can resemble drought stress. Adult feeding mimics damage caused by rose chafer and other skeletonizing beetles.

Plants attacked: More than 300 species of flowers, trees and shrubs.

Management strategies: Birds and toads help keep these insects under control. Be careful using pesticides that will harm these natural predators. And think twice about using traps. They seem to attract more insects than they control. Milky spore bacteria can be used in the soil to control this pest. It only works on Japanese beetles, not other troublesome grubs, and takes several years to become established and provide control. Other grub controls must be applied in late spring or early fall, when grubs are near the soil surface. Handpick and destroy adult beetles. Throw them in soapy water to slow them down before smashing them, or place in a sealed jar. Chemicals labeled for beetles can be applied to plants when the adults are present.

Sawflies

Damage: Large sections or whole leaves and needles missing.

Time of damage: Differs throughout the season, depending on species.

The pest: Caterpillar-like insects that usually feed in colonies. They often "dance", swaying to and fro, when disturbed. Sawflies have three pairs of true legs and one pair of false legs (prolegs) on each remaining body segment. The adult, a fly-like insect, causes no damage.

Look-alikes: Caterpillars.

Plants attacked: Various trees and shrubs; varies with species.

Management strategies: Sawflies are easy to control, since they like to feed in colonies. Prune off and destroy the infested branch, sawflies and all. Or, don a leather glove and smash the sawflies with your hand. It's disgusting, but effective. Make insecticides your last choice. Do not use *Bacillus thuringiensis*. This kills only true caterpillars, not sawflies.

Sawfly larvae

Slugs and Snails

Damage: Holes in leaves.

Time of damage: Any time, but especially during wet weather.

The pest: Nocturnal feeders that leave a slime trail on leaves as they feed. Slugs are gray and slimy, without shells. Snails look similar but carry a protective shell.

Look-alikes: Earwigs, caterpillars and sawflies cause similar damage.

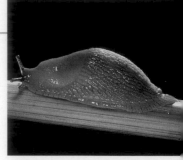

Orange garden slug

Plants attacked: Various plants, especially hostas and other shade plants.

Management strategies: Invite slug- and snail-eating toads into your garden with plenty of moisture and cover. To trap these mollusks, sink a shallow container into the ground and fill it with beer. They are attracted to the beer, crawl in and drown. Or, empty half a bottle of beer and lay it on its side. This provides a built-in roof so the beer doesn't become diluted or need replacing during wet weather. Some new granular products contain iron phosphate, which kills slugs and snails without harming other wildlife. Gardeners have reported good control with less frequent applications. On hostas, you may want to sprinkle it under the leaves to discourage birds from eating it.

Slug damage on hosta

Tent Caterpillars

Damage: Webby nests in trees and shrubs filled with caterpillars.

Time of damage: Varies with species.

The pest: There are several tent-forming caterpillars. The most common are the Eastern and Western tent caterpillars, fall webworm and euonymus caterpillar.

Look-alikes: Often mistaken for the gypsy moth.

Plants attacked: Different species feed on different plants. Euonymus tent caterpillars feed mainly feeds on euonymus. The rest feed on fruit trees,

Tent caterpillar in apple tree

walnut, birch and other ornamentals.

Management strategies: Birds, parasitic wasps and disease help keep these insects under control. Most healthy plants will re-leaf once the insect is done feeding. Use a stick to dislodge the tent and smash the caterpillars. Or, spray the tent and several feet surrounding it with *Bacillus thuringiensis*. Do not burn tents while they are still in the tree. Fire causes more damage than the hungry caterpillars.

Sucking Insects

LOOK FOR speckled, yellow or stunted leaves and distorted growth.

Aphids

Damage: Speckled and/or yellow leaves.

Time of damage: Most of the season; more of a problem during hot, dry weather.

The pest: Aphids, also known as plant lice, are small, teardrop-shaped and come in a wide range of colors. They have two small tailpipe-like projections on their backsides. Females can give birth to live aphids without mating. This factor, combined with a short life cycle, allows populations of aphids to build quickly.

Look-alikes: Spider mite damage; herbicidal damage; environmental stress.

Plants attacked: Virtually all plants.

Management strategies: Ladybugs, lacewing larvae and other predatory insects eat aphids. Summer showers or a strong blast of water from the garden hose can dislodge and help control them. Insecticidal soap, which kills insects but is gentle on plants, will control these and other soft-bodied insects. Repeat applications may be necessary. Or, set out a yellow dish of soapy water. Aphids, which are attracted to anything yellow, will go into the water and drown.

Aphids on nasturtium

Les Campbell/Positive Images

Leafhoppers

Damage: Yellow or speckled leaves, often with brown tips known as hopper burn.

Time of damage: Summer.

Leafhopper

The pest: Wedge-shaped insects that hop sideways when disturbed. Color varies with species. Leafhopper saliva is toxic to some plants, causing the characteristic hopper burn. The aster leafhopper is a carrier of aster yellow disease.

Look-alikes: Drought or other environmental stress.

Plants attacked: Flowers, vegetables, trees, shrubs and lawns.

Management strategies: Healthy plants can tolerate small infestations. Control leafhoppers on plants susceptible to aster yellow. Insecticidal soap can help keep populations down. Systemic and other pesticides can be used where damage is significant or aster yellow is a concern.

Mealybugs

Damage: Yellow leaves; honeydew present.

Time of damage: Throughout season, depending on species.

The pest: A soft-scale insect covered with white cottony filaments. Present outdoors throughout the South and in greenhouses throughout the United States. The immature stage is a translucent nymph. There may be several generations per season.

Look-alikes: Scales.

Plants attacked: Apples, avocados, citrus, grapes and other fruits; some ornamental and tropical plants.

Management strategies: Insecticidal soap will control the immature stage. Horticultural oils will control nymphs and adults. Several applications may be necessary.

Long-tailed mealybugs

Mites

Damage: Speckled or silvery foliage. Leaves may appear yellow and feel gritty. Webbing appears over time and with high populations.

Time of damage: Summer through fall, especially in hot, dry weather.

Spider mites

The pest: Mites are very small relatives of the spider. You may need a magnifying glass to see them. They have two body parts and eight legs, like other spiders. Confirm their presence by shaking a damaged leaf over a piece of white paper. If you see small specks racing across the paper, you have spider mites.

Look-alikes: Nutritional or moisture deficiencies.

Plant attacked: Most plants.

Management strategies: Don't wait for webbing to start treatment. A strong blast of water from the garden hose can dislodge and control mites. Insecticidal soap works, too. Repeat applications will be needed, since the soap kills only the insects it touches.

Plant Bugs

Damage: Speckled leaves, often accompanied by brown spots and brown leaf edges.

Four-lined plant bug (above) and damage to veronica (left)

Time of damage: All season; varies with species.

The pest: Plant bugs are true bugs—a group of insects that feed on plants and problem insects. Look closely at their backs to identify them. True bugs have a triangular marking just below the head. You may have encountered the four-lined plant bug on your mint, or the phlox plant bug that causes circular spots on garden phlox. The ash and honeylocust plant bug distorts leaves and makes itself a nuisance by falling from the tree and landing on you.

Look-alikes: Mite and aphid feeding; drought stress.

Plants attacked: Various flowers, shrubs and trees.

Management strategies: Healthy plants can tolerate feeding. Treatment is only needed when populations are high, damage is evident and plants are unhealthy or already stressed. Insecticidal soap will control populations and minimize damage. Several applications may be needed. Other insecticides also are effective.

Scales

Damage: Yellow leaves, stunted growth, lack of vigor.

Time of damage: Throughout growing season; varies with species.

Scales

The pest: Mature scales have hard white, brown or black shells and can be scraped off the plant. Immature scales are translucent. They move around a plant, looking for a place to feed and form the hard shell after they begin feeding. Females lay eggs under the shell.

Look-alikes: Galls; mealybugs.

Plants attacked: Flowers, ground covers, shrubs and trees.

Management strategies: Dormant treatments can be used to kill overwintering eggs. Insecticidal soap or horticulture oils are effective at killing nymphs. Systemic insecticides are applied to the soil, absorbed by the plant and eventually ingested by the scales. No matter what type of control you use, timing is critical for success. Check the label for specifics.

Spittlebugs

Damage: Looks as though someone has spit on the plant. Plants look fine otherwise.

Time of damage: Summer; varies with species.

Spittlebug

The pest: A small insect, sometimes called a froghopper, sucks plant juices. It uses its legs as bellows to make its liquid secretions frothy.

Plants attacked: Various plants.

Management strategies: Spittlebug populations generally remain low and plants are not damaged, so no treatment is needed. If populations rise and damage occurs, a strong blast of water or insecticidal soap provides sufficient control.

Whiteflies

Whiteflies

Damage: Yellow, stunted plants, often with honeydew on leaves.

Time of damage: Year-round in greenhouses and warm regions; summers only in colder areas.

The pest: The adult is a small white flying insect. When disturbed, large numbers often fly away in a white cloud. Immature whiteflies are translucent and resemble immature scales.

Plants attacked: Flowers, vegetables, citrus and various ornamentals.

Look-alikes: Mite and aphid damage; environmental stress.

Management strategies: Most healthy plants can tolerate feeding, and cold winter temperatures will kill any whiteflies in Northern gardens. Control only if plants are showing signs of stress or damage. Sticky traps can be used, but cover traps to keep birds off while allowing insects in. Neem, horticultural oils and other insecticides also can be used.

Borers

INSECTS THAT BORE into the stems and trunks of trees interfere with the flow of water and nutrients between the leaves and roots. Plants infested by borers begin to wilt, the leaves turn brown and branches die. Sometimes borers kill the entire plant.

Stalk Borers

Damage: Leaves and growing tips wilt, yellow and brown or break off in high winds. Sawdust-like droppings may be found at base of plant.

Time of damage: Summer and fall; varies with species.

The pest: Larvae of several different insect species.

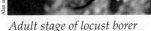

Adult stage of locust borer

Look-alikes: Drought stress; root rot.

Plants attacked: Lilies, potatoes and other thick-stemmed ornamentals and vegetables.

Management strategies: Control weeds throughout the growing season, prune out infested areas and clean up the garden and surrounding area in fall. Destroy borer-infested stems. Don't put them in the compost pile.

Tree and Shrub Borers

Damage: Upper leaves and branches wilt, yellow and brown. Infested branches may wither and die. Plant goes into decline and may die.

Time of damage: Spring through fall, depending on species.

The pest: Caterpillars, grubs and beetles.

Look-alikes: Drought stress; decline.

Plants attacked: Borers usually attack trees and shrubs stressed by weather, the environment and other pests.

Management strategies: Select the right plant for existing growing conditions and provide proper care to keep it healthy and borer-resistant. Prune out dead branches and stems. If a borer attacks, consult a certified arborist. Timing and proper application are critical for chemical control.

Miscellaneous Pests

Ants

Damage: Mounds of soil that make mowing difficult or expose plant roots to drying.

Time of damage: All season.

Anthill

The pest: Ants can be red, brown or black, from 1/6 to 3/4 inch long. They have pinched waists. Ants eat sugars and proteins. Many build their nests underground.

Look-alikes: Drought stress.

Plants attacked: Ants are more active in stressed lawns and gardens.

Management strategies: Some ants are insect predators, making them a friend to gardeners. Some can signal the presence of aphids, as they feed on the honeydew secreted by these pests. Try living with them. You can use commercial baits or insecticides to control troublesome infestations.

Gall-Forming Insects

Damage: Bumps on leaves and stems; other distorted growths. Plants look fine otherwise.

Time of damage: Much of the feeding occurs in early spring; growths become evident later in the season.

The pest: Aphids, mites and psyllids (small sucking insects) feed on flowers, emerging leaves and other plant parts. The feeding stimulates plant growth. The

Oak gall

lumps and bumps, called galls, are actually part of the plant. The insect spends part of its life inside the gall.

Look-alikes: Canker scale.

Plants attacked: Various galls are found on maples and oaks. Other varieties include ash flower gall, hackberry nipple gall and many more.

Management strategies: No treatment is necessary. The galls look bad, but usually do not affect plant health. Dormant oil sprays will kill many of the overwintering insects that cause galls, but this is done strictly for aesthetics.

Leaf Miners

Damage: Trails and blotches in leaves.

Time of damage: Spring and summer, as new leaves emerge.

The pest: Larvae of flies, sawflies, butterflies and beetles.

Leaf miner damage to hibiscus

Plants attacked: Arborvitae, columbine, birches, hollyhocks, beets, spinach and others.

Look-alikes: Viral disease.

Management strategies: Treatment is usually not needed and often doesn't succeed anyway, since it's too late to treat once the damage is noticed. Adjusting planting times, covering susceptible plants or pruning back affected foliage will help eliminate damage on some crops. Systemic insecticides can be applied to the soil for stressed and declining plants.

Thrips

Damage: Brown streaks, yellow leaves, distorted leaves and flowers.

Time of damage: Summer.

The pest: A small insect with a long, narrow body and fringed wings. You'll need a magnifying glass to see it.

Look-alikes: Mite and aphid damage; drought stress; disease.

Plants attacked: Gladiolus and other flowers; trees and shrubs.

Management strategies: Some thrips are predators of aphids and other harmful insects. Others serve as disease vectors, spreading viruses from sick to healthy plants. Discard or treat thrip-infested gladiolus corms before storing for winter. Chemical treatment is recommended where the spread of disease is a concern.

Thrips (below) and damage (right)

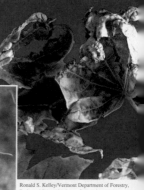

Ronald S. Kelley/Vermont Department of Forestry, Parks and Recreation/www.forestryimages.org

Jack T. Reed/Mississippi State University

The *Plant Doctor* is in

Q: Ants have invaded my lawn. I occasionally find them in my home. Someone told me to pour boiling water over the nest. What do you think?

A: Boiling water usually gets the ants to quickly abandon their nest, but they generally set up housekeeping in another spot in your yard. Improving the health of your lawn will reduce problems.

You can help keep ants out of the house by using a solution of water and vinegar. This solution destroys the scent trail and prevents scout ants from leading others into your home. Ants are more of a nuisance than a hazard, but if you can't tolerate their presence, commercial traps and insecticides provide the most effective control.

Q: Is there anything I can spray in my yard to prevent insects from damaging my flowers, trees and shrubs?

A: There are a few soil systemics that are applied in fall to control insect damage the following spring and summer. These products are labeled for specific pests and many require a certified pesticide applicator.

However, it's best to avoid preventative sprays. They can waste your time and money, since you may be applying a product for a problem that will never occur. They're often ineffective, too, because the spray and the insect aren't in the landscape at the same time. Let nature take care of insect prevention. Birds, toads and insects eat troublesome pests. Spraying in advance often kills the predators, allowing the pests to feed freely. The less spraying we do, the more nature can help.

Q: Can I use any soap to kill the insects on my plants?

A: Insecticidal soap is basically soap that has been developed for killing insects without damaging most plants. Dish washing and laundry soaps have been evaluated for cleaning dishes and clothes, not for killing insects or use on plants. If you want to try a homemade soap-and-water solution, test it first by spraying a leaf or two. Wait a day and watch for brown spots or other indications the plant was dam-

aged. If it's unharmed, set this bottle of detergent aside for use on your plants. But test every new bottle before spraying. Manufacturers often change formulas to improve cleaning power, and these changes may damage your plants. I prefer to buy insecticidal soap and let someone else do the testing.

Q: My paper birch has bronze birch borer. Is there anything I can do?

A: A healthy tree is the best defense against borers. This goes for infested trees as well. Remove the grass around the base of your tree to reduce the competition for water and nutrients. Mulch the soil with wood chips, or plant ground covers or low-growing shrubs under the tree canopy. This will help keep the roots cool and moist. Make this tree a high priority and water thoroughly whenever the soil starts to dry. Prune out any dead branches and watch for further damage. If dieback continues, you'll need to consult a certified arborist to save the tree. These professionals have access to materials that may control the borers.

Keeping a paper birch tree healthy is the best defense against bronze birch borers.

Chapter 11
It's a Zoo Out There

A deer lifts her head, startled by the sound of your footsteps. She lifts her tail, quickly surveys the landscape and bolts into the woods.

It's a beautiful sight anyone would love—until you realize the gentle creature was feasting on your tulips, roses and other flowers.

Now cue the cute bunnies with their numerous offspring. They'll polish off the rest of your plants.

Don't get me wrong—I like to see backyard wildlife. But I also understand the frustration these creatures cause gardeners.

Rural, suburban and even city gardeners may be surprised to find a variety of wildlife dining on their landscape. I've seen fox, deer, coyotes and other animals where I live—right in the heart of a busy metropolitan neighborhood.

I've stopped complaining about the damage they do since I've seen the photos *Birds & Blooms* readers share of moose eating their petunias and bears raiding bird feeders! That kind of wildlife makes the bunnies and squirrels look like minor pests!

As we talk about managing these creatures, keep this in mind: They were here first.

The more we build in their habitat, the more we force them to live in smaller spaces, making it more difficult for them to find food and shelter. And as they become used to us, it becomes more difficult to keep them out of our yards, garages, gardens and even our homes.

I really appreciate wildlife's beauty and place in our world, but my job is to help you find ways to co-exist with animals *and* keep your garden alive. So we'll tread lightly as we find common ground for enjoying wildlife while minimizing their damage.

Preventing Wildlife Invasions

KEEPING ANIMALS from eating your landscape plants is a huge challenge. Some plants, such as lilies, are like candy to deer and rabbits, while other plants, like daffodils, are usually left alone.

I find that animals' eating preferences vary from season to season, which may explain why there are so many discrepancies among lists of plants susceptible to animal damage. And if populations are high and food is limited, most animals will eat just about anything to survive.

I recommend starting your own list. Monitor plants that animals tend to let be, so that you can consider those as replacements for the plants in your garden that are devoured.

I also welcome predators into my landscape. Owls, hawks and other birds can't help with deer, but they do a good job reducing the voles, rabbits and other small mammal populations.

But if you want to attract songbirds as well, I recommend adding plenty of plantings for protective cover. That way, predators will focus on the unwanted wildlife, not the birds you're trying to attract.

Rolling Up the Welcome Mat

Wildlife, like people, need food, water, shelter and space. It's become quite common for gardeners to create ideal habitat to maximize their viewing opportunities. In fact, the National Wildlife Federation certifies yards as Backyard Wildlife Habitats for homeowners who provide these exact resources for animals.

But, if you want to keep the critters out, you'll need to do the exact opposite—create a not-so-inviting yard. Take a look around to see if you're providing a welcome mat for wildlife you'd rather not have. Here are some simple steps to help:

- **Brush piles.** They're great for attracting birds, but they're also perfect hiding spots for rabbits.
- **Patch holes and cracks.** Do this in the garage or other outbuildings.
- **Close doors and windows.** We ended up with three kittens this spring because someone left the garage door open.
- **Eliminate sources of water.** The birdbath, weed bucket left in the rain or tiny water garden all provide this basic element for survival.

If you want to attract more songbirds, put out a birdbath. But you'll also have to deal with the raccoons that visit in the evenings. To keep geese from ponds, try to grow tall grasses and other plantings around them.

- **Don't provide easy food sources.** Skunks and raccoons love birdseed or dry dog and cat food. Keep these in critter-resistant containers. You'll also want to use baffles on your bird feeders to keep these raiders from stealing your food.

Some people have tried the opposite approach—they feed animals in an attempt to keep them out of the garden.

My friend Val Heidenreich, a Master Gardener from West Allis, Wisconsin, buys peanuts for the

chipmunks and squirrels. She insists this keeps them out of her vegetable garden.

Just be wary—not all creatures are as considerate as Val's. Feeding certain animals, like deer, may be illegal in your community and may attract more critters besides. You may lure them in with an appetizer, only to find they use your garden for the main course.

Putting Up Barriers

If changing habitat doesn't work, try fencing. The key is to have a fence high enough that critters can't crawl or jump over, and low enough that they can't slither or burrow under.

Rabbits need at least a 4-foot fence that's snug to the ground. Those baby bunnies can squeeze through the tightest openings. And voles can excavate their way to your plants, so bury the fence several inches deep.

And while this sounds like an exaggeration, deer really need a fence 10 feet high or they will be able to jump it. That's not very practical or attractive.

Try fencing smaller areas with a 5-foot-high fence. Deer seem to avoid entering small spaces, even though they can easily jump the barrier.

I know what you're thinking—"I don't want an ugly fence blocking the view of my flowers." There is an item called deer fencing (a black mesh-type material) mounted on attractive wrought-iron posts that keeps out the deer with little obstruction of the view. Sure, it would be nicer without the fence, but it's better than looking at plants sheared to the ground by animals.

Electric fences can help keep animals from larger areas. These produce a mild shock when touched, and it doesn't take long for animals to steer clear of it. Check with your local community for any possible restrictions.

Applying Repellents

Whether you have a homemade recipe or you buy them, repellents are designed to fend off wildlife with odor and bad taste.

I've tested several of these products and concoctions and found that effectiveness varies with location and time of year.

Urban animals, surrounded by people and our smells, are less responsive to repellents than animals in more rural areas. Wherever you live, it's important to monitor the product's effectiveness. What works for your neighbor might not work for you.

Water is essential for wildlife survival. Birdbaths provide the perfect spot for raccoons to drink and wash their food.

Homemade Repellents

MANY GARDENERS have resorted to homemade repellents to keep wildlife at bay. When mixing any concoction, follow this green-thumb rule: Make sure it's safe for you, your children, pets and wildlife. We want to scare animals away, not make them sick.

As with commercial repellents, monitor effectiveness and make changes when needed. Many of these remedies will need to be replaced after rainfall.

● **Hair:** A handful of human hair placed in an old nylon stocking can be hung from the lower branches of trees or on fence posts. This has proven to be an effective deterrent in some areas. Ask your barber or hairstylist to save a bag of clippings for you.

● **Hot pepper:** Sprinkle cayenne pepper on plants. To make a spray, mix 1 to 2 tablespoons pepper powder or Tabasco sauce and 2 tablespoons of Spreader Sticker (an odorless additive), a wetting agent, soap or horticultural oil in a gallon of water. Gardeners have reported commercial versions of this product seem to last longer.

● **Rotten eggs:** Recipes abound for mixing eggs and water to sprinkle on your plants, but be careful to avoid food poisoning. Always wash your hands afterward—a good idea with any repellent—and keep the mixture off edible plants.

● **Garlic:** Chop, mince and place in a permeable

container or mix with water and spray onto plants.

● **Mothballs:** Some gardeners find this a great repellent for rabbits and squirrels, but I've had an equal number tell me they've found wildlife rolling on them (this controls body lice). You decide. Just tuck them away out of reach of children, pets and desirable wildlife. Several commercial repellents contain naphthalene, the stuff mothballs are made of.

● **Bar soap:** Strongly scented deodorant soaps (above) may keep animals away. Some gardeners slice or grate it up and sprinkle it throughout the garden. Others hang bars of soap in net bags from trees, posts and structures near prime feeding areas.

● **Used cat litter:** Some gardeners find that cat odor helps keep wildlife out. Wear rubber gloves to spread litter box contents around your plants. Several cat diseases can affect people.

● **Dog droppings:** Use gloves to distribute and when working in areas where you've placed them.

A landscaper I know had great success using cayenne pepper to ward off deer. He bought the hottest pepper available through Mexican restaurant supply companies. His crews wore goggles and gloves and applied the pepper early in the morning, when dew was still on the plants. It worked like a charm.

When I told my horticulture class this story, one student said the nearby golf course where he worked used the same pepper technique and found the deer actually *preferred* the peppered plants. I guess they were ready for a little spice in their life!

I've learned that these methods will be more effective if you apply them before the animals start feeding and vary the repellents used.

Keep records of what works and what doesn't. Some repellents may be more effective against certain animals at different times of the season. Building on your experience will improve future results. But remember, if they're hungry enough, wildlife will eat anything, no matter how it tastes or smells.

Scare Tactics

If bad tastes and smells don't do the trick, resort to plan B—scare tactics. Try whirligigs, rubber snakes, inflatable owls, plastic bags, foil pans, scarecrows, motion-sensing items—the list goes on and on.

Gardeners and groundskeepers often employ these and other scare tactics. Many say they work, while others have had little to no success. My personal experience has been the latter.

Once I attended a fund-raiser at Boerner Botanical Gardens in Hales Corners, Wisconsin. The tent was filled with more than 200 people, dinner was being served and the band was so loud you couldn't hear the conversation at your own table. Then someone returned to our table to inform us the deer had joined in the fun. Not 50 feet away, deer were eating the roses! So much for the sound and smell of humans scaring away wildlife.

As with repellents, use a variety of tactics so the animals don't get used to them. This will help improve success. Wildlife will venture into the garden if the inflatable owl or rubber snake sits in the same spot too long. Mix things up.

This is one advantage of motion-sensing devices. Flashing lights, spraying water or noisemakers triggered by an animal's motion add randomness and the element of surprise.

Setting Traps

To me, trapping is a last resort. Many gardeners think that using "live traps" and relocating the wildlife is a more humane alternative, but it can actually be less humane if done improperly.

Being trapped and moved to a different location can be extremely stressful for all animals. Mothers and babies are often separated, and the result is starvation. Or, some people forget to check the trap regularly and the animals become dehydrated or starve.

The other problem with live trapping is where to release them once you have an animal in the cage. Park personnel, farmers and landscape managers don't want any extra wildlife—they have enough of their own to deal with.

Even if you find a spot, another animal is probably on its way to your yard to claim the vacant territory. I've personally witnessed this myself when I worked with the city forestry department. One of our gardeners redesigned the plantings outside the municipal building, which included a few known favorites of rabbits.

Rather than protect the plants, the gardeners trapped and removed the rabbits to prevent damage. A short time later, I received a call from an amused resident across the street who said, "Look out the window—

they're headed your way."

Sure enough, there was a rabbit hopping across a busy four-lane city street to get to the newly renovated garden buffet.

I guess the *real* last resort is poison, snap trapping and suffocation. Think carefully before choosing any of these options.

First, you should contact the Department of Natural Resources in your area to find out if your community, state or the federal government has any regulations on trapping and destroying wildlife in your area. All native birds and many animals are protected by local, state or federal laws.

Then stop and think about the environmental consequences and potential risk to other wildlife, pets and children.

Snap traps baited with peanut butter and oats are effective against ground squirrels and chipmunks. Hide them in PVC pipe or under cover to keep songbirds and other wildlife away. Trapping can be tough to do, though, when the rodent has a furry tail and looks like Disney's Chip and Dale.

Gas cartridges, available at garden centers, are often used for burrowing animals. Read and follow all label directions, and never use these in burrows under or next to the foundation of the house. Block all but one entryway, toss in the cartridge and cover the last hole. Following the directions will improve your success and ensure your safety.

A friend of mine, who shall remain nameless, did not heed the label warnings. He filled the woodchuck holes, inserted the cartridge and waited. He didn't think it was working, so he lit a kerosene-soaked rag and threw it into the hole.

When the explosion hit, he finally realized he was

Live traps are available for purchase at garden centers and farm supply companies. Some local health departments and humane societies will rent these traps as well.

standing next to an unplugged hole. Luckily, he escaped injury, though he was more than a little surprised. And I think the woodchuck got a chuckle as he watched.

Coordinated Efforts

The most successful wildlife control is a coordinated approach. I once read about a family that installed a tall decorative fence around the gardens near their home. The remaining 8 acres were planted with trees, shrubs and flowers the wildlife seemed to ignore.

The family used repellents and scare tactics on a few special or new plantings. They still had some damage, but the important point is that it was tolerable. They could still enjoy their landscape and the wildlife they'd moved to the country to see.

Most of us don't have such large properties to manage, but even a small city or suburban lot can have its challenges. And chances are if the wildlife is feeding in your backyard, they're also doing the same on the entire block or neighborhood. That means quite a few people need to manage the wildlife.

Start by working together. Make sure one neighbor isn't attracting wildlife for the others to trap and haul away. Neither you or your neighbor will be successful or happy when you're working toward opposite goals in small nearby spaces.

Wildlife Resources

THERE'S NEVER ENOUGH space to share everything I would like, and there's always so much more for all of us, myself included, to learn.

As you begin battling wildlife or decide to invite some into your landscape, you may need more information. Start by contacting your local Extension office and Department of Natural Resources. Here are a few additional resources you may find useful:

• Wildlife Damage Management Fact Sheet Series from Cornell University Extension: *www.dnr.cornell.edu/ext/wildlifedamage/publications.htm*

• The North Dakota Game and Fish Department's site on building nesting structures and various feeders includes many of the same birds and animals found elsewhere in the U.S.: *www.npwrc.usgs.gov/resource/tools/ndblinds/ndblinds.htm*

• The U.S. Department of Agriculture's Animal and Plant Health Inspection Service resources, including publications: *www.aphis.usda.gov/*

• USDA's Natural Resource Conservation Service tips on attracting wildlife: *www.nrcs.usda.gov/feature/backyard/*

• USDA's Wildlife Habitat Management Institute: *www.ms.nrcs.usda.gov/whmi/*

Who's Eating My Plants?

DAMAGE AND EVIDENCE	WILDLIFE
Damage to beehives	Bears, skunks
Burrows, tunnels	Chipmunks, ground squirrels, moles, woodchucks
Droppings	Birds, free-ranging domestic cats, dogs, geese
Eaten flowers, vegetables	Birds, bears, chipmunks, deer, elk, moose, ground squirrels, squirrels, voles, woodchucks
Eaten bark and branches	Bears, deer, elk, moose, rabbits, voles
Rubbed or stripped bark	Deer, elk, moose, bears, squirrels, woodchucks
Turf damage	Armadillos, moles, raccoons, skunks, voles

Wildlife Profiles

Armadillos

Damage: Root in lawns and gardens looking for food.

Evidence: Twilight feeder. Look for trails to den and three-toed tracks.

Nine-banded armadillo

Habitat: Brushy areas and woodlands near rivers and creeks.

Food preferences: Earthworms, insects, insect larvae, tender roots and shoots.

Control strategies: Clear brush, remove food source (insects in the lawn). Trap but handle with care—may have transferable disease.

Bears

Damage: Chew and claw saplings; pull large strips of bark from trees and eat cambium layer; tear up turf; damage beehives and bird feeders.

Evidence: Nocturnal feeders. Look for damage, tracks and droppings.

Habitat: Heavily wooded areas.

Food preferences: Trees, shrubs, vegetables, nuts, fruits and honey. May tear up turf looking for insects.

Control strategies: Clean up and secure food. Loud noises may provide temporary relief. Check with DNR before taking more aggressive action.

Black bear

Birds

Damage: Eat seedlings, vegetables and fruit; pluck leaves and flowers for nesting material; build nests in hanging baskets.

Evidence: Nests, droppings, flocking.

Habitat: Dense plantings of evergreens, fruiting trees, bushes and berries.

Food preferences: Varies with species.

Control strategies: State and federal laws protect all native birds. Start control strategies as soon as damage appears. Cover plants with netting to prevent damage. A variety of sound and motion scare tactics may help.

Northern mockingbird

Free-Ranging Domestic Cats

Damage: Use gardens as litter box and hunt songbirds and small mammals you may be trying to attract to your garden.

Evidence: Digging, droppings and smell (males spray their territories).

Habitat: Abandoned buildings, junked cars, brush piles, culverts and other covered and protected locations.

Food preferences: Birds, mice and small rodents.

Control strategies: First, be aware that domestic cats are considered private property if tagged and registered. Otherwise, they are considered feral and the property of the landowner where they reside.

Clean up junk piles, brush piles and other areas that provide food and shelter. Repellents may protect small areas. Contact your local humane society for other recommendations.

Domestic cat

Eastern chipmunk

Chipmunks

Damage: Dig in gardens and retaining walls; feed on seeds, plants and flower bulbs; restless hibernator in winter and may continue to feed on stored food.

Evidence: Usually visible as they run through the landscape with tail in the air. Look for an accumulation of seed hulls.

Habitat: Mature woodlands and woodlot edges; also found in and around suburban and rural homes.

Food preferences: These omnivores primarily eat grains, nuts, berries, seeds, mushrooms, insects and salamanders. May eat bird eggs or nestlings.

Control strategies: Avoid continuous ground covers and garden plantings that connect wooded areas to your home's foundation. Scare tactics and repellents usually aren't effective. Snap traps are an option, but can be dangerous to songbirds and other wildlife in your backyard.

Other Ground Squirrels

Damage: Similar to that of chipmunks, which often are blamed for ground squirrels' feeding. They hibernate in winter. In summer, they dig new plantings, eat seeds and vegetables and burrow in lawns and under buildings.

Evidence: Daytime feeder; runs with its tail down.

Habitat: Prefers grassy areas like parks, cemeteries and lawns.

Thirteen-lined ground squirrel

Food preferences: Feeds on a variety of seeds, plants and insects.

Control strategies: Chase them out by flooding or tilling their burrows. Some gardeners report luck with using dried blood and mothballs as repellents. Poisonous baits may require special permission or a certified applicator and may be harmful to predatory birds. Fumigants and live or snap traps are a last resort and may be harmful to songbirds and other wildlife.

Deer, Elk and Moose

Damage: Rub on trunks; trample small trees; eat just about everything, including tree branches, bark, small trees (feeding damage leaves a telltale curl of wood) and various flowers and vegetables.

Moose

Evidence: Tracks, droppings, sightings.

Habitat: Deer at forest edge; elk near forests by natural clearings; moose in dense mixed forest near water.

Food preferences: Will eat almost any plant material. Eating habits can vary throughout the season and from year to year.

Control strategies: Try a combination and variety of repellents and scare tactics. Tall fences (over 8 feet), electric fencing and short fences around small gardens can protect valuable plantings. Many communities restrict feeding and are trying to manage populations in heavily populated or agricultural areas.

It's a Zoo Out There

Canada goose

Geese

Damage: Eat field crops; messy droppings. Aggressive nature can cause conflicts with people.

Evidence: Droppings, sightings.

Habitat: Ponds surrounded by mowed grass, farm fields and parks.

Food preferences: Grains.

Control strategies: The Migratory Bird Treaty of 1918 protects geese. Grow tall plants near ponds and water features, and don't feed the birds. Repellents are showing some success. Noise, dogs, swans and other scare tactics may help.

Moles

Damage: In summer, dig temporary surface feeding tunnels that damage lawns and other plants by exposing the roots. In winter, they're harmless because they hibernate. Often blamed for plant damage caused by voles.

Evidence: Look for heart-shaped molehill by burrow entrance.

Habitat: These loners live in underground burrows in cool, moist, well-drained soils.

Food preferences: Insects and worms.

Control strategies: Tamp soil to destroy tunnels or flood them. You can remove their food source — grubs in the lawn—although this will harm beneficial insects as well. Trapping with choker or harpoon traps will require persistence and repeated attempts; move and reset trap if no success in 2 days. Other options include thiram-based repellents or gas cartridges for fumigation.

Eastern mole

Rabbits

Damage: Eat flowers, fruits, leaves, bark and stems of many ornamental and edible plants.

Evidence: Droppings; when they feed on branches, they leave a clean cut at a 45-degree angle.

Habitat: Brushy fence-rows, field edges, brush piles and similar shelter.

Rabbits

Food preferences: Variety of flowers and vegetables, branches, small shrubs and trees; tree bark in winter.

Control strategies: The term "multiplying like rabbits" is true—one female can produce six litters of six bunnies each per season. Install tree guards of 1/2 inch wire mesh around trees and shrubs at least 3 to 4 inches in the ground and 4 feet high. Fence gardens with chicken wire at least 4 feet high. Cats, dogs, owls, fox and hawks are natural predators. Remove piles of brush, stones or junk. For repellents, try homemade or commercial formulas, mothballs or blood meal. Trapping and shooting should be a last resort; check local ordinances. Rabbits carry disease, so do not handle.

Raccoons

Damage: Eat a variety of vegetables, making a mess in the process; disturb turf when rooting for grubs; raid gardens, garbage cans and bird feeders; and invade homes, garages and outbuildings.

Raccoon

Evidence: Pawprint (looks like a small human hand); dog-like droppings.

Habitat: Forests near water and in sewer systems in urban areas.

Food preferences: These omnivores are night feeders and will eat whatever they can find.

Control strategies: Store birdseed, cat and dog food indoors or in sealed containers. Try scare tactics; use repellents like mothballs, blood meal or dog droppings (handle with care). You can trap and move them to a site at least 10 miles away, but raccoon populations are too high for this to be effective. Raccoons carry rabies, so it's best not to handle them.

Gray squirrel

Evidence: Sightings; leafy nests in trees.

Habitat: Wooded areas, parks, landscapes with trees.

Food preferences: Fruits, nuts, vegetables and bark.

Control strategies: Thiram-based repellents and mothballs may help. Temporarily wrap tree trunks with metal sheeting or install squirrel baffles. Use baffles or squirrel-resistant bird feeders. Cover bulbs with chicken wire at planting. Catch with live or snap traps, but be careful. These traps are dangerous to other wildlife and songbirds in your yard.

Skunks

Damage: Disturb and damage turf when rooting for grubs; damage beehives; and spray offensive odor.

Evidence: Night feeder; watch for tracks with 5 toes on front and hind paws. Droppings usually show undigested insect parts.

Habitat: Clearings, open areas. Skunks seek shelter in open logs, thickets, under decks and in window wells.

Striped skunk

Food preferences: They prefer insects, but also eat plants, rodents and small mammals.

Control strategies: Remove dog and cat food from outside dishes. Cover window wells and pits. Put skirting on decks and close off other elevated structures to keep skunks from nesting beneath them. Elevate beehives. Fence yard or garden at least 2 feet above ground and 12 inches deep, or 6 inches down and 6 inches outward. Mothballs may drive them away.

Squirrels

Damage: Dig bulbs; eat and disturb plants as they bury seeds; plant black walnuts and other unwanted trees; and strip tree bark, which they use for food and nests.

Voles/Meadow Mice

Damage: Feed day and night, year-round, on seeds, bulbs and rhizomes. Most damage to landscape plants occurs in winter. Voles may chew tree and

Meadow vole

shrub bark near soil surface; wear trails into the turf over winter; and chew roots of hostas, Siberian iris and other fleshy-rooted perennials. Populations peak every 2 to 5 years.

Evidence: Winter damage is evident in spring as snow recedes—tooth marks at different angles, varying from light scratches to indentations.

Habitat: Grassy areas.

Food preferences: Seeds, bulbs, rhizomes; in winter, tree trunks and shrub stems.

Control strategies: Protect seedlings, young trees and shrubs with tree guards made of 1/2 inch wire mesh sunk 3 to 4 inches into the ground and 4 feet high. Remove weeds, tall grass and debris, which can provide cover. Repellents do not seem effective. Try placing poisonous baits and snap traps baited with peanut butter and oats in PVC pipe or similar object to prevent harming songbirds, pets and other wildlife.

Yellow-bellied marmot

Woodchucks and Marmots

Damage: Quickly eat plants to the ground; strip bark off young trees; burrow under plantings, exposing and drying roots; excavate under structures. They hibernate in winter.

Evidence: Burrows with a large mound of earth at the entrance; trails from feeding areas to dens. Prefer to feed in early morning and evening.

Habitat: Woodland edges and grassy areas with well-drained soils; burrows under sheds and porches in urban areas.

Food preferences: Eat almost any plant.

Control strategies: Eliminate brush piles and overgrown areas, although this will eliminate habitat of desirable wildlife as well. Fence gardens with at least 10 to 12 inches of fencing below ground and 4 feet above ground, with the top bent outward, or try electric fencing 4 to 5 inches above ground. Gas cartridges sold at garden centers can be used if burrows *are not* located next to or under buildings (be sure to read label directions). Check with your Department of Natural Resources before trapping or shooting; some states have laws protecting these animals.

Woodpeckers

Damage: Drill holes in wood siding; make noise during spring breeding and when hunting for food in fall.

✔ *Melinda's Tips*

IF GARDEN INVADERS are eating your hostas, try substituting lungwort (*Pulmonaria*). Lungwort has a similar growth habit and appearance. The leaves are green, blotched or variegated, and the white, mauve or purple flowers are a nice surprise in early spring. Deer and rabbits seem to leave this plant alone, although slugs won't.

Evidence: Pounding sound; feeding damage.

Habitat: Wooded areas.

Food preference: Insects in trees and untreated cedar-sided homes.

Control strategies: Take action as soon as damage begins. Noisemakers, balloons and other scare tactics may work if started immediately. Treat siding to kill insects and repel woodpeckers; remove ledges and other footholds. Cover drain spouts, siding or tree trunks with burlap or other material to deaden sound. Cover damaged areas with screening. Federal and state laws protect all woodpeckers.

Pileated woodpecker

The *Plant Doctor* is in

Q: *Every spring, my lawn is covered with trails of dead and disturbed grass. Are moles causing this damage? How can I stop it?*

A: Moles are often blamed, but they are not the problem. Voles, also called meadow mice, were busy running around your lawn looking for food, while the moles spent their winter hibernating underground.

Gently tamp the disturbed grass back in place. The surrounding grass will quickly fill in these worn trails. You can speed up the process by overseeding large damaged areas.

Q: *The animals are destroying my garden. A fence doesn't seem to keep them out. Are there any repellents that work on food plants?*

A: Check your fence for weak spots. Tears or small openings near the soil line or by the gate can provide sufficient space for some animals to enter. Noise-makers and motion-sensing sprinklers may give added benefits.

Use a coordinated effort to reduce animal damage. You can include Hinder, Hot Pepper Wax, Deer Off or other repellents labeled for use on food crops, but wash them well so they don't repel you, too.

Line your garden fence with chicken wire to keep critters out.

Q: *Squirrels keep digging up my bulbs. Is there any way to stop them?*

A: I have the same problem. I find a few of my tulips each spring in the adjacent park. Try using some naphthalene flakes, hot pepper or other repellents labeled for this problem. If this doesn't work, you may want to try creating a barrier. Dig the planting hole to the proper depth. Set bulbs in the bottom of the hole and cover with an inch of soil. Place chicken wire over the top of the bulbs, with the sides bent around the edges. Finish filling the planting hole with soil. This will discourage squirrels, chipmunks and ground squirrels from doing any unwelcome transplanting.

Q: *Voles destroyed my hostas, Siberian iris and a few other perennials this winter. Someone suggested I cut them down in fall to prevent this type of damage next year. I love the winter interest these plants provide. Is there any other solution?*

A: I have been informally surveying gardeners on just this topic. Most gardeners who let their perennials stand all winter don't experience vole damage. The few who did experience damage started cutting their perennials back in fall.

To reduce the risk, monitor vole populations in fall. You may want to use snap traps baited with peanut butter and oats when the populations are high. Place these in a PVC pipe or other containers to prevent harm to birds, pets and other wildlife. Check plants as soon as the snow recedes. Remove damaged portions of plants and replant the healthy divisions.

Q: *The trunks of several of my trees are riddled with holes. I think sapsuckers are killing them. How can I make them stop?*

A: Sapsuckers tap tree trunks looking for tree sap. Their shallow feeding rarely harms trees. Provide the plant with proper care to keep it healthy and better able to recover from the feeding. If you're very concerned, you can wrap the feeding area with burlap or hardware cloth to discourage the birds. Try installing a few scare tactics if you're unable to wrap the trunk.

Chapter 12
Keeping Plants Healthy and Fit

Shirley Bryant; opposite page: Alan and Linda Detrick

"My juniper has been slimed!" No, it's not a scene from *Ghostbusters*. It's cedar-apple rust fungus, which attacks red cedars (*Juniperus virginiana*) in landscapes across the country.

This and many other slimy, rotting and disgusting things grow on and in trees, shrubs and flowers. Despite their ugly appearance, most are not harmful to the long-term health of your plants. So don't let all this slime stop you from gardening.

Like insect problems, many diseases are related to the weather and are often cyclical in nature. We can't adjust the weather, but we can adjust our selection and care of plants to minimize problems.

Diseases caused by living organisms (fungi, bacteria and viruses) can cause harmful and abnormal growths. These may show up as spots, blotches and lumps on leaves, stems and roots.

Weather, pollution, nutrient deficiencies and environmental stresses also can produce these symptoms, but we'll talk about these causes in the next chapter.

Three Parts to Plant Disease

FOR A DISEASE to become established in a plant, it needs all three parts of the "disease triangle" —a disease-causing organism (pathogen) in an infectious stage of development; proper weather conditions for it to grow and multiply; and a susceptible plant at the right stage of *its* development. Remove or change one of the three factors, and plant disease can't develop.

Plant diseases are more difficult to

Susceptible Plant

DISEASE

Pathogen

Weather Conditions

identify than insects and weeds. The pathogen is usually microscopic and hidden within the plant, so the symptoms are our only visible clues. Common plant disease symptoms are listed on page 186.

Like insects, diseases have a life cycle. Understanding how diseases infect plants, grow and reproduce can help you keep them out of your garden or keep them under control if they invade.

The first step is inoculation, where the pathogen contacts the host. Wind, rain, running water, birds, insects and wildlife are nature's way of spreading disease. We help out by transporting pathogens on our garden tools, feet and hands. A few pathogens can move short distances on their own.

Once the pathogen reaches a susceptible plant, it needs to find a way inside. Wounds, pores and other natural openings provide access. Some pathogens create their own entryways by secreting an enzyme that dissolves a portion of the leaf surface.

Pathogens may be ready to enter the plant as soon as they arrive. Others, like fungi, must grow penetration pegs to enter these openings. Many types of bacteria are carried into a plant through water, while others depend on insects or humans to help it get inside. The same is true for other pathogens.

Infection occurs once the pathogen has established a parasitic relationship with the host plant. We don't observe the symptoms until the plant shows signs of responding to the pathogen, which may take a few days, weeks or longer.

Controlling Diseases

SINCE WE DON'T SEE disease symptoms until after pathogens have already invaded and established themselves, disease control is difficult.

Most chemicals that kill pathogens inside the plant are damaging or deadly to the plant itself. That's why most disease-controlling chemicals can only prevent infection, not cure existing disease.

Record keeping and an understanding of the disease triangle are critical for successful management of sick plants. These pieces of information will help you track past problems, predict the risk of future infection and create a management strategy that's effective and environmentally friendly. This is where the Plant Health Care System comes in—again.

Prevention

I know you're tired of hearing this, but a healthy plant is the best defense. Selecting a plant that's suited for the growing conditions and providing proper care reduces the risk of disease.

Here are some ways to prevent disaster in your landscape:

• **Don't use plants susceptible to known diseases.** Replacing a crabapple killed by fireblight with a pear that's vulnerable to the same disease is just asking for trouble. Instead, look for plants that are fireblight-resistant, such as a Japanese tree lilac.

• **Know if the disease needs more than one host plant.** Some diseases, like the cedar-apple rust men-

tioned earlier, need two different host plants to complete their life cycles. Without both hosts, the disease cannot survive.

• **Diversify your landscape.** Managing a yard is just like managing a retirement portfolio. Use a variety of plants with different disease resistance and you'll assure yourself of long-term success.

Creating a garden filled with plants that can all catch the same disease can be devastating. All you need is one or two seasons with the pathogen present and the right environmental conditions, and you'll have your own version of an undiversified portfolio in your landscape. Remember Dutch elm disease?

• **Use disease-resistant varieties whenever possible.** Many crabapple cultivars have been selected for their resistance to apple scab and fireblight. Selecting a resistant crabapple will eliminate the need to rake fallen leaves, prune out dead branches and spray to keep the plant looking good.

• **Never buy disease-infested plants.** You may save a little on such "bargains", but you'll end up spending more money and time down the road. Avoid buying plants with pale leaves, stunted growth, spots and other disease symptoms. Isolate questionable plants to prevent infecting your healthy garden. If you're the type of person who likes to bring sick plants back to health, consider creating an "intensive-care garden" quarantined from your other plants.

• **Give your plants plenty of room to grow.** I find this the hardest practice for most gardeners, my-

Common Garden Pathogens

MANY OF THESE may sound familiar, since your health can be affected by similar organisms. Fortunately, we can't "catch" anthracnose, black knot or other diseases from our plants.

Bacteria—Invasive single-celled organisms that lack chlorophyll cause damage by using plant cells for their own growth and nourishment. Bacteria enter through pores and wounds and cause a variety of symptoms.

Some types of bacteria block the vascular system, which carries water and nutrients, causing the plant to wilt. Others trigger abnormal growths called galls. Bacteria can cause leaf spot and root, fruit and stem rot.

Fungus—The most common cause of plant disease. Fungus is a plant, but it lacks chlorophyll. It reproduces by spores, which are spread by wind, rain, animals and people (primarily from our garden tools). Fungus has a filamentous growth habit.

Good fungi help break down plant debris and turn it into compost. Problem species cause leaf spot as well as root, fruit and stem rot.

Mycoplasma—These and the closely related phytoplasm, formerly known as mycoplasma-like organisms, are similar to bacteria. They're too small to see even with a compound microscope and difficult to culture in a lab. They cause yellowing or other abnormal coloring, stunting and distorted growths in plants. Insects carry many. Aster yellows is probably the most well-known pathogen.

Nematodes—These microscopic roundworms are often grouped with insects, but sometimes are listed with disease organisms. I guess no one but brave nematologists really wants to claim these organisms.

Beneficial nematodes can control insect pests. Most of the harmful species live in the soil, feeding on plant roots. Infested plants are discolored, stunted and often have malformed roots.

Parasitic plants—These plants are closely related to those we grow. Most have chlorophyll, but depend on other plants for their nutrients, which usually weakens the host plants. Dodder is an example of such a plant (see Chapter 9).

Virus—This submicroscopic bit of cellular material can grow and multiply only inside a plant, where it disrupts growth. Many are moved from infected plants to healthy plants by aphids, leafhoppers and other insects. Controlling the vector—the insect carrying the disease—is often the only control for viral diseases. Viruses also can move from plant to plant on garden tools or through propagation techniques.

Infected plants are stunted, discolored and malformed. Some of the discoloration occurs in rings, mosaics and other attractive patterns.

---

self included, to follow. The temptation to squeeze in one more plant in my small yard is often more than I can resist. Or, maybe you have trouble visualizing that little plant growing into a 40-foot-wide, 60-foot-tall shade tree. Proper spacing shows off your plants, reduces the need to prune and reduces disease by allowing air and light to reach all parts of the plant.

● **Give plants the proper care.** Too much water and fertilizer can increase the risk of diseases like fireblight and root rot. Adjust pruning times and techniques to reduce disease problems. Dormant-season pruning can reduce the risk of nectria canker on honeylocust and oak wilt on oaks. Make proper cuts (see pruning instructions in Chapter 5) so wounds can close quickly and keep out disease.

Scouting the Landscape

Make it a habit to check your plants any time you mow the lawn, deadhead or enjoy the view. And pay special attention to disease-susceptible plants.

Check out everything, including the lower leaves, plants at the back of the bed and other hard-to-see spots. The leaves, stems and plants hidden from view are usually the first to show symptoms. Catching the disease early may mean the difference between removing a few leaves and spraying or removing the whole plant.

Look for signs of aster leafhoppers, thrips and other insects that spread disease. Controlling them is the only cure for aster yellows and many viruses. Catching pests early may keep these deadly diseases out of your garden.

Watch the weather as well. Certain conditions are more conducive to disease problems. Cool, wet weather increases the risk of anthracnose and apple scab. Heavy rains and poorly drained soils increase the risk of root rot. Increase your garden inspections when all three parts of the disease triangle are present.

Monitor the progression of any disease over time and in relation to the weather. Note where the symptoms first appeared and how they developed throughout the plant. This will help you, or the professional you hire, make a quick and accurate diagnosis.

Disease Identification

Matching the symptoms and progression of the disease with potential pathogens is the first step. Start by studying the disease profiles at the end of this chapter.

Then look at your troubled plants and try to find symptoms and conditions that match a profile. If you can do this, you're on your way to managing the disease. If not, check other diseases with similar symptoms. That second guess may provide the solution.

You may need to look for additional help if your plant problem does not match the common ones listed here. Universities and Extension services across the country have wonderful Web sites with information and pictures to help. Your local Extension service, garden center or landscape professional may help diagnose disease.

Once you've unraveled the clues and identified the disease, you need to decide if control is needed. In most cases, this means preventing further damage or waiting for the appropriate time to apply a preventative treatment so it won't be a problem next season. Once a plant is infected, your control options are limited.

Healthy plants are able to tolerate occasional outbreaks of many diseases. Don't be too concerned if your plant has been healthy, the disease is not life threatening and your plant hasn't been infected before.

A few summers ago, our area had perfect weather conditions for powdery mildew. By the end of the season, almost every perennial in my front yard was infected. The plants looked bad by fall, but I knew they'd be fine the next season because this wasn't an ongoing problem. The plants were generally healthy and they were receiving enough light. Lo and behold, they were fine the next year.

On the other hand, if your plant is continually attacked by a disease and loses its leaves by midsummer, you may want to provide some control. This may mean marking your calendar to apply a preventative treatment next season.

Apple scab, for example, infects susceptible crabapples, causing leaves to spot and eventually drop. Trees that have been infected for consecutive seasons can be weakened and are more likely to develop life-threatening problems. Treatment must begin before the disease is evident, at bud break—when the bud scales peel back and leaf tissue just begins to appear.

Sometimes we opt to treat plants for our own benefit and peace of mind. Maybe the tree has sentimental value or is in a key area of the landscape. Perhaps your child doesn't understand why the leaves on his "birthday tree" are missing or spotted, or you can't enjoy shade on your patio because the adjacent tree lost all its leaves in mid-July.

Whatever your motivation, be certain treatment will work before proceeding. Spraying the wrong chemical or treating at the wrong time wastes time and money, and it's bad for the environment. The disease must be present and at a certain phase of development for control to work. For some diseases, ground-level pruning is the only control.

Outsmarting Disease Without Chemicals

Disease control varies from simple sanitation measures to therapeutic injections. The pathogen, disease history and value of the plant will help you determine the best course of action.

• **Sanitation is a good starting point.** Remove infected leaves as soon as they appear so the dis-

Common Plant Disease Symptoms and Causes

SYMPTOM	POSSIBLE DISEASE
Spots on leaves	Anthracnose, apple scab, black spot, botrytis blight (gray mold), rust
Discolored leaves	Aster yellows, virus
White substance on leaves	Powdery mildew, botrytis blight (gray mold), southern blight
Sudden death of flowers, leaves and stems	Fireblight, botrytis blight, southern blight
Growths on twigs and stems	Black knot, crown gall
Sunken and discolored areas on trunk, branches and stems	Canker
Sudden wilting of seedlings	Damping off
Wilting and leaf discoloration	Root rot, verticillium wilt, Dutch elm disease, southern blight, canker, fireblight

ease doesn't spread. Clean up garden debris, especially infected materials, in fall to reduce the source of disease next season.

Sometimes sanitation is a little more work. You may need to dig out a diseased plant or prune it to ground level.

- **Eliminate host plants.** Certain rust fungi need two different hosts to complete their life cycle. Remove one, and you've eliminated the problem. Unfortunately, the other host plant is often in the neighbor's yard.

- **Rotate plantings just like farmers**. Disease organisms build up in the soil when the same crop is planted each season. Mixing up your plantings re-

Here Comes the Sun

HEAT has long been used as a means of managing plant diseases. Seeds can be heat-treated to eliminate disease problems.

I don't recommend this for home gardeners—it's too easy to cross the fine line between controlling disease in seeds and roasting them.

Organic gardeners have reported some success with controlling fusarium, southern blight and nematodes with the use of clear plastic to heat up the soil. Start by removing all vegetation from the garden. Then rake the soil smooth and water until the earth is moist. Cover the garden with clear plastic and leave it in place for 6 to 14 weeks during the hottest part of the season.

The heat should destroy the harmful organisms and provide several years of control. After planting, you should continue monitoring for disease symptoms. You may lose a growing season, but you'll protect plants for seasons to come from these diseases.

moves the food source and reduces the buildup of disease. Replace infested plantings with unrelated and resistant plants the next season.

- **Manage your plants.** Many diseases can be prevented or controlled with a simple change in landscape management. Bee balm and garden phlox are notorious for powdery mildew. If you can't bear to replace your existing plants, change your maintenance practices. Remove one-third of the stems in spring to open up the plant for better airflow and light penetration. This reduces powdery mildew problems.

- **Disinfect tools.** This needs to be done between pruning cuts, or at least between plants. Do this to reduce your part in spreading disease. Make this a habit when pruning or at least when pruning diseased plants. Dipping tools in a solution of 1 part bleach and 9 parts water or alcohol will kill pathogens, and may save your plant.

This wasn't the case at one landscape I visited. A gardener had pruned into a fireblight canker on a crabapple, then pruned the rest of the tree with the same contaminated tool. A month or 2 later, the branches were wilting and turning black. The only solution was to prune out the diseased portions and hope we caught the problem in time. You can be sure the tools were disinfected between each cut the second time around.

- **Water the right amounts at the right time.** Make sure you're providing the right amount of water at proper intervals. Adjusting watering practices can help prevent and reduce rot problems and many leaf spot diseases. See Chapter 5 for tips on maintaining healthy plants and reducing disease problems.

Watering in the morning or relying on soaker hoses is another way to help plants because wet foliage can increase the risk and spread disease. When you water in the morning, the leaves have plenty of

Amazing Baking Soda

CORNELL UNIVERSITY RESEARCHERS have found baking soda provides good control of powdery mildew. Home gardeners and a few botanical gardens have discovered it helps with some other diseases as well. Application is easy, too. Add 1 tablespoon baking soda and 1 to 1-1/2 teaspoons horticulture oil or insecticidal soap to 1 gallon of water. Mix thoroughly and spray on plants weekly, being sure to cover both the tops and bottoms of the leaves.

time to dry before dark. And when you water at the roots, the plant stays dry.

- **Control insects.** Eliminating disease-carrying insects is often the only solution to a plant disease. Thrips, aphids and leafhoppers often spread pathogens from sick to healthy plants as they feed. Remove diseased plants and kill the insect vectors with insecticidal soap or some other environmentally friendly product.

The Last Resort—Chemicals

I FEEL chemicals should be your last resort for disease control. They usually require properly timed and repeated applications for them to work.

Most of us don't have the time, desire or dedication to spray throughout the growing season. If you miss an application, the disease will come right back, which means you wasted time and chemicals in the process.

Products with copper are often used to control some fungal and bacterial diseases. These are rated as nontoxic, but can cause damage when misused.

Sulfur dusts and sprays help prevent spores from germinating and infecting plants. However, they can harm beneficial mites and damage leaves in hot weather, so you need to be careful when using them.

There are many newer, more environmentally friendly products on the market. Neem and other plant-derived oils have shown good control for various fungal diseases. As with all chemicals, you'll need to read and follow label directions carefully. Even plant-derived products can be harmful if misapplied.

A few fungicides will control certain diseases after they enter the plant. Oaks and elms are often injected with a fungicide to prevent or cure oak wilt and Dutch elm disease, but the plant must be disease-free or showing only minor symptoms. Special equipment and exact timing are required for effectiveness. Hire a certified arborist with experience in tree injection.

Finally, don't just prune off a branch or spray your rose and walk away. As I said earlier, you'll need to continue to monitor for problems, evaluate the effectiveness of the control and make adjustments if needed.

Write down what control you used and how well it worked. Mark next year's calendar as a reminder to scout for certain diseases or apply preventative controls that are absolutely needed. This will help you grow a healthier landscape next season.

Disease Profiles

Anthracnose

Symptoms: Brown to purple irregularly shaped spots. Shaded and lower leaves most affected. Sycamore and dogwood may experience twig dieback.

Pathogen: Several species of fungi.

Susceptible plants: Various trees, including maple, ash, oak, sycamore and black walnut; some shrubs, such as dogwood and brambles; occasionally seen on flowers, vegetables and turf.

Jerry Howard/Positive Images

Favorable conditions: Cool, wet spring and fall weather.

Look-alikes: Scorch, tar spot, other fungal leaf spots.

Control strategies: Healthy trees are better able to tolerate anthracnose. Avoid high-nitrogen fertilizers that stimulate lush, disease-susceptible growth. Rake and destroy fallen leaves to reduce the source of future infections. Chemicals are needed only in severe cases, or for sycamores and dogwoods with twig dieback. Apply fungicides labeled for controlling anthracnose on the plants you're treating. Apply as directed by the label, usually at bud break and during leaf expansion.

Apple Scab

Symptoms: Leaves develop olive green to black spots, then yellow, brown and drop prematurely. Fruit can develop rough brown spots.

Pathogen: Several strains of a fungus, which overwinters in fallen leaves and fruit.

✔ *Melinda's Tips*

TAKE THIS TEST before spraying your large trees. Use the garden hose and plain water to thoroughly wet the tree's leaves.

Are you wet? How about the surrounding plants? If the answer is yes to either question, seriously consider hiring a certified arborist for the job. They have the equipment and training to do such a large job correctly and safely. Log on to *www.isa-arbor.com* for a list of certified arborists, or check the "tree care" or "tree services" listings in the yellow pages.

Susceptible plants: Apples, crabapples, hawthorns, and mountain ash.

Favorable conditions: Wet weather.

Look-alikes: Other leaf spot diseases.

Control strategies: Plant scab-resistant cultivars whenever possible. We are seeing loss of scab resistance in some varieties, so look for the latest disease-resistant recommendations for your area.

Rake and destroy fallen leaves and fruit to reduce future infections. Fungicides can be applied starting at bud break and continuing through early fruit development. Do not use spray containing both fungicides and insecticides, such as home orchard sprays, when the plant is in bloom.

Aster Yellows

Symptoms: Scattered plants have yellow leaves, stunted growth and/or green, twisted or distorted flowers and stems.

Pathogen: Phytoplasm, formerly thought to be a virus, then a mycoplasma-like organism. Carried by leafhoppers.

Susceptible plants: Many flowers and vegetables. Other yellows diseases attack trees and shrubs.

Favorable conditions: Presence of leafhoppers. These pests overwinter in the South and blow into the North on spring winds. Hot, dry weather increases populations.

Look-alikes: Root rots and viruses.

Control strategies: Remove infected plants as soon as they are found. Control leafhoppers to prevent spread of disease.

Black Spot

Symptoms: Black spots develop on lower leaves and spread upward through plants. Leaves turn yellow and drop.

Pathogen: Fungi that overwinter in leaf debris and on stems.

Susceptible plants: Roses; many shrub roses are resistant.

Favorable conditions: Heavy dews, warm weather, high humidity, rain.

Look-alikes: Environmental stress.

Control strategies: Fall cleanup helps reduce the source of this disease. Mulch and avoid overhead watering. Once a plant is infected, it becomes a yearly problem. Spray with a fungicide labeled for black spot. Start before the first sign of disease and continue throughout the season. Vary fungicides to avoid resistance, or replace susceptible plants with resistant species.

Black Knot

Symptoms: Black knobby growths on branches and stems.

Pathogen: *Dibotryon* fungus.

Susceptible plants: Ornamental and edible plums, cherries and other stone fruits.

Favorable conditions: Cool—near 55°—and wet.

Look-alikes: Canker.

Control strategies: Sanitation may help slow the spread. Unfortunately, there are many wild plums and cherries to infect your trees. Prune at least 2 to 4 inches below the black knots. Remove immature knots in late winter to prevent spore release.

Some pathologists recommend cutting the knots out of major branches and trunk at least 1 inch below and 1/2 inch beyond the knot, but this may be more hazardous to the tree than the disease.

Dormant, spring and early summer fungicide treatments may provide some relief. If you have badly infected trees with knots on the trunk, you may want to eliminate them for the health of your other plants.

Botrytis or Gray Mold

Symptoms: Browning of leaves, stems, crowns, flowers or fruit. Masses of gray or silver spores may accumulate on leaf surface.

Pathogen: Several different fungi, which overwinter in infected plant debris.

Susceptible plants: Wide variety of annuals, perennials, strawberries and vegetables.

Favorable conditions: Cool, rainy spring and summer weather with temperatures near 60°.

Look-alikes: Other leaf spot diseases.

Control strategies: Sanitation is usually sufficient. Remove affected leaves as they appear and clean up thoroughly in fall.

Fungicides labeled for controlling this disease can be applied as a preventative. Follow label directions for exact timing.

Canker

Symptoms: Sunken and discolored areas in trunk, branches and stems. Leaves on infected branches wilt, yellow and brown.

Pathogen: Several fungi.

Susceptible plants: Various plants, including evergreens, ornamentals and fruit plants.

Favorable conditions: Most common after drought.

Look-alikes: Borer and drought stress.

Control strategies: Keep trees healthy and properly watered during drought. Avoid wounds that create

entryway for disease. Limit pruning of susceptible plants to the dormant season and dry weather. Prune out infected branches as soon as possible during dry weather. Make cuts at least 6 to 8 inches below the canker and disinfect tools.

Crown Gall

Symptoms: Knobby growth on stem or roots; plants may be stunted, decline and eventually die.

Pathogen: Several species of *Agrobacterium*, a soilborne bacterium brought into the landscape on infected plants or soil.

Susceptible plants: A variety of ornamental and fruit plants; often seen on euonymus, grapes, raspberries and apricots.

Favorable conditions: Bacteria in soil.

Look-alikes: Insect galls.

Control strategies: Thoroughly examine plants you buy; choose only those that are disease-free. Avoid injuring roots and stems during planting. Remove infected plants and the soil around them. Disinfect tools.

Use resistant plants such as andromeda, barberry, birch, boxwood, cedar, firethorn, golden-rain tree, holly, maidenhair tree, mimosa, mountain laurel, redbud, smoke tree, sweet gum and tulip tree. Select plants suited to your growing conditions and landscape design.

Damping Off

Symptoms: Seeds fail to germinate; seedlings suddenly collapse and die; older plants may appear wilted.

Pathogen: Several fungi.

Susceptible plants: Seedlings.

Favorable conditions: Contaminated and cool, wet soils.

Look-alikes: Bird or animal damage may be blamed for poor sprouting; other rot diseases.

Control strategies: Avoid problems by starting with quality seeds. Indoors, use sterile soil and clean containers. Bottom heat speeds germination and reduces disease risk. Outdoors, plant in well-drained soils. Use row cover fabrics to warm soils for plants that need warm soil to germinate. Cultural controls are usually sufficient. When these techniques fail, fungicides labeled for damping off can be applied as a soil drench.

Dutch Elm Disease

Symptoms: Tips of a few branches wilt, yellow and brown from early spring through summer. Symptoms spread throughout the tree. Death can come quickly, within one season, or take several years.

Pathogen: Two species of *Ophiostoma* fungi can attack the vascular system, entering the tree through root grafts or on the European elm bark beetle.

Susceptible plants: All native elms. American elm is most susceptible; red or slippery elms are somewhat less susceptible.

Favorable conditions: Diseased trees in the vicinity provide the pathogen. Pruning cuts and wounds attract disease-carrying insects.

Look-alikes: Elm yellows and bacterial leaf scorch.

Control strategies: When adding new elm trees, plant resistant hybrids or the American Liberty variety to minimize disease risks.

For existing trees, practice good sanitation. Remove weakened or susceptible branches immediately. Remove infected trees as soon as possible to avoid spreading the disease. Sever root grafts between healthy and diseased trees before removal. Use infected firewood immediately or pull off the bark and tarp securely for storage.

Chemical injections of some fungicides can prevent the disease and even cure a tree if less than 5% of it is infected.

Fireblight

Symptoms: Leaves suddenly wilt and turn brown or black as if burned. Stem ends curl like a shepherd's crook. Cankers develop on infected branches.

Pathogen: *Erwinia* bacterium that overwinters in cankers on the bark. Transferred by wind, bees and pruning tools to other trees.

Susceptible plants: 75 species in the rose family, including apples, crabapples and pears.

Favorable conditions: High humidity and temperatures near 65°.

Look-alikes: Drought stress; borers.

Control strategies: Plant resistant varieties and species whenever possible. Avoid excess nitrogen, which can promote the lush, succulent growth that's most susceptible. Avoid pruning during wet weather when the disease is active. Prune out infected branches at least 12 inches below the canker. Disinfect tools between cuts.

Bordeaux—the fungicide, not the wine—and copper-containing fungicides applied at the silver tip stage (when buds swell and show silver through the tips) may provide some protection.

Powdery Mildew

Symptoms: Leaves covered with powder-like substance; they may turn yellow or brown and dry up.

Pathogen: Eight different types of fungi; each have a narrow host range. Overwinters in debris and on stems.

Susceptible plants: A variety of indoor and outdoor plants. Often found on lilac, garden phlox, bee balm, zinnia and grass.

Favorable conditions: This disease is caused by fluctuations in humidity, not water on the foliage. The fungus needs high humidity to infect plants and low humidity to spread. Shade and poor air circulation increase the risk.

Look-alikes: Spray residue.

Control strategies: Use resistant cultivars and species whenever possible. Fall infestations are unsightly but not life threatening. Avoid excess nitrogen; this results in lush growth that is more susceptible. Thin crowded plants and move regularly infected plants to sunnier locations.

Chemical control is usually not needed or practical. Start with the baking soda mix on page 187 or a plant-derived fungicide. Repeat applications will be needed from the first sign of the disease until the end of the season for control.

Root Rot

E.L. Barnard/Florida Division of Forestry/www.forestryimages.org

Symptoms: Leaves wilt, yellow and brown, while roots rot.

Pathogen: Various soil fungi and bacteria.

Susceptible plants: Any plant can succumb to this disease.

Favorable conditions: Waterlogged soils.

Look-alikes: Wilt diseases and environmental stresses.

Control strategies: Avoid problems with proper soil preparation. Plants growing in well-drained soils are less likely to develop rot diseases. Water thoroughly, but less frequently. A few fungicides are labeled for use as a soil drench against root rot-causing fungi.

Rust

Alan and Linda Detrick

Symptoms: Bright orange-yellow spots develop on the leaves and eventually develop swellings full of reddish-orange spores.

Pathogen: Several fungal species; often need two different host plants to complete life cycle.

Susceptible plants: Roses; various trees, including apple, crabapple and juniper; various flowers, including daylily; and turf.

Favorable conditions: Extended wet periods.

Look-alikes: Other leaf spot diseases, but the orange color makes this disease easy to identify.

Control strategies: This is usually more of an aesthetic issue on trees and shrubs but can be detrimental to daylilies. Healthy plants can tolerate the disease. Remove alternate host, if applicable and possible. Fall cleanup will help reduce overwintering spores.

Fungicides labeled for controlling rust can be used as preventative sprays. Remove or aggressively treat daylily rust. This disease is new to the United States, and its potential spread and threat are not fully known.

Southern Blight

Clemson University/USDA Cooperative Extension Slide Services/ www.forestryimages.org

Symptoms: Leaves yellow and wilt due to basal or root rot. A white filamentous growth (mycelium) may be present near the soil line.

Pathogen: *Sclerotium* fungus.

Susceptible plants: A wide variety of annuals and perennials; some fruit, trees and shrubs.

Favorable conditions: Hot, humid weather. Has been found to survive in northern regions with mild winters or good snow cover.

Look-alikes: Other root rots.

Control strategies: Hard to control because of the wide range of hosts. Prevent problems by buying disease-free plants. Move plants or soil from infected gardens to disease-free planting beds. Disinfect tools and equipment when moving from diseased to non-diseased areas.

Use resistant species such as abutilon, alyssum, baby's breath, bells of Ireland, cleome, cockscomb, English daisy, four o'clock, freesia, fritillaria, globe amaranth, hyacinth, lavender, moss rose, primrose, statice, tansy, Virginia bluebells and wild geranium.

Verticillium Wilt

Symptoms: Leaves on one or several branches suddenly wilt, brown and die. Internal streaking may be found on pencil-sized infected twigs.

Pathogen: *Verticillium* fungus on plants and in soil.

Susceptible plants: Wide range of plants including maple, ash, catalpa, golden-rain tree, Pistache, pepper trees, elm, linden, Russian olive, smoke tree, redbud, tulip trees, barberry, various flowers, vegetables (tomatoes and potatoes) and fruit. See the University of California publication, *Plants Resistant or Susceptible to Verticillium Wilt*, available on-line at *http://ucce.uc davis.edu/freeform/VegCD/documents/PDF_docs_for_CD ROM1101.pdf*, or by calling 1-800-994-8849.

Favorable conditions: Infected soils, plants and weeds in the landscape.

Look-alikes: Stress from drought.

Control strategies: Use resistant plants like evergreens, manzanita, birches, hickory, rockrose, sycamores, California laurel, lindens, willows and oaks. (The University of California publication has a more complete list.) Keep plants healthy and minimize stress so they can fight off the disease. Remove and de-stroy infected plants and weeds as soon as they are found. Disinfect tools between cuts.

Virus

Symptoms: Discolored leaves of yellow, light and dark green or attractive patterns.

Pathogen: Various viruses, many carried by insects.

Susceptible plants: Most plants are susceptible to some type of virus.

Favorable conditions: Presence of virus, host plant and insects or organisms that help spread it.

Look-alikes: Root rot; aster yellows.

Control strategies: Remove infected plants, control insects and always disinfect tools and wash hands when moving from a diseased area to a disease-free part of the landscape. Cigarette smoke can spread tobacco mosaic to susceptible plants.

The *Plant Doctor* is in

Q: My beautiful mountain ash tree died 5 years ago. I've been trying to grow another ever since, but three have died. Any suggestions?

A: In general, it's a good idea to avoid replacing dead plants with the same or related species. If a pest killed the first one, there's a good chance it's still around and waiting to attack the next victim. Try planting the mountain ash in another location far from the first tree. Make sure to water during dry periods, avoid excess nitrogen, prune only during the dormant season and in dry weather and mulch the soil. This will help keep it healthy and avoid the risk of fireblight disease.

Q: Can I spray my landscape in fall to prevent disease problems next season?

A: It may make you feel better, but it won't reduce disease problems. The disease must be in an active stage of growth for the fungicide to work. Spraying the dormant spores will not kill them. By the time the weather conditions are right for infection to occur, the fungicide will be gone.

Q: I have trouble calculating the amount of spray I need for my apples. Can I save what's left over for the next application ?

A: Once mixed, fungicide needs to be used as soon as possible. Leftover mixtures won't provide adequate control. Keep records of what you use and what's left over to help you mix the right amount the next time. If you still have too much, maybe your neighbors would appreciate your help in controlling diseases on their apples.

Q: Can I use wood chips from diseased trees?

A: Chipping and shredding diseased tree parts dries out the fungus, eliminating the risk of spreading the disease. If you're the cautious sort, use the chips in areas away from other susceptible plants. Or, compost the chips and use them as a soil amendment in the future. It will take several years and patience on your part for the chips to decompose. Special care is needed for storing and using firewood from trees with oak wilt, Dutch elm disease or other diseased trees that can serve as a source of future infection. Remove the bark and cover with a tarp. Anchor the edges with soil to prevent beetles from spreading the diseases.

Chapter 13
Weathering Plant Stresses

Heat, drought, floods, frost and assorted weather conditions can wreak havoc on our gardens.

Many of the problems I see each season can be traced to some significant weather event or an ongoing stressful period. I'm sure there are times when people think I just blame the weather because I don't have a better answer. But I hope that after you read this chapter, we'll agree that weather is one of the biggest challenges facing gardeners and plants.

Plants Tough It Out

FORTUNATELY, plants have been able to survive nature's extremes and surprises for thousands of years. As their caretakers, we can only try to minimize the impact and repair the damage.

Weather factors include temperature, moisture and seasonal events. Whenever I visit a botanical garden or nature center, I buy weather calendars. They give me great insight into that area's weather history, extremes and norms. This information is also available from several sites on the Internet.

Consider starting a weather calendar for your own backyard. It's a great place to record significant weather events and its impact on plants. I used to be able to keep this information in my head. But that "file drawer" is a bit overloaded.

Writing the information down makes it easier for me to access when I need it. Since I have better intentions than follow-through, I even buy a weather calendar for my own city. It lists the past year's weather, norms, extremes and significant events. With this baseline data, I just need to add a few notes of my own to have a useful garden reference.

Visits from Jack Frost

Most North American gardeners can relate to this weather event. We wait for the last spring frost so we can plant our tender annuals. In fall, we keep our fingers crossed for just a few more days of frost-free weather—unless you're ready for a break from a long growing season.

Frost damage seems obvious: The temperature drops to 32° and plants are damaged. But it's a bit more complex than that.

As the sun sets, the ground begins to radiate heat. If it's a clear night, this heat given off by the ground keeps rising as air temperatures continue to drop. That's when frost occurs.

Young transplants that have not been hardened off and tropical plants are the first to be damaged. Cabbage, pansies, perennials and other cold-tolerant plants are unaffected by light frosts. As temperatures drop toward the mid-20s, however, even these tough plants become damaged.

Location also influences frost. Plantings near buildings, under shade trees and in other protected spots are the last to freeze.

Frost leaves early and comes late to gardens in the "heat islands" known as cities, and near large bodies of water. You can often squeeze another few weeks of growing season out of these areas.

But if you're in a low area where cold air settles, you'll need to protect your plants earlier in fall and later in spring. Lack of attention could result in loss of tender new plants or a spectacular floral display that's reaching its peak.

Young twigs and leaves are the first to show damage. They wilt, turn off-color to black and may shrivel. Sensitive plants, like impatiens or coleus, can completely die when temperatures drop below 32°.

In other cases, frost damage may not show for several weeks. As buds break and leaves begin expanding, they're very sensitive to frost. Cold temperatures can damage the exposed leaf tissue, while the inner portion is protected. As leaves open, they're riddled with holes resembling insect damage. Unlike insect damage, however, frost damage won't progress. Monitor closely if you're not sure of the cause.

Spruce trees can have a similar response. New growth exposed to freezing temperatures can wilt and eventually brown, which is often mistaken for Roundup damage. This is where being a weather watcher and a good note taker pays off. Compare weather reports and spraying records to determine the culprit.

FROST-TOLERANT PLANTS

Clarkia	Petunia
Cornflower (*Centaurea*)	Pinks (*Dianthus*)
Dusty Miller	Snapdragon
Kale	Spike (*Dracaena*)
Larkspur	Stock (*Matthiola*)
Lobelia	Sweet alyssum
Love-in-a-mist (*Nigella*)	Sweet pea
Pansy	Viola

Patience Pays Off

Wait to plant tender annuals until the soil has warmed and danger of frost has passed. Those first few warm days of spring make us quickly forget about late frosts, and a few years with mild temperatures may lull us into a false sense of security. Then one spring, *WHAM*, we're caught off guard and lose plants to a late frost.

If you've jumped the gun and planted early, be sure to protect young plantings, frost-sensitive plants and tropicals whenever frost is expected. Cover them with an old sheet, row cover or newspaper in late afternoon and wait until frost disappears before removing.

Row covers can be left in place until the danger of frost has passed. See Chapter 17 for more tips on lengthening short seasons.

Some professionals use sprinklers, believe it or not, to keep their plants from freezing. As the water on the plants turns to ice, heat is given off, keeping the temperature of the plant above freezing.

This method can only provide a few degrees of protection and is best for lower-growing crops. On

Keep plastic frost protection off plants for best results. Ventilate on warm and sunny days and when you water.

trees, the weight of the freezing water may cause damage. This method is best left to professionals or those with large areas to protect. Sheets and newspapers will do the trick for the rest of us.

Cold Temperatures

Unusually cold winter weather can catch many gardeners by surprise. As temperatures drop, ice begins to form inside plants and between the cells. This is what causes the most damage to plants. The impact of cold weather and ice formation varies with the type of plant and rate of temperature change.

Hardy species form very little or no ice during cold weather. To prevent or at least minimize cold-weather damage, select hardy plants suited for your climate (check the Plant Hardiness Zone Map on page 52).

I realize this is easier said than done. I think all gardeners are guilty of what my friend Deborah Brown, a garden writer in Minnesota's Twin Cities, calls "zone envy". We all want to grow plants that are better suited for zones warmer than our own.

The rate at which the temperature drops or climbs also influences the amount of ice that forms within plants. The faster the change, the greater the risk of damage. A gradual shift allows the cells to adjust to the internal changes and minimize damage—much like what happens when you harden off annuals in spring.

We can't change the weather, but winter mulching (see Chapter 5) will help to minimize temperature extremes and rapid fluctuations. Record rapid temperature changes on your weather calendar. When damage shows up in spring, you'll know why.

Vertical cracks that develop in tree trunks, known as frost cracks, also are related to temperature changes. As the sun or reflected heat from buildings and sidewalks warms the tree trunk, the cells warm. Then, when the sun sets, temperatures drop and the cells quickly freeze, causing injury and eventually a crack.

Tree wraps don't help. Research has found that flush cuts and deep planting cause weak points in the trunk that are more likely to crack. Proper pruning and planting will reduce the risk of frost cracking and help trees recover from the damage if it does occur.

Turning Up the Heat

The other temperature extreme—heat—can be equally harmful to plants. As temperatures rise above 86°, we start to see internal changes. Some plant systems become overactive and release toxins into the cells, while others begin to shut down. Selecting heat-hardy plants (review plant selection tips on page 59 in Chapter 4) is just as important as choosing cold-hardy ones. Heat-hardy plants are less likely to develop scorch, root and twig dieback and other heat-related damage.

Wood chips, pine needles or other organic mulches will help conserve moisture and keep soil and plant roots cooler. Make sure plants receive sufficient moisture during hot spells. This is even more important when humidity is low, and plants lose moisture quickly.

Even properly mulched and watered plants will show signs of heat stress. Scorch, a browning of leaf edges, occurs when plants lose water faster than they can pull it up from the soil. Even if plants are getting watered, they can't absorb it fast enough.

In the summer of 1995, many areas of the country experienced prolonged record high temperatures. Bare soil reached temperatures of 100°. The roots and crowns of many herbaceous plants died or declined. Other plants struggled through the season and even the following year before dying.

Hardening off will help plants adjust to heat as well as cool temperatures. Gradually exposing plants to change always helps minimize sunburn, frost damage and other negative environmental responses.

Dealing with Drought

Selecting drought-tolerant plants (see Chapter 15) saves two valuable resources—water and time. Using plants suited to these growing conditions will give you a good-looking garden that thrives on existing rainfall.

You may need to add some water after planting, but once the plants are established, they'll develop deep drought-tolerant root systems.

Proper care will help plants through dry periods. Again, mulching will help conserve moisture. And thorough, less frequent waterings will help. Shallow, frequent watering encourages development of shallow, less drought-tolerant roots that stay near the soil's surface, the first area to dry out.

I guarantee these tips will result in amazing improvement in your plants' health and appearance.

After the Flood

Mother Nature has a way of giving us too much of a good thing, including water.

Floods can damage plants immediately or affect their long-term health. Damage depends on the species, age of the plant and the duration of flooding.

Young seedlings are the least tolerant of flooding. Their small root systems rot and the plants die. Or, they're washed away in rushing water along with the valuable topsoil.

Wait until the soil dries out before replanting. Consider adding organic matter to flood-damaged soils, since many of the valuable microorganisms may have died. Adding compost, aged manure and similar materials improves drainage, adds nutrients and replaces some microorganisms.

Drought-resistant plants such as Mexican hat and yarrow create a beautiful drought-tolerant garden in New Mexico.

Develop a good working relationship with a tree care company, so when damage occurs, like from this hurricane, you will be at the top of their service list.

And, as we discussed earlier, flooded soils also lack the oxygen plants need to absorb nutrients and water. The resulting lack of oxygen can cause nitrite buildup in the soil, and the absorption of toxins that may harm plants. Lower leaves begin to yellow or drop. Some develop brown patches or black wet spots on the leaves.

Most established plants can tolerate a week of flooding. Longer periods can cause long-term visible damage. Root rot is common in waterlogged, oxygen-deficient soils. This results in aboveground symptoms like yellow leaves, twig death and other signs of decline.

When floodwaters recede, don't break out the chainsaw and start pruning immediately. Wait for things to settle a bit.

Remove only broken and hazardous branches. Then wait to see what happens. Plants often send out new growth or buds to replace those that were lost. If a branch is pliable, buds are firm and both show signs of green, your plant is on its way to recovery. More leaves mean the plant can produce more energy to repair the damage.

Contamination from sewage can be a concern, but most of it should wash off over time. Let nature do this, or wait until the soil dries before washing plants and watering.

The edible parts of vegetables and fruits exposed to contaminated floodwaters do pose a safety risk. You may want to dispose of these.

Waterlogged soils, as opposed to flooded soil, can cause problems, too. Tomatoes are one of the best indicators. Circular rings and growth cracks develop at the stem end of the fruits when soils are wet or temperatures are high.

Geraniums and other ornamentals may develop oedema when soils are wet and weather is cool or cloudy. The plant absorbs more water than it loses through the leaves. Small blisters form on the underside of leaves and eventually become brown and corky. Though not life threatening, oedema does get your attention. If you're the one responsible, avoid overwatering. If Mother Nature is in charge, you'll have to wait for the weather to change.

Winds of Change

High winds can tatter leaves, break branches and uproot trees. Once damage occurs, it's just a matter of repair or removal.

Remove broken branches by cutting flush with the branch bark collar (see page 85 in Chapter 5). Ripped and torn branches may have destroyed this area, so do the best you can to repair it.

Hanging and loose bark should also be removed, but try not to cut into healthy bark attached to the tree. Oaks are the only trees I recommend using pruning paint on. And that's only when the wounds or cuts happen during the growing season.

Large cracks in major branches and trunks may require cabling and bracing to prevent further damage and loss of a major part of the plant. Damaged areas can be secured with rods and bolts or cables, but hire an experienced arborist to do this. (Though some gardeners have tried, duct tape will not work in this situation.) Find a professional who stays current with developments in the field through continuing education and membership in professional organizations.

Large uprooted trees are done for, but smaller trees (less than 25 feet tall) may sometimes be salvageable. Lift the tree back in place as soon as possible and stake to give it needed support until the roots are re-established.

Remove any broken or dead branches immediately. Mulch the soil and water properly to speed recovery. Don't fertilize—this could injure the already stressed roots. Then wait. Some branches may die back, depending on the amount of root damage. Again, patience will tell you if the plant will recover.

Proper planting and care will minimize wind damage. Trees planted too deeply, and those with

✔ *Melinda's Tips*

FOR DETAILED INFORMATION on storm-damaged landscapes, check out this great Web site: *http://bluestem.hort.purdue.edu/plant/stormdamage.html*

girdling roots are the most likely to topple in the wind. Avoid mower and weed whip injury to trunks and stems. These create wounds and increase the risk of disease and decline. A damaged root flare—the area where roots extend from the trunk—can rot and snap during high winds.

Monitor your trees' health and general structure, and prune regularly to avoid wind damage. Removing damaged branches and those with narrow crotch angles to reduce risk.

Avoid overwatering—that can lead to root rot and a smaller, less supportive root system. Waterlogged soil also provides less support for plants. Have you ever noticed that more uprooting occurs after prolonged wet periods?

Staking doesn't prevent wind damage. In fact, done improperly, it can increase the risk. Stake only newly planted trees with large canopies and small root systems, or those in very exposed sites. Don't leave the stakes on for more than a year.

Tattered and scorched leaves may appear on plants exposed to windy conditions. Young tender leaves are the most susceptible. The drying winds and leaf movement result in brown leaf edges and holes in the leaves. It may look bad, but it's not life threatening. Besides, there's nothing you can do to correct the damage. As always, proper care is your best insurance.

Hail Damage

Ice falling from the sky is not good for plants, or for people or cars. The impact of falling hail rips and shreds leaves and injures stems and branches, creating entryways for insects and disease.

You can't stop hail damage, but afterward you can monitor your plants' health. Young seedlings may not recover from severe damage. Wait a few days to see if there is any sign of life. If not, replace them.

Hail-damaged leaves should not be removed from plants. They may not look pretty, but as long as they have green tissue, they're still creating energy to help the plant grow and, more importantly, recover. Some plants put out another flush of leaves that help mask the damage.

A few years ago, we had a bad hailstorm in late May. Many of our spring plantings and early perennials were damaged. The hostas looked like the slugs had already taken over. But the plants survived, even if they looked bad.

Ice and Snow

Captured in cards and paintings, a snow-covered landscape looks tranquil. What those pictures don't show is the aftermath of a winter storm with wet, heavy snow and ice that breaks branches, splits upright evergreens and creates a cleanup nightmare.

Snow on the ground is an asset, however. It blankets the soil, insulating it and preventing frost heaves caused by fluctuating temperatures. As the snow melts in spring, it provides moisture for plants.

The problems come with the snowstorms. The weight of "wet" snow (and ice) on stems and branches of landscape plants creates lots of damage.

Once the stuff has landed, there's little you can do. Many gardeners try to shake off the snow and ice, but moving frozen branches can cause internal and external cracks to form, resulting in death and dieback.

If you really feel you must do something, get out the broom. Lightly brush the snow off the branches as it falls. Once it freezes in place, it's time for you to go inside, fix a cup of cocoa and enjoy the scenery.

After the storm, when the weather clears, prune any broken or hazardous branches. Regular pruning will reduce the risk of snow and ice damage. Establish and maintain a strong framework of branches that are better able to manage the extra weight.

Loosely tying upright yews, arborvitae and junipers in fall will help prevent snow loads and splitting. For more tips on winter protection, see Chapter 5.

Icy patches on lawns and gardens are another problem. Since ice is a poor insulator, the covered plants are subject to winterkill.

Heavy snow and ice can damage both evergreen (above) and deciduous plants. Many will bounce back after the snow melts, while others may require pruning.

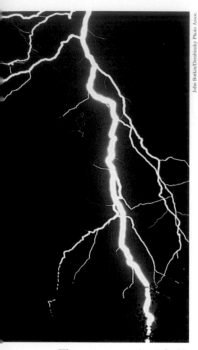

There are approximately 30 million cloud-to-ground lightning strikes each year in the U.S.

When Lightning Strikes

Lightning strikes the earth about 100 times each second. It occurs when negative charges in the clouds meet positive charges from the ground in the air. Lightning looks for the path of least resistance to the ground. Tall trees provide natural pathways.

Lightning travels through the tree's water and sap, so it moves through the parts of the tree with the most moisture. This can be in the center, just under the bark or on the tree's outer surface.

Lightning traveling through the center of the tree often causes it to explode. If only the bark flies off the tree, the lightning traveled through the vascular system. And if there was plenty of moisture on the trunk, it may skim over the surface, traveling down to the soil.

Damaged trees may die immediately or decline over several years. The bark damage, known as lightning scar, creates an entryway for insects and diseases, which can move in and finish off an already stressed tree.

To reduce the stress and increase your tree's survival chances, do not paint lightning scars. Research shows the paints often trap moisture and pests in the trunk rather than keep them out.

Work with a certified arborist to install a lightning-protection system in extremely tall and valuable trees that may be at risk. A series of wire cables are run from the top of the tree down the trunk and then grounded at a safe distance from the tree.

Other Environmental Stresses

WEATHER IS ONLY ONE aspect of environmental stress. Light, soil, pollution, nutrient deficiencies and maintenance practices also can adversely affect plants. Damage can resemble problems caused by weather, insects or disease. A close examination of the site and maintenance practices can help you discover the cause.

Planting Levels

Trees, shrubs and flowers planted too deep can suffer root and crown rot. Affected plants are often stunted, color prematurely in fall and eventually die.

It's not too late to do something about it. Perennials that are planted too deeply can be lifted and replanted at the right depth.

Shrubs are a bit more forgiving than trees. Just try not to plant them too deep in the future, and avoid adding to the problem by burying the crown with wood chips.

Planting trees too deeply puts them at greater risk of developing frost cracks and other diseases. The impact of improper planting shows up years later and is often overlooked as the cause of the problem. See Chapter 4 for tips on proper planting.

Construction and Grade Changes

Changing the soil level around your trees can also have negative results. Whether you're building a raised bed, enlarging the house or regrading for drainage, the results are the same. As little as an inch of extra soil can kill some trees.

The damage does not appear until 5 to 10 years later. People often forget these distant events and blame something more recent for the damage and repeat the process.

What are the telltale signs? Leaves will be smaller, the crown will thin and part or the entire tree may change color earlier than usual in fall. Over the next few years, the symptoms intensify until the tree dies.

To prevent this, don't build raised beds around existing trees and shrubs. Mulch the soil or plant perennials and ground covers in the existing soil. (See the "Plant Doctor is in" section on page 69 for more details.)

When new construction, widened roads or other factors make it necessary to change the grade around your trees or shrubs, preserve as much of the existing root zone as possible. Keep large equipment and materials as far from the trunk as possible. Small tree wells will keep the soil away from the trunk, but they don't prevent damage to the roots. Try to preserve the original grade of soil under the tree's drip line (a diameter as large as the crown of the tree.)

Construction has other negative effects on a landscape. Heavy equipment and material storage compacts the soil. You'll have some damage even if you protect your trees to the drip line. Tree roots go way beyond the drip line—as much as 2-1/2 to 5 times the height of the tree away from the trunk.

More visible damage like ripped branches, gashed trunks and other mechanical injuries can

Michael Wendt

occur, too. Large equipment always wins when the two make contact, so fence off valuable plants and work with the contractor to preserve your landscape. Have the damage repaired and soil aerated as soon as possible, and continue to monitor the tree's health.

Girdling Roots, Vines and Twine

Anything that restricts plant growth can cause problems. It can be another plant, a manmade object or part of the plant itself. No matter what the cause, the result is the same—decline. The plant is stunted, enters dormancy early and dies prematurely.

Girdling roots are one of the most common culprits. These roots grow around the trunk instead of away from it and into the surrounding soil. As the trunk and roots enlarge, they eventually make contact. The roots press on the trunk, preventing water and nutrients from traveling between the roots and leaves.

The leaves on the girdled side of a tree are often stunted and change color early in fall. The trunk may be flat on that side, too.

Once these symptoms are noticeable, it may be too late to treat, though some arborists will excavate the soil and sever the girdling root. Success depends on the extent of the damage and the arborist's ability to find and sever all the offending roots. Proper care may prolong the tree's life, but it won't solve the problem.

Girdling roots may be hidden below the soil or visible at the soil surface (above).

Prevent problems at planting time by immediately removing any girdling roots. Create a shallow but wide planting hole as discussed in Chapter 4. Loose soil encourages the roots to grow into the surrounding soil instead of encircling a narrow planting hole. Plant the tree at the proper height to avoid girdling roots developing above the buried root flare.

Other plants can cause similar problems. Twining vines can encircle another plant's stems or tree's

Brown leaves can be the result of drought, root rot, pollution or winter damage, as seen on this boxwood.

Alan and Linda Eznick

Weather and Environmental Stress Symptoms

Symptom	Possible Environmental Cause
Blisters on leaves	Oedema
Brown leaf margins	Scorch, flooding, drought, deicing salt, mower blight, pollution, frost
Chlorosis	Nutrient deficiency, high pH, flooding, drought, pollution, girdling root
Cracks in tree trunks	Cold (frost cracks), lightning
Decline	Weather extremes, change of grade, construction damage, deep planting, girdling roots
Early fall coloration	Girdling root, deep planting, change of grade, construction damage
Holes in leaves	Hail, wind, frost
Twisted/distorted growth	Herbicide damage, frost, pollution
Wilted plants	Black walnut toxicity, excessive or insufficient water, construction damage

trunks. As both plants grow, the vine girdles the other plant, preventing water and nutrients from traveling between the leaves and roots. The supporting plant begins to decline and eventually dies.

Twine, plant tags, tree wraps, holiday lights and other materials can do the same thing. As the branches, stem or trunk expand, these materials don't. Take a few minutes to walk through your landscape and look for any of these. Pull back the mulch and soil around the base of plants. Make sure the twine was removed.

Now check for plant labels you may have overlooked. Write the plant names on your landscape plans or in your garden journal and remove the restricting tag. And don't believe ads—those expandable tree wraps don't expand as quickly as the tree.

Look for any stray holiday lights you may have wrapped around and left on plant stems and branches. Loosen or remove them. If you have birdhouses, hanging baskets or other items mounted on plants, make sure the mounting devices aren't harming the trees.

Mower Blight

Lawn mowers and weed whips are a major cause of plant decline and death. Every time equipment takes a nick out of a plant, it creates an entryway for insects and diseases.

Mower-damaged trees and shrubs are among the first plants to show drought stress. Insects and diseases begin to attack the stressed trees, decline continues and the trees eventually die.

The solution is simple and actually saves you work: Mulch around your trees and shrubs. This means less grass to mow, no hand trimming and, best of all, no mower blight.

Marie Mills/David Cummings/Unicorn Stock Photos

Mower blight is one of the major contributors to urban tree death.

Nutrient Deficiencies

Pale green or chlorotic leaves may signify a nutrient deficiency. This can be caused by a lack of nutrients in the soil, or the plant's inability to get those nutrients out.

Start with a soil test (review Chapters 1 and 2). This will tell you whether you need to add more nutrients or adjust your pH, so the plants can use the nutrients that are already there.

If the soil is fine, look for environmental conditions that would prevent the plant from taking up nutrients. Anything that damages roots or prevents movement of nutrients into or through the plant can cause similar symptoms.

Drought, poorly drained soils, root rot, pollution damage, borers, root-eating grubs and several diseases can cause the same symptoms. Find the cause and correct the problem. Adding more fertilizer won't help if the plant can't use it.

Black Walnut Toxicity

Plant wilting, stunted growth and eventual death are often clues there is a black walnut in the vicinity. Their roots, leaves and nuts contain a substance called juglone. When the roots of a susceptible plant contact the juglone, usually within 1 to 2 months of planting, injury occurs.

Most publications recommend keeping sensitive plants at least 50 feet away from black walnuts. However, I've seen damage to plants over 200 feet away.

Create planting beds as far from black walnuts as possible—at least 50 to 60 feet. Consider creating a raised bed lined with weed barrier fabric to keep out the black walnut roots.

Using resistant plants will minimize problems. There are several lists of plants observed growing or dying under black walnuts. Though no one list is complete, Ohio State University has one of the better ones. Check out: *http://ohioline.osu.edu/hyg-fact/1000/1148.html*.

You may have to do a little experimenting if the plant you want to grow is not on the list. Plant one in the area of the black walnut and wait a season. If the plant is unaffected, it's safe to plant more.

Black walnut wood chips can be used as mulch around resistant plants. Leaves and wood chips can be composted, but not the husks. When fully decomposed, they're safe to use in the garden. I prefer to compost things like this in a separate pile and use the compost on resistant plants. That way, if my compost isn't ready, no harm will be done.

Removing the tree will not give you immediate results. It takes 5 to 10 years for black walnut roots to decompose and lose their toxicity. The next time a squirrel gives you a free black walnut tree, you may want to say, "No, thanks".

Black Walnut Toxicity

Paul Wray/Forestry Extension, Iowa State university/www.forestryimages.com

DO NOT PLANT NEAR BLACK WALNUTS

Alder, European
Apple
Asparagus
Azalea
Baptisia
Basswood or linden
Birch species
Blackberry
Blueberry
Cabbage
Chokeberry, red
Chrysanthemum,
  some species
Columbine, wild and
  Colorado
Crabapples
Eggplant
Hackberry, northern
Hydrangea
Lilac
Lilies (especially Asian
  hybrids)
Mountain laurel
Norway spruce
Peony, some
Peppers
Petunia, some
Potato
Potentilla
Privet
Red pine
Rhododendron
Rhubarb
Yew

RESISTANT PLANTS* THAT CAN BE PLANTED NEAR BLACK WALNUTS

Arborvitae
Astilbe
Beans
Bee balm (*Monarda*)
Begonia, wax
Bellflower
Black raspberry
Bugleweed (*Ajuga*)
Carrots
Catalpa, southern
Clematis, some
Coralbells (*Heuchera*)
Corn
Crocus
Daphne, some
Daylily
Euonymus
Ferns, some
Forsythia, some
Geranium, perennial
Ginger, European
Grasses, most
Hemlock, Canadian
Hosta, some
Hyacinth, grape and
  common
Lungwort
Maple, Japanese
Melon
Pansy
Peach
Pear
Pot marigold
  (*Calendula*)
Redbud, Eastern
Rose of Sharon
Sedum, some
Snowdrop
Squash
Squill
Sundrops
Sweet woodruff
Tulips
Viburnum, some
Winter aconite
  (*Galanthus*)
Zinnia

*These plants have been observed growing within 50 feet of a black walnut.

Weathering Plant Stresses ———

Pollution Problems

It's not uncommon near larger cities to be warned of "ozone alerts" on especially hot days. While we may think of these days in terms of our own health, high concentrations of ozone, sulfur dioxide and other pollutants can damage plants, too.

Symptoms and intensity vary with the type and concentration of the pollutant, duration of exposure, plant species and how close the plant is to the source.

Damage usually appears very soon after exposure. Symptoms can include mottled leaves, scorch, twig dieback, stunted growth, premature leaf drop and flower loss. These injuries can be confused with problems caused by insects, nutrition, weather or disease.

The most recently matured leaves are often the ones that show symptoms. Keeping track of pollution exposure may help you correctly identify the problem.

Proper care is your only recourse for minimizing pollution stress. Gardeners who live in areas with frequent ozone alerts should select the most pollution-resistant plants available. For a detailed description of major pollutants, their damage and resistant plants, log on to *www.aces.edu/department/ipm/poldmge.htm.*

Deicing Salts

Winter means ice, snow and lots of deicing salts in northern areas. If drought, floods and wind don't kill our plants, a dose of these chemicals is sure to finish them off.

Salt spray on stems, needles and buds can cause browning, twig death and brooming, a proliferation of fine twiggy growth near the tip of the branch.

Deicing salts that enter the soil cause desiccation. Damage usually shows up in spring, when the soil thaws. New growth may have brown leaf edges, needles may be partially or totally brown and there may be some tip dieback.

To minimize damage, select salt-tolerant plants and change your maintenance practices. See pointers at the end of Chapter 5.

Herbicide Damage

TWISTED GROWTH, strap-like leaves and brown or dead plants can indicate herbicide damage. Prevent problems by applying chemicals properly and follow these rules:

● **Never spray herbicides or pesticides on windy days.** The spray may drift over to other plants. Keep herbicides away from gardens, or treat in fall, when many of the plants will be dormant or done for the season.

● **Use separate sprayers for weed killers and other chemical applications.** It's difficult, if not impossible, to clean all residue from a sprayer, and a little bit of remaining herbicide may be all it takes to injure or kill your prized plants.

● **Don't use grass clippings treated with a weed killer as mulch.** Chemicals can leach from the grass clippings into the soil and damage your plants. Leave clippings on the lawn to add nutrients to that soil. About 4 to 6 weeks after the lawn has been treated, you can begin collecting clippings again.

● **Always read the labels.** A very nice couple once brought me samples of beans and tomatoes from their vegetable garden. The twisted plants and strap-like leaves showed classic broadleaf weed killer damage. I discovered they used a weed-and-feed product to kill weeds growing in the pathways inside their garden. It's always important to read labels carefully.

Proper structural pruning will reduce storm damage, allowing you to enjoy the beauty of a snowstorm without the worry.

The *Plant Doctor* is in

Q: I've been trying to grow shrubs near my home. Nothing will grow—not even weeds. Do you have any suggestions?

A: Take a look up. I'll bet you have an overhang. These are great for keeping water away from the house, but make it difficult to grow plants. A lack of water—and, in some cases, excess shade—creates a hostile environment for plants.

Consider expanding the planting bed beyond the overhang. Mulch the area next to the house and grow your plants on the outer edge, where they can get light and rain. Once the plants start to grow, no one will realize there is a bare space in back. This also gives you a potential storage area and great access to the back of the plantings.

Q: I think my tree is planted too deeply. Is there anything I can do to help?

A: This is a difficult problem to fix. Removing soil around the trunk to expose the surface roots may create a sink that collects water. This excess water can lead to root rot.

Manipulating the planting depth on older, established trees could actually cause more problems. Small newly planted trees can be transplanted with the root flare at the surface. Otherwise, do whatever you can to keep the tree healthy. Remove the grass around it and plant ground covers or mulch the soil.

Q: My white oak and red maple have pale green and yellow leaves with dark green veins. This year a few leaves turned brown and the trees are not looking good. Please help.

A: Start with a soil test. It appears the soil is alkaline and tying up the iron and manganese your plants need. Add chelated forms of these nutrients (sold as Miracid and Greenol) for a quick green.

Then start working on a long-term solution. Remove the grass under the tree (at least a 10-foot by 10-foot area). Add elemental sulfur (see chart in Chapter 2) and mulch. In 2 or 3 years, the trees will start showing improvement. Or, consult a certified arborist who can use sulfuric acid to lower the pH.

Research has found this gives long-lasting results.

Q: Will the high iron content in our well water harm my plants? I regularly water during the growing seasons.

A: The iron content in well water is usually not harmful to common landscape plants. This is especially true where the soil pH is 7.0 (neutral) or higher (alkaline or sweet). Iron toxicity is more likely to occur, if at all, in acid soils.

Have your soil tested if plants exhibit unexplained brown spots, or you want to be sure the levels are safe for healthy plant growth. Contact your local office of the Extension service for soil test information.

Q: My forsythia has yet to bloom after many years of waiting. How can I get this shrub to unfurl its bright-yellow flowers in early spring?

A: The flower buds of most forsythia are not winter hardy in the North. The plants will survive extreme cold, but the flower buds won't. Add some of the newer forsythias that have cold-hardy buds for reliable spring bloom. "Meadowlark" is 9 feet tall and hardy in areas in Zone 3. "Northern Sun" and "Vermont Sun" are also large shrubs and hardy in Zone 4. "Sunrise" is smaller, urban tolerant and hardy to areas in Zone 4.

Reader's Digest Assoc. Inc./GID

In cold areas, forsythias will survive extreme cold, but their beautiful sunny flower buds won't.

Challenging Locations

Photos: Superstock; inset (from left)—Mark Turner; Jerry Howard/Positive Images; Faith Bemiss; Karen Bussolini

Chapter 14
Made in The Shade

Faith Komsis; opposite page: Alan and Linda Detrick

The dense canopy of a shade tree provides a cool hideaway on a hot summer day. What it doesn't provide is enough light for grass and many flowers to grow. But don't get out the saw or pack away your garden tools—you can have your shade and garden, too.

Study the Light

BEFORE YOU BEGIN PLANTING in a shady area, you should first evaluate the light conditions. There may be more sun than you realize. I have a spot in my side yard that I thought was too shady to grow sun-loving plants. One spring I overbought and ended up placing some sun-loving okra and flowers in this location. To my amazement, they bloomed all summer. To my family's disappointment, the okra even produced fruit. Apparently there was enough early morning and indirect light for these plants to thrive.

Check your landscape throughout the day, season and year. Some areas of your yard may be shady when you leave for and return from work each day, so you might not see the sun that reaches these areas while you're gone. On your day off, do a little detective work. You may discover there's more sun than you realize.

Then think about the seasonal changes in the landscape. Tree leaves can cast lots of shade in summer, but there may be enough sunlight in spring for those early season, sun-loving bulbs and perennials. And the angle and intensity of the sun change throughout the year, too.

Don't forget to reevaluate the light conditions over time. Shade slowly creeps into the yard, often unnoticed, as trees grow or structures are added. Check out the neighbors' yards as well. In my neighborhood, we all cast a little shade on each other's gardens.

Now consider the other factors that influence a plant's ability to grow in sun or shade. The sun is

Types of Shade

WHEN YOU READ gardening books or plant tags, they may recommend growing a plant in full, partial, light or other types of shade. But what do these terms really mean? What is "light shade", and how much sun does a "full shade" plant really need? There is some agreement, but a fair amount of variation, in defining different types of shade.

● **Dappled:** A type of light shade cast by open structures or trees with small leaves and open canopies, like honeylocust or birch. As the sun moves over the tree, the pattern of sun and shade

changes. Plants growing in these conditions receive some direct light, some bright light and some shade throughout the day.

● **Filtered:** The same as dappled shade.

● **High:** Another kind of light shade cast by tall trees with a high canopy. This allows light to reach plants under the tree for all but a few hours each day.

● **Light:** Plants in light shade receive less than 4 hours of shade each day. The type could be filtered, dappled or high shade. A wide variety of sun and shade plants grow in these conditions.

● **Partial, medium or semi-shade:** Plants receive 4 to 6 hours

of sun each day. This is similar to a woodland edge or areas on the east and west sides of buildings.

● **Full:** No direct sunlight reaches plants, as with the shade cast by maples and oaks or the north side of a building. Hydrangeas, hostas and other shade-loving plants will grow here.

● **Dense:** Found in the darkest corners of your landscape, under the deck or beneath a stand of evergreens. Only a few very shade-tolerant ground covers and ferns will grow here. You may want to mulch or grow a moss garden rather than fight the odds.

more intense in the South, allowing (or forcing) gardeners to provide more shade than those gardening in the North. High humidity and cool temperatures in the Pacific Northwest allow shade lovers to move into full sun. Consider all these factors when evaluating light conditions and selecting plants for your yard.

Using Plants as Indicators

Still confused about how much sunlight your plants really need to grow? I use other plants to help me determine how much light is available and what will tolerate the conditions. When a gardener complains of difficulty with a plant, I always ask what

Annual impatiens brighten any shade garden. Mix a few with ferns and hostas for a more informal look.

else thrived or died in that location. If geraniums, zinnias and other sun lovers died but the impatiens thrived, it's probably a shady location.

Make notes about light conditions and planting successes in your garden journal. Over time, you'll be able to tell how much light you really have in a given location and what plants will tolerate that amount of sun or shade. Experience will add to your success in following directions on plant tags or in a book.

Letting in the Light

Gardeners are never happy with the weather, soil or other growing conditions. It could always be warmer, cooler, drier or even sunnier. Although they

can't remove the clouds, some gardeners have come up with some ingenious techniques for increasing light in their gardens.

One was a Master Gardener I worked with many years ago. In his backyard, he created plots that were 4 feet square, then crafted a portable light system for them. He mounted a 4-foot fluorescent light fixture on a stand and ran the lights all day, moving them from plot to plot. I think the electric bill (and his spouse) eventually convinced him to rent a plot in a community garden and replant his backyard with hostas and ferns.

Rooftop gardens have helped others move their plants into the light. A large bag of potting soil makes the perfect container. It may not be the most attractive, but it works—and the plastic provides a built-in mulch. Slice a few drain holes in one side of the bag, then plant lettuce, strawberries or another summer crop in the other.

Decorative containers filled with flowers can add beauty and color to your rooftop garden. Make sure that your roof can support the weight of the pot, wet soil and mature plants. Develop a maintenance plan first. Remember, you'll have to water every day, fertilize throughout the summer, deadhead, manage pests, harvest and tend to other garden-related chores.

Your last resort is pruning your trees to increase the light reaching the garden. As a certified arborist, I'm always hesitant to recommend pruning for this reason alone. Low branches and full canopies have lots of leaves for producing energy for the tree. What's more, such trees are less likely to become hazardous and more likely to stay healthy. If you must remove a few of the lower branches or thin the canopy, consult a certified arborist who can do the job safely and maintain the tree's health, while increasing the light below.

Really Tough Spots

You know you have difficult growing conditions when even the weeds won't grow. The area under your spruce or pine tree may have become a sea of needles and nothing else. In these locations, shade is just part of the problem.

Take a closer look under that tree. Many gardeners worry about the acid soil caused by the needles. But that overlooks the two biggest factors that really keep out grass and weeds: shade and mulch. The dense canopy and fallen needles block the light, which prevents grass from surviving and weeds from sprouting. Either enjoy this mulch that nature replenishes each year, or try using shade-tolerant

This mixture of native and cultivated shade lovers creates a welcoming edge to this shady pathway.

Use a mixture of shrubs, perennials, bulbs and ground covers to create several layers of color, texture and interest under your shade trees.

ground covers in these challenging locations.

That's what fellow horticulture instructor Carol Bangs did. We were walking through her yard in Mequon, Wisconsin one day when she asked, "Know what grows under a spruce tree?" She lifted the lowest branch off the ground and said, "Ginger." Sure enough, she had a healthy stand of wild ginger thriving under the tree. Now *that* is a shade-tolerant plant.

Norway maples and oaks present a different challenge. Check the soil under these trees after a heavy rain. You'll be amazed to see that very little, if any, rain penetrates the heavy canopy. And both trees' extensive root systems compete heavily for water and nutrients. If you want to plant something beneath these trees, try ground covers like lamium that are suited to dry shade. Or, give up the fight and mulch with shredded bark or wood chips. It's better for the tree and may be easier for you to maintain.

The overhang presents one of the more difficult gardening sites. The shade and lack of moisture affect plant growth and soil health. Many gardeners plant these areas intending to water on a regular basis. Unfortunately, I know from experience that good intentions don't keep your plants alive.

Try some creative lower-maintenance solutions. Expand the planting bed next to your house. Give up planting in the dark, dry area under the overhang. Instead, mulch it to keep the dust down and plant your shrubs, small trees and flowers in the planting area beyond the overhang. This area will receive more light and moisture, while hiding the view below the overhang.

A few clever gardeners have screened these areas with trellises and vines, which make a nice backdrop for other flowers and shrubs. And if you're like me, any added growing and flowering space is welcome.

Growing Grass in Shade

Beautiful lawns and shady conditions are not the best match. I've met many gardeners who struggle to grow grass under maple or oak trees. Every spring they prepare the soil, plant the seed and are encouraged as a few blades start to appear. But that's about all they see. The new lawn remains thin and barely

The variety of textures and shades of green create an inviting garden that tempts the visitor to stop and reflect at the garden bench.

has more leaf surface to capture the limited sunlight reaching the ground.

Reduce fertilization to compensate for the slower growth. Lawns growing in shadier locations need about half the fertilizer of lawns growing in full sun. Check your soil test report and see Chapter 7 for more details on fertilizing and caring for your lawn.

Water thoroughly to encourage deep rooting, but only when needed. Wait until the top 4 to 6 inches of soil starts to dry before you water again. This is when the grass starts to wilt and footprints remain. Overwatering is bad for the grass and harmful to the tree.

The Ground Cover Option

If the grass still won't grow under your trees, try shade-tolerant ground covers. These provide greenery and flowers, don't need mowing and create a healthy growing situation for your trees. Just be careful not to damage your tree in the process.

First, kill any remaining grass with a total vegetation killer, remove it with a sod cutter, or cover it with newspaper and wood chips. Do not till deeply or add soil. Deep cultivation can damage the tree's feeder roots, which grow in the top 12 inches. Adding as little as an inch of topsoil over the roots can injure or even kill some trees.

Plant ground covers in the existing soil. Dig a wider hole and add organic matter if necessary. Plant

makes it through the season. Next spring, they're met with bare soil and a chance to start the process over again.

To help stop this vicious cycle, use a shade-tolerant grass seed. Most lawn grasses do best in full sun, but a few—fine fescues in the North and St. Augustine grass in the South—will grow in shadier conditions.

Once the grass becomes established, you'll need to adjust your maintenance practices. Mow the grass at the tallest height possible—3 inches or more for both fescue and St. Augustine grass. Taller grass

Spring flowering shrubs, perennials and bulbs create a colorful display before the trees leaf out and cast their shade.

with the crown at the soil surface and gently tamp. Mulch the area with wood chips, shredded bark or other organic material. This will keep the weeds out, conserve moisture and improve the growing conditions for both the tree and ground cover. Water thoroughly and only as needed.

If the spot is too shady for ground cover and you don't like the look of mulch, consider a moss garden.

Moist, shady conditions are perfect for growing moss. If you look closely, nature may have already started this garden for you. Maintain the shade and moisture, add a few flagstones and you have a low-maintenance shade garden. If you have the shade but no moss, just get a piece from a friend. Place it on the soil, water often enough to keep it moist and soon you'll have a fuzzy green carpet.

Choosing and Caring for Shade Plants

WHEN YOU SELECT PLANTS for a shade garden, of course you want shade-tolerant plants. But otherwise, the principles are the same as for sunny gardens. Choose plants that are hardy to your area, tolerant of the soil conditions and provide seasonal interest. Many shade plants can add color with foliage, flowers and fruit.

A mixture of textures adds interest to a predominantly green landscape, and light-colored flowers and foliage brighten it. Trish Little of Racine, Wisconsin plants yellow moneywort (*Lysimachia nummularia 'Aurea'*) under her hostas. It's a great combination—the chartreuse foliage of the moneywort makes the hostas pop out in the shade.

Once your plants are in place, you may be tempted to overcompensate by giving them more water and more fertilizer. This is the last thing they need. Shady conditions slow plant growth, so they need less water and energy.

Use organic mulches and compost for ground covers and perennials. Add a little fertilizer, if needed, in spring or summer. For fertilizer, follow your soil test report or use half the amount recommended on the product label. You can always add more—but if you feed your plants too much, you can't take it away.

Water only as needed, when the soil starts to dry. Check the top 4 to 6 inches of soil before reaching for the hose. Some shady locations stay damp even when those under certain trees and evergreens dry out.

Trish uses the weather as her guide. Right after a good rain, she heads out to the shade garden under a Norway maple. If the soil is dry, she drags out the hose and waters thoroughly. She says her neighbors think she's a little daft, but when you look at her garden, it's clear her technique is working.

Shade-Tolerant Ground Covers

Here are a few shady characters you may want to try growing under trees or in other shady spots. The plant name is followed by its cold hardiness zones and, where this information is available, heat hardiness zones.

Ajuga or Bugleweed (*Ajuga*): Cold hardy zones 3 to 9, heat hardy zones 8 to 2. Clumps of solid green, bronze or variegated foliage topped with blue flowers in late spring to early summer. Be careful—it likes to creep into the lawn.

Ajuga

Bearberry (*Arctostaphylos*): Cold hardy zones 2 to 8, heat hardy zones 9 to 3. The evergreen foliage (except *A. alpina*) provides a nice background for the white or pink spring flowers and red fruit in fall. Prefers acid soil.

Creeping Oregon Grapeholly (*Mahonia repens, Mahonia pumila*): Cold hardy zones 5 to 8, heat hardy zones 8 to 2. The common name tells you a lot about this plant. The evergreen leaves look like holly, and the yellow spring flowers are followed by blue-black fruit that looks like grapes.

Epimedium or Barrenwort (*Epimedium*): Cold hardy zones 4 to 8, heat hardy zones 8 to 5. Delicate red, white or yellow flowers, red fall color and evergreen foliage give this plant year-round appeal. Slow to establish.

Epimedium

Ginger (*Asarum*): Cold hardy zones 4 to 9, heat hardy zones 9 to 3. Evergreen and deciduous plants grown for their foliage. Interesting flowers, but you must lift a leaf in early summer to find them.

Lady's Mantle *(Alchemilla).* Cold hardy zones 3 to 8, heat hardy zones 7 to 1. Clump- or mat-forming perennials with soft green leaves and chartreuse flowers in summer or fall.

Periwinkle *(Vinca minor):* Cold hardy zones 4 to 9. Evergreen vines cover the ground. Foliage can be green or variegated. Spring flowers are either periwinkle blue, white or dark blue. Can be invasive.

Lamium or Deadnettle *(Lamium maculatum):* Cold hardy zones 4 to 8, heat hardy zones 8 to 1. Variegated foliage lights up the shade throughout the growing season. The white or mauve flowers are an added bonus. Good in dry shade.

Lamium

Lily-of-the-valley

Lily-of-the-Valley *(Convallaria majalis):* Cold hardy zones 4 to 9, heat hardy zones 9 to 1. A long-time favorite of gardeners. The spring display of fragrant white bell-shaped flowers is followed by red berries. Grows in dense shade, but will move into areas where it is not invited or welcome. Poisonous.

Lilyturf *(Liriope):* Cold hardy zones 5 to 11, heat hardy zones 8 to 3. Forms small clumps of grass-like leaves with spikes of white or purple flowers in summer.

Pachysandra or Japanese Spurge *(Pachysandra terminalis):* Cold hardy zones 4 to 8, heat hardy zones 8 to 3. Evergreen foliage topped with white flowers in spring.

Partridgeberry *(Mitchella repens):* Cold hardy zones 3 to 9, heat hardy zones 9 to 1. White fragrant flowers followed by red berries. Needs acid soil.

Sweet Woodruff *(Galium odoratum):* Cold hardy zones 4 to 8. Pretty, fragrant white flowers in spring. Flowers and leaves used to make May wine.

Winter Creeper *(Euonymus fortunei* varieties or cultivars*):* Cold hardy zones 4 to 9, heat hardy zones 9 to 5 (some cultivars may suffer winter damage in the North). Low-growing to mounding evergreen ground covers and shrubs.

Small Trees and Shrubs

If your shade problem requires a bigger solution, think vertical. Shade-loving small trees and shrubs can provide height, structure, flowers and fruit. Avoid sun-loving plants in these spaces—they'll produce fewer flowers, limited fruit and poor fall color.

Here are just a few options and their cold hardiness zones, followed by heat hardiness zones if available.

Aucuba or Japanese Laurel *(Aucuba):* Cold hardy zones 7 to 10, heat hardy zones 12 to 6. Grows 6 to 10 feet tall with green, speckled or variegated foliage.

Chokeberry *(Aronia):* Cold hardy zones 3 to 9, heat hardy zones 9 to 4. Grows 6 to 10 feet tall with white flowers in spring; red or black fruit. Glossy green foliage turns red in fall.

Clethra, Summersweet, Sweet Pepperbush or White Alder *(Clethra* species*):* Cold hardy zones 4 to 9, heat hardy zones 10 to 1. Grows 3 to 12 feet tall (tropical species grow up to 20 feet). Fragrant white flowers in summer or fall.

Dogwood *(Cornus* species*):* Cold hardy zones 2 to 8. Grows to 20 feet. Colorful stems, spring flowers and bird-attracting fruit make these nice additions to any landscape or garden.

Euonymus, Burning Bush or Wahoo *(Euonymus* species*):* Cold hardy zones 4 to 9, heat hardy zones 9 to 5. Mature heights of 1 to 20 feet, depending on species. Glossy green or variegated foliage. Some have attractive fruit and red fall color.

Dogwood

Fothergilla *(Fothergilla):* Cold hardy zones 4 to 9, heat hardy zones 9 to 2. Grows 3 to 8 feet tall. Covered with fragrant white flowers in spring or early summer and colorful leaves in fall.

Hemlock *(Tsuga canadensis):* Cold hardy zones 3 to 8, heat hardy zones 7 to 3. Can reach 40 feet or more. One of the few shade-tolerant needled evergreens. Soft texture makes it a nice plant for the woodland edge and back of the garden. Dwarf varieties work well in perennial gardens.

Hydrangea species *(Hydrangea):* Cold hardy zones 4 to 9. Heights of 3 to 20 feet, depending on species. Flowers readily in shade. Pink and blue species are not reliably hardy in the North, and white ones can't change color except with the help of spray paint.

Kerria (Kerria japonica): Cold hardy zones 4 to 9, heat hardy zones 8 to 3. Grows up to 10 feet tall. Brightly colored chartreuse stems provide winter interest. White or yellow flowers add color to spring gardens.

Lindera or Spicebush (Lindera species): Cold hardy zones 4 to 9, heat hardy zones 8 to 1. Grows 10 to 20 feet tall, depending on species. Attractive flowers in spring followed by red berries on the female plants.

Nandina or Heavenly-Bamboo (Nandina domestica): Cold hardy zones 6 to 9, heat hardy zones 9 to 3. Grows to 6 feet. Glossy green foliage turns red and often persists from fall through winter. Large panicles of white flowers are followed by red fruit.

Oregon Grapeholly (Mahonia species): Cold hardy zones 5 to 8, heat hardy zones 8 to 2. Grows up to 15 feet tall. Evergreen holly-like foliage, yellow flowers and blue fruit give this plant year-round beauty. Northern gardeners should plant it in a protected location.

Pittosporum (Pittosporum): Cold hardy zones 8-10, heat hardy zones 12 to 3. Grows 10 to 12 feet tall. Glossy green or variegated evergreen leaves are a nice backdrop for its own flowers (some are fragrant) and others in the shade garden.

Rhododendron (Rhododendron): Cold hardy zones 4 to 8, heat hardy zones 9 to 5. Grows 3 to 40 feet tall, depending on species and location. More than 500 species provide a colorful early season display in the garden.

Rhododendron

Russian Arborvitae (Microbiota decussata): Cold hardy zones 3 to 7. Low-growing evergreen that grows 3 feet tall but up to 15 feet wide. Leaves turn bronze in winter.

Viburnum (Viburnum species): Cold hardy zones 2 to 8, heat hardy zones 8 to 1. Grow 3 to 15 feet tall. Flowers, fruit and fall color make these plants standouts in the shade garden.

Winterhazel (Corylopsis): Cold hardy zones 5 to 9, heat hardy zones 9 to 2. Grows 4 to 15 feet tall. Produces fragrant bell-shaped flowers.

Witch Hazel (Hamamelis): Cold hardy zones 3 to 9. Grows up to 12 feet tall. Fall or winter blooms are a nice surprise.

Witch hazel

Color Your Spring with Bulbs

Even shade gardeners can use spring-flowering bulbs, which signal the gardening season is on its way. These beauties often receive enough light to create a colorful display before the shade sets in for the season. Try a few to see how far you can push the plants and your gardening skills. Hardy bulbs, which need a cold period to flower, include:

Daffodil (Narcissus): Cold hardy zones 3 to 8; heat hardy zones 9 to 2. White, yellow, salmon and peach flowers.

Daffodil   *Squill*

Squill (Scilla): Cold hardy zones 3 to 8. Blue, purple or white flowers.

Virginia Bluebells (Mertensia virginica, now known as Mertensia pulmonarioides): Cold hardy zones 3 to 8; heat hardy zones 7 to 1. Blue or white flowers; large leaves fade in late spring.

Wild Hyacinth (Camassia): Cold hardy zones 3 to 10. White or blue spikes of flowers in late spring or summer.

Tropical bulbs, which need to be stored indoors in cold regions, include:

Caladium (Caladium species): Cold hardy zones 10 to 11. Grown for the colorful foliage. See the plant profile on page 217.

Calla Lily (Zantedeschia): Cold hardy zones 9 to 11. Large green or spotted leaves and fragrant white, yellow, pink or red blooms. Tolerates wet soil.

Tuberous Begonia (Begonia x tuberhybrida): Cold hardy zones 9 to 11. Large leaves, stout stems covered with large rose-like blooms of yellow, pink or red.

Shade Plant Profiles

THERE ARE MANY PLANTS that will tolerate shade. This list covers a few that will work in most gardening regions. Heat hardiness ratings are given where available, but those ratings do not yet exist for all plants. Be patient—it will take a few years to evaluate and collect this data on all the new and existing landscape plants.

Astilbe

Astilbe

Other common names: False spirea.
Botanical name: *Astilbe*.
Plant type: Perennial.
Bloom time: Summer into fall.
Hardiness: Cold, zones 3 to 9; heat, zones 8 to 2.
Flower color: White, red, pink, salmon, lavender.
Flower shape: Feathery plumes.
Height: 8 to 48 inches.
Width: 8 to 36 inches.
Light needs: Full to partial shade.
Soil type: Moist, well-drained.
Planting tips: Divide in early spring.
Notes: Nice ferny foliage with bonus of flowers in summer or fall. Combines well with hostas, ferns and other shade lovers. Most will scorch in hot, dry soils and full sun.

Begonia

Other common names: Wax begonia, fibrous-rooted begonia.
Botanical name: *Begonia*.
Plant type: Tender perennial grown as annual in most locations.
Bloom time: Summer through fall.
Hardiness: Cold, zone 11; heat, zones 12 to 1.
Flower color: White, pink, red.
Flower shape: Clusters

Begonia

of two-petaled flowers.
Height: 5 to 16 inches.
Width: 6 to 12 inches.
Light needs: Shade to sun.
Soil type: Moist, fertile.
Planting tips: Seeds are very small. Start indoors 12 weeks before last frost. Plant outdoors after danger of frost.
Notes: Waxy leaves, abundant flowers and low maintenance have kept this a popular bedding plant. Keep soil mulched and moist when grown in full sun. Bronze-leafed varieties are more sun-tolerant.

Bergenia

Bergenia

Other common names: Pigsqueak.
Botanical name: *Bergenia*.
Plant type: Perennial.
Bloom time: Spring.
Hardiness: Cold, zones 4 to 9; heat, zones 9 to 2.
Flower color: Rose, white.
Flower shape: Round clusters of bell-shaped flowers.
Height: 12 to 18 inches.
Width: 12 to 24 inches.
Light needs: Partial shade to full sun.
Soil type: Moist, well-drained.
Planting tips: Sow seeds outdoors in late fall or early spring. Divide in early spring.
Notes: Large cabbage-like leaves are evergreen, often turning reddish-purple in winter. The bold leaf texture, early bloom and fall color make them a year-round beauty.

Bleeding Heart

Bleeding heart

Botanical name: *Dicentra*.
Plant type: Perennial.
Bloom time: Spring and summer.
Hardiness: Cold, zones 3 to 9; heat, unavailable.
Flower color: White and pink to crimson.
Flower shape: Heart-shaped on

terminal stems.
Height: 15 to 36 inches.
Width: 12 to 30 inches.
Light needs: Partial shade.
Soil type: Moist, humus soil.
Planting tips: Sow seeds outdoors in late fall. Divide in late summer.
Notes: The common bleeding heart is an old-fashioned favorite. Large plants (*D. spectabilis*) usually die back in midsummer. Fringed bleeding-heart (*D. eximia,* also known as *D. formosa*) has fern-like leaves that persist all season and blooms that can last all summer.

Bugbane

Bugbane

Botanical name: *Cimicifuga.*
Plant type: Perennial.
Bloom time: Summer or fall.
Hardiness: Cold, zones 3 to 8; heat, zones 12 to 1.
Flower color: White.
Flower shape: Spike.
Height: 3 to 7 feet.
Width: Up to 2 feet.
Light needs: Full sun to shade.
Soil type: Moist, well-drained, fertile.
Planting tips: Sow stratified (cold-treated seed) in spring. Divide in spring.
Notes: One of the few tall plants that will bloom in shade. Fern-like foliage is green or purple and looks good all season. If planted in full sun, keep soil moist.

Caladium

Caladium

Botanical name: *Caladium.*
Plant type: Tender perennial grown as annual in most locations.
Bloom time: Grown for foliage, not flowers.

Hardiness: Cold, zones 10 to 11; heat, unavailable.
Flower color: Grown for white, cream, green and red foliage.
Flower shape: Not applicable.
Height: 24 inches.
Width: 24 inches.
Light needs: Partial to full shade.
Soil type: Moist, organic, well-drained.
Planting tips: Start tuber, knobby side up, in February or March. Transplant outdoors after last frost.
Notes: A colorful container plant or addition to shade garden. Mulch and water to keep roots cool and moist, especially where summers are hot. Pack tubers in peat moss and store in cool, dark location for winter.

Coleus

Coleus

Botanical name: *Solenostemon scutellarioides.*
Plant type: Tender perennial grown as annual.
Bloom time: Grown for foliage, not flowers.
Hardiness: Cold, zones 10 to 11; heat, unavailable.
Flower color: Grown for red, green, yellow and purple foliage.
Flower shape: Not applicable.
Height: 6 to 36 inches.
Width: 6 to 36 inches.
Light needs: Shade to sun.
Soil type: Moist, organic, well-drained.
Planting tips: Start from seeds indoors 6 to 8 weeks before last frost. Move transplants into garden after danger of frost has passed.
Notes: Pinch off any flowers that appear. This will keep plants full and compact. Many new "sun-tolerant" cultivars have been introduced. I find most coleus will tolerate the sun if they are mulched and receive sufficient moisture. Take cuttings and over-winter your favorites as houseplants.

Columbine

Botanical name: *Aquilegia.*
Plant type: Perennial.
Bloom time: Spring to midsummer.
Hardiness: Cold, zones 3 to 9; heat, unavailable.
Flower color: Blue, yellow, white, red solid or bicolor.

Flower shape: Nodding or upright with spurs.
Height: 8 to 36 inches.
Width: 4 to 18 inches.
Light needs: Shade to full sun.
Soil type: Moist, well-drained.
Planting tips: Sow seeds outdoors spring through early summer.
Notes: Keep soil mulched and moist in full sun and hot locations. Great in woodland settings. Deadhead to prevent cultivars from seeding offspring that may be more aggressive and less desirable.

Columbine

Coralbells

Coralbells

Botanical name: *Heuchera*.
Plant type: Perennial.
Bloom time: Late spring to summer.
Hardiness: Cold, zones 3 to 8; heat, zones 8 to 2.
Flower color: Coral, pink, white, green.
Flower shape: Light, airy panicles of tiny bell-shaped flowers.
Height: 4 to 30 inches.
Width: 5 to 24 inches.
Light needs: Shade to sun.
Soil type: Fertile, moist, well-drained.
Planting tips: Sow seeds outdoors in late fall or early spring. Divide in fall.
Notes: A popular plant grown both for foliage and flowers. Bronze- and purple-leafed cultivars tend to scorch in full sun. Check and reset any plants that frost-heave over winter.

Daylily

Botanical name: *Hemerocallis*.
Plant type: Perennial.
Bloom time: Summer through fall.
Hardiness: Cold, zones 3 to 10; heat, unavailable.

Flower color: Wide range—white, yellow, salmon, peach, orange, lavenders, pinks, purples.
Flower shape: Lily-like with variations that are flat, triangular or spider-shaped.
Height: 1 to 4 feet.
Width: 2 to 3 feet.
Light needs: Partial shade to full sun.
Soil type: Tolerates most soils; prefers moist, well-drained.
Planting tips: Sow seeds outdoors in late fall or early spring (need cold treatment if started indoors). Divide in spring or fall.
Notes: Each bloom lasts one day, but numerous blossoms make each floral display last a month. Use several varieties with varying bloom times to extend flowering, or look for repeat bloomers to extend blossoms through summer and fall.

Daylily

Elephant's Ear

Botanical names: *Colocasia* and *Alocasia*.
Plant type: Tender perennial grown as annual.
Bloom time: Grown for foliage, not flowers.
Hardiness: Cold, zone 10; heat, unavailable.
Flower color: Grown for colorful foliage.
Flower shape: Not applicable.
Height: 1 to 15 feet.
Width: 2 to 4 feet or more.
Light needs: Best in partial shade.

Elephant's ear

Soil type: Moist, organic, well-drained.
Planting tips: Start corms indoors 4 to 6 weeks before last frost, or plant directly outdoors after danger of frost passes. Set corms 2 to 3 inches deep.
Notes: Mulch and keep soil moist when grown in full sun and hot regions. Some gardeners with lots of room grow the plants indoors for winter. The tuberous roots also can be overwintered like other tender bulbs in a cool, dark location.

Ferns

Botanical names: Various, including *Matteuccia* and *Osmunda*.
Plant type: Perennial.
Bloom time: Grown for foliage, not flowers.
Hardiness: Cold, zones 2 to 10; heat, zones 9 to 1.
Flower color: Not applicable.
Flower shape: Not applicable.
Height: 4 to 48 inches.
Width: 8 to 36 inches.
Light needs: Full to partial shade.
Soil type: Moist, organic soils.
Planting tips: Divide in spring or propagate from spores (see Chapter 6).
Notes: Ferns can provide texture, form and a backdrop for your shade garden. Select a species that fits the space and your garden design.

Ferns

Forget-Me-Not

Botanical name: *Myosotis*.
Plant type: Annual or biennial that self-seeds and acts like a perennial.
Bloom time: Spring to early summer.
Hardiness: Cold, zones 4 to 8; heat, zones 7 to 1.
Flower color: Blue with yellow center.
Flower shape: Clusters of small round flowers.
Height: 4 to 12 inches.
Width: 6 to 12 inches.
Light needs: Partial shade to full sun.
Soil type: Moist, well-drained.
Planting tips: Start seeds outdoors in late summer or early fall for spring flowers.

Forget-me-not

Notes: Mounds of greenery topped with lots of dainty blue flowers. Nice addition to woodland and shade gardens. Water during dry periods.

Foxglove

Botanical name: *Digitalis*.
Plant type: Biennial, short-lived perennial.
Bloom time: Late spring to summer.
Hardiness: Cold, zones 5 to 9; heat, zones 10 to 1.
Flower color: Purple, pink, salmon, yellow, white.
Flower shape: Large spikes of trumpet-like flowers.
Height: 2 to 6 feet.
Width: 1 to 2 feet.
Light needs: Partial shade.
Soil type: Moist, well-drained.
Planting tips: Sow seed outdoors in spring or early summer. Divide in spring or fall.
Notes: Colorful spires rise above the foliage to provide a vertical accent in shade

Foxglove

gardens. Though short-lived, they put on a good show. All parts can cause digestive discomfort.

Fuchsia

Botanical name: *Fuchsia*.
Plant type: Tender perennial grown as an annual in most areas.
Bloom time: Summer to fall.
Hardiness: Cold, zones 8 to 10; heat, unavailable.
Flower color: White, pink, purple, red and combinations.
Flower shape: Pendulous, tubular flowers.
Height: 1 to 5 feet.
Width: 1 to 3 feet.
Light needs: Full to partial shade.
Soil type: Moist, organic.
Planting tips: Sow seeds in spring; root softwood cuttings in spring.

Fuchsia

Notes: A favorite hanging basket. Also works well in containers mixed with other annuals. Try upright types in the garden. Deadhead to prolong blooming.

Goatsbeard

Botanical name: *Aruncus.*
Plant type: Perennial.
Bloom time: Spring.
Hardiness: Cold, zones 3 to 9; heat, zones 10 to 1.
Flower color: Cream.
Flower shape: Airy plumes, 1 to 6 feet.
Width: 1 to 4 feet.
Light needs: Partial to full shade.
Soil type: Moist, rich loam.
Planting tips: Divide in early spring or fall. Self-seeds.
Notes: A large, shrub-sized perennial with nice ferny foliage. Deadhead for tidier appearance and to prevent reseeding, unless you want more plants.

Goatsbeard

Hosta

Hosta

Botanical name: *Hosta* (species and cultivars).
Plant type: Perennial.
Bloom time: Summer; a few species bloom in fall.
Hardiness: Cold, zones 3 to 9; heat, zones 9 to 2.
Flower color: White or lavender.
Flower shape: Spikes of trumpet-shaped flowers.
Height: 4 to 48 inches.
Width: Up to 5 feet.
Light needs: Full to partial shade.
Soil type: Moist, well-drained.
Planting tips: Dig and divide late summer or early spring. Sow seeds in spring.
Notes: Grown for its attractive foliage. The variegated, puckered or blue leaves are great additions to any shade garden. Some have fragrant flowers.

Impatiens

Other common names: Busy Lizzie, Balsam.

Impatiens

Botanical name: *Impatiens wallerana.*
Plant type: Tender perennial grown as annual in most areas.
Bloom time: Summer through fall.
Hardiness: Cold, zone 11; heat, 12 to 1.
Flower color: Variety, including white, orange, red, pink, violet and coral. New yellow varieties have just been introduced.
Flower shape: Flat, with five petals.
Height: 6 to 24 inches.
Width: 6 to 18 inches.
Light needs: Full to partial shade.
Soil type: Moist, well-drained.
Planting tips: Start seeds indoors 3 to 4 months before last frost, or buy transplants.
Notes: A popular annual shade plant. This nonstop bloomer can brighten up the shade in planters, hanging baskets or gardens. Mulch roots and keep soil moist when growing this plant in a sunnier location.

Lungwort

Botanical name: *Pulmonaria.*
Plant type: Perennial.
Bloom time: Late winter or early spring.
Hardiness: Cold, zones 4 to 8; heat, zones 8 to 4.
Flower color: Pink when they first open, then turning blue or white.
Flower shape: Small clusters of bell-shaped flowers.
Height: 6-18 inches.
Width: 2 feet.
Light needs: Full to bright shade.
Soil type: Moist, well-drained.

Lungwort

Planting tips: Divide after flowering or in fall.
Notes: Appears to be deer-resistant. Solid green, spotted or variegated evergreen leaves. Remove old leaves after flowering.

Meadow Rue

Botanical name: *Thalictrum.*
Plant type: Perennial.
Bloom time: Summer.
Hardiness: Cold, zones 3 to 10; heat, zones 9 to 1.
Flower color: Creamy white, yellow, pink, purple.
Flower shape: Panicles or clusters of star-shaped or daisy-like flowers.
Height: 8 inches to 8 feet.
Width: 12 to 24 inches.
Light needs: Full shade to full sun.
Soil type: Moist, rich.
Planting tips: Sow seeds outdoors in fall or spring. Divide in early spring as growth begins.
Notes: Texture and color of the blue-green foliage provide relief from other shade greenery. Small plants are good for rock gardens; tall ones make a nice back-

Meadow rue

ground or vertical accent in the flower border.

Monkshood

Botanical name: *Aconitum.*
Plant type: Perennial.
Bloom time: Summer to fall.
Hardiness: Cold, zones 3 to 8; heat, unavailable.
Flower color: Blue, white, bicolor, yellow.
Flower shape: Spikes of little flowers that look like a monk's hood.
Height: 3 to 6 feet.
Width: 1 to 2 feet.
Light needs: Partial shade to full sun.
Soil type: Moist, organic.

Monkshood

Planting tips: Sow seeds outdoors in late fall or early winter. Seeds need 3 weeks of cold treatment if started indoors. Divide in early spring.
Notes: Unique flower shape makes this a fun and attractive addition to the back of the garden. Taller varieties may need staking. Poisonous.

Primrose

Primrose

Botanical name: *Primula.*
Plant type: Perennial.
Bloom time: Early spring, often repeating in fall.
Hardiness: Cold, zones 3 to 8; heat, zones 7 to 3.
Flower color: Almost every color.
Flower shape: Round clusters of five-petaled flowers.
Height: 2 to 24 inches.
Width: 8 to 24 inches.
Light needs: Partial shade.
Soil type: Moist loam.
Planting tips: Sow hardy types outdoors in late fall or early spring.
Notes: Size and hardiness vary with variety. The plants are evergreen in milder areas and benefit from mulch in colder regions.

Solomon's Seal

Botanical name: *Polygonatum.*
Plant type: Perennial.
Bloom time: Late spring.
Hardiness: Cold, zones 3 to 9; heat, zones 9 to 1.
Flower color: Greenish-white.
Flower shape: Tiny bells in pairs beneath the stem.
Height: 1 to 6 feet.
Width: 1 to 2 feet.
Light needs: Full to partial shade.
Soil type: Moist, rich soil.
Planting tips: Start seeds indoors 6 to 8 weeks before last frost. Sow outdoors after danger of frost has

Solomon's seal

passed. Divide in spring when growth begins.
Notes: Native to the eastern half of the United States. The graceful arching stems add structure and texture to shade gardens. Fragrant flowers are followed by blue berries. Try the variegated cultivar to brighten shade. False Solomon's seal has white flowers at the end of the stem, followed by red berries.

Chapter 15
Some Like It Hot

Those of you in the South and Southwest may be wondering what a gardener from the Great Lakes region knows about hot, dry weather and dealing with watering restrictions. Readers in my part of the country may be thinking about skipping this chapter and moving on to something more relevant—but please don't. Water is an important resource that we all share and that our plants need.

I haven't lived through years of extremely hot, dry summers. But like most gardeners, I've suffered through seasonal droughts.

A summer working in Southern California helped me appreciate the summer rains and numerous lakes and rivers that cover the upper Midwest. Then there were the years hauling water buckets, or filling and driving the old Army surplus water truck to remote garden sites. That was way too much work, and I decided there had to be a better way. After all, I am a low-input (not lazy!) gardener.

We'll use the philosophy of Xeriscaping as the basis for our discussion. This idea started in Colorado in 1981, when a Denver Water Department task force started creating attractive landscapes with water-efficient plants. The task force believed that with proper plant selection and management strategies, gardeners could cut their water use in half.

This is a great goal for all of us to share. Saving time, money and a valuable resource benefits us all. You've already started the process if you've been following the recommendations in this book. (See Chapter 5 for more watering and Xeriscaping ideas.) With a little more information, you can make a concerted effort to efficiently use water in your yard.

Cooling Off The Landscape

START WITH a landscape plan. Walk around your yard and neighborhood to discover the direction of the prevailing winds, sun and shade patterns and any microclimates that may exist. Now work to improve the good features and eliminate or modify those that create a harsher growing environment.

Use drought-tolerant trees and shrubs to create windbreaks. Staggering the plants to create double or triple rows will give even better results.

Windbreaks can affect plant growth in an area 2 to 10 times the height of the windbreak. So if your windbreak of trees and shrubs is 6 feet tall, plants within 12 to 60 feet of the leeward side may benefit. If space is limited, try a trellis and some vines. Though less effective than three rows of trees, it's better than nothing.

Add a little cooling shade with arbors, pergolas and other outdoor structures. Grow a vine or two over the structure, and you'll increase the shade even more. Use drought-tolerant trees, shrubs and ornamental grasses to provide shade to nearby plants.

Providing just a little relief from the afternoon sun reduces moisture loss, extends the time between waterings, and just may save a plant or two. Don't worry about your sun lovers. Maintain a few beds for them. Southern gardeners dealing with intense light can grow quite a few sun-loving plants in the shade.

Move the more heat-sensitive and moisture-loving plants to the east side

of the house or other areas that receive only morning sun. This way, plants will receive plenty of cool morning sun but escape the hot afternoon rays.

Group your plants into beds, gardens or areas of the yard based on moisture needs. This is better for your plants, and you'll spend less time hand-watering individual plantings scattered throughout the landscape. It also decreases the risk of accidentally over-watering a neighboring plant that prefers dry conditions. And if the plants are all equally suited to the conditions, they're more likely to live in harmony and not outgrow their partners and take over the bed.

Limit the number of sentimental favorites that need lots of moisture. If you just can't resist, plant moisture lovers near the house and water supply. This will make them easier to tend and give you the greatest cooling and aesthetic value for the water and effort used.

Selecting Water-Efficient Plants

Selecting the right plants is the next step in creating a Xeriscape. Take a look at the plants growing in nature preserves, wildlife refuges and your own backyard. Note the ones that seem to survive what-

These drought-tolerant perennials—flowering tobacco, penstemon and artemesia—provide color and texture in the landscape with minimal need for moisture.

ever Mother Nature dishes out—especially heat and drought. These are plants you may want to add to your list. Once established, they won't need much supplemental water, so you'll spend less time dragging hoses and more time enjoying your garden.

Native plants are a good starting point. If they developed naturally in your region, they should be adapted to the weather. Visit the Lady Bird Johnson Wildflower Center's Web site at *www.wildflower.org* for a listing of native plants for your part of the country.

Whether selecting native or cultivated plants, make sure they are suited to your growing conditions. Since humans have stepped in, the natural environment has gone through some big changes.

Soils have been destroyed during construction, temperatures have increased in and around urban "heat islands", wind patterns have changed and the growth in paved areas has increased water runoff. This is no longer the same environment in which our native plants initially developed and thrived.

I still recommend native plants when they're suited to the environment in your yard. If you choose "domestic plants", as my naturalist friends call them, make sure they're water-efficient as well. I've listed a few in this chapter, though there are many more to try.

Consider conducting your own drought stress

Put Limits on the Lawn

LOOK FOR OPPORTUNITIES to replace water-loving turf with more drought-tolerant ground covers, mulches or other moisture-conserving materials. Save grass for play areas, where it serves a needed function.

If you feel you must have green grass to make your landscape complete, these strategies will help reduce water consumption:

• Use a drought-tolerant lawn grass like Bermuda in the South, and fine or tall fescues in the North.

• Grow grass at the tallest recommended mowing height. Tall grass forms deeper roots, making it more drought-tolerant.

• Sharpen the mower blade so it cuts the grass instead of tearing it. A clean cut loses less moisture and closes faster.

• Leave clippings on the lawn. They add moisture and nutrients back to the soil.

• Let your lawn go dormant during hot, dry spells. This is how it survives adverse conditions. Once the weather cools and the rains return, the grass will green back up. Avoid walking on dormant grass.

Steven Nikkila/Perennial Favorites

Using Trees to Save Energy

PLANT PLACEMENT has a great impact on year-round energy use as well as water conservation. Plant shade trees on the west and east side of the house to reduce heating and cooling costs. In summer, they shade the sunniest windows, helping to keep things cool. In the winter, they won't block the sunlight from the south that helps warm our homes.

test. Get out your journal and record the names of plants that thrive, those that just survive and those that die during hot, dry weather. I do this in my yard.

I water my plants as needed during the establishment period. After that, they're pretty much on their own. Some call it survival of the fittest, but I prefer to call it "low-maintenance evaluation testing". That sounds more scientific and socially acceptable. I "test" plants the same way to see how they handle winter cold.

Evaluate all the features of the plant, not just drought tolerance. When an ad or catalog description of a plant sounds too good to be true, it probably is. Most plants that will grow anywhere, survive anything and still look good usually do it at the expense of surrounding and native plants. Ask about invasive tendencies. Internet sites and your local Extension service or Department of Natural Resources can help you avoid bringing problems into your landscape and community.

Amend the Soil

That amazing stuff known as organic matter can help with drought, too. Add compost and other organic matter to the top 12 inches of soil to improve water-holding capacity and the growing environment. A garden growing in properly prepared soil

can survive most droughts and out-compete the weeds (for a review of how to improve soil, see Chapters 1 to 3).

You don't have to fix all problem areas at once. Make soil preparation a priority for any new gardens you install. Then redo one garden at a time, starting with the worst—you know, the ones that are mostly weeds and have just a few pathetic plants barely clinging to life. Don't worry, we've all had one of those beds.

In the meantime, mulch your gardens that don't have organic matter. As the mulch breaks down, the earthworms, ground beetles and other good insects work it into the soil around the plant roots.

Mulching also helps conserve moisture, reduce erosion and keep plant roots cool. Once you water or it finally rains, it will keep the moisture by the plant roots, where it's needed. You also want to keep the soil you've worked so hard to improve in place. Mulch softens the force of pounding rains or high-pressure watering (remember the last time you didn't change the nozzle?), reducing soil and water runoff.

Recycling Water in the Landscape

The era of the rain barrel may be returning. Gardeners all across the country are starting to recycle

judywhite/GardenPhotos.com

Covered rain barrels capture rain from the roof, while keeping mosquitoes out.

water from downspouts and other areas. The Lady Bird Johnson Wildflower Center in Austin, Texas recycles enough water from its roofs to provide most of the water needed, if not all, for the landscape and trial gardens.

If you live in an arid region, try capturing your own roof runoff for use in the garden. Gardeners in wetter regions may want to divert water from the storm sewers and put it to better use in the landscape.

There are many new systems available to make this an attractive, space-efficient and mosquito-free process. The Department of Natural Resources and Parks in King County, Washington has useful information at *http://dnr.metrokc.gov/wlr/PI/rainbarrels.htm*. Check with your local municipality for any ordinances and restrictions on collecting and using this type of water.

A rain garden is another way to recycle water from the roof to the landscape and back into the groundwater. See page 239 for more information on this emerging trend.

Installing an Irrigation System

Irrigation systems and Xeriscapes sound like they don't belong in the same book, let alone the same chapter. But when used with Xeriscaping, a well-designed, properly installed sprinkler system can actually help conserve water.

Irrigation systems can apply the proper amount of water at the best time based on the weather and plant needs. The key is using these watering systems properly.

Consider a system with several watering zones for various types of plants. More drought-tolerant plants, for example, should be in a different zone than drought-sensitive ones. This way, you apply water only where it's needed, instead of wasting it on the whole landscape.

Select a system that adjusts to the weather as well—it's disheartening to watch a sprinkler running during a rainstorm. Use a shovel or trowel to monitor your irrigation method. The soil should be drier on top and moist several inches below. Adjust your system so the topsoil just starts to dry before it begins watering again.

To find a professional installer, check the yellow pages. Ask about training, membership in professional organizations and customer references.

— *Heat-Tolerant Trees and Shrubs* —

Note: *Heat hardiness ratings are given where available, but these ratings do not yet exist for all plants.*

Trees

Acacia (*Acacia*): Cold hardy, zones 9 to 11; heat hardy, zones 12 to 1. Grows 20 to 60 feet. Fast grower; often short-lived. Tolerates heat and seaside conditions; flowers.

Reader's Digest Assoc. Inc/GID

Bottlebrush buckeye

Ash (*Fraxinus*): Cold hardy, zones 4 to 9; heat hardy, zones 8 to 2. Grows 45 to 80 feet.

Buckeye (*Aesculus*): Cold hardy, zones 3 to 7; heat hardy, zones 8 to 4. Grows 20 to 40 feet.

Catalpa, Indian Cigar or Bean Tree Catalpa (*Catalpa*): Cold hardy, zones 4 to 9. Grows 30 to 60 feet. Orchid-like flowers, beanpod-type fruit; some gardeners don't like the mess.

Cedar (*Cedrus*): Cold hardy, zones 5 to 9; heat hardy, zones 7 to 2. Grows to 100 feet or more.

Crape-Myrtle (*Lagerstroemia indica*): Cold hardy, zone 7 to 9; heat hardy, zone 10 to 2. Grows 7 to 25 feet. Pink, white, rose or purple flowers in late summer; attractive exfoliating bark.

Desert Willow (*Chilopsis*): Cold hardy, zones 8 to 10; heat hardy, zones 11 to 7. Grows 10 to 25 feet. Snapdragon-like flowers in spring; willow-like leaves. Native to arid Southwest.

Eucalyptus or Gum Eucalyptus (*Eucalyptus*): Cold hardy, zones 9 to 10. Grows to 100 feet. Many have fragrant foliage. Colorful bark.

Golden-Rain Tree (*Koelreuteria paniculata*): Cold hardy, zones 5 to 9; heat hardy, zones 8 to 5. Airy yellow flowers followed by seedpods.

Hackberry (*Celtis*): Cold hardy, zones 3 to 9. Grows 40 to 60 feet. Elm-like growth habit; tolerant of urban environments.

Juniper (*Juniperus*): Cold hardy, zones 2 to 9; heat hardy, zones 9 to 1. Grows 6 inches to 60 feet. Comes in low-growing, spreading and upright forms.

Kentucky Coffeetree (*Gymnocladus dioicus*): Cold hardy, zones 4 to 8. Grows 60 to 75 feet. Attractive scaly bark; large leaves with lots of small leaflets. Visually ineffective, but female trees have fragrant flowers and brown pods.

Mescal bean *(Sophora secundiflora):* Cold hardy, zones 8 to 10. Grows 15 to 30 feet. Fragrant blue or white flowers.

Oak *(Quercus):* Cold hardy, zones 4 to 8; heat hardy, zones 9 to 2. Grows 40 to over 100 feet. Some of the most drought-tolerant are holly oak (*Q. ilex*); cork oak (*Q. suber*), a desert variety; and bur oak (*Q. macrocarpa*).

Oak

Pine *(Pinus):* Cold hardy, zones 2 to 10; heat hardy, zones 9 to 1. Grows 6 to 90 feet. Bristlecone, Afghanistan, pinyon and ponderosa are most drought-tolerant.

Poplar *(Populus):* Cold hardy, zones 4 to 9; heat hardy, zones 9 to 3. Grows 40 to 90 feet. Fast-growing, weak-wooded. Tolerates salt and pollution.

Silver Linden *(Tilia tomentosa):* Cold hardy, zones 4 to 7. Grows 50 to 70 feet. Silver-backed leaves, yellow fragrant flowers.

Smoke Tree *(Cotinus coggygria):* Cold hardy, zones 5 to 9; heat hardy, zones 9 to 3. Grows 10 to 15 feet. Pollution tolerant with attractive flowers and seed heads.

Wafer Ash *(Ptelea trifoliata):* Cold hardy, zones 3 to 9. Grows 15 to 20 feet. Wafer-shaped fruit once used as a substitute for hops.

Shrubs

Barberry *(Berberis):* Cold hardy, zones 4 to 9; heat hardy, zones 9 to 2. Grows 18 inches to 8 feet. Deciduous varieties are more drought-tolerant.

Beautybush *(Kolkwitzia amabilis):* Cold hardy, zones 4 to 8. Grows 6 to 10 feet. Pink bell-shaped flowers.

Bluebeard or Blue Mist Spirea *(Caryopteris x clandonensis):* Cold hardy, zones 5 to 9; heat hardy, zones 9 to 2. Grows 1-1/2 to 5 feet.

Broom *(Cytisus):* Cold hardy zones 6 to 8; heat hardy zones 8 to 4. Grows 1-1/2 to 6 feet tall. Evergreen with creamy yellow flowers.

Killiney Salmon broom

Butterfly Bush or Summer Lilac *(Buddleia or Buddleja):* Cold hardy, zones 5 to 9; heat hardy, zones 10 to 4. Grows 6 to 20 feet. Fragrant flowers in summer and fall. Grown as subshrub in North; invasive in milder regions.

Cassia or Wild Senna *(Cassia):* Cold hardy, zones 4 to 7. Grows to 6 feet. Yellow flowers; perennial and shrub forms. Tropical species in zones 10 to 11 grow much taller.

Cotoneaster *(Cotoneaster):* Cold hardy, zones 3 to 9; heat hardy, zones 8 to 3. Grows 1 to 15 feet; tolerates drought and seaside conditions. Best fruiting in poor, dry soils.

Germander *(Teucrium):* Cold hardy, zones 8 to 11; heat hardy, zones 12 to 4. Grows 6 to 18 inches. Used as perennial or small shrub.

Juniper *(Juniperus):* Cold hardy, zones 2 to 9; heat hardy, zones 9 to 1. Grows 6 inches to 60 feet. Comes in low-growing, spreading and upright forms.

Lavender Cotton *(Santolina):* Cold hardy, zones 6 to 9; heat hardy, zones 12 to 1. Grows 18 to 24 inches. Used as low hedge or perennial.

Juniper with yellow foliage

Lilac *(Syringa vulgaris):* Cold hardy, zones 3 to 8; heat hardy, zones 8 to 3. Grows 3 to 30 feet. Fragrant white, blue, purple, pink and red flowers.

Nandina or Heavenly-Bamboo *(Nandina domestica):* Cold hardy, zones 6 to 9; heat hardy, zones 9 to 3. Grows to 6 feet. Shade- and drought-tolerant. Good year-round interest.

Potentilla *(Potentilla fruticosa):* Cold hardy, zones 3 to 8; heat hardy, zones 9 to 4. Grows 1 to 4 feet. Summer-blooming shrub with yellow or white flowers.

Sumac *(Rhus typhina):* Cold hardy, zones 4 to 9; heat hardy, zones 9 to 5. Grows 8 to 30 feet. Aggressive; good fall color; winter interest.

Rock Rose (*Cistus*): Cold hardy, zones 8 to 10; heat hardy, zones 12 to 1. Grows 3 to 5 feet. Resistant to fire.

Rose *(Rosa species)*: Cold hardy, zones 4 to 9; heat hardy, zones 9 to 3. Grows 1-1/2 to 20 feet. Shrub roses, flower, fruit.

Rosemary *(Rosmarinus officinalis)*: Cold hardy, zones 8-10; heat hardy, zones 12 to 2. Grows 6 inches to 7 feet. Grows as an annual or potted plant that can be wintered indoors in the North.

Snowberry and Coralberry (*Symphoricarpos*): Cold hardy, zones 3 to 7. Grows 2 to 6 feet. Blue-green leaves, white or coral berries. Shade- and drought-tolerant.

Spirea *(Spiraea):* Cold hardy, zones 3 to 8. Grows 1 to 10 feet. Spring- and summer-blooming varieties.

Tamarisk *(Tamarix)*: Cold hardy, zones 2 to 8. Grows 10 to 15 feet. Salt-tolerant. Fine-textured foliage; rosy-pink airy flowers.

Vitex or Chaste Tree *(Vitex)*: Cold hardy, zones 5 to 10; heat hardy, zones 10 to 1. Grows to 20 feet. Treated as subshrub in North.

Grasses, Cacti and Such

Foliage is as important in the sunny garden as it is in the shade. Many heat- and drought-tolerant plants are coated with white hairs to help them conserve moisture. Gray foliage is often a good sign the plants will grow in these difficult conditions.

Artemisia (*Artemisia*): Also known as wormwood, silvermound or mugwort. Cold hardy, zones 3 to 9.

Artemisia

Grown as annuals, perennials and shrubs. The attractive, fragrant foliage adds texture and color (mainly green and gray) to the garden; plants also can be used in garden crafts.

Dusty Miller *(Senecio cineraria)*: Cold hardy, zones 8 to 10. Grown as an annual in the North and shrub in the South. A popular bedding plant that's been paired with almost every other sun-loving annual.

Hens and Chicks *(Sempervivum tectorum)*: Cold hardy, zones 5 to 10. Another hardy succulent found in the North as well as southern regions of the U.S. Often used in planters and as ground covers.

Pampas grass

Ornamental Grasses: Many are native to the prairie and well-adapted to hot, dry conditions. Select those that are hardy for your area, fit the available space (they can get big) and blend with the rest of your landscape.

Prickly-Pear Cactus *(Opuntia species)*: Found growing throughout much of the U.S., including an excellent planting at the Minnesota Landscape Arboretum in Chanhassen.

Yucca or Adam's Needle *(Yucca):* Cold hardy, zones 4 to 10. The sword-shaped leaves and long flower stems covered with large bell-shaped flowers make a statement in any garden. Evergreen foliage provides a strong vertical accent.

Bulbs

Many spring-flowering bulbs will survive in hot, dry locations, since the worst of the weather strikes while they lie dormant. Mulch the soil or cover them with other plants to keep them safely tucked away. Here are a few that survive and thrive in the heat.

Desert Candle or Foxtail Lily *(Eremurus)*: Cold hardy, zones 5 to 9; heat hardy, zones 8 to 1. The rosette of strappy leaves and long, wide spike of flowers provide the look and feel of the desert.

Torch flower

Needs winter cold to set flowers.

Lily-of-the-Nile *(Agapanthus)*: Cold hardy, zones 8 to 11, or treated like a tender bulb in cold regions; heat hardy, zones 12 to 1. Domed clusters of blue or white flowers top a rosette of straplike evergreen leaves. Grow as a perennial in mild areas and a tender bulb in colder regions.

Torch Flower or Red Hot Poker *(Kniphofia)*: Cold hardy, zones 5 to 9, but needs protection during first winter in the North. Grow in full sun or light shade and well-drained soil.

Ground Covers

Bearberry *(Arctostaphylos species)*: Cold hardy, zones 2 to 8; heat hardy, zones 9 to 3. This heat-, drought- and shade-tolerant ground cover also flowers and fruits. Prefers acid soil.

Catmint *(Nepeta x faassenii)*: Cold hardy, zones 3 to 9; heat hardy, zones 12 to 2. Gray foliage and long-lasting blue flowers look like lavender in the garden. Spreads slowly and does not seem to invade the garden like other catmints.

Juniper: See listing under **Shrubs.**

Lamb's Ears *(Stachys byzantina)*: Cold hardy, zones 4 to 9; heat hardy, zones 9 to 1. Grown for the foliage covered with soft white hairs. Remove flowers to keep the tidy appearance or buy non-flowering types like Big Ears and Silver Carpet.

Lamium or Deadnettle *(Lamium maculatum)*: Cold hardy, zones 4 to 8; heat hardy, zones 8 to 1. Shade-, heat- and drought-tolerant. Variegated foliage with white or mauve flowers are an added bonus.

Lilyturf *(Liriope)*: Cold hardy, zones 5 to 10. Forms clumps or mats of grasslike leaves; topped with short spikes of violet or white flowers in late

Lamb's ears

summer or fall.

Sedum or Stonecrop *(Sedum)*: Cold hardy, zones 3 to 10; heat hardy, zones 8 to 3. Various species good as ground covers, in rock gardens or as perennials. Most have attractive flowers.

Thyme *(Thymus)*: Cold hardy, zones 3 to 9; heat hardy, zones 9 to 1. Low-growing herb often used around stepping-stones to provide a pleasant fragrance underfoot.

Adding different heights and textures to your Xeriscape is an excellent way to add more interest to your backyard.

Plant Profiles for Hot, Dry Areas

HOT, DRY WEATHER have your garden wilting? Then consider Xeriscaping, which means landscaping with plants that will tolerate parched conditions. Listed here are plants that require less water, yet still provide a beautiful flower show.

Note: *Heat hardiness ratings are given where available, but these ratings do not yet exist for all plants.*

Giant Hyssop

Botanical name: *Agastache.*
Plant type: Perennial.
Bloom time: Summer.
Hardiness: Cold, zones 4 to 11; heat, zones 12 to 5.
Flower color: Purple, red-purple, blue, white.
Flower shape: Short stout spikes.
Height: 2 to 5 feet.
Width: 1 to 3 feet.
Light needs: Full sun to light shade.
Soil type: Well-drained.
Planting tips: Sow seeds indoors 10 to 12 weeks before last frost. Divide in spring or fall. Self-seeds.
Notes: Fragrant foliage and attractive flowers make these suitable for flower and herb gardens.

Giant hyssop

Rose Vinca

Other common names: Annual vinca, Madagascar periwinkle.
Botanical name: *Catharanthus roseus.*
Plant type: Tender perennial grown as annual.
Bloom time: Summer through frost.
Hardiness: Cold, zones 9 to 11; heat, zones 12 to 1.

Rose vinca

Flower color: White, purple, pink, red.
Flower shape: Flat with 5 petals.
Height: 6 to 24 inches.
Width: 12 to 24 inches.
Light needs: Full sun to partial shade.
Soil type: Well-drained.
Planting tips: Sow seeds indoors 12 weeks before last frost.
Notes: A good substitute for impatiens in dry, sunny locations. Also tolerates dry shade found under trees and on the leeward sides of fences and buildings.

Can be overwintered indoors in cold regions where it often continues to flower.

Blanket Flower

Botanical name: *Gaillardia.*
Plant type: Annual, biennial and perennial.
Bloom time: Summer through fall.
Hardiness: Cold, zones 3 to 9; heat, zones 12 to 1.

Blanket flower

Flower color: Red or yellow, with yellow or purple centers.
Flower shape: Daisy-like.
Height: 1 to 3 feet.
Width: 6 to 24 inches.
Light needs: Full sun.
Soil type: Well-drained to dry.
Planting tips: Sow perennial types in spring or early summer. Start annual types indoors 4 to 6 weeks before planting outdoors. Wait for frost danger to pass before planting outside.
Notes: Old-fashioned favorite, good for cutting. Deadhead for continuous bloom.

Butterfly Weed

Botanical name: *Asclepias tuberosa.*
Plant type: Perennial.
Bloom time: Summer.
Hardiness: Cold, zones 3 to 9; heat, zones 10 to 2.
Flower color: Orange, yellow.
Flower shape: Clusters of tiny flowers.
Height: 2 to 3 feet.
Width: 1 foot.
Light needs: Full sun.
Soil type: Well-drained.
Planting tips: Sow seeds outdoors in the spring or early summer.

Notes: This plant is slow to emerge in spring. Plant spring-flowering bulbs next to them to mark their location and prevent accidental digging. I find that butterfly weed self-seeds and picks the location it prefers in the garden.

California poppy

California Poppy

Botanical name: *Eschscholzia californica.*
Plant type: Annual.
Bloom time: Spring to fall.
Hardiness: Cold, annual; heat, zones 9 to 2.
Flower color: Yellow, orange.
Flower shape: Poppy-like flowers.
Height: 4 to 12 inches.
Width: 6 to 8 inches.
Light needs: Full sun.
Soil type: Dry.
Planting tips: Sow seeds outdoors in spring, or in autumn in warmer regions.
Notes: A native to California and the Southwest, this commonly appears in wildflower mixes. Reseeds readily in warmer areas.

Celosia

Other common names: Cockscomb.
Botanical name: *Celosia.*
Plant type: Annual, perennial.
Bloom time: Summer through fall.
Hardiness: Cold, zones 10 to 11; heat, zones 9 to 2.
Flower color: Mostly red, yellow, orange, gold.
Flower shape: Large and small plumes, barley-like spikes, crested.
Height: 6 to 36 inches.
Width: 6 to 18 inches.
Light needs: Full sun.
Soil type: Well-drained.

Celosia

Planting tips: Start seeds indoors 4 weeks before last frost or outdoors after danger of frost passes.
Notes: These long-lasting flowers are good for cutting and drying.

Cosmos

Botanical name: *Cosmos bipinnatus.*
Plant type: Annual; tender perennial.
Bloom time: Summer to frost.
Hardiness: Cold, zone 11; heat, zones 12 to 1.
Flower color: White, purple, pink.
Flower shape: Daisy-like.
Height: 1 to 6 feet.
Width: 8 to 24 inches.
Light needs: Full sun to light shade.
Soil type: Well-drained to dry.
Planting tips: Sow seeds outdoors after frost, or start indoors 5 to 7 weeks before last frost.
Notes: Finely dissected foliage is a foil for other flowers. Dwarf varieties are available. Reseeds readily.

Cosmos

Dahlberg Daisy

Botanical name: *Thymophylla tenuiloba* (also sold under its former name, *Dyssodia tenuiloba).*
Plant type: Annual.
Bloom time: Summer through fall.
Hardiness: Cold, annual; heat, unavailable.
Flower color: Yellow.
Flower shape: Small daisy-like flowers.
Height: 12 inches.
Width: 12 inches.
Light needs: Full sun.
Soil type: Well-drained to dry.
Planting tips: Start indoors in mid-spring or sow seeds outdoors in late spring.
Notes: Tolerates fall frost. Works well in containers. Reseeds.

Dahlberg daisy

Flax

Flax

Botanical name: *Linum.*
Plant type: Perennial.
Bloom time: Summer.
Hardiness: Cold, zones 5 to 9; heat, zones 8 to 2.
Flower color: Blue, white, gold.
Flower shape: Cup-shaped.
Height: 12 to 24 inches.
Width: 6 to 18 inches.
Light needs: Full sun to light shade.
Soil type: Well-drained.
Planting tips: Sow seeds outdoors in spring or early summer.
Notes: This short-lived perennial reseeds readily and may be a longtime resident of your garden. Though each blossom lasts only one day, there are enough flowers to put on a show for at least 6 weeks. Must have good drainage in winter to survive.

Lantana

Lantana

Other common names: Shrub verbena.
Botanical name: *Lantana.*
Plant type: Evergreen shrubs and perennials; grown as annuals in the colder regions.
Bloom time: Summer to fall.
Hardiness: Cold, zone 9; heat, unavailable.
Flower color: White, orange, pink, red, yellow.
Flower shape: Clusters of small tubular flowers.
Height: 1 to 6 feet.
Width: 1 to 6 feet. (Some species grow into large perennials or shrubs in milder regions.)
Light needs: Full sun.
Soil type: Well-drained.
Planting tips: Sow seeds indoors 12 weeks before the last frost.
Notes: Plants can be overwintered indoors in colder regions. Grow as a houseplant in a sunny window or under artificial lights.

Lavender

Botanical name: *Lavandula.*
Plant type: Perennial, grown as small shrub.
Bloom time: Summer.

Lavender

Hardiness: Cold, zones 5 to 10; heat, zones 12 to 7.
Flower color: Purple.
Flower shape: Spike.
Height: 1 to 4 feet.
Width: 1 to 4 feet.
Light needs: Full sun.
Soil type: Well-drained to dry.
Planting tips: Start seeds indoors 6 to 8 weeks before last spring frost, or outdoors after danger of frost passes. Place transplants in the garden in spring for early establishment and increased chance of winter survival.
Notes: Gray foliage, fragrant flowers. Has long been used as a scent to mask odors and promote relaxation. May survive some winters in zone 4.

Liatris

Other common names: Gayfeather.
Botanical name: *Liatris.*
Plant type: Perennial.
Bloom time: Summer into fall.
Hardiness: Cold, zones 3 to 9; heat, zones 9 to 2.
Flower color: Purple, white.
Flower shape: Spikes; individual flowers open from top down.
Height: 1 to 6 feet.
Width: 1 to 2 feet.
Light needs: Full sun to light shade.
Soil type: Well-drained.
Planting tips: Sow seeds outdoors in fall. Divide in spring.
Notes: A nice vertical accent in natural or perennial gardens. Good for cutting, naturalizing and wildlife. Reseeds readily; one plant will give you many in a short time.

Liatris

Mexican Sunflower

Botanical name: *Tithonia rotundifolia.*
Plant type: Annual.
Bloom time: Summer to frost.
Hardiness: Cold, annual; heat, zones 12 to 2.

Mexican sunflower

Flower color: Orange.
Flower shape: Daisy-like.
Height: 2 to 6 feet.
Width: 1 to 1-1/2 feet.
Light needs: Full sun.
Soil type: Well-drained.
Planting tips: Start seeds indoors 6 to 8 weeks before last frost. Sow directly outdoors after danger of frost; do not cover seeds.
Notes: Nice orange color for the garden. Shorter varieties are making it easier to add to smaller gardens.

Penstemon

Other common names: Beardtongue.
Botanical name: *Penstemon.*
Plant type: Perennial.
Bloom time: Summer.

Penstemon

Hardiness: Cold, zones 3 to 9; heat, zones 9 to 1.
Flower color: White, yellow, orange, red, pink, purple.
Flower shape: Tubular; similar to foxglove.
Height: 18 to 36 inches.
Width: 12 to 24 inches.
Light needs: Full sun to light shade.
Soil type: Well-drained.
Planting tips: Sow seed outdoors from late winter through early summer. Divide in spring.

Notes: Taller species make nice additions to perennial border. Use smaller ones in rock gardens.

Poppymallow

Other common names: Winecup.
Botanical name: *Callirhoe.*
Plant type: Annuals and perennials.
Bloom time: Summer.
Hardiness: Cold, zones 3 to 10; heat, zones 7 to 1.
Flower color: Rosy red to violet.
Flower shape: Poppy-like.
Height: 6 to 48 inches.
Width: 12 to 24 inches.
Light needs: Full sun.
Soil type: Well-drained.

Poppymallow

Planting tips: Sow seeds of annuals outdoors in spring, and perennials in early spring.
Notes: All species thrive in heat and tolerate drought.

Portulaca

Other common names: Moss rose, purslane.
Botanical name: *Portulaca.*
Plant type: Mostly annuals.
Bloom time: Summer to fall.
Hardiness: Cold, annual; heat, unavailable.
Flower color: Red, purple, pink, yellow, white.
Flower shape: Cup- to rose-shaped.
Height: 4 to 8 inches.
Width: 6 to 24 inches.
Light needs: Full sun.
Soil type: Well-drained to dry.
Planting tips: Sow seeds outdoors in spring after the last frost. Start seeds indoors in midspring.
Notes: The thick, fleshy leaves can be flat or narrow and moss-like. Flowers close in low light.

Portulaca

Prairie coneflower

Prairie Coneflower
Other common names: Mexican hat.
Botanical name: *Ratibida* species.
Plant type: Perennial.
Bloom time: Summer.
Hardiness: Cold, zones 3 to 9; heat, zones 9 to 1.
Flower color: Yellow with brown center.
Flower shape: Daisy-like.
Height: 1-1/2 to 5 feet.
Width: 1 to 2 feet.
Light needs: Full sun to partial shade.
Soil type: Well-drained to dry.
Planting tips: Sow seeds in coldframe in spring. Divide young plants in spring.
Notes: Use in flower, meadow or cutting gardens. The long cone and drooping petals reveal the origin of the common name.

Purple Coneflower
Botanical name: *Echinacea purpurea.*
Plant type: Perennial.
Bloom time: Summer to fall.

Purple coneflower

Hardiness: Cold, zones 3 to 9; heat, zones 12 to 1.
Flower color: Purple, white, pink.
Flower shape: Daisy-like with brown cone in center.
Height: 2 to 4 feet.
Width: 2 to 3 feet.
Light needs: Full sun to light shade.
Soil type: Well-drained.
Planting tips: Sow seed in fall, spring or early summer. Divide in spring or fall.
Notes: One plant can quickly fill a garden as it spreads and reseeds. Great for cutting, winter interest and bird food.

Rudbeckia
Other common names: Black-eyed Susan.
Botanical name: *Rudbeckia* species.
Plant type: Annuals, biennials and perennials.
Bloom time: Summer to fall.
Hardiness: Cold, zones 3 to 9; heat, zones 9 to 2.
Flower color: Yellow with brown center.
Flower shape: Daisy.
Height: 1-1/2 to 5 feet.
Width: 1 to 3 feet.
Light needs: Full sun to light shade.
Soil type: Well-drained.
Planting tips: Sow annual seeds indoors in midspring. Sow biennials and perennials outdoors in fall or spring.

Rudbeckia

Notes: Most species reseed readily, allowing these plants to dominate the garden. Good for cutting, winter interest and wild bird food. Look for mildew-resistant varieties.

Russian Sage
Botanical name: *Perovskia atriplicifolia.*
Plant type: Perennial.
Bloom time: Summer to fall.
Hardiness: Cold, zones 4 to 9; heat, zones 9 to 4.
Flower color: Blue.
Flower shape: Airy panicle.
Height: 3 to 4 feet.
Width: Up to 3 feet
Light needs: Full sun.
Soil type: Well-drained.

Russian sage

Planting tips: Sow seed indoors in spring.
Notes: This large plant is treated as a subshrub. Prune it back to about 4 to 6 inches in late March. This removes any winterkill and prevents floppy growth. Provides fragrant foliage, blue flowers and winter interest.

Sunflower

Botanical name: *Helianthus.*
Plant type: Annual and perennial.
Bloom time: Summer to frost.
Hardiness: Cold (perennials), zones 4 to 9; heat, zones 11 to 3.

Sunflower

Flower color: Yellow, white, red, rust, gold; brown center.
Flower shape: Daisy-like.
Height: 2 to 15 feet.
Width: 1 to 3 feet.
Light needs: Full sun.
Soil type: Well-drained.
Planting tips: Sow seeds directly outdoors after the last frost.

Notes: A fun plant for the whole family. It also attracts visiting wildlife and birds.

Yarrow

Botanical name: *Achillea.*
Plant type: Perennial.
Bloom time: Summer.
Hardiness: Cold, zones 3 to 9; heat, zones 9 to 2.
Flower color: Yellow, white, red, pink.
Flower shape: Round, flat-topped clusters.
Height: 6 to 52 inches.
Width: 12 to 24 inches.
Light needs: Full sun.
Soil type: Poor, well-drained to dry.

Yarrow

Planting tips: Sow seed directly outdoors in spring or early summer. Divide in spring.
Notes: Long-lasting cut and dried flowers. Some species, such as *A. millefolium*, can become a weed in the garden and landscape.

Zinnia

Botanical name: *Zinnia.*
Plant type: Annual.
Bloom time: Summer to frost.
Hardiness: Cold, annual; heat, zones 12 to 1.
Flower color: Yellows, reds, pinks, reds, salmons, cream, lime, purple.
Flower shape: Daisy-like.
Height: 6 to 36 inches.
Width: 8 to 24 inches.
Light needs: Full sun.
Soil type: Well-drained.
Planting tips: Sow seeds indoors 6 weeks before last frost. Sow outdoors after danger of frost.
Notes: Good for cutting. Select disease-resistant cultivars to avoid mildew and leaf-spot diseases.

Zinnia

Chapter 16
Wet and Wonderful

*Water, water everywhere . . .*and in this case, there's plenty for plants to drink. For most gardeners, it seems that rainfall comes in waves of too much or not enough.

It would be wonderful if we could time it so our gardens received that magical inch of water each week, preferably with an early morning delivery. This isn't happening in my garden, and I'm guessing it isn't for most of you.

But rainfall is only part of the problem. Soil drainage, slope and the type of surrounding surfaces also influence the moisture content and drainage of our garden's soil.

Waterlogged soils can be harmful to plants. Most plants can tolerate a week of wet soil, but after that, root rot, stress and other damage starts to occur. Symptoms can show up soon after the flooding or appear gradually over time, but eventually the leaves will turn yellow and often brown. In time, the plant will appear stunted and less vigorous. Then borers, other insects and diseases like root rot may move in to finish them off—not a pretty sight.

ing. It's much easier to flip a switch or preset an irrigation system to turn on automatically. And the ease of watering makes it harder to recognize that you're overdoing it.

Someone once called me about some landscape problems that sounded like they were caused by overwatering. The gardener insisted that was not possible because the irrigation system had been set up so carefully. When I went out to take a look, the lawn was so wet it squished beneath our feet, and the water filled our footprints. We had to reset the irrigation system and develop some monitoring techniques.

Evaluate the Problem

Take some time to evaluate water flow and drainage patterns in your yard. Note where water collects, when it's a problem (after snow melts or rainstorms?), how often it occurs and what, if anything, will grow there.

Once you know these things, you can start tracking down the cause and focus on potential solutions. Fixing only part of the problem may lead to other drainage dilemmas in a different area of your yard.

Serious problems warrant calling in a professional. Check the government listing in the phone book to find the nearest Natural Resources Conservation Service (NRCS) office. The people at this office, formerly known as the Soil Conservation Service, often help property owners with drainage concerns. They and the Department of Natural Resources can also tell you about any guidelines, restrictions or regulations for managing water problems in your area.

Another alternative is to contact a qualified engineer or a landscaping company with a good reputa-

Turn Off the Sprinkler

SOMETIMES the cause and cure are the same. In this case, it's the gardener in charge of watering. We think we're doing our plants a favor by watering every day. This is the worst thing we can do.

Most of the plant problems I diagnose are related to improper watering. I've pulled many new trees out of planting holes filled with water. The intentions were good, but the results were detrimental.

The one concern I have about irrigation systems is that they make it too easy to overwater. Hauling buckets of water or hauling the hose to the far reaches of your yard makes you think twice about water-

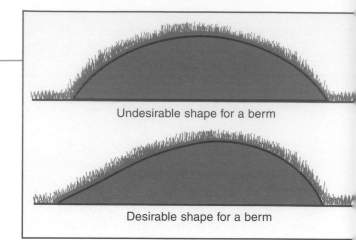

Undesirable shape for a berm

Desirable shape for a berm

Asymmetrical berms (above) blend in to the landscape for a more natural look.

tion for solving drainage problems. You'll still need to talk to the DNR and your local municipality to make sure you have permission to implement a solution.

Amending the Soil

After your inspection, you may realize the problem lies in your soil. Clay and compacted soils do not allow water to pass through quickly. Instead, moisture is trapped near the roots for long periods of time. Well-drained soil is able to move water from the surface, past the plant roots and beyond, in a timely fashion.

To improve drainage, add organic matter to the soil. This amazing material separates soil particles to improve drainage and relieve compaction. Core aerate lawns if water seems to run off the surface or collect in certain spots. Top-dress the lawn with compost after aeration to help amend the soil and further improve drainage.

If amending the soil isn't enough, creating raised beds should improve drainage. At the very least, it

Wood, stone or other materials can be used to contain the soil in raised beds.

will elevate plant roots above the waterlogged soil. See Chapter 2 for details on creating raised beds.

Increased air flow around raised beds helps them warm up earlier in spring and drain faster. If you're frustrated by spring rains and cool temperatures, you can get an earlier start with a raised bed, which helps dry and warm the soil.

Creating a Berm

Many gardeners don't stop at just raising the bed. They bring in truckloads of soil to create raised areas called berms. Done correctly, this can resolve

some poor growing conditions and beautify the landscape. Done incorrectly, it can create other drainage problems and an eyesore.

Size is the most common mistake. Many people create small berms that look like an afterthought. Keep them in scale with the size of your landscape and the plants you'll use. This means a substantial investment in soil, but it pays off with healthier plants and a better-looking addition to the landscape.

Design the berm so it follows the forms and lines of the rest of the landscape design. Use height and form that imitate what might be found in the area. Asymmetrical berms appear more natural and blend in more easily. Slope the sides at a 4:1 or 5:1 ratio for easier mowing and visual appeal. (A 4:1 slope means the height drops 1 foot for every 4 feet of width.)

Plant trees on berms with a 7:1 slope. Other plants can grow on a 3:1 slope, but you may experience more water runoff. Consider 4:1 or 5:1 as your minimum to prevent wood chips and soil from washing off. Shredded bark or long wood chips will help minimize runoff.

Monitor drainage patterns before, during and after the berm construction. Elevating part of your landscape can affect water flow and drainage in the surrounding area. Work with the NRCS to ensure you are not creating more—or different—drainage problems in your yard or neighborhood.

Installing Drain Tiles

If going up isn't appealing—or working—you may need to look down for solutions. Farmers have long used drain tiles to move excess water away from their fields. The buried tiles collect water and direct it away from wet areas. Soil type and grade will help determine the location and slope. Proper design and installation make the difference between a functioning drainage system and a pipe buried in the ground.

A French drain sounds exotic, but it's just a variation on the drain tile system. A narrow channel is

A rain garden, like the one illustrated above, is designed to capture runoff for plant use. Water is filtered through the soil instead of filling up storm sewers.

dug in the landscape at a slope of 1:100 (a drop of 1 foot for every 100 feet in length). The width and depth can vary, so consult with the NRCS for the best design for your particular situation.

Fill the bottom of the channel with gravel. Cover the gravel with landscape fabric to keep out soil, which can filter into the gravel and interfere with drainage. Fill the rest of the channel with high-quality topsoil and then plant. You'll need at least 6 inches of soil, preferably 12, for most plants. Better drainage will be the only clue this has been added to the landscape.

Some gardeners create a larger drainage space to serve as a temporary collection area until the moisture can slowly drain away. Combining this method with drainways may help you manage larger volumes of water. Consult a professional so you don't dig your way into a poorly drained mess.

Rain Gardens

If you're looking for a natural and attractive way of managing runoff from roofs, patios and other hard surfaces, consider planting a rain garden.

This idea uses garden space and plants to catch surface water and redirect it into the groundwater. This not only reduces water runoff but improves water quality. The soil acts as a natural filter, removing pollutants and other impurities as the water seeps through.

Place the garden in an area near the source of runoff—an overhang, patio, sidewalk or other hard surface. Remove the grass and create a slight indentation in the center of the garden. This will direct the water into the garden—just the opposite of what happens in a raised bed.

As you prepare the soil, maintain the depressed center. Use natives and garden plants tolerant of temporary flooding. Many of those listed in the plant profiles will work.

The Progressive Dane organization provides more details and planting recommendations at *www.prodane.org/committees/environment.*

Plant Profiles for Wet Areas

WHETHER YOU'RE BUILDING a rain garden or just trying to help your plants survive a wet space, plant selection is the first step to success. Here are a few plants that will tolerate moist to wet soil conditions:

Note: *Heat hardiness ratings are given where available, but these ratings do not yet exist for all plants.*

Baneberry

Baneberry
Botanical name: *Actaea.*
Bloom time: Late spring to early summer.
Hardiness: Cold, zones 4 to 8; heat, unavailable.
Flower color: White.
Flower shape: Airy spikes.
Height: 2 to 3 feet.
Width: 2 feet.
Light needs: Partial shade.

Soil type: Moist.
Planting tips: Sow seeds in cold frame in fall. Divide plants in spring.
Notes: The fruit—clusters of white, red or black berries—put on a real show. But don't eat them; they're poisonous.

Blue Cardinal Flower
Botanical name: *Lobelia siphilitica.*
Plant type: Perennial.
Bloom time: Late summer to mid-fall.

Calla lilies

Hardiness: Cold, zones 4 to 7; heat, zones 9 to 2.
Flower color: Bright blue.
Flower shape: Spikes of tubular flowers.
Height: 2 to 4 feet.
Width: 1 to 2 feet.
Light needs: Full sun to partial shade.
Soil type: Moist.
Planting tips: Sow seeds in fall. Divide plants in spring.
Notes: Grows well in moist garden areas and along ponds and streams.

Blue cardinal flower

Boneset

Botanical name: *Eupatorium perfoliatum.*
Plant type: Perennial.
Bloom time: Late summer to fall.
Hardiness: Cold, zones 3 to 9; heat, unavailable.
Flower color: White; often tinged purple.
Flower shape: Loose, rounded clusters of tiny flowers.
Height: Up to 5 feet.
Width: 2 to 3 feet.
Light needs: Full sun to partial shade.
Soil type: Moist.
Planting tips: Sow seed indoors or in cold frame in spring. Divide plants in spring.
Notes: Large plants suited for the back of the perennial garden or more naturalized plantings. Flowers are attractive to insects.

Boneset

Calla Lilies

Botanical name: *Zantedeschia.*
Plant type: Tropical bulb.
Bloom time: Spring and summer.
Hardiness: Cold, zones 8 to 11; heat, unavailable.
Flower color: White, yellow, pink, red, purple.
Flower shape: Funnel-like.
Height: Up to 30 inches.
Width: Up to 12 inches.
Light needs: Full sun to shade.
Soil type: Moist, organic.
Planting tips: Set rhizomes 4 inches deep in spring. Start indoors in colder regions for earlier bloom.

Notes: Many are fragrant. Northern gardeners must dig in fall and store indoors for winter. This plant is native to South Africa, where it grows in and alongside streams.

Cardinal Flower

Botanical name: *Lobelia cardinalis.*
Plant type: Short-lived perennial.
Bloom time: Summer to early autumn.
Hardiness: Cold, zones 3 to 9; heat, zones 9 to 2.
Flower color: Red.
Flower shape: Tubular flowers in spike-like arrangement.
Height: 3 feet.
Width: 1 foot.
Light needs: Full sun or partial shade.
Soil type: Moist.
Planting tips: Sow seed outdoors in fall. Divide plants in spring.

Cardinal flower

Notes: Sometimes difficult to find the perfect growing locations. Keep trying—it's worth the effort.

False Spirea

Botanical name: *Astilbe x arendsii.*
Bloom time: Summer to fall.
Hardiness: Cold, zones 4 to 8; heat, zones 8 to 2.
Flower color: White, pink, red, purple.
Flower shape: Airy panicles.
Height: 1-1/2 to 4 feet.
Width: 2 feet.
Light needs: Partial to full shade.
Soil type: Moist, organic.

False spirea

Planting tips: Sow seeds indoors in mid-spring. Divide in early spring.

Notes: All astilbes prefer moist soil but the *arendsii* group are the most tolerant of wet soils. These plants can scorch and decline in full sun and hot conditions.

Houttuynia

False Sunflower

Botanical name: *Heliopsis.*
Plant type: Perennial.
Bloom time: Summer through fall.
Hardiness: Cold, zones 4 to 9; heat, zones 9 to 1.
Flower color: Yellow to orange with gold or brown center.
Flower shape: Daisy-like.
Height: 3 to 6 feet.
Width: 2 feet.
Light needs: Full sun.

False sunflower

Soil type: Moist.
Planting tips: Sow seeds in cold frame in spring. Divide plants in spring or fall.
Notes: Large plants that bloom continuously without deadheading. Divide older plants to keep the continuous bloom.

Ferns

Many ferns are tolerant of moist soils. See the plant profiles on page 219.

Forget-Me-Not

Details on this shade- and moisture-tolerant plant appear in the plant profiles on page 213.

Ginger

This plant tolerates moist and shady conditions and is suitable for use as a ground cover or in a woodland garden or perennial bed. See listing under "Shade-Tolerant Ground Covers" on page 213.

Houttuynia

Botanical name: *Houttuynia cordata.*
Bloom time: Summer.
Hardiness: Cold, zones 5 to 11; heat, unavailable.
Flower color: White.
Flower shape: Flat with four petals.
Height: 6 to 12 inches.
Width: Wide-spreading.
Light needs: Full sun to light shade.
Soil type: Moist to wet.
Planting tips: Sow seeds in cold frame in late summer. Divide in spring.
Notes: The straight species is very aggressive, the

cultivars less so. Use in areas where it can be confined, or plant in a large pot sunk in the ground. *H. cordata* 'Chameleon' has attractive green, yellow and red leaves.

Japanese Coltsfoot

Other common names: Sweet coltsfoot, butterbur.
Botanical name: *Petasites.*
Plant type: Perennial.
Bloom time: Late winter or early spring.
Hardiness: Cold, zones 5 to 9; heat, unavailable.
Flower color: Yellowish-white or purple.
Flower shape: A cluster of small star-shaped flowers appear before or with the leaves, depending on species.

Sweet coltsfoot

Height: 1 to 4 feet.
Width: Up to 5 feet.
Light needs: Partial to full shade.
Soil type: Moist to wet.
Planting tips: Divide in spring or fall.
Notes: Grown for its large leaves; makes quite an impression along the water's edge. Aggressive, so use with care. Deadhead and plant in sunken containers to control spread. Early nectar source for bees.

Joe Pye Weed

Botanical name: *Eupatorium maculatum, E. fistulosum.*
Plant type: Perennial.
Bloom time: Summer to fall.

Joe Pye weed

Hardiness: Cold, zones 3 to 9; heat, zones 9 to 1.
Flower color: Dusky rose, purple.
Flower shape: Flat-topped or rounded clusters of small tubular flowers.
Height: 5 to 7 feet.
Width: 2 to 3 feet.
Light needs: Full sun.
Soil type: Moist.
Planting tips: Sow seed in spring. Divide plants in spring.
Notes: Big and bold, these plants make an impact in the back of the perennial garden, near a water feature or in a naturalized setting. Consider one of the shorter cultivars for smaller areas.

Marsh Marigold

Botanical name: *Caltha palustris.*
Plant type: Perennial.
Bloom time: Mid-spring.
Hardiness: Cold, zones 3 to 7; heat, zones 7 to 3.
Flower color: Yellow.
Flower shape: Buttercup-like.
Height: 10 to 24 inches.
Width: 18 inches.
Light needs: Full sun to partial shade.
Soil type: Rich; wet to moist.
Planting tips: Sow seeds outdoors in spring or early summer.
Notes: Found growing along streams and even in water. Plants go dormant in late summer, making them more drought-tolerant.

Marsh marigold

Ornamental Rhubarb

Botanical name: *Rheum.*
Plant type: Perennial.
Bloom time: Spring or summer.
Hardiness: Cold, zones 5 to 9; heat, unavailable.
Flower color: Yellow-green, white, red.
Flower shape: Plumes.
Height: 3 to 8 feet.
Width: 2 to 8 feet.
Light needs: Full sun or partial shade.
Soil type: Moist.
Planting tips: Sow seed in cold frame in fall. Divide plants in spring.
Notes: Grown for the large green, bronze or variegated leaves as well as the flowers.

Ornamental rhubarb

Pearly everlasting

Pearly Everlasting

Botanical name: *Anaphalis.*
Plant type: Perennial.
Bloom time: Summer to fall.
Hardiness: Cold, zones 3 to 9; heat, zones 8 to 3.
Flower color: White.
Flower shape: Clusters of small round flowers.
Height: 1 to 3 feet.
Width: 1 to 2 feet.
Light needs: Full sun to partial shade.
Soil type: Moist.
Planting tips: Sow seeds outdoors in fall or spring; or start indoors in spring. Divide plants in early spring.

Queen of the Prairie

Botanical name: *Filipendula rubra*.
Plant type: Perennial.
Bloom time: Summer.
Hardiness: Cold, zones 3 to 9; heat, zones 8 to 1.
Flower color: Pink.
Flower shape: Fluffy panicles.
Height: 6 to 8 feet.
Width: 4 feet.
Light needs: Full sun to partial shade.
Soil type: Moist.
Planting tips: Sow seed in fall or spring. Divide plants in spring or fall.
Notes: Needs constant moisture.

Queen of the prairie

Sedge

Botanical name: *Carex*.
Plant type: Perennial.
Bloom time: Summer.
Hardiness: Cold, zones 3 to 9; heat, zones 12 to 1.
Flower color: Green to brown.
Flower shape: Various; grown for leaves, not flowers.
Height: 6 to 60 inches.
Width: 10 to 36 inches.
Light needs: Sun to partial shade.
Soil type: Moist to wet.
Planting tips: Sow seeds in spring. Divide plants in spring or early summer.
Notes: Sedges are native to moist and wet regions. Use these with hostas, next to a water feature or to provide the look of grass in any garden that's too wet and shady.

Sedge

Siberian Iris

Botanical name: *Iris siberica*.
Plant type: Perennial.
Bloom time: Mid-spring to early summer.
Hardiness: Cold, zones 4 to 9; heat, zones 8 to 4.
Flower color: White, blue, purple.
Flower shape: Typical iris.
Height: 2 to 4 feet.

Width: 2 to 3 feet.
Light needs: Full sun to partial shade.
Soil type: Moist.
Planting tips: Sow seeds in fall in cold frame. Divide in early spring for best results.
Notes: Provides year-round interest in the landscape. Nice grass-like foliage, early season bloom, fall color (leaves turn gold) and seedpods persist for winter. Blue flag iris (*I. versicolor*) also tolerates wet soils.

Siberian iris

Skunk Cabbage

Botanical name: *Symplocarpus foetidus*.
Plant type: Perennial.
Bloom time: Late winter to early spring.
Hardiness: Cold, zones 3 to 7; heat, unavailable.
Flower color: Mottled brownish-purple.
Flower shape: Shell-like spathe.
Height: 1 to 2 feet.
Width: 1 to 2 feet.
Light needs: Sun to partial shade.
Soil type: Moist to wet.
Planting tips: Plant in spring or summer.
Notes: Large cabbage-like leaves appear after the flower. Lysichiton, another group of plants known as skunk cabbage, also tolerates wet soils. These have white or yellow flowers and are hardy to zones 7 to 9.

Skunk cabbage

Swamp rose mallow

Swamp Rose Mallow

Botanical name: *Hibiscus moscheutos.*
Plant type: Perennial.
Bloom time: Summer to fall.
Hardiness: Cold, zones 4 to 10; heat, zones 12 to 1.
Flower color: White, pink, red.
Flower shape: Funnel-shaped, like tropical hibiscus.
Height: Up to 8 feet.
Width: Up to 3 feet.
Light needs: Full sun.
Soil type: Moist, organic.
Planting tips: Sow seed or divide plants in spring.
Notes: Needs long, hot summer for best flowering. Apply mulch for winter in Northern areas.

Swamp Sunflower

Botanical name: *Helianthus angustifolius.*
Plant type: Perennial.
Bloom time: Fall.
Hardiness: Cold, zones 5 to 9; heat, zones 11 to 3.
Flower color: Yellow with purple-brown center.
Flower shape: Daisy-like.
Height: 5 to 7 feet.
Width: Up to 4 feet.
Light needs: Full sun.

Swamp sunflower

Soil type: Moist.
Planting tips: Sow seeds outdoors in spring. Divide in spring or fall.
Notes: This large plant provides a colorful display for 4 to 6 weeks in fall. Tolerates hot weather and moist soils.

Sweet Flag

Botanical name: *Acorus calamus.*
Plant type: Perennial.
Bloom time: Midsummer; grown for foliage.
Hardiness: Cold, zones 3 to 11; heat, zones 12 to 2.
Flower color: Yellow-green.
Flower shape: Horn-shaped; insignificant.
Height: 6 to 60 inches.
Width: 4 to 24 inches.
Light needs: Full sun to partial shade.
Soil type: Moist to wet.
Planting tips: Allow seeds to dry before sowing. Divide in spring.
Notes: Grown for attractive grass-like foliage, which may be solid green or variegated. Thrives in wet areas along streams and water features.

Sweet flag

Tall Meadow Rue

This plant blooms in summer, with white flowers. See "Meadow Rue" in the plant profile on page 221.

Touch-Me-Not

Other common names: Rose balsam.
Botanical name: *Impatiens balsamina.*
Plant type: Annual.
Bloom time: Summer to fall.
Hardiness: Cold, annual; heat, unavailable.
Flower color: White, pink, red, purple.
Flower shape: Cup-shaped; somewhat hooded.

Touch-me-not

Height: Up to 30 inches.
Width: Up to 18 inches.
Light needs: Full to partial sun.
Soil type: Moist.
Planting tips: Sow seeds indoors in early spring.
Notes: An old-fashioned favorite that might be a bit hard to find. Most gardeners are happy to share a

Turtlehead

cutting or seeds. Mulch and keep soil moist if growing in a sunny location.

Turtlehead

Botanical name: *Chelone.*
Plant type: Perennial.
Bloom time: Mid- to late summer.
Hardiness: Cold, zones 3 to 9; heat, zones 9 to 3.
Flower color: White, pink, purple.
Flower shape: Somewhat like a turtle's head.
Height: 1 to 4 feet.
Width: 1-1/2 to 2 feet.
Light needs: Partial shade to sun.
Soil type: Tolerates clay and moist to wet soils.
Planting tips: Sow seeds in cold frame in spring. Divide plants in spring.
Notes: Native to marshes, stream banks and moist woodlands, making them adaptable plants for many garden situations.

Valerian

Botanical name: *Valeriana.*
Plant type: Perennial.
Bloom time: Summer.
Hardiness: Cold, zones 3 to 9; heat, zones 9 to 1.
Flower color: White or pink.
Flower shape: Cluster of small tubular flowers.
Height: 4 to 6 feet.

Width: 1-1/2 to 3 feet.
Light needs: Full sun or dappled shade.
Soil type: Moist.
Planting tips: Sow seeds indoors 10 to 12 weeks before last frost. Divide plants in spring or fall.
Notes: An old-time favorite that seems to be making a comeback. Fragrant, lacy foliage and light, airy flowers make it nice for the garden and cutting.

Valerian

Willow Amsonia

Other common names: Willow blue star.
Botanical name: *Amsonia tabernaemontana.*
Bloom time: Late spring to midsummer.
Hardiness: Cold, zones 3 to 9; heat, zones 8 to 4.
Flower color: Blue.
Flower shape: Star.
Height: 2 to 3 feet.
Width: 2 to 3 feet.
Light needs: Full sun to partial shade.
Soil type: Moist.
Planting tips: Sow seeds in cold frame in fall or spring. Divide in spring (roots are thick and fleshy).
Notes: Leaves turn bright yellow in fall. Plant rarely needs staking. Avoid high-nitrogen fertilizers, which can cause floppiness. The variety *A. tabernaemontana salicifolia* has much finer leaves.

Willow amsonia

Chapter 17
Too Short a Season

Most gardeners long for a few more days, weeks or even months of good gardening weather. As a Northern gardener, I occasionally find myself lamenting our short season and cold winters. Then I remember the Extension agents I met from Alaska at a National Master Gardener Conference.

The agents showed a video on gardening in Alaska. It opened with the agents walking out to the garden in snowshoes, with snow shovels in hand. The first step, they said, was to remove the snow and thaw the soil. At that point, I quit whining and was grateful for my relatively long season and mild winter.

I may not be whining anymore (well, not too much), but I do keep trying new ways to extend the season. There are simple and cheap techniques, or more complex and expensive methods you can try. The choice is yours.

plants growing outdoors year-round.

Garden supply catalogs and some garden centers sell ready-to-use cold frames, often made of aluminum, fiberglass or similar lightweight materials. These should be anchored to the ground and insulated for added winter warmth. Wood frames are expensive and difficult to find, but relatively cheap to make.

Whether you make your own cold frame or buy one, it should fit the space available. Most cold frames are at least 2 feet wide and 4 feet long with an open bottom. The opening provides added flexibility, so the frame can be used over plants in the garden or flats and containers on their way to the garden. Make sure it will accommodate all the pots and flats you plan to grow in it at one time. Allow enough height for your tallest plants, pot and all.

To maximize light penetration, design your cold frame with the back taller than the front. The back wall should be at least 18 to 30 inches and the front slightly lower, about 12 to 24 inches. Adjust to fit your plants. Frames can be temporarily raised by placing them on bricks. Cover the exposed area with plastic to keep the heat in and cold out.

Cold Frames and Cloches

GARDENERS HAVE ALWAYS TRIED to cheat nature. Old books and experienced gardeners suggest covering plants with clear glass jars to create mini greenhouses in the garden. The goal is to use solar heat to warm the soil and air around the plants. It works most of the time. Problems occur when temperatures get too warm inside the covering, or we forget to deal with the rest of the plant's needs, such as water.

Cold Frames

Gardeners have used cold frames—an improvement on the glass-jar method—for years. You can use these structures to start seeds, harden off transplants, protect plants from frost or extend the growing season in spring and fall. Cold frames can even help gardeners in warmer regions keep some of their

This homemade cold frame is used right in the garden to get a jump on the growing season.

This tunnel cloche allows for easy access—slide the plastic up over the hoops for watering and ventilation.

Place the cold frame against the house, garage or an outbuilding for added heat and shelter. Face it with the low end toward the south to maximize light penetration and solar heating.

Heating Up and Cooling Down

Additional heat can be used to further extend the season or aid in plant propagation. Commercially available heating cables can be used in the bottom of the frame to warm the soil, and along the sides of the frame to heat the air. Make sure the system you select is safe for this type of use.

You can create your own heat with fresh manure or compost. Pile the manure around the outside of the cold frame. As it ages, the compost will give off heat, warming and insulating the air inside the frame. This may not be a practical or socially acceptable option for urban gardeners like me. My neighbors are probably relieved that I don't have easy access to fresh manure.

Composting under the cold frame can generate heat, too. Dig a hole and fill with green and brown materials like grass clippings, fall leaves, rinds, straw, other plant debris and natural or organic fertilizer. Mix with soil until the hole is filled. Cover the area with soil, level and place the cold frame over it. As the materials start composting, the pile will heat up and the cold frame will hold the heat around the tender plants. This short-term warming can give you a couple more weeks of outdoor gardening.

Invest in a maximum-minimum (high-low) thermometer to help monitor temperatures inside the cold frame. Keep a watchful eye throughout the growing period. Sunny days, both warm and cool, can overheat the cold frame. Lift the lid and let some of the warm air out, and lower the lid when temperatures return to the desirable level.

You may want to purchase an automatic ventilation system that monitors temperature and raises and lowers the cold frame lid as needed. The small investment is worth it for busy and forgetful gardeners.

Cloches and Row Covers

If all this sounds like it involves too much effort, space or construction, there is hope. Many homemade or commercially available cloches (protective plant covers) work, too—and they're effective on flowers as well as vegetables.

One popular and inexpensive cloche is the plastic gallon milk jug. Gardeners cut off the bottom and one side or enlarge the opening on top of the jug. The containers are placed over young transplants to protect them from frost and speed up rooting.

You also can build a larger shelter from a tomato tower and plastic. Wrap the tower in plastic and place over the plant. The open top prevents heat

Recycle milk jugs, water bottles and other containers to help your plants get a quick start. Be sure to provide a large enough opening for water and ventilation.

An Aqua Dome

buildup and lets in the rain. Cover the top during very cold weather.

Wall-of-Water and Aqua Dome are two products that use water as solar collectors. Wall-of-Water has two layers of plastic with narrow vertical columns. The columns are filled with water and the cloche is placed over the plants. Many gardeners add a little interior support to keep the cloche in place. I find an extra set of hands and easy access to water make a quicker and drier installation. When you're done using the cloches, just empty the water, allow them to dry and store flat in a dark location.

The Aqua Dome looks like a double-walled plastic version of a rose cone, with an open top for ventilation and watering. Set the dome over the plant and fill the space between the walls with water. These are a little more expensive, but they're long-lasting and easy to use. Stack them in a corner of the garage for easy storage.

Row covers and tunnel cloches use these ideas on a broader scale. Use wire hoops to create a support system over a row of plants, cover with plastic and you have a mini greenhouse in the garden. Lift one end of the plastic to ventilate and water. Perforated plastic covers are self-ventilating, but you may still need to reach under the cover to water. For winter storage, just place the hoops against a wall or other small space. Replace the plastic when it tears and becomes discolored.

To add solar collectors, place several black-painted containers filled with water 20 to 50 feet apart in the tunnel cloches. The containers help collect heat for rerelease in the evening. This added heat may provide just the edge your garden needs.

My favorite row covers are the floating types sold as Harvest-Guard, ReeMay or Grass-Fast. These lightweight spun fabrics let air, light and water through while trapping heat below. This means no ventilation is needed, and moisture can reach the plants through the cover. Loosely cover the plants, allowing enough slack for them to grow. Anchor the fabric to the ground with pipes, boards, large rocks or other materials.

As the plants grow, they will lift and support the material. Leave the material in place until day and night temperatures warm. (I leave my cabbage and broccoli covered all season to protect them from cabbage worms.) Remove the fabric as soon as flowering plants like melons and tomatoes start to bloom. The bees need to reach the flowers for pollination and fruit formation.

Most fabrics last one or two seasons. Once they rip, they lose their insulation value. I extend the life of mine by cutting the torn pieces into smaller sections and reusing them.

Warming the Soil

Air temperature is only one concern. Cold soils can cause delayed growth, poor rooting, rot and even plant death. Warm the soil before planting to get faster results.

Place cloches over the planting area 1 to 2 weeks before planting to warm the soil and create a friendlier environment for the plants. Replace the cloche immediately after planting to keep the air and soil warm.

To warm larger planting beds, use clear plastic. Prepare the site for planting, then cover it for 2 weeks before planting. When you remove the plastic, lightly cultivate to remove any weeds that may have

Row covers are so easy to use that farmers in Vermont and the northeast United States have used them to shorten the time from tomato planting to harvesting by a much as 1 month.

sprouted. Plant seeds and transplants in the warmed soil, then cover with a tunnel cloche or other season extender. You'll be amazed at the difference this makes.

Factors to Consider

Before buying or making a season extender, make sure you're not creating more work and headaches for yourself. Consider the following features when selecting or making season extenders:

- **Watering.** Closed covers or those made from non-permeable materials don't let the heat out or the rain in. You'll need to lift the cover to water, or run a soaker hose under the frame.

- **Ventilation.** The goal is to keep the plants and soil warm by trapping the sun's warmth. This can be a problem when temperatures under the cover get too warm. Some season extenders must be opened or tipped to release the hot air. Others have open tops or perforated covers for built-in ventilation. See if the ventilation system matches your gardening style.

- **Storage.** Find out the space and conditions needed for storage. Some materials stack or fold up flat for easy storage, but others require much more space.

- **Longevity.** Some season extenders will last for years. Others are meant to be just a one- or two-season investment. Know which is which when comparing prices.

- **Cost.** Price is usually considered first, but it should be just one of many factors in your decision. Look for a product with good value and the features you need.

High-Altitude Gardening

SHORT SEASONS are only one of the challenges high-altitude gardeners face. The cold nights, thin and rocky soils and beautiful but hungry wildlife make gardening even more difficult.

Elevation and latitude further influence these conditions. Gardens growing at higher elevations and latitudes experience a shorter growing season and colder temperatures. Frost dates and temperatures are also influenced by large bodies of water, surrounding vegetation and other environmental factors. But there's hope. Season-extending techniques can lengthen the season and speed up your floral display or garden harvest.

Spring-flowering bulbs like daffodils,

squills and grape hyacinths tolerate these growing conditions, and animals tend to leave them alone. Tulips and crocus also work, but I've found these are favorites of deer, rabbits and other wildlife.

Select plants that will tolerate your conditions, especially cold- and drought-tolerant plants that grow, flower and fruit in a short period of time. This will pay off with less maintenance and better-looking plants. Although the growing season at high altitudes is often compressed, it's very impressive.

Take a look at the plants that survive and thrive in the surrounding area and in neighbors' gardens. From a distance, many alpine plants create a floral tapestry with colorful flowers held above short tufts of green leaves. When hovering above the alpine species, you may want to move in for a closer inspection to appreciate their form and beauty.

Many garden plants also will survive at high altitudes. Select those that are hardy to your area and tolerant of adverse high-altitude conditions. The list on page 251 offers a few plants with which high-altitude gardeners have had success. For a list of herbs, vegetables and wildflowers suited for high elevations, check out Seeds Trust's High Altitude Gardens catalog. It's available online at *www.high altitudegardens.com.*

Then get out your garden journal and do a little testing of your own. Try a few of the natives and some of the plants listed on the next page. Record how they perform, add some new ones and trade those you don't like. Soon you'll have a beautiful high-altitude garden of your own.

Hardy animal-resistant bulbs, like the daffodils above, provide welcome color in high-altitude gardens.

High-Altitude Plants

THESE ARE JUST A FEW PLANTS that have performed well at higher altitudes and in drier soil. Select those that are hardy to your climate, fit the space available and provide the desired look. Cold hardiness is followed by heat hardiness where available.

Trees and Shrubs

Alpine Currant (*Ribes alpinum*): Cold hardy, zones 2 to 7. Grows 3 to 6 feet. Twiggy upright shrub that tolerates shearing and shade.

Cotoneaster

Cotoneaster (*Cotoneaster* species): Cold hardy, zones 4 to 7. Includes creeping, spreading and upright forms.

Green Ash (*Fraxinus pennsylvanica*): Cold hardy, zones 3 to 9. Grows 50 to 60 feet. Tolerates difficult growing conditions. Reseeds readily, finding its way into other planting beds.

Hackberry (*Celtis occidentalis*): Cold hardy, zones 3 to 9. Grows 40 to 60 feet. Tolerates adverse conditions.

Juniper (*Juniperus*): Cold hardy, zones 3 to 9. Upright and spreading shrub and tree forms vary in size, depending on species and cultivar. Heat- and drought-tolerant.

Poplar (*Populus* species): Cold hardy, zones 3 to 9. Fast-growing trees that can reach heights of 40 to 100 feet.

Potentilla (*Potentilla fruticosa*): Cold hardy, zones 2 to 7. A 1- to 4-foot shrub topped with yellow flowers all summer. Heat- and drought-tolerant.

Rugosa Rose (*Rosa rugosa*): Cold hardy, zones 2 to 7. A fast-growing, hardy shrub rose with rose-colored to white flowers and attractive orange-red fruit (hips). Grows 4 to 6 feet.

Siberian Pea Shrub (*Caragana arborescens*): Cold hardy, zones 2 to 7. Grows 15 to 20 feet. Produces bright yellow flowers as leaves emerge in spring. Tolerates cold, poor soils and dry conditions.

Sumac (*Rhus* species): Cold hardy, zones 3 to 9. Upright or spreading types; 3 to 15 feet. Most are aggressive growers; place in an area where they can be contained.

Flowers

Arctic Poppy (*Papaver croceum*): Cold hardy, zones 2 to 8. A 1-foot-tall plant with blue-green leaves and fragrant yellow, white, orange or red flowers.

Alpine Aster (*Aster alpinus*): Cold hardy, zones 5 to 7. A 10-inch-tall perennial producing violet flowers with yellow centers.

Bellflower (*Campanula* species): Cold hardy, zones 3 to 8. Spreading, clump-forming and upright types available. Grows from 3 to 30 inches.

Blanket flower (*Gaillardia* species): Annuals and perennials. The latter are cold hardy in zones 3 to 8. Grows to 36 inches and is heat- and drought-tolerant.

Columbine (*Aquilegia* species): Cold hardy, zones 3 to 8. Grows 1 to 3 feet. Attractive flowers above the foliage in late spring and early summer.

Columbine

Gilia (*Ipomopsis rubra*): Cold hardy, zones 5 to 9. A drought-tolerant biennial or perennial producing spikes of scarlet flowers in summer. Reaches 6 feet in bloom.

Lupine (*Lupinus* species): Cold hardy, zones 4 to 9. Reaches heights of 4 inches to 3 feet. Attractive foliage covered with spikes of yellow, white, pink, red, purple or blue flowers.

Penstemon (*Penstemon* species): Cold hardy, zones 2 to 10. Plants produce spikes of foxglove-like flowers and prefer good drainage. Most are drought-tolerant.

Peony

Peony (*Paeonia* species): Herbaceous types cold hardy in zones 3 to 8. Bushy perennial that grows to 3 feet. White, pink, red and salmon flowers, often fragrant, in spring and early summer.

Phlox (*Phlox* species): Cold hardy, zones 3 to 9. Mat-forming and upright perennials that bloom in spring or summer.

Pinks (*Dianthus*): Cold hardy, zones 3 to 10. Low-growing perennials with mainly white, pink or red flowers that are often fragrant.

Soapwort (*Saponaria*): Cold hardy, zones 3 to 9. Low-growing spreading or upright plants up to 2 feet tall. White, pink or purple flowers. Drought-tolerant.

Index

Index

263